# Groundless Grounds

# Groundless Grounds

## A Study of Wittgenstein and Heidegger

Lee Braver

The MIT Press
Cambridge, Massachusetts
London, England

MIT Press books may be purchased at special quantity discounts for business or sales promotional use. For information, please email special_sales@mitpress.mit.edu or write to Special Sales Department, The MIT Press, 55 Hayward Street, Cambridge, MA 02142.

This book was set in Stone Sans and Stone Serif by the MIT Press. Printed and bound in the United States of America.

Library of Congress Cataloging-in-Publication Data

Braver, Lee.
Groundless grounds : a study of Wittgenstein and Heidegger / Lee Braver.
    p.  cm.
Includes bibliographical references (p.   ) and index.
ISBN 978-0-262-01689-6 (hardcover : alk. paper)
1. Wittgenstein, Ludwig, 1889–1951. 2. Heidegger, Martin, 1889–1976. I. Title.
B3376.W564B72  2012
192—dc23
2011028984

10  9  8  7  6  5  4  3  2  1

For my wife, whom I love

The difficulty is to realize the groundlessness of our believing.

At the foundation/ground [*Grunde*] of well-grounded belief lies belief that is not grounded.
—Ludwig Wittgenstein

Insofar as being essentially comes to be as ground/reason [*Grund*], it has no ground/reason. However this is not because it founds itself, but because every foundation—even and especially self-founded ones—remain inappropriate to being as ground/reason. . . . Being *qua* being remains ground-less. . . . As what is to be thought, it becomes, from out of its truth, what gives a measure. The manner in which thinking thinks must conform to this measure.

Being "is" in essence: ground/reason [*Grund*]. Therefore being can never first have a ground/reason which could supposedly ground it. . . . Being "is" the abyss [*Abgrunde*] in the sense of such a remaining-apart of reason from being. To the extent that being as such grounds, it remains groundless.
—Martin Heidegger

# Contents

Acknowledgments    xi
Abbreviations    xiii

Introduction    1

1   What Is Philosophy?    13

2   What Is a Thing?    53

3   The Whole Hurly-Burly of Human Actions    81

4   What Is Called Thinking?    119

5   The Essence of Ground    173

Conclusion: Original Finitude    223

Notes    241
References    325
Index    351

# Acknowledgments

I want to thank Jonathan Beale, Charles Guignon, Iain Thomson, Jim Edwards, Jon Cogburn, and John Koritansky for helpful comments and suggestions on drafts. Any errors are, of course, entirely their fault. An NEH Summer Seminar helped my early work on it. Andy Paiko made the beautiful glassworks which he graciously allowed me to use on the book's cover. I also want to thank my editors, Philip Laughlin and Judy Feldmann, for making the process remarkably smooth and painless. And I thank my children, Sophia, Ben, and Julia for their patience, and my wife Yvonne, who benefits me in more ways than I could name.

# Abbreviations

## Martin Heidegger

| | |
|---|---|
| AM | *Aristotle's* Metaphysics Θ 1–3 (Heidegger 1995) |
| Basic | *Basic Concepts* (Heidegger 1993) |
| BaT | *Being and Truth* (Heidegger 2010) |
| BCAP | *Basic Concepts of Aristotelian Philosophy* (Heidegger 2009) |
| BP | *The Basic Problems of Phenomenology* (Heidegger 1982) |
| BQ | *Basic Questions of Philosophy: Selected "Problems" of "Logic"* (Heidegger 1994) |
| BT | *Being and Time* (Heidegger 1962) |
| BW | *Basic Writings* (Heidegger 1993) |
| CP | *Contributions to Philosophy* (Heidegger 1999) |
| CPC | *Country Path Conversations* (Heidegger 2010) |
| CT | *The Concept of Time* (Heidegger 1992) |
| DT | *Discourse on Thinking* (Heidegger 1966) |
| EF | *The Essence of Human Freedom: An Introduction to Philosophy* (Heidegger 2002) |
| EGT | *Early Greek Thinking* (Heidegger 1975) |
| EHP | *Elucidations of Hölderlin's Poetry* (Heidegger 2000) |
| ET | *The Essence of Truth* (Heidegger 2002) |
| FCM | *The Fundamental Concepts of Metaphysics* (Heidegger 1995) |
| FS | *Four Seminars* (Heidegger 2003) |
| H | *Heraclitus Seminar* (Heidegger 1993) |
| HCT | *History of the Concept of Time* (Heidegger 1985) |
| HH | *Hölderlin's Hymn "The Ister"* (Heidegger 1996) |
| HPS | *Hegel's* Phenomenology of Spirit (Heidegger 1994) |
| HR | *The Heidegger Reader*, ed. Günter Figal (Heidegger 2009) |
| ID | *Identity and Difference* (Heidegger 1969) |
| IM | *An Introduction to Metaphysics* (Heidegger 1959) |

| IPR | *Introduction to Phenomenological Research* (Heidegger 2005) |
| ITP | *Introduction to Philosophy—Thinking and Poetizing* (Heidegger 2011) |
| KPM | *Kant and the Problem of Metaphysics*, 5th ed. (Heidegger 1990) |
| LEL | *Logic as the Question Concerning the Essence of Language* (Heidegger 2009) |
| LQT | *Logic: The Question of Truth* (Heidegger 2010) |
| MFL | *The Metaphysical Foundations of Logic* (Heidegger 1992) |
| MHC | *Martin Heidegger in Conversation* (Heidegger 1977) |
| M | *Mindfulness* (Heidegger 2002) |
| N | *Nietzsche*, 4 vols. (Heidegger 1979–1987, volume denoted by Roman numeral) |
| OBT | *Off the Beaten Track* (Heidegger 2002) |
| OG | Der Spiegel *Interview with Martin Heidegger,* previously known as "'Only a God Can Save Us'" (In HR) |
| OWL | *On the Way to Language* (Heidegger 1971) |
| P | *Parmenides* (Heidegger 1992) |
| PIA | *Phenomenological Interpretations of Aristotle: Initiation into Phenomenological Research* (Heidegger 2001) |
| PIK | *Phenomenological Interpretation of Kant's* Critique of Pure Reason (Heidegger 1997) |
| PS | *Plato's Sophist* (Heidegger 1997) |
| PLT | *Poetry, Language, Thought* (Heidegger 1971) |
| PM | *Pathmarks* (Heidegger 1998) |
| PR | *The Principle of Reason* (Heidegger 1991) |
| PRL | *The Phenomenology of Religious Life* (Heidegger 2010) |
| PT | *The Piety of Thinking* (Heidegger 1976) |
| QT | *The Question Concerning Technology and Other Essays* (Heidegger 1977) |
| STF | *Schelling's Treatise on the Essence of Human Freedom* (Heidegger 1985) |
| Supp | *Supplements: From the Earliest Essays to* Being and Time *and* Beyond (Heidegger 2002) |
| TB | *On Time and Being* (Heidegger 1972) |
| TDP | *Towards the Definition of Philosophy* (Heidegger 2000) |
| WCT | *What Is Called Thinking?* (Heidegger 1968) |
| WIP | *What Is Philosophy?* (Heidegger 1956) |
| WT | *What Is a Thing?* (Heidegger 1967) |
| Zo | *Zollikon Seminars: Protocols—Conversations—Letters* (Heidegger 2001) |

## Ludwig Wittgenstein

| | |
|---|---|
| AWL | *Wittgenstein's Lectures: Cambridge, 1932–1935*, ed. Alice Ambrose (Wittgenstein 2001) |
| BB | *The Blue and Brown Books: Preliminary Studies for the* Philosophical Investigations (Wittgenstein 1969) |
| Conv | *Wittgenstein Conversations 1949–1951* (Wittgenstein 1986) |
| CV | *Culture and Value* (Wittgenstein 1980) |
| LC | *Lectures and Conversations on Aesthetics, Psychology and Religious Belief* (Wittgenstein 1967) |
| LFM | *Wittgenstein's Lectures on the Foundations of Mathematics: Cambridge 1939* (Wittgenstein 1976) |
| LLP | *Wittgenstein's Lectures on Philosophical Psychology, 1946–47* (Wittgenstein 1989) |
| LO | *Letters to C.K. Ogden with Comments on the English Translation of the* Tractatus Logico-Philosophicus (Wittgenstein 1973) |
| LWL | *Wittgenstein's Lectures: Cambridge, 1930–1932*, ed. Desmond Lee (Wittgenstein 1980) |
| LWVC | *Ludwig Wittgenstein and the Vienna Circle: Conversations Recorded by Friedrich Waismann* (Wittgenstein 1979) |
| LWPPI or II | *Last Writings on the Philosophy of Psychology*, 2 vols. (Wittgenstein 1982, 1992) |
| NB | *Notebooks, 1914–1916* (Wittgenstein 1961) |
| OC | *On Certainty* (Wittgenstein 1969) |
| PG | *Philosophical Grammar* (Wittgenstein 2005) |
| PI | *Philosophical Investigations*, 3rd ed. (Wittgenstein 2001) |
| PhR | *Philosophical Remarks* (Wittgenstein 1975) |
| PO | *Philosophical Occasions, 1912–1951* (Wittgenstein 1993) |
| RC | *Remarks on Color* (Wittgenstein 1977) |
| RFM | *Remarks on the Foundations of Mathematics*, rev. ed. (Wittgenstein 1983) |
| RPPI or II | *Remarks on the Philosophy of Psychology*, 2 vols. (Wittgenstein 1980) |
| T | *Tractatus Logico-Philosophicus* (Wittgenstein 2001) |
| Z | *Zettel* (Wittgenstein 1970) |

## Other

| | |
|---|---|
| C1 | *Critique of Pure Reason* (Kant 1929) |
| GB | *Translations from the Philosophical Writings of Gottlob Frege* (Frege 1960) |

HE              *Enquiries Concerning Human Understanding and Concerning the*
                *Principles of Morals*, 3rd ed. (Hume 1975)
HT              *A Treatise of Human Nature*, 2nd ed. (Hume 1978)
NE              *Nicomachean Ethics* (Aristotle 1985)
PFM             *Prolegomena to Any Future Metaphysics*, rev. ed. (Kant 1950)
WWRI or II      *The World as Will and Representation*, 2 vols. (Schopenhauer
                1966, 1969)

# Introduction

First, let's get the obligatory biographical parallels out of the way. Martin Heidegger and Ludwig Wittgenstein were both born in 1889 in adjacent German-speaking countries (Germany and Austria, respectively). After flirting with other occupations (priesthood and engineering), they both came to study under leading philosophers of the day (Edmund Husserl and Bertrand Russell), each of whom recognized in his pupil not only an heir apparent but the savior of philosophy as a whole.[1] Both published a first book in the 1920s (*Being and Time* and *Tractatus Logico-Philosophicus*) which employs their mentors' method (phenomenology and logical analysis) while criticizing their mentors' conception of it. Full of enigmatic claims written in a cryptic style (hyphenated neologisms and diamond-dense numbered statements, respectively), each book established its author as preeminent within a branch of philosophy. While Heidegger and Wittgenstein came to be dissatisfied with these works, they continued to exert astonishing influence, giving birth to entire movements (existential phenomenology and logical positivism) that largely shaped the next several decades of their respective traditions.

Few thinkers in the history of philosophy have been sufficiently forceful and original to give rise to an entire movement, but far fewer have spawned two. Both Heidegger and Wittgenstein grew dissatisfied with their early work and underwent what Heidegger calls a *Kehre* or "turning," the exact nature and extent of which continues to be the subject of vast scholarly contention. Amazingly, abandoning their celebrated early work for even more mysterious writings only expanded their influence. Ordinary language philosophy and what has been called "post-analytic" philosophy are deeply indebted to Wittgenstein's later philosophy, while postmodernism and post-structuralism arose in the wake of Heidegger's later thought. Their teaching styles were unorthodox and spellbinding,[2] and inspired many of their students to fruitful careers themselves.[3] They remain leading contenders for the (dubious) title of "greatest philosopher of the twentieth century" and, on a personal note, both have fascinated me in a way that no other philosophers have.[4]

One reason for their importance is that they both developed powerful critiques of traditional philosophical theories. Heidegger and later Wittgenstein undermine the Cartesian conception of the self, reality, and the relationship between them. Now, this project is hardly remarkable; digging up Descartes in order to kill him off yet again has been a rather popular pastime among philosophers for some time now. He is, to change genres, the Margaret Dumont of modern philosophy. What is distinctive about Heidegger's and Wittgenstein's work is the way in which they construct thorough alternatives which do not so much refute Cartesian ideas as prevent them from arising in the first place. They both try to show that the underlying ideas, far from being self-evident and foundational, actually rest on and perpetuate a whole host of misguided presuppositions. And as we will see, Heidegger and Wittgenstein do not just share a common enemy: they employ startlingly similar ideas and methods to help us dispense with it and move on with our intellectual lives.

This agreement is particularly important in light of their typical classification in different branches of contemporary philosophy—namely, continental and analytic—which diverge significantly on such basic matters as what it means to philosophize, which topics are philosophically important, and what counts as a legitimate reason or argument. By now, these branches have grown so far apart that many who are educated in one know little about the other (beyond the fact that it isn't worth wasting time on) and yet, this book will argue, these two central thinkers make similar arguments for similar views on a wide range of fundamental issues. And where they disagree, we can bring them into dialogue and compare their reasons. If a load-bearing bridge can be built between Heidegger and Wittgenstein, perhaps this will facilitate dialogue between analytic and continental thinkers in general, making the traditions intelligible to each other, thus allowing a fruitful crosspollination.[5] At times, I admit, I could almost imagine myself as Henry Drummond at the end of *Inherit the Wind*, clasping *Being and Time* and *Philosophical Investigations* together to my chest. In this sense, I am continuing the project begun in my first book, *A Thing of This World: A History of Continental Anti-Realism* (2007), albeit with a different strategy. That work devised a common vocabulary to show that continental and analytic philosophers have been working on the same topic. Here, I focus on two thinkers to give a deep-bore (hopefully, in only one sense of the term) analysis of a single dialog. This limitation in scope allows an increase in depth.

My strategy of using perhaps the most obscure representative of each tradition to enable communication may appear, let us say, less than self-evident. But I have found that examining these two difficult bodies of work together proves mutually illuminating rather than compounding the darkness. Revealing the sympathy that underlies their very different styles, terms, and perspectives, as well as examining certain points where they diverge, enriches our understanding of each—itself no small benefit when it comes to figures this difficult and this important. Stanley Cavell makes this point with his usual eloquence:

Since it is reasonably apparent that both Wittgenstein and Heidegger incessantly philosophize by putting the language of philosophy under fire . . . and equally apparent that these fires are not the same (both are progeny of Kant's, but not both are progeny of Hegel's), the question is bound to arise (if, that is, one regards these figures as principal voices of the present of philosophy) whether both or neither of the fires will survive when they are turned upon one another. Since I do not believe that the question has yet been fully engaged, I philosophize, to the extent that I do, within the sense of a split in the spirit of philosophy, of two live, perhaps dying, traditions that are to an unmeasured extent blank to one another. (1995, 143–144)

As usual, Cavell's sentences are very rich, and very long. The points I want to emphasize here are that Wittgenstein and Heidegger represent the "principal voices of the present of philosophy," that the question of how their thoughts interact has not "yet been fully engaged," and that the contemporary traditions of philosophy are largely "blank to one another."

Cavell goes on to write that since "the rift within the philosophic mind . . . seems to me . . . a reality of Western philosophizing now," the way to address this state is to "give incomprehension palpability" rather than offering "more translations from one bank to the other" (1995, 179). I'm not quite sure how one would perform the former task and, to the degree that I grasp it, I don't see its value; personally, I find the mutual incomprehension at present sufficiently palpable. I think that mutual translations can be quite useful and, at least regarding Wittgenstein, I am hardly alone: many continental figures have found Wittgenstein's work congenial. Jean-François Lyotard uses Wittgenstein's notion of language-games in *The Differend*. Hans-Georg Gadamer, fascinated by both games and language, writes that "Wittgenstein's concept of 'language games' seemed quite natural to me when I came across it."[6] Scholars have paired Wittgenstein with many continental partners, including Derrida (Garver and Lee 1995; Staten 1986; Glendinning 2001), Saussure (Harris 1988), Hegel (Lamb 1980), Kierkegaard (Creegan 1989; Schönbaumsfeld 2007), Merleau-Ponty (Dwyer 1997), Gadamer (Horn 2005; Lawn 2007; Arnswald in Malpas, Arnswald, and Kertscher, 2002), critical theory (Brill 1994), and phenomenology (Gier 1981; Overgaard 2006).

Conversely, Wittgenstein's relationship to analytic philosophy has always been problematic, down to his classification as an analytic philosopher at all—an astonishing predicament, given how deeply involved he was in its early formation.[7] If we use the dubious criteria of clarity of style and rigor of argumentation to define analytic philosophy, Wittgenstein fails miserably.[8] His writing style is perhaps the most obscure of all the great analytic figures, leading to an unusual state of affairs: "one of the most striking characteristics of the secondary literature on Wittgenstein is the overwhelming lack of agreement about what he believed and why."[9] Already in 1961, the literature on the *Tractatus* was compared to literary scholarship in dissension and sheer mass.[10] His opaque prose and sparse argumentation have given rise to a cottage industry of exegetical work and scholarly contention that focuses on accurately capturing his ideas rather than evaluating or applying them to contemporary topics—the kind of scholarship that is often pejoratively imputed to continental philosophers.[11] Who but Wittgenstein could be compared to a "creative artist . . . a religious prophet or a seer"[12] by Carnap, and have it be a compliment?

One way to know a philosopher is by the company she keeps—whose ideas does she critique or develop? Whom is she engaging in conversation?—and in this too Wittgenstein is an anomaly. Frege and Russell figure prominently in his early thought, both as sources of ideas adopted (such as Frege's context principle) and models followed (such as Russell's theory of descriptions), as well as subjects of criticism. Their strategy of solving the confusions created by ordinary language by constructing a proper logical language determined much of Wittgenstein's early agenda and, to the degree that his later work responds to this project, it continued to figure prominently in his discussions.

But this is only part of the story, albeit the part that has dominated most interpretations of his early work until fairly recently. Wittgenstein mixed these logical concerns with the mysticism and ethics of Schopenhauer[13] within a broadly Kantian framework. The explicit goal of the *Tractatus* is critical: it draws the limits of thought by locating the limits of thought's *expression*; we cannot say what cannot be said, but we can survey the entirety of the sayable and thereby plot its outer boundary from the inside. The new logic developed by Frege, Peano, and Russell takes for Wittgenstein the place of Euclidean geometry and Newtonian physics in Kant's system, simultaneously revealing the nature of sensible language and intimating transcendent subjects such as ethics or aesthetics by ejecting them from the domain of expression. And, again like Kant, what lies on the far side of the boundary far outweighs the statements of contingent facts within.[14] This shows how profoundly some members of the Vienna Circle misunderstood the *Tractatus* when they used its theory of language to deride the kind of ethics and mysticism contained in its final pages. It was such misreadings that led Wittgenstein to shockingly defend Kierkegaard and Heidegger at one of their meetings.[15]

Russell's prominence in Wittgenstein's personal life, the development of modern logic, and the history of analytic philosophy in general framed the initial reception of Wittgenstein's early work.[16] But where Frege, Russell, and Moore were polemically erecting analytic philosophy on the corpse of idealism, Wittgenstein took no notice of the divide they were creating. Kant represents one of Frege's and Russell's great adversaries,[17] but it is Kant's work that supplies the framework for the *Tractatus*.[18] Although Wittgenstein read little in the history of philosophy,[19] what dabbling he did was "markedly eclectic" in Ayer's opinion (1985, 13), ranging far beyond the (emerging) analytic canon to figures like William James,[20] Sigmund Freud, and James Frazer. He appreciated Kierkegaard, while expressing impatience with his repetitive writing style (a valid objection, I'd say),[21] as well as Tolstoy's religious works, both of whom make prominent appearances in *Being and Time*.[22]

Wittgenstein's later work also confounds customary categories of analytic philosophy. As the *Tractatus* was initially lumped in with "logical positivism," so his later work was originally seen as a form of "ordinary language philosophy," a method developed by a loosely allied group of Oxford thinkers who form a prime example of a family resemblance. *The Blue and Brown Books* were popular at Oxford (Hacker 1996, 162–182), and one can find plenty of statements in Wittgenstein's work which are sympathetic with the ethos of this movement: "the philosophy of logic speaks of sentences and words in exactly the sense in which we speak of them in ordinary life," for example, or "what *we* do is to bring words back from their metaphysical to their everyday use."[23] However, Wittgenstein differs greatly from Ryle or Austin in his conception of ordinary language and its role in his overall project.

But it's not just that Wittgenstein's work doesn't fit neatly into "ordinary language philosophy" or "logical positivism" before it. As the years and secondary literature pile up, it becomes increasingly apparent that Wittgenstein is simply not the kind of thinker who can be assimilated to movements or schools. To put it simply, Wittgenstein is a genius—a term that is perhaps outmoded or suspect, but which seems appropriate, even unavoidable here. Good philosophers take up positions and explore their ramifications, developing them in new directions or offering original arguments for or against them. Such thinkers survey the positions that are on the board at the time, determine the best ones, and think creatively and productively about them. These are difficult and valuable tasks but they are, at bottom, conservative, incrementally filling out extant conceptual contours.

Great thinkers, on the other hand, uncover the ideas presupposed by all parties to a dispute, premises so basic and self-evident that they have escaped notice until then and, by challenging these ideas, create entirely new games. Whence their influence: we see everything anew in the wake of revolutionary work, and set to work mapping the new landscape. One may, like Nietzsche, scorn these lesser philosophical workers scurrying about underfoot those who bestride the history of philosophy like a colossus, especially if one has Nietzsche's gifts; or one may, like Locke, humbly accept the role of under-laborer—but either way, the vast majority of us embroider along philosophy's fringes. Geniuses work in a fundamentally different way. As one commentator puts it, "the young Wittgenstein had learned from Frege and Russell. His problems were in part theirs. The later Wittgenstein, I should say, has no ancestors in the history of thought. His work signalizes a radical departure from previously existing paths of philosophy."[24] Read "Kant, Kierkegaard, and Husserl" for "Frege and Russell," and the statement applies to Heidegger as well. While he develops his own thoughts in an ongoing conversation with the history of philosophy, a study that frequently uncovers partial anticipations of his own ideas, the way he carries out this project and the ideas he "discovers" in the canon are profoundly original.

There is something inexhaustible about their work, so that it can never be neatly dissected and definitively classified. This is why Wittgenstein and Heidegger remain so puzzling, and so provocative; this is why they have been categorized in so many contradictory ways, and why their work maintains its vitality. The unconventionality of their positions also explains their unusual writing styles, since they must battle the connotations of a vocabulary suited to inherited notions. Wittgenstein struggles to communicate his ideas, often sounding perverse in rejecting both sides of what appear to be exhaustive options[25]: "it is not a *something*, but not a *nothing* either" (PI §304), rejecting both realism and idealism, often in evasive terms[26] that get him accused of being "a behaviourist in disguise" (PI §307) or of wanting to deny things he has no intention of denying.[27] Heidegger talks a lot about the fact that "we lack not only most of the words but, above all, the 'grammar'" to discuss the ideas he wants to, leading him to coin new terms, use old ones in odd ways, or devise peculiar orthographic maneuvers such as crossing words out.[28]

Wittgenstein's insistence that "we must avoid accepting party lines"[29] is echoed by Heidegger (KPM 207), who also rejects both realism and idealism due to their shared assumptions: "in elucidating these positions it is not so much a matter of clearing them up or of finding one or the other to be the solution, but of seeing that both can exist only on the basis of a neglect: they presuppose a concept of 'subject' and 'object' without clarifying these basic concepts."[30] The classification of Heidegger's early work as "existentialist" follows the same pattern as the scholarly categorizations of Wittgenstein: an initial assimilation is followed by an increasing appreciation of the way in which its originality cannot be neatly subsumed, even under the school it helped create.

Continental philosophy is more tolerant of the indigestible genius who turns accepted ideas inside out rather than developing them. Indeed, every great continental philosopher seems to feel the need to forge a new vocabulary, a new history of philosophy, a new agenda, almost as a necessary criterion of greatness. To use Kuhn's terms, continental philosophy remains in perpetual revolution, whereas much of analytic philosophy settles into normal mode where thinkers work at common puzzles with fairly established methods. Analytic progress wields analysis in the Cartesian sense: breaking issues down to their smallest parts and then dividing up the labor on these conceptual atoms.

This approach fits Russell and Moore's anti-idealist commitment to the doctrine of external relations (that is, that many properties and relations are contingent and can be changed without fundamentally altering the underlying entity) and what Dummett later identifies as realist bivalence (that is, that each statement has a determinate truth-value, regardless of our ability to ascertain it), leading Russell to proclaim "that an isolated truth may be quite true"[31] as a battle cry. This atomism leads to a quasi-scientific conception of philosophy as divisible into branches, specific problems, and even components of problems, which can then be farmed out to individuals. It portrays texts as bundles of arguments and thinkers as committed to sets of theses. To understand a thinker is to grasp her doctrines and her reasons for them, and these can be transplanted from past texts to contemporary issues regardless of context, like cutting a block of ice out of a frozen Arctic sea and bringing it back to make ice cubes in mint juleps. Thus has Wittgenstein become a philosopher of language, or of mind, logic, mathematics, and so on.

It is one of the great ironies of Wittgenstein scholarship that a philosopher who continuously emphasized the distortive effects of removing elements from their context is frequently studied in precisely that way. Scholars often sift out discrete arguments with premises and conclusions that can be stated and evaluated on their own.[32] This is particularly problematic due to the fact that, except for the *Tractatus*, one immediately retracted essay,[33] and the first 188 paragraphs of the *Philosophical Investigations*, Wittgenstein's publications have been assembled by editors from remarks he wrote down in notebooks or collected in shoeboxes, and often extensively and repeatedly revised. Which of these he planned to publish, however—and which version of them, and in what order or grouping—is unknown.[34] We know in particular that he rearranged the *Philosophical Investigations* in several different ways over the years, making the version we have merely the last rather than the definitive edition.

I will treat Wittgenstein's and Heidegger's works holistically, placing their published texts within the "whole hurly-burly" of their thought. I have found Wittgenstein's *Nachlass* and Heidegger's lecture notes tremendously helpful, clarifying remarks that, removed from or isolated within their *oeuvre* proper, become more obscure than they need be.[35] This approach is more natural to continental philosophers, who tend to be more holistic in their approach to philosophy and philosophers. We continentalists typically view a thinker's ideas as interrelated, so that, as the "hermeneutic circle" has it, we can only understand particular views in light of the thinker's overall stance, even if this stance in turn is grasped via these views.

Looking at a thinker's work as a whole not only clarifies individual ideas; when drawn together, widely distributed and seemingly disparate notions can bring out her most basic insights, the roots from which her various views arise, the core beliefs that inspire and guide her work. This is part of what Nietzsche means when he says that "at the bottom of us, really 'deep down,' there is, of course, something unteachable, some granite of spiritual *fatum*, of predetermined decision and answer to predetermined selected questions. Whenever a cardinal problem is at stake, there speaks an unchangeable 'this is I'" (1966, §231). It is not just in tragedy, but in philosophy too that character is fate. My overarching thesis is that Heidegger and Wittgenstein, so different on the surface, end up with similar views because of their agreement on these spade-turning, lowest-level convictions.

The more I have read and reread their works, the more I have come to see their ideas as emerging from the idea that we are finite creatures and that everything about us must reflect this fact. While they make many, very different criticisms of traditional theories, their basic objection is that philosophy has been practiced in a way that is fundamentally inappropriate for creatures like ourselves. Human reason has been understood as a limited version of divine intelligence; infinitude has determined the finite/infinite contrast. Wittgenstein and Heidegger construct a notion of *original* finitude, finitude without a contrast—or at least not the unavailable contrast with infinitude. Nietzsche writes that even after God has been killed and buried, it will take centuries to finish scrubbing his shadows from our minds, cutting out the vestigial concepts of earlier times. I take this to be one of the great projects of the last two centuries and one that still lies before us, and I will try to show in this book that the works of Wittgenstein and Heidegger offer some of the richest resources we can draw upon to think about it.

The book divides into three phases: the wrong, the right, and the moral of the story. Chapters 1 and 2 explain the form of philosophy and a number of prominent ideas that both thinkers oppose; chapters 3 and 4 lay out the alternatives they advocate; and finally, chapter 5 and the conclusion discuss what we learn from their work.

Each chapter begins with an examination of the early Wittgenstein, who then serves as the foil for his own later work and, to some degree, stands in for many of the problems that Heidegger attacks. One of the ideas organizing this book is that Wittgenstein's *Kehre* from his early to his later work parallels (imperfectly, of course) Heidegger's early critique of traditional thought. The Heidegger portions of chapters are generally shorter than Wittgenstein's because discussions of the latter set out conceptual material that I use to discuss the former. Earlier drafts of this study covered both thinkers' early and later phases, but this proved unwieldy. Now I focus on Heidegger's early thought because it makes a better interlocutor with Wittgenstein, bringing in the later Heidegger's work where especially relevant. This is somewhat unfortunate, both because, as I have argued elsewhere, I consider Heidegger's later work more important than his early, and because of my own regulative goal of producing exhaustive accounts in my scholarship. Hopefully the loss in comprehensiveness will be compensated by gains in comprehensibility, as well as in brevity and unity.

We begin in chapter 1 with Wittgenstein's and Heidegger's views on philosophy—how they understand the enterprise they are engaged in—which provides an overview of the enterprise itself. Heidegger and Wittgenstein sharply distinguish how they practice philosophy from how it has traditionally been done, represented by Heidegger's incessant readings of the canon on the one hand, and the *Tractatus*, and Russell and Frege's work on the other. While pointing out the errors of the past is a fairly standard move, Wittgenstein's and Heidegger's indictments cut unusually deep, with both calling for the end of philosophy and problematizing the very act of making philosophical claims. Both locate the fundamental problem in the way philosophizing suspends our ongoing engaged behavior in the world, with its tacit knowledge of how to use words and interact appropriately with different types of entities, to take up a disengaged theoretical stance. Without our normal mastery of words and things, bizarre pictures and theories step in to command our assent and guide our philosophizing; the cure is to remind us of what we already know.

Chapter 2 focuses on the philosophical notion most responsible for displacing our thoughts from the everyday situations where we know our way around. Wittgenstein singles out what he sometimes calls "meaning-objects," a Platonic view of meaning as contained within a rule, word, or thought which remains constant regardless of changes in context or application. Heidegger accuses traditional metaphysics of focusing exclusively on "present-at-hand" objects—that is, unchanging entities which are unaffected by their surroundings. These notions underwrite atomism and private languages on the one hand, and metaphysics' focus on unvarying features and, more broadly, the atemporal in general on the other hand. Due to its method, such philosophy finds only bare inert objects which cannot account for our meaningful world and language.

After chapter 2 examines the distortions that result from theoretical disengagement, chapter 3 lays out the notions of meaning and being that actually occur in and sustain our normal behavior and understanding. The central idea here is, in contrast with substantial objects, a holistic interdependence of words and entities with each other and their context. Wittgenstein argues that words only have meaning within specific language-games, which then expands into an entire language and ultimately a form of life. The traditionally neglected modes of being that *Being and Time* focuses on—"existence" and "readiness-to-hand"—are both defined by holism: tools only function and make sense within their instrumental chains and the world these form, a world that largely defines Dasein. Restoring this pre-reflective holism returns us to philosophical sanity and keeps false problems like skepticism from getting off the ground.

Chapter 4 puts forward a new conception of thinking that fits this view of meaning. Our primary relationship to reality has traditionally been portrayed as one of knowledge, which ought to be purified and actualized as much as possible. Besides being untrue to what actually occurs, this picture creates insurmountable aporias such as the rule-following paradox, skepticism, and solipsism. Heidegger and Wittgenstein alike emphasize the spontaneous immediacy and responsiveness of our reactions in normal ongoing activity, even within high-level abstract contemplation, which bypasses thematic consideration altogether. Thought necessarily rests upon nonrational and ultimately unjustifiable factors like our socialization and our particular susceptibility to socialization. These factors are intrinsic to us and our world rather than contaminants we need to burn off in the white-hot fire of pure reason. This chapter also briefly shows how Aristotle's notion of *phronêsis* anticipates some of these ideas.

Chapter 5 explores the ramifications of this new conception of thinking, especially for foundationalism. While factors like arbitrary grammar and historical understandings of being ground our thinking by supplying its most basic laws—Wittgenstein focuses on the Law of Non-Contradiction, Heidegger on the Principle of Reason—these factors cannot themselves be justified. Wittgenstein stops the infinite regress of rule-following at the place where our spade is turned, where we can only say, "This is what we do." Heidegger traces all thought back to the fore-structures of understanding and, in his later work, to the historical epochs we have been "thrown" into. We cannot argue for such an encompassing sense of what is and how to think, since such reasoning already presupposes certain answers to these questions. Both thinkers emphasize, however, that this lack of justification does not rob thinking of its legitimacy; rather, it makes certain factors and structures "groundless grounds." The important point about this phrase is that *both* terms are in effect: while the grounds of all thinking lack the kind of foundation philosophers have long dreamt of, and thus are groundless, they still function as grounds for finite creatures like us. Making another historical detour, I present Hume's thoughts on these ideas.

Finally, in the conclusion, I will draw together the insights gathered to try to understand what Heidegger and Wittgenstein have to teach us. Like Kierkegaard, a thinker both admired, they strive to construct a new conception of reason itself—one that is free of the illusions of the past, one that is appropriate to the kind of beings that we are.

# 1 What Is Philosophy?

Naming appears as a *queer* connexion of a word with an object.—And you really get such a queer connexion when a philosopher tries to bring out *the* relation between name and thing by staring at an object in front of him and repeating a name or even the word "this" innumerable times. For philosophical problems arise when language *goes on holiday*.

—Wittgenstein, *Philosophical Investigations*, §38

When we merely stare at something, our just-having-it-before-us lies before us *as a failure to understand it any more*. This grasping which is free of the "as," is a privation of the kind of seeing in which one *merely* understands. It is not more primordial than that kind of seeing, but is derived from it.

—Heidegger, *Being and Time*, 190/149

The topics philosophers discuss are as diverse as the types of things there are in the universe, and plenty of them ignore even that restriction. But there is one topic that all great philosophers address, and that is philosophy itself. This issue carries personal significance for Wittgenstein and Heidegger since their methodological innovations were partially undertaken in rebellion against their mentors. *Being and Time* struck Husserl as a personal betrayal, especially since Heidegger had concealed the extent of his apostasy while Husserl was furthering his career.[1] Russell was, for a time, broken by Wittgenstein's criticisms, abandoning the book he had been writing to leave the future of philosophy to his young pupil.[2]

It is here, with their understanding of philosophy, that I will begin examining Wittgenstein's and Heidegger's thought, starting with their suspicion of the way it has traditionally been practiced. While demands to change the course of philosophy are a relatively constant feature of this course, Wittgenstein and Heidegger are unusually severe in their critiques. It is not a matter of individual mistaken claims or flawed methods in need of repair; the entire project has been misconstrued from the ground up, building certain errors and distortions into the structure of the discipline itself. Heidegger comes to call his later work "thinking" to emphasize its distance from traditional philosophy.

Both consider the negative step of disassembling received views to be a necessary preparation if their positive work is to avoid perpetuating these perennial problems. For later Wittgenstein, this means disenchanting various "pictures" that have taken over one's thinking about a subject, while early Heidegger proposes the *Destruktion* or "dismantling" of traditional theories, a process that would have formed the second half of *Being and Time* had he completed that work.

## The Right Signs

Wittgenstein's work needs to be read as a whole.[3] The later works, largely written in reaction to his early views, often illuminate his highly compressed early writings. While he comes to attack a number of "grave mistakes"[4] in the *Tractatus*, that book serves more as an example of the *type* of philosophy he later takes aim at, rather than his specific target. In Schlick's copy of the book, Wittgenstein described it as "the symptom of a disease,"[5] a disease he sets out to eradicate by finding what *gives rise* to the philosophical impulse in general. The *Tractatus* thus represents a paradigmatic example of a phenomenon that is pervasive,[6] which means that studying the former will help us grasp the latter, as Wittgenstein advises: "I should publish those old thoughts and the new ones together: that the latter could be seen in the right light only by contrast with and against the background of my old way of thinking" (PI x).

While Russell's introduction depicts the *Tractatus* as seeking "the conditions which would have to be fulfilled by a logically perfect language,"[7] Wittgenstein—who disliked Russell's contribution (NB 131)—is actually after the conditions of *any* successful description of reality. Any language that can represent reality by forming propositions which assert the existence or non-existence of states-of-affairs is perfectly legitimate and needs no support from an ideal system of communication fashioned to more rigorous standards, the way Russell and Whitehead constructed a logical basis for mathematics. In other words, "all the propositions of our everyday language, just as they stand, are in perfect logical order."[8]

To say that everyday language is in perfect *logical* order, however, is not quite the same as saying that it is in perfect order *simpliciter*, and on that slender difference hangs the entire endeavor. Everyday language evolved in mundane situations to serve practical purposes, not to display its form with maximal clarity, with the unfortunate result that "language disguises thought" (T 4.002). A thought is "a logical picture of facts" (T 3) whose structure is isomorphically embodied in language's most basic semantic units, elementary propositions.[9] But ordinary statements act like loose apparel on a body, concealing the underlying structure.[10] Although all propositions must contain the correct logical form somewhere within them to be able to assert at all, slippage betwixt logical and linguistic form lets the latter mislead us about the former. In sum, "symbols are not what they seem to be."[11]

Wittgenstein credits Russell with this insight. Russell's theory of descriptions, which Wittgenstein assured him in 1913 "is *quite undoubtedly* right" (NB 128), peels back the misleading surface of definite descriptions ("The present king of France") to reveal more basic assertions concealed within like two dwarves hiding in a long overcoat ("There is an *x*, such that *x* is the present king of France," and "For all *y*, if *y* is the present king of France, then *y* is equal to *x*"). These propositions are transparent, honestly wearing their logical structure on their sleeves which turns their reference to a nonexistent entity from troubling nonsense to mundane falsity. The theory thus demonstrates "that the apparent logical form of a proposition need not be its real one" (T 4.0031) and offers an enticing example of how analysis can melt longstanding, seemingly intractable problems. While every legitimate linguistic outfit contains a sound logical body, a little tailoring wouldn't hurt.[12]

Russell's solution to this particularly thorny kind of phrase opens the door to an entire way of doing philosophy for the young Wittgenstein,[13] who attributes the very existence of philosophical problems to misunderstandings of "the logic of our language."[14] He points out a number of confusions that result from our getting tripped up by language's loose clothing,[15] often when the same or similar signs are used for different functions and thus lead us to mistake one type of linguistic apparatus for another. Generally, "distrust of grammar is the first requisite for philosophizing" (NB 93).

The diagnosis naturally suggests the cure: "in order to avoid such errors we must make use of a sign-language that excludes them . . . that is to say, a sign-language that is governed by *logical* grammar—by logical syntax" (T 3.325). Because the problems result from confusions about "the logic of our language," a limpid presentation of that logic would eliminate such misunderstandings, ending millennia of philosophical rainbow-chasing. Like Kant's critical reform of "any future metaphysics" by drawing the limits of permissible thought,[16] Wittgenstein proclaims all genuine philosophy to be "a 'critique of language'" (T 4.0031). Many traditional problems do not get solved but dissolved when they are shown not to be real problems in the first place.[17] The critique of linguistic reason consists in "the clarification of propositions" (T 4.112) because philosophical problems, like mushrooms, only grow in the dark. Since a proper symbolic notation would prevent grammatical disorientation, there is an important role for something like an ideal language in the *Tractatus*, just not the one that Russell described.[18] As with the meaning of life, once language is rightly understood "there are then no questions left, and this itself is the answer."[19] Grammatical analysis promises to exorcise the ghosts of philosophy's past, suggesting a vision of its future that partially inspired the logical positivists.

Our task then is to master a logic whose propositions are tautologies that, saying nothing,[20] show the combinatory possibilities of their symbols. With all informational content removed, we can see through these pseudo-propositions to look upon the face of logic itself.[21] This solves the *Tractatus*'s great internal problem that, according its claims, its own claims commit nonsense by attempting to express the inexpressible logical features of language.[22] If these features *show* themselves in the way symbols combine, they need never be spoken, thus avoiding the nonsense that results from attempts to do so.[23] Wittgenstein scolds works on logic for breaking their stream of proofs with discussions in everyday language.[24] The correct method is to link well-constructed signs correctly and thereby let the rules of their combination shine forth,[25] while illegitimate combinations exhibit their illicitness by their absence. Explicit exclusions backfire the way Frege's horse concept does,[26] but this method lets us remove counterfeit propositions from circulation without having to commit nonsense by saying them ("The following statements cannot be said: '. . .'"). The consistent logician's correction must emulate the builder's response to requests for a broken piece in the *Investigations*, and silently shake his head (PI §41).

Logic can only manifest itself transparently in "a suitable notation." Unlike ordinary language's deceptive attire, skin-tight apparel exhibits logical properties without saying what cannot be said.[27] Such a notation would clearly display: formal concepts,[28] logical entailments among propositions (T 5.13), the difference between propositions and names (T 5.515), the difference between tautologies and factual propositions (6.113), the limited number of existing objects (by having a limited number of names or elementary propositions),[29] and the identity of apparently different things (by using a single sign for it).[30] It would prevent us from taking the sign of a logical operation as the name of an object,[31] and it would make evident the way in which complex propositions are the products of logical operations upon elementary propositions.[32] I imagine Wittgenstein pictures proper symbols a bit like puzzle pieces that only fit with certain other pieces, as is readily visible from their shape. Perspicuous notation would free logic from the problems of self-reference common to Frege's "horse"-concept, Russell's paradox, and the *Tractatus*'s own nonsensical discussion of logic (in the philosophy of logic, it is Narcissus rather than Dionysus who brings madness and anarchy). Honest signs wear their identity openly, which both ensures that we understand them correctly and relieves us of the need to speak of them. Hence Wittgenstein's "fundamental idea": operators do not *represent* logical relations; they *live* them.[33]

With the typical white dwarf compression of his early work, Wittgenstein packs this entire line of thought into a pair of statements:

4.1212   What *can* be shown, *cannot* be said.

4.1213   Now, too, we understand our feeling that once we have a sign-language in which everything is all right, we already have a correct logical point of view.

According to the book's numbering system, these are both comments on 4.121: "propositions cannot represent logical form: it is mirrored in them. . . . Propositions *show* the logical form of reality." It is the crossing of these wires—saying what can only be shown—that causes the *Tractatus* to perpetrate nonsense, but the same distinction also yields the solution. The right notation isomorphically lines up signs on the page with the thoughts in our heads on one side, and the facts in the world on the other. Once calibrated, "logic must look after itself," such that in a well-designed language "any possible proposition is legitimately constructed."[34] Policing the border between sense and nonsense is no longer needed when illegal immigrants cannot disguise themselves and citizens are compliant by their very nature. With the right set-up, the laws of logic require no more enforcement mechanisms than do the laws of nature.[35] Like Russell's analyzed definite descriptions, this ideal language can certainly make false assertions, but all of its products will have sense.

To sum up, while everyday language successfully describes the world, the fact that it conceals its structure causes a certain form of confusion, what most of us just call "philosophy." Were language's deep syntax to be lucidly embodied in a system of signs, it would completely illuminate logical relations, leaving no shadows where confusion could hide. In this way, "logic is . . . a field . . . in which the nature of the absolutely necessary signs speaks for itself. If we know the logical syntax of any sign-language, then we have already been given all the propositions of logic."[36] Just as puzzle pieces only fit together in the one way that produces a picture, so appropriate signs could only combine in ways that make possible pictures of the world. Nonsense would not arise since mismatched pieces would conspicuously clash. Russell is not far off in his introduction: "a perfect notation would be a substitute for thought."[37]

## One Form of Language

The structure of the *Tractatus*, as many have noted, is basically that of a Kantian transcendental inquiry: given an actual phenomenon, the necessary conditions for it to be possible must also hold.[38] The book retro-engineers language, logic, and the nature of reality from the linguistic prototype we use every day. In such a project, the nature of the phenomenon in question guides the inquiry into its conditions: what the phenomenon does governs the investigation into how it does it. In this case, the given is language's ability to describe the world, so the majority of the book is spent examining just what this means.

Strategically speaking, the project's beginning point is "the most general propositional form" which gives "a description of the propositions of *any* sign-language *whatsoever*" (T 4.5). The comprehensive scope of the claim is important. We can be sure that we will find a single set of transcendental conditions enabling language to do what it does because, essentially, language does but one thing: assert or deny the existence of states-of-affairs. All other, more complex functions are constructed out of these building blocks by means of logical operations, making all legitimate uses of language mere consequences of the nature of propositions.

Wittgenstein uncovers the three elements that comprise language's genetic code—the general form of all propositions, the most basic elements that have this form, and the formula for producing all complex propositions out of them. When combined, these three elements—the Tractarian trinity—puff up to encompass all that language is and can ever be, like a Hoberman expanding sphere.

Once we have perfectly grasped just *one* logical particle we know *all* logical particles. The discovery of further logical particles is inconceivable. In a certain sense all of them are there at the same time. They form a system whose scope and limits we can survey perfectly clearly from the outset. . . . Here we have the feeling that everything springs from *one* root. If we know the principle on which a system is based, then we know the *entire* system. . . . If we know the operation in question, we can, starting from one propositional form, generate all others.[39]

Capturing all that can be said lets us limit language from the inside rather than from the outside, which would require us to say the inexpressible and to determine language's conditions once and for all without the possibility of later revision. It is this exhaustive determination that leads to the imperious tone echoing throughout the *Tractatus*, a book that defines the world in its first sentence, declares "to have found, on all essential points, the final solution of the problems" addressed with a truth "unassailable and definitive" (T p. 4) in its preface, and closes the door on all further discussion with its final sentence.

The first step in this expansion to contain all possible language is the determination of the general form of all propositions, that is, the essence that makes something a proposition, which is to assert or deny the existence of a precisely circumscribed piece of the world. The most basic complete unit of language, the elementary proposition, correlates with the smallest complete unit of reality, states-of-affairs. Second, the law of the series (T 6) gives us the logical operators which constitute all legitimate ways of connecting elementary propositions. Feeding (1) the set of all elementary propositions into (2) the set of all combinatory operations generates in principle (3) all possible propositions—that is, language as a whole. Wittgenstein lays out this overarching strategy when he announces the general form of all propositions: "suppose that I am given [1] *all* elementary propositions: then I can simply ask what propositions I can [2] construct out of them. And there I have [3] *all* propositions, and *that* fixes their limits."[40] When propositions fall outside these limits, as many standard philosophical theses do, we can simply discard them as illicit pseudo-propositions, thereby pulling out the semantic rug from under traditional philosophy's feet. This forms the heart of the *Tractatus*, the crowning achievement of its project, and the target of much of Wittgenstein's later work.

## Impurities

Having conclusively solved all philosophical problems both past and future, Wittgenstein retired from the profession to teach elementary school in a remote Austrian village, an interlude that went rather badly. This disappointment, combined with an awakening sense that he may not have laid philosophy to rest quite as definitively as he had thought, lead to his return to the profession in 1929. The transitional period of 1929 to 1933 sees Wittgenstein shedding previous convictions at an astonishing rate as he haltingly puts together an entirely new way of thinking about philosophy and language, with occasional attempts to salvage elements from his previous work. Perhaps the single most consequential change is his abandonment of the idea that language has a single function: the singularity of this function had been essential to his ability to draw the limits of language in the *Tractatus*. Once this idea loosened its grip on him, he unleashed repeated and merciless attacks on it for the rest of his life.

As discussed above, Wittgenstein's early attempt to delimit language began with (1) the single form that all legitimate propositions must take; this allowed him to select the complete set of linguistic atoms which, along with (2) the complete set of their combinations, set the limit of (3) language itself. But he now believes that "the word 'proposition' does not signify a sharply bounded concept,"[41] undermining the very foundation of the Tractarian project. If (1) what counts as an elementary proposition can vary, then the function's domain or input loses its rigor, which in turn smudges the boundaries of (3) the range or output, that is, the "limited whole"[42] of all possible propositions, which in turn blurs the crucial distinction between sense and nonsense.[43] To paraphrase the old computing slogan: vagueness in, vagueness out.

The second Tractarian element, the legitimate logical combinations, also came under attack. One of the events that brought Wittgenstein back to philosophy was a 1928 lecture by L. E. J. Brouwer,[44] whose intuitionist mathematics rejects the kind of Platonic realism staunchly upheld by Frege and Russell.[45] As I will discuss in chapter 5, Wittgenstein became deeply suspicious of the idea of a rigid calculus that univocally determines its own application and so predetermines its results in a special sense. The confusion lies in moving from the mastery of a technique that reliably yields agreed-upon results, to the notion that the set of numbers or propositions satisfying the operation already exists, that all its members have already been branded like metaphysical cattle. Turning the indefinite *expandability* of a mathematical formula into its infinite *expansion* tempts us to misleading metaphysical pictures.[46]

Wittgenstein now argues tirelessly that calculi do not univocally determine their products in advance, independently of the way we calculate, at least not in any sense more exciting than the fact that the vast majority of competent people (a group that cannot be defined noncircularly) typically get the same results. The right extension does not timelessly exist in a transcendent Platonic heaven, but only within our practices of recognizing the right answer.[47] Thus falls the second piece of the Tractarian trinity, the idea that perspicuously symbolized rules unambiguously apply themselves.[48]

Once he has discarded (1) the fixed set of elementary propositions (since various candidates can count as propositions and as elementary), and (2) the fixed set of legitimate combinations of elementary propositions (since their correct application is not predetermined), the prospect of reaching (3) a cleanly delimited totality of language goes too. Wittgenstein now finds that "what is called 'language' is made up of heterogeneous elements and the way it meshes with our lives is infinitely various."[49] Like games, language has neither a fixed essence at its core nor firm borders at its limits to keep the barbarians from invading and wreaking nonsense on the law-abiding denizens inside,[50] In Wittgenstein's adaptation of *Hamlet*, "there just are many more language-games [than] are dreamt of in the philosophy of Carnap and others."[51]

Identifying language's one function had sifted sense from nonsense, but if no essence defines language then there can be no paternity test for the purity of linguistic DNA. What counts as legitimate and what bastardized is, metaphysically speaking, up for grabs (this needs qualification, as we will see in chapters 4 and 5). "If 'proposition' was not 'sharply bounded,' 'sense' was not 'sharply bounded' either. . . . Where we say 'This makes no sense' we always mean 'This makes nonsense *in this particular game'*" (PO 66). A single true form impanels a permanent tribunal of logic to pass judgment on all statements; a teeming sea of incommensurable games does not. Instead of an absolute division between games and non-games, there are only different games. "For me one calculus is as good as another. . . . If the games are really distinct from each other, then one game is as good, that is as interesting, as the other. None of them is more sublime than any other."[52] Without the one thing that language essentially *does*, we have no way to legislate what particular instantiations of language *ought* to do.

Wittgenstein clearly indicates the central error of his early work.

I had the mistaken idea that propositions belong to just one calculus. There seemed to be *one* fundamental calculus, viz., logic, on which any other calculus could be based. This is the idea which Russell and Frege had, that logic was the foundation of mathematics. The task was to exhibit what is characteristic of this one fundamental calculus, to show what logic is. . . . If one has the idea of a single logic then one must be able to give one general formula of logic, the general formula of a proposition. I thought I had found this formula. . . .

The idea that logic gives the general form of a mathematical statement breaks down when one sees there is no such thing as one idea of a proposition, or of logic. One calls lots of things propositions.[53]

This messy mass of statements shatters the Tractarian dream of surveying propositions once and for all from the superior vantage point of logic. Thus ends Wittgenstein's early philosophical project; thus arises a very different one.

## Tacit Mastery, Troubled Articulation

Throughout his career, Wittgenstein sees philosophy as consisting of more than just argumentation. The roots of belief reach far beneath the claims

being attacked or defended, so persuasion requires more than mere refutation. After all, he had hardly been unaware that language is used in many
different ways during his early period, so bringing this fact to his attention
would not have shaken his faith that a single function must lie beneath
the apparent diversity. In order to cure the strange monomania of philosophers, we must discover its etiology, that is, why he had ever found such an
obviously false idea "unassailable."

A philosopher is not a man out of his senses, a man who doesn't see what everybody sees; nor on the other hand is his disagreement with common sense that of
the scientist disagreeing with the coarse views of the man in the street. That is, his
disagreement is not founded on a more subtle knowledge of fact. We therefore have
to look round for the *source* of his puzzlement.[54]

Having broken the spell of his early beliefs, Wittgenstein wants to understand how he had ever fallen under it.

In place of an absolute distinction between sensible propositions and
nonsense, Wittgenstein now posits a mobile division between the use of
words in normal situations and in highly unusual conditions, with philosophical problems typically arising from unwittingly crossing this line.
We start with a word's meaning in ordinary circumstances, the "everyday
use" of a word which forms "its original home"[55] where our use of it is
unproblematic and in harmony with everyone else's. Philosophical questions, however, take words into strange situations, well past where we have
a sense of how to use them. For example, competent adults understand
what it means to know a fact, under what kinds of circumstances we may
claim to know something, when to deny another's claim, and so on, but
epistemology pushes the issue far beyond such mundane situations. It asks
what knowledge we could still claim if, say, a demon were systematically
deceiving us. Unsurprisingly, the word's grammar is unprepared for such a
scenario, leaving us disoriented, unsure what to say. I have seen goldfinches
in gardens, in books, and in the rain, but never in a demon's dream, so
I don't know what kinds of allowances to make for such a scenario. It is
this move—from the everyday circumstances in which we know our way
around to thought experiments that dispense with the features that anchor
our normal usage—that makes queries philosophical, and that makes philosophical queries so perplexing.[56]

We allow these scenarios to stretch words until they tear for three reasons. The first is due to the nature of linguistic understanding, which Wittgenstein considers to be a know-how rather than a know-that, a tacit skill
rather than the explicit awareness of a fact: "to understand a language

means to be master of a technique."[57] Competence allows us to perform tasks unthinkingly: when we greet a neighbor or answer the telephone or yell at the dog we pay no more attention to the words themselves than to the muscular manipulations making them.[58] Often, nothing at all goes on in our minds while we speak, a point Wittgenstein emphasizes with examples of spontaneous, unreflective speech such as shouting "Help!" when drowning or casually noting an object's color.

The trouble with words such as "understanding" comes through thinking of a few cases and trying to carry over their analogy to all other cases. For example, conscious mental acts do play a great role in understanding, but we should not try to make every case of understanding look like these cases. For there are cases where no conscious experience mediates between understanding an order, say, and carrying it out.[59]

Explicitly thinking about knowledge places explicit thought in the foreground, shouldering out the far more common mode of acting on autopilot, thus creating a distorted sense of knowledge. As in the standard interpretation of quantum mechanics, the act of observing affects the observed.

Wittgenstein considers the focus on a single type of example to the exclusion of all others to be one of philosophy's general professional deformations. In this case, people "are surprised that one can know something and not be able to say it" due to their fixation on the kind of information that can easily be put into words, such as the height of a mountain. This model transfixes our thinking, filtering out forms that resist expression such as the indescribable but perfectly recognizable way "a clarinet sounds."[60]

The height of a mountain and the sound of a musical instrument mark opposite ends on the spectrum of articulation, between which Wittgenstein places grammatical know-how. His portrayal of understanding as mastery of a technique complements his connection of meaning with use[61] and his comparison of words to tools[62] since, as Heidegger demonstrates, the use of tools is an excellent example of mindlessly competent activity. We "forget" this kind of inarticulate understanding when reflecting on knowledge precisely because it eludes reflection and expression. In Heidegger's words, "these [tools] are intelligible because we ourselves move among and operate with them, although we do so in such a taken-for-granted way that we forget this state of affairs in its basic structure as constituting these things."[63] In fact, attempts to put this implicit knowledge into words can actually inhibit and distort it, the way consciously controlling one's legs makes one walk like Frankenstein. This heretically places Wittgenstein's sympathies with Socrates' interlocutors who blame the philosopher's questions for their own intellectual paralysis. "We know how to use the word 'not'; the trouble comes when we try to make the rules of its use explicit. Correct use does not imply the ability to make the rules explicit. Understanding 'not' is like understanding a move in chess."[64] Our normal understanding evades direct scrutiny the way a dim star vanishes when we focus on it.

This tacit mastery of grammar guides our engaged activity and speech smoothly through familiar situations but philosophical inquiry halts this flow, transporting us to situations that sheer off those ordinary features that provide purchase for normal usage. What aspect of us could exist without our bodies? Is a God who exists more perfect than one who does not? Do chairs exist when no one is looking at them? Baffled, we stop and, brow furrowed, think intensely at the words: if we could just understand what existence *really* meant, we could figure out whether it's a perfection or not. When detached contemplation fails to yield a clear answer we are astonished, both at our present ignorance and at our former competent use, suddenly rendered mysterious. Entire philosophical schools spring up to teach new employments of the words by piping in intuitions from analogous areas where we do know our way about. The peculiar nature of philosophical issues renders them immortal, allowing philosophers to go on proposing one model after another, century after century. It's no wonder Wittgenstein discouraged students from pursuing the discipline professionally.[65]

In addition to the tacit nature of skills, Wittgenstein cites a second reason why linguistic understanding proves difficult to articulate.

The aspects of things// of language// which are philosophically most important are hidden because of their simplicity and familiarity. (One is unable to notice something because it is always (openly) before one's eyes.) The real foundations of his inquiry do not strike a man at all. Unless that fact has at some time struck him. . . . And this means he fails to be struck by what is most striking. . . . This must also relate to the fact that I can't give any explanations of the variable "sentence."[66]

Some phenomena are difficult to examine not because they are rare or hard to find, but precisely because of their constant presence; their ubiquity is their invisibility, their manifestness their camouflage. In Heidegger's wording, "that which is closest . . . for just this reason . . . is ontologically"—that is, explicitly and thematically—"that which is farthest" (BT 36/15). Following Heidegger, I will call these phenomena "inconspicuous."[67]

Along with a number of basic facts about human behavior and the world, Wittgenstein's primary inconspicuous topic is grammar: we have difficulty grasping it explicitly because it is constantly within our grasp, like a ring on one's hand that one forgets about. Whereas the *Tractatus*'s logical form of propositions had been hidden beneath an obscuring linguistic screen, grammar is, like Poe's purloined letter, *too* obvious. Our ever-present know-how generally renders conscious rumination on proper use unnecessary, leaving us unpracticed at dredging up and articulating it, which leads to incomplete and distorted formulations.[68]

A third difficulty in discerning the rules of word-usage is that no abstract formula could possibly regulate the open-ended and endlessly adaptive nature of real-life practice.

After all, there is not one definite class of features which characterize all cases of wishing (at least not as the word is commonly used). If on the other hand you wish to give a definition of wishing, that is, to draw a sharp boundary, then you are free to draw it as you like; and this boundary will never entirely coincide with the actual usage, as this usage has no sharp boundary.[69]

However firm we think the distinction between what does and what doesn't count as an instance of a class—Frege's requirement for a concept to be meaningful at all, upheld in Wittgenstein's early work[70]—borderline cases can always arise to unsettle the idealized taxonomy. Knowing how to apply words is a matter of knowing one's way around mundane applications which are highly various, often held together by a family resemblance rather than a set of specific and hence specifiable traits. Attempts to extract a firm rule of usage makes apparently straightforward solid words sublime into clouds of exceptions and *ceteris paribus* conditions usually invisible as we pass through these semantic minefields without a scratch. Such loose, patchwork definitions may disappoint the philosophical obsession with crystalline clarity, but they are perfectly serviceable, often preferable to ones with greater precision. "In the flux of life, where all our concepts are elastic, we couldn't reconcile ourselves to a rigid concept. Indeed, mustn't any concept simply of behavior be formulated imprecisely if it is more or less to serve the game with such concepts?" (LWPPI §§246–247).

The fact that our seemingly firm vocabulary is tunneled through with vagueness should not make us dissatisfied with our tacit mastery of it, which works quite well, but rather with the incoherent ideal of absolutely determinate definitions.

We are not at all *prepared* for the task of describing the use of e.g. the word "to think." (And why should we be? What is such a description useful for?)

And the naïve idea that one forms of it does not correspond to reality at all. We expect a smooth contour and what we get to see is ragged. Here it might really be said that we have constructed a false picture.[71]

The goal of Wittgenstein's early project was to shake us from our lazy complacency with the looseness of ordinary language, which lets meaning slosh around and spill out, to spur us to work arduously for absolute determinacy and clarity. His later work marks a nearly complete reversal of this project. Far from being an unwelcome burden we must be forced to take up, the way Plato's philosopher must pull prisoners from his mythic Cave kicking and screaming, there is something in us that is intrinsically drawn to this quest for perfect clarity, that yearns for the ideal and scoffs at mere shadows—and it is *this* infatuation that Wittgenstein now fights. In general, contentment with rough and ready everyday meanings is fully appropriate, and this attitude must be protected from enticing promises of transcendent perfection. In this sense, he sides with the prisoners still in the cave—the philosopher's dazed scorn for the shadows of everyday life is the sign of a peculiar kind of malady, not a superior wisdom. As Robert Stern writes, Wittgenstein wants "to bring out the priority of our prephilosophical relation to the world, and to turn to investigating how we were tempted out of it in the first place" (Stern 1995, 25). As this applies to Heidegger's project as well, let us now turn to him.

## Tacit Use of Ready-to-Hand Tools, Explicit Study of Present-at-Hand Substances

Heidegger's conception of philosophy differs in many ways from Wittgenstein's, including his estimation of its worth. Where Wittgenstein both early and late would like to consign it to the dustbin of history as a nest of confusions, Heidegger considers philosophy "one of the few great things of humanity."[72] Rather than an artificial break from or meddling interloper in our normal lives, philosophy represents the highest expression and culmination of our very way of being.[73] Heidegger no less than Wittgenstein aims to dissolve pseudo-problems, but this task exhausts Wittgenstein's project whose success, early and late, is defined as the cessation of philosophical questioning,[74] whereas Heidegger regards this step as the preliminary clearing of the ground for something more important to take root. However, there is more agreement between them than may initially be apparent, both on their critiques of philosophy as traditionally practiced and on their proposed alternatives.

The primary goal of *Being and Time* as we have it (only one third of the proposed book was published) is to correct the understanding of ourselves that has, with minor variations, dominated two and a half millennia of philosophy. Partly as a cause of this received self-understanding and partly as its effect, we are estranged from ourselves, alienated from our proper way of living; Heidegger's existential project is to dismantle this long-held view in order to reintroduce us to ourselves and establish a more appropriate or "authentic" (*eigentlich*) way of life. Prejudices lead us to think we experience what we think we should be experiencing, but phenomenology's careful and open-minded attention can reveal "the things themselves" as we actually do experience them. Heidegger uses the German term *Dasein* for the kinds of beings we are in order to create a conceptually sterile environment, one that minimizes contamination by the philosophical implications packed into standard terms such as "man" or "consciousness."

Like Wittgenstein, Heidegger sees an "unbalanced diet" as one of the principle sources of philosophical error, especially the idea formed in ancient Greece that our fundamental relationship to the world is one of knowledge which achieves its highest state in disengaged study. Abstract reasoning is taken to define our essence or what is greatest within us, which trails a comprehensive epistemological and metaphysical system in its wake: "Being is that which shows itself in the pure perception which belongs to beholding, and only by such seeing does Being get discovered. Primordial and genuine truth lies in pure beholding. This thesis has remained the foundation of western philosophy ever since."[75] This view leads to the methodological stance that has long ruled philosophy: Socrates makes contemplation the epistemo-ethical ideal because it most successfully turns us away from our mortal body's distractions to look upon Truth; Descartes retires from worldly concerns in order to ruminate in the quiet solitude of his study,[76] and so on. This interconnected view perpetuates itself by sifting out all counterevidence: if only disinterested contemplation shows us the world as it is, fluctuating qualitative features become mere subjective projections, ghosts passing through the machinery of the world.[77]

Heidegger argues that extensive complexes of ideas and practices like this one emerge from particular understandings of being—that is, what it means for anything to be, the way things behave, the categories appropriate for understanding them, and so on.[78] Heidegger calls the mode of being that has steered philosophy for these many centuries "presence-at-hand." Present-at-hand objects are basically substances: they are self-sufficient and so independent of other entities; their real properties are those that remain the same across time, environmental changes, and perceivers; and they are what show up for disengaged theoretical investigations, including metaphysics and science.[79] While he accepts this mode as a legitimate way that beings are when contemplated, itself a perfectly natural stance for Dasein to take up, philosophy has focused on it to the exclusion and degradation of all other ways of being and acting, thus profoundly distorting accounts of ourselves and our relationships. This perspective misconstrues a number of phenomena, as I will discuss in chapter 2,[80] but *Being and Time* focuses primarily on the view of ourselves as present-at-hand.[81]

Heidegger's project faces a dilemma similar to Meno's paradox: either we have access to the correct understanding of ourselves, in which case it becomes mysterious why such a wildly inaccurate idea ever became the standard view, or we lack it, in which case it becomes mysterious how to acquire it, and how we will recognize it if we do. Like Wittgenstein, he must explain how philosophical confusion has come about and how it can be removed.[82] Both end up adapting Socrates's response to Meno, positing an intermediate sort of understanding between simply knowing or not knowing something which Heidegger calls "*pre*-ontological—that is to say, not conceived theoretically or thematically."[83] Phenomenology unearths the meanings flowing through our behavior which evaporate under the light of theoretical reason. Just as Wittgenstein says that true philosophical theses would not be contested by anyone since they consist in universally known but inconspicuous facts,[84] so Heidegger believes that these phenomena command immediate recognition once they have been brought to our attention, our pre-ontological understanding serving as a partial inoculation against bad ontology.[85] Phenomenology acts like Platonic *maieutics,* helping us recollect the knowledge we have unknowingly known all our lives by removing the prejudices covering our experience.[86] If the beginning point of wisdom for Socrates is the realization that you don't know what you think you know, for Plato it is that you do know what you think you don't—you just don't know that you know it. We are ignorant not of the relevant facts, but of the fact that we are not ignorant of them. Thus is the Socratic acknowledgment of ignorance replaced by the recollection and recognition of one's concealed knowledge.

In order to avoid traditional biases, Heidegger examines Dasein in its "average everydayness," that is, amidst the mundane activities that fill our days.[87] In spite of philosophy's overwhelming emphasis on abstract theoretical thinking, the briefest glance at our daily conduct shows that "the kind of dealing which is closest to us is as we have shown, not a bare perceptual cognition, but rather that kind of concern which manipulates things and puts them to use; and this has its own kind of 'knowledge.'"[88] Heidegger calls this noncognitive, nontheoretical, inconspicuous understanding "circumspection," and defines it as a tacit know-how[89] that "'comes alive' in any of [Dasein's] dealings with entities."[90] We understand the three kinds of beings—tools, objects, and people—because we're constantly dealing with them in very different ways; Oliver Sacks' patients excepted, we rarely mistake people for tools or vice versa. These three regional ontologies collectively constitute our understanding of being, which does not consist in learning an esoteric doctrine but in being proficient at living a human life.[91] In order to behave as humans do, we must know how to use some form of equipment, how to communicate with others, and how to examine objects—which means that every Dasein has mastered these three ways of being. This skillful engagement with the world represents our most basic kind of understanding, grounding all abstract thematic thought.[92] Heidegger pursues ontology by studying Dasein for the same kind of reason that Willie Sutton robbed banks: because that's where the understanding of being is.[93]

Heidegger explains why traditional theories have so consistently gotten it wrong with his famous description of equipment's mode of being, "readiness-to-hand." Even though we're constantly using tools (broadly conceived), they have the peculiar characteristic of "withdrawing" from conscious attention. Absorbed in smooth operations, explicit awareness of the tool, our understanding of it, and even of ourselves recede.

The original way of encountering the environing world evidently cannot even be directly grasped . . . this phenomenon is instead typically passed over. This is no accident, inasmuch as Dasein as being-in-the-world in the sense of concern *is absorbed* in its world in which it is preoccupied, is so to speak exhausted by that world, so that precisely in the most natural and the most immediate being-in-the-world the world in its worldhood is not experienced thematically at all.[94]

Centuries of philosophers haven't been stupid for missing it; this experience is elusive, resistant to examination by its very nature. Like Wittgenstein's tacit grasp of grammar, tools and the interrelated whole they constitute, which Heidegger calls "world" or "worldhood," deflect attention and articulation. "The world as already unveiled in advance is such that we do not in fact specifically occupy ourselves with it, or apprehend it, but instead it is so self-evident, so much a matter of course, that we are completely oblivious of it."[95] The world is too much with us, escaping notice not because it is hidden but because it is too obvious; it is inconspicuous. Some have called this phenomenon—that the nearest is for that reason the farthest—the first law of phenomenology.[96]

I generally use tools more or less automatically. I do not *decide* to sit at my desk with my morning coffee, but unthinkingly glide along the grooves my daily activities have worn into my usual surroundings. Explicit thought springs up when we pause, often due to some sort of obstacle or problem halting the flow of our activity, at which point "the context of equipment is lit up. . . . The world announces itself."[97] Now we peer at what is in front of us and the connected strands of the world. We can fix the problem and sink back into the job at hand, sealing the hole ripped in our ongoing engagement. But when nurtured, this seed of thematic attention can grow into a full "change-over" in our attitude and in the considered being's mode of being. Like Medusa, our focused gaze turns dynamically interconnected ready-to-hand tools into static, isolated present-at-hand objects with little sign of their former equipmental life and liveliness. Ontologies define reality as present-at-hand things because these are what show up to the cerebral stare. Contemplation's congealing effect constitutes philosophy's professional deformity: the method biases the data, in that the attempt to grasp reality sheers off much of it: "speaking about it somehow *solidifies* itself in such a way that the chalk is now simply *there*."[98]

Whereas readiness-to-hand inconspicuously eludes study, presence-at-hand has the opposite vice of being *too* conspicuous: it presses itself on us as the one and only form of reality. Looking back at our absorbed activities, we conclude that the tools were *really* lumps of inert stuff onto which we projected usefulness, that "only by reason of something present-at-hand, 'is there' anything ready-to-hand."[99] Like a Lockean substance, a present-at-hand object must lie beneath qualities to support them, "as if some world-stuff which is proximally present-at-hand in itself were 'given subjective colouring.'"[100] I will call this way of explaining phenomena afterward, according to the demands of particular theories one is committed to, a Retrospective Rational Reconstruction (RRR). In this case, the reconstruction slips present-at-hand objects underneath tools and explicit knowledge beneath circumspective know-how.[101] Presence-at-hand has an intrinsic tendency to retrospectively reinterpret experience: "once entities have been uncovered, they show themselves precisely as entities which beforehand already were."[102] Once this view is in place, it casts all experience in its image—much as, for later Wittgenstein, philosophical expectations are imposed upon experience rather than arising from it.[103] The owl of Minerva does indeed spread its wings at dusk, but it kicks up a heck of a lot of dust in the process.

If flowing absorption characterizes normal use, stopping and staring are exemplary modes of philosophical observation.

We must keep in mind that knowing is grounded beforehand in a Being-already-[amid]-the-world.[104] . . . Proximally, this Being-already-[amid] is not just a fixed staring at something that is purely present-at-hand. . . . When concern holds back from any kind of producing, manipulating, and the like, it puts itself into what is now the sole remaining mode of Being-in, the mode of just tarrying alongside. . . . This kind of Being towards the world is one which lets us encounter entities within-the-world purely in the *way they look* (ειδος),[105] just that.[106]

Upon halting an activity to stare, the richly meaningful, interconnected world we live and act in recedes, leaving behind beached inert, present-at-hand objects. Like Wittgenstein's claim that the philosopher knows less than the average person because disengagement suspends her usual mastery of grammar, Heidegger sees this kind of observation as a reduction in comprehension, rather than its highest or purest form. "When we merely stare at something, our just-having-it-before-us lies before us *as a failure to understand it any more.* This grasping which is free of the 'as,' is a privation of the kind of seeing in which one *merely* understands. It is not more primordial than that kind of seeing, but is derived from it."[107] Understanding lives in use, much the way understanding how to ride a bicycle occurs in riding it and vanishes if we attempt to do so intentionally or to articulate this ability. Stripping off a tool's "subjective qualities" and meaningful relations with other entities does not give us reality distilled, but diluted. Phenomenology dredges up our implicit understanding so that we can construct theories on *its* basis, rather than on what shows up to the theoretical gaze; phenomenology lets metaphysicians heal themselves.

Wittgenstein singles out similar unusual behaviors, especially repeating a phrase or word over and over to oneself[108] and focusing intently (often introspectively) on something like the experience of reading ("as it were attending closely to what happened in reading, you seemed to be observing reading as under a magnifying glass").[109] An epistemological tragedy ensues: the very attempt to achieve a clear view of matters by suspending usage renders them opaque, like shining light on a developing picture. This is what Wittgenstein means by his famous claim that "the confusions which occupy us arise when language is like an engine idling, not when it is doing work."[110] As long as language is working an honest job in plain circumstances, its use comes easily; it is when we stop and stare that it baffles. PI §38 brings these themes together in relation to naming, one of the central topics of the *Tractatus*:

naming appears as a *queer* connexion of a word with an object.—And you really get such a queer connexion when a philosopher tries to bring out *the* relation between name and thing by staring at an object in front of him and repeating a name or even the word "this" innumerable times. For philosophical problems arise when language *goes on holiday.*

Wittgenstein also gets behind Retrospective Rational Reconstructions (RRR). Look at his analysis of the experience of being guided in drawing something:

But now notice this: *while* I am being guided everything is quite simple, I notice nothing *special*; but afterwards, when I ask myself what it was that happened, it seems to have been something indescribable. *Afterwards* no description satisfies me. It's as if I couldn't believe that I merely looked, made such-and-such a face, and drew a line.—But don't I *remember* anything else? No; and yet I feel as if there must have been something else; in particular when I say *"guidance," "influence,"* and other such words to myself. "For surely," I tell myself, "I was being *guided*."—Only then does the idea of that ethereal, intangible influence arise.[111]

While performing the action, everything flows smoothly with nothing particularly noteworthy occurring. *"Afterwards"* however, when reflecting on what happened, I find that I cannot satisfactorily explain how I was able to do it, rendering it miraculous. Now I feel compelled to find queer entities, "ethereal, intangible" things to shore up my flimsy retrospective account.[112] We appeal to the queer not because it can be found in our experience, but precisely because it cannot. Something *had* to have been there to accomplish the now-mysterious deed, and none of the garden-variety phenomena we do find there seems up to the job. We move from the fact that no description satisfies to the positing of something indescribable, the description of which can fuel entire careers. In general, "the past tense is deceptive" (PG 103) because "our use of the past tense creates the delusion that something else happened at the time . . . than actually did."[113] RRRs propagate mental denizens like an Occam's Hair Tonic, if you will.

One of Wittgenstein's favorite examples of an RRR concerns the act of meaning something:

We easily overlook the distinction between stating a conscious mental event, and making a hypothesis about what one might call the mechanism of the mind. All the more as such hypotheses or pictures of the working of our mind are embodied in many of the forms of expressions of our everyday language. The past tense "meant" in the sentence "I meant the man who won the battle of Austerlitz" is part of such a picture, the mind being conceived as a place in which what we remember is kept, stored, before we express it.[114]

It is only afterward that we are perplexed—"thought does not strike us as mysterious while we are thinking, but only when we say, as it were retro-spectively: 'How was that possible?'" (PI §428)—which leads us to insert queer entities or activities to explain how such an event, now enigmatic, was accomplished. David G. Stern connects Wittgenstein's analysis of reading with Heidegger's analysis of equipment breakdown:

in most cases of proficient reading, we just get on with it and do it. Here we have an example of what Heidegger calls "readiness-to-hand": our ordinary use of everyday things does not call for reflective awareness of what we are doing. We only become aware of these things when something goes wrong or some other unusual circumstance draws our attention to them, making them "present-at-hand." . . . If we try to understand the cases in which we are proficient on the model of what goes on in abnormal or problematic cases, we shall inevitably look at what goes on when we make an effort to read as revealing the essence of being influenced, an essence that is concealed in normal usage. (Stern 1995, 123–124)

Just as metaphysics takes theory-induced presence-at-hand as the paradigm of reality, so epistemology focuses exclusively on the kind of thinking that occurs when we pay thematic attention, even though this sort of attention was absent in the event under investigation.

Wittgenstein's agreement with Heidegger on the diagnosis brings them together on the cure as well. Since these reconstructions make us "forget" what "we have always known,"[115] we need to restore our memory with careful descriptions of what actually occurred, the fundamental tool of phenomenology. Close attention to "what my memory tells me really happened"[116] dispels retrospectively raised apparitions.

We must do away with all *explanation*, and description alone must take its place. . . . The problems are solved, not by reporting new experience, but by arranging what we have always known. Philosophy is a battle against the bewitchment of our intelligence by means of our language. (PI §109)

Since we actually understand the relevant subject matter, we don't need explanations or theories, but "reminders" (PI §127). This anamnestic method runs throughout Wittgenstein's later writings: "learning philosophy is *really* recollecting. We remember that we really used words in this way."[117] Like Dasein's pre-ontological understanding of being, our everyday grammatical proficiency contains all that we need; we simply need to recognize and return to it. Wittgenstein compares our situation to a man desperately trying to get out of a room without realizing that an exit lies behind him; he must simply turn around to see that he is not actually locked in at all. One of Heidegger's only two mentions of Wittgenstein refers to this image.[118]

In one of his rare engagements with the philosophical canon, Wittgenstein accepts Augustine's contrast in *Confessions* XI between confidently understanding time and, when asked to define it, feeling at a loss—but Wittgenstein reverses the polarity. Where Augustine, like Socrates, believes that the inability to define exposes a serious deficiency in his knowledge, Wittgenstein considers the everyday competent reckoning with time—knowing how to read a clock, successfully meeting a friend for coffee at three o'clock—to be the real understanding of time. Instead of plugging the hole with a theory of time, the proper solution is to return to the expertise embodied in our ability to deal with time in mundane circumstances. "We remind ourselves, that is to say, of the *kind of statement* that we make about phenomena. Thus Augustine recalls to mind the different statements that are made about the duration, past, present or future, of events. (These are, of course, not *philosophical* statements about time)."[119] The inability to answer philosophical questions does not *reveal* ignorance; it manufactures it. Wittgenstein is implicitly siding with Aristotle's argument against Socrates and Plato[120] that, for example, a soldier can be courageous without being able to define courage, since *phronêsis* guides our application of concepts in concrete situations in a way that cannot be put into a precise formula. I will return to this comparison at the end of chapter 4.

This analysis constitutes a profound challenge to core philosophical ideas. Philosophers have often seen their task as being to articulate and judge the unexamined presuppositions we irresponsibly presuppose or act upon. This goal prominently and explicitly informs the projects of such figures as Socrates, Descartes, and Kant. Heidegger argues that the kind of understanding we constantly depend upon not only does escape attention, but must do so to be effective. Moreover, he brilliantly accounts for the prevalence of theory and presence-at-hand, despite the fact that they represent an atypical, derivative mode of being. We derive our "ontological orientation" (BT 129/96) from this mode because it is what shows up to the disengaged cognitive stance of philosophical analysis, which then interprets everything in its terms.[121] To adapt the saying that to someone with a hammer everything looks like a nail, to a philosopher who only has the concept substance, nothing looks like a hammer. We always approach phenomena with particular preconceptions,[122] and the one most "ready-to-hand" to theory is the one that springs up when we observe. Ultimately, this ontology enjoys such a disproportionate share of philosophical attention for the same reason the proverbial drunk searches for his keys under the streetlight, even though he dropped them down the road: this is where the world is lit up.

## Sources of Confusion

As we have seen, Wittgenstein's diagnosis of and cure for philosophy arise from the contrast between the taken-for-granted understanding embodied in our mundane use of language and the queer ideas fostered by disengaged contemplation—the same division that underlies Heidegger's analysis of Dasein. Heidegger, however, considers the contemplation that gives rise to theoretically oriented epistemology and presence-at-hand metaphysics to be a natural stance of Dasein's, giving it a limited legitimacy. The problem isn't that it's false, but that over the centuries, philosophers have massively expanded its estate, shouldering out other more common aspects.[123] Wittgenstein contrasts the two much more sharply, branding the problems of philosophy simply foreign to mundane life.[124] Their very existence is due to this separation, to the disorienting extrapolation from our usual sense of a term to situations where no proper usage has been settled (supported by an idea I will call "Meaning-Object," which will be the topic of chapter 2): "we learn to use the word 'think' *under particular circumstances*. If the circumstances are different we don't know how to use it."[125] This view raises a problem for Wittgenstein that Heidegger does not face: if philosophical theories clash so strikingly with our normal experience, why are we so susceptible to them?[126] Although we touched on this above, we now need to discuss a particularly important factor in Wittgenstein's explanation of philosophical confusion—pictures.

One way to come up with something to say when mired in a philosophical conundrum is to consult what Wittgenstein calls a picture: "a full-blown pictorial representation of our grammar . . . as it were illustrated turns of speech" (PI §295) that often employs queer, fantastic imagery to depict an idea. As is so often the case in his later work, Wittgenstein stops short of a blanket condemnation of pictures as intrinsically harmful; by and large they are perfectly innocuous and can often be quite helpful in unpacking and communicating what we mean.[127] Most of the time we don't even notice them since our tacit understanding rarely needs to consult auxiliary sources of information.

But when philosophy hampers our usual sure-footedness, we seize on pictures as our map through these strange and treacherous terrains.

But then where did our queer ideas come from? Well, I shew you the possibility of a movement, say by means of a *picture* of the movement. . . . We mind about the kind of expressions we use concerning these things; we do not understand them, however, but misinterpret them. When we do philosophy we are like savages, primitive people, who hear the expressions of civilized men, put a false interpretation on them, and then draw the queerest conclusions from it.[128]

Once we have left our ordinary understanding behind, we rely upon pictures far beyond their capacity, unwittingly jumping the track from the way we actually use the word to usage appropriate to the picture. Taking them literally, we conjure strange metaphysical beasts to perform the tasks rendered mysterious by our disengaged staring, not realizing how difficult it will be to tame these queer creatures; we become ensorcelled by the shades we summoned up to clarify matters.[129] The wakefulness of reason produces metaphysical monsters.

In the absence of our knowing how to talk about these matters, we must rely on conscious thought which, as we have seen, is ill-suited to this task.

The characteristic trouble we are dealing with is due to our using language automatically, without thinking about the rules of grammar. In general the sentences we are tempted to utter occur in practical situations. But then there is a different way we are tempted to utter sentences. This is when we look at language, consciously direct our attention on it. And then we make up sentences of which we say that they also ought to make sense. . . . Thus, for example, we talk of the flow of time and consider it sensible to talk of its flow, after the analogy of rivers.[130]

Much of Wittgenstein's later work consists in precise descriptions of the mental images and analogies he associates with various phrases, in the expectation that readers, recognizing similar notions in their own thought, will realize what flimsy support their ideas have, changing their disguised nonsense into patent.[131] We start with a model that seems able to guide any application, but when removed from its natural context, it dissipates, leaving us confused about what to say in these new situations. A philosopher theorizing is a bit like a dog trying to fetch a snowball thrown into a snowbank, looking up quizzically when no amount of digging unearths it. The great philosophical debates represent, for Wittgenstein, divergent applications of pictures that have been carried far beyond their legitimate role.

Another cause of philosophical confusion is the tangled web of connections between words as "a result of the crossing of different language-games."[132] Wittgenstein believes that language is permeated by the furrows and grooves of analogies, with words overlapping and tying into each other in all sorts of complex and, often, purely coincidental ways. We become linguistically disoriented without a grammatical roadmap which, for reasons discussed above, we rarely possess, at least not consciously. The *Tractatus* noted this untidiness,[133] but in order to contrast it with the ideal of a pure logic where "the solution to all my questions must be *extremely* simple."[134] In Wittgenstein's later works, this snarled skein of words is all there is to language, with no core of clean crystalline clarity beneath the labyrinthine surface. The source of confusion has changed from linguistic disguise to complexity. The *Tractatus* warns of the outer edges of the map of logical space where there be dragons of absurdity; *Philosophical Investigations* guides us through language's tangled maze of "little streets and squares, of old and new houses, and of houses with additions from various periods" (PI §18).

Whereas the early work considered the complications of language an unfortunate accident we should clear up in order to unearth its essence, Wittgenstein now rejects the idea of hidden depths in need of plumbing. Similar to Heidegger's phenomenological ontology which identifies beings with their appearance instead of with never-revealed noumena, language's manifestations exhaust it. Of course, this hardly makes our task easier: "in logic nothing is hidden. . . . What is difficult is to make the rules explicit."[135] Although everything there is to know about language lies out in the open rather than concealed within deceptive clothing, we lack a clear overview (*übersehen*) of this sprawling, knotted mess due to "the immensely manifold connections they are caught up in."[136]

### The Inner-Outer Picture

For Heidegger, our ontological orientation toward presence-at-hand plays the same role as Wittgenstein's pictures: it seizes our thinking precisely when we consider ourselves to be most faithful to reality or reason,[137] forcing our thoughts down inappropriate lines of interpretation while manufacturing supporting evidence. One particular confusion that both discuss extensively is the picture of the mind as an interior.

This simile of "inside" or "outside" the mind is pernicious. It is derived from "in the head" when we think of ourselves as looking out from our heads and of thinking as something going on "in our head." But *we then forget the picture and go on using language derived from it.* Similarly, man's spirit was pictured as his breath, then the picture was forgotten but the language derived from it retained. We can only safely use such language if we consciously remember the picture when we use it.[138]

We start with a common expression: "I have a thought in my head." There is nothing particularly wrong with this phrase, but note ("consciously remember") that the picture is one of spatial containment.

Under certain circumstances—especially in the thin air of philosophical contemplation—pictures metastasize into malignant ideas that take over and structure our thinking about a topic. Removed from the firm ground of normal usage, they surreptitiously lure us away from how we talk about thinking to how we talk about one physical object located inside another. "We aren't able to rid ourselves of the implications of our symbolism. . . . We are led into puzzlement by an analogy which irresistibly drags us on."[139] A wormhole opens up between heterogeneous regions of our language, which is why "the phrase 'in the mind' has caused more confusion that almost any other in philosophy."[140] It suggests a homunculus crouching inside the "dark closet" of the skull (in Locke's description), peering out through the eyeballs as through a pair of gelatinous binoculars. We end up talking about thinking in terms and concepts borrowed from spatial location without realizing that a substitution has occurred.

Heidegger also considers this conception of the mind as a closed-off interior, which he lays at Descartes's feet, to be particularly influential and harmful, labeling it a "cancerous evil" late in his life.[141] We appear to be a present-at-hand object (*res cogitans*) with the capacity to think because this is what replaces the selfless flow of engaged activity when thematized.[142] This conception then gives rise to problems as unsolvable as they are artificial.

Let's compare their analyses directly. Here is how Wittgenstein explains the genesis of philosophical befuddlement on the topic:

> how does the philosophical problem about mental processes and states and about behaviourism arise?—The first step is the one that altogether escapes notice. We talk of processes and states and leave their nature undetermined. Sometime perhaps we shall know more about them—we think. But that is just what commits us to a particular way of looking at the matter. For we have a definite concept of what it means to learn to know a process better. (The decisive movement in the conjuring trick has been made, and it was the very one that we thought quite innocent.)—And now the analogy which was to make us understand our thoughts falls to pieces.[143]

It is the initial conception of mental states in accord with the inner/outer picture—the step that "altogether escapes notice," that appears to take place before the real work gets going—that organizes the rest of the analysis, sealing its fate before it even starts. From that point on, "one uses inappropriate concepts to form the *picture* of the processes" (RPPI §193). For instance, first- and third-person asymmetry—that is, the idea that I transparently know what goes on inside myself but can only infer what is happening in you—gets cast as signaling a process hidden deep in the recesses of my mind, screened off from others' view by my body. But this "fact" which is cited as the supporting evidence for the picture is actually a consequence of it.

> "You can never know what's going on in his soul."—That seems to be a truism. And it is, in the sense that the picture we just used already contains the sentence. But of course we have to call the sentence into question just as much as the picture.
>
> The expression "Who knows what is going on inside him!" The interpretation of outer events as consequences of unknown ones, or merely surmised, inner ones.[144]

This picture is what makes skeptical worries about whether we can ever know what another is feeling, or even *if* feelings course through the passages of another's heart, plausible, pressing, and unsolvable. One short step then takes us to external-world skepticism.

Heidegger's account matches Wittgenstein's point for point. Let me quote it at length:

Inasmuch as knowing belongs to these entities and is not some external characteristic, it must be "inside."[145] Now the more unequivocally one maintains that knowing is proximally and really "inside" and indeed has by no means the same kind of Being as entities which are both physical and psychical, the more one believes that one is proceeding without presuppositions in the question of the essence of knowledge and in the clarification of the relationship between subject and Object. For only then can the problem arise of how this knowing subject comes out of its inner "sphere" into one which is "other and external." . . . The question of the kind of Being which belongs to this knowing subject is left entirely unasked, though whenever its knowing gets handled, its way of Being is already included tacitly in one's theme. Of course we are sometimes assured that we are certainly not to think of the subject's "inside" and its "inner sphere" as a sort of "box" or "cabinet."[146] But when one asks for the positive signification of this "inside" of immanence in which knowing is proximally enclosed . . . then silence reigns. . . . The knowing which presents such enigmas will remain problematical unless one has previously clarified how it is and what it is.[147]

Here too it is the portrayal of the phenomena in spatial and, for Heidegger, present-at-hand terms that lays the ground for the problems as the metaphor hardens into presupposition and then dogma. Philosophers pass over this initial characterization, lumping the mind in with other kinds of objects without ever seriously investigating subjectivity's distinctive mode of being,[148] but Heidegger pegs this as the fateful step. Once "Dasein is tacitly conceived in advance as something present-at-hand" (BT 150/115), the other pieces of the picture fall into place with the inexorable force of the self-evident. Moreover, "precisely by its being inexplicit, it possesses a peculiar stubbornness" (BCAP 187). This conception perpetuates itself by presenting all experience in its terms and papering over any conflicting evidence, especially the easily ignored, inconspicuous experience of our daily lives.

Even though Being-in-the-world is something of which one has pre-phenomenological experience and acquaintance, it becomes *invisible* if one interprets it in a way which is ontologically inappropriate.[149] This state of Dasein's Being is now one with which one is just barely acquainted (and indeed as something obvious), with the stamp of an inappropriate interpretation. So in this way it becomes the "evident" point of departure for problems of epistemology.[150]

Skepticism then appears inevitable and, within this framework, insurmountable.[151]

But skepticism only takes root in the ground of a specific ontology. Showing it to be groundless by reminding us of what we already know through a close examination of our normal way of living exposes it as a pseudo-problem.

The contention that there is no longer a problem of knowledge, if it is maintained from the outset that Dasein is involved with its world, is really not a contention but only the restoration of a datum which any unbiased seeing sees as obvious. Moreover, it is nowhere prescribed that there must be a problem of knowledge. Perhaps it is precisely the task of a philosophical investigation ultimately to deprive many problems of their sham existence.[152]

In other words, skepticism is a fake problem that must be dis-solved by restoring us to our normal, seamless state of being-in-the-world, rather than solved by bridging an illusory gap between inner and outer realms.[153]

Once regained, the pre-ontological understanding of our mode of being disperses philosophy's bewitchment and pseudo-issues, just as Wittgenstein's perspicuous overview of terms' grammar, the tacit knowledge of which is shown by our ability to use the words properly in normal circumstances, can pop the speculative bubbles we felt trapped within. Since proper philosophy merely brings these quasi-unconscious competencies to the surface, Wittgenstein says that no one would disagree with genuine philosophical theses (PI §§128, 599), just as phenomenology reminds us of a "datum which any unbiased seeing sees as obvious." Like Heidegger's *Destruktion*, Wittgenstein dismantles the preconceptions that orient our thinking by a close description of how we actually use words, a grammatical phenomenology if you will: to the words' themselves! "The scrutiny of the grammar of a word weakens the position of certain fixed standards of our expression which had prevented us from seeing facts with unbiased eyes. Our investigation tried to remove this bias, which forces us to think that the facts *must* conform to certain pictures embedded in our language."[154] In Heidegger's words, "rightly considered, the idea of an inner and an outer world does not arise."[155]

## Ethics

This leads us to a significant difference between the way these thinkers view philosophy and its relationship to ethics, broadly conceived. Wittgenstein views philosophy, both early and late, as a negative enterprise. I don't go as far as some interpreters who read the *Tractatus* as a *reductio* of all of its apparent claims to nonsense *simpliciter* rather than as useful or informative nonsense, or that the *Investigations* is a fundamentally skeptical book, balancing voices against each other to escape commitment to any theses.[156]

I explained above how I understand Wittgenstein's claim that everyone would agree with philosophical theses, connecting it to phenomenological recognition. It is true however that his work, early and late, seeks to eliminate philosophical questions rather than answer them. The *Tractatus*'s singular combination of haughty arrogance and metaphysical self-deprecation results from Wittgenstein's belief that he has definitively solved all philosophical problems once and for all—and how little this means, as this solution leaves all important questions untouched. In fact, it is the very act of not broaching these topics or, more precisely, gesturing cryptically at them while forbidding their discussion, that is their solution. The discussion of logic and language which takes up the majority of the *Tractatus* clears away traps and obstructions, leaving neither answer nor question—which is itself the answer.[157] A bit like Heidegger's focus on what is unsaid in philosophical works,[158] Wittgenstein's early writings outline the transcendent precisely by *not* discussing it, the way the edges of an object in a painting's foreground outline the background, and vice versa. As he wrote to Paul Engelmann in 1917, "if only you do not try to utter what is unutterable then *nothing* gets lost. But the unutterable will be—unutterably—*contained* in what has been uttered!"[159] And for Wittgenstein and Heidegger alike, the key to the riddle of life lies in the correct understanding of the self.

Wittgenstein's early work darkly intimates a Schopenhauerian distinction between the transcendent self "outside" world, space, and time, and the empirical self, linked together by the will. I identify myself with my empirical, physical self, and steer it around to procure satisfaction of its desires. Everything that takes place in this world is absolutely contingent, however, including my ability to get what I want,[160] so hanging my happiness on getting what I desire and avoiding what I do not is a sucker's game. The dice are loaded—determined, even—and the house always wins in the end. Even the most fortunate face the inescapable sufferings endemic to human life. The only strategy that is entirely within our control is to withdraw from the game, to quiet the will and mute its preferences and protests. We win by becoming indifferent to winning.

Thus the only secure form of happiness, which is the same thing as moral goodness or "the right way of living" (PO 38), consists in accepting the way things turn out. Suicide represents "the elementary sin" (NB 91) because it betrays one's belief that worldly states determine one's happiness. If we rise above the circulation of pleasures and pains then nothing can harm us, as attested to by one of Wittgenstein's paradigmatic experiences of moral goodness: "the experience of feeling *absolutely* safe. I mean the state of mind in which one is inclined to say 'I am safe, nothing can injure me whatever happens.'"[161] As Stoics and Buddhists argue, this is the only truly reliable way to achieve genuine freedom and happiness.[162]

Like the Buddhist doctrine of *anātman* or no-self, the empirical self for Schopenhauer has no substantial essence underlying changes, making attachment to its prosperity not just a recipe for discontent, but an ontological error. Even the bond between my willing an action and my empirical self's performing it is inexplicable and contingent, as Hume argued.[163] But the transcendental self presents problems of its own. For one thing, we cannot experience the experiencing self any more than we can see our seeing eye.[164] Russell and Frege try to render the Kantian transcendental self superfluous by relieving it of the role Kant assigned it, namely, unifying subjects and predicates in judgments.[165] Frege sees this assignment as the first step toward psychologism, that is, making logic depend on contingent facts about our minds, so he makes logical judgments snap together on their own: the pegs of the complete parts slide into the holes of the unsaturated parts while we just observe.[166] Wittgenstein's early work gets considerable mileage from this solution: if the speaker has no effect on propositions ("'A believes that *p*' . . . [is] of the form '"*p*" says *p*'"), then we can remove the thinker from the empirical world ("this shows too that there is no such thing as the soul—the subject, etc.—as it is conceived in the superficial psychology of the present day") and solve Frege's problem of intensional nonsubstitutability at the same time.[167] This motivates Wittgenstein's constant refrain that we must let logic take care of itself, which I will discuss in chapter 2.

In early Wittgenstein's nimble fingers, Frege's dry logic and Schopenhauer's angst-soaked metaphysical ethics dovetail as if they were made for each other, just as *Being and Time* makes the union of Husserl and Kierkegaard feel inevitable rather than a crime against nature. Logic shows worldly events to be uncontrollable contingent facts, entirely lacking in any kind of value, making them irrelevant to ethics.[168] Reconciling ourselves to what *does* happens rather than trying to coerce what *should* happen, releases us from misery; as tautologous as it sounds, appreciating that "'everything is what it is and not another thing'" is the inexpressible (for how could it be any other way?) essence of ethics.[169] This tranquil acceptance of all that is the case is embodied in the totality of true propositions which mirror, untroubled, the world as a limited whole.[170]

We achieve this perspective when we stop identifying ourselves with that bit of dying flesh and rise above the vicissitudes of fortune to see the world from outside, *sub specie aeterni* (T 6.45; NB 83), and our empirical self as just another piece of the world whose fate is no more or less important than anything else.[171] We identify instead with a world-soul (NB 49, 85) which, in one sense, is transcendent in virtue of the fact that it is not an item within the world, or in space and time at all (NB 74, 86). In another sense, the soul *is* the world in that the transcendent seer is completely absorbed into and exhausted by its seeing of the spectacle of the world: "what brings the self into philosophy is the fact that 'the world is my world.'"[172] Wittgenstein is fascinated with experiences that offer tastes of this Schopenhauerian absorption in those moments we dwell entirely in the present when something completely fills our attention.[173] These tiny, perfectly shaped droplets of eternity yield a kind of quasi-immortality, a momentary suspension of care, time even. One then identifies not with the little metal top hat on the game board, but with the transcendental self who knows we're playing with fake money, who neither suffers nor prospers since she knows that no state-of-affairs affects it. The aim of Wittgenstein's early philosophy is to show this self, trapped in the world as in a fly-bottle, the way out.

This is genuine ethics, as transcendent as logic (T 6.13, 6.421). Just as a tautology's lack of content about the way things are lets logic shine through, so emptying the will of all preferences for how things should be allows us to wonder that the world is at all.[174] This change, not in actions but in attitude, makes our world a happy one without altering its contents in any way.[175] Indeed, just as it is the cessation from asking philosophical questions that is their answer, it is the very refraining from attempts to alter its contents that *makes* the world that of the happy man, the one who accepts whatever happens to him the way a tautology will "admit *all* possible situations" (T 4.461, 4.462). The logical tautology "it is either raining or not raining" gives no information about the weather, and the happy man has no preference come rain or come shine. It may rain on the just and unjust alike but, in light of their differing attitudes, the same rain does not befall them both.

Like Wittgenstein, Heidegger's early work weaves together highly disparate influences. I have been emphasizing Heidegger's phenomenological attempt to restore our pre-reflective skillful coping when, disengaged, we acknowledge only present-at-hand objects and theoretical knowledge—an analysis that is, I have been trying to show, in considerable agreement with Wittgenstein's later thought. However, this dichotomy is primarily to be found in division I of *Being and Time*. Division II, on the other hand, turns to existentialist worries about conformism and "the oblivious passing of our lives," states facilitated by just the kind of autonomic flow praised in the first division.[176]

And here we find much that diverges from Wittgenstein's early ethics. Where early Wittgenstein follows Schopenhauer in valuing the stilling of desires as the road to happiness and our true self, early Heidegger follows Kierkegaard (and Augustine) in *defining* the self as caring about what happens to her.[177] Our pre-ontological understanding of being—the necessary condition for us to do anything and be anyone at all—comes from Dasein's unavoidable investment in her own wellbeing, her future; our encounters with others, tools, and objects receive their intelligibility within the context of our quest to be a certain kind of person. Where Wittgenstein adheres to Schopenhauer's quest to distance me from myself, Heidegger agrees with Kierkegaard in making *Jemeinigkeit*, "mineness," essential to our form of life. We must cultivate this identification, not starve it. Mineness lays the ground for the possibility of authentically taking "ownership" of our lives and owning up to our ontological responsibilities, as shown by the term for authenticity: *Eigentlichkeit* or "ownedness" builds on *eigen* or "own."[178]

The two thinkers warn us of intrinsic tendencies running in opposite directions—Wittgenstein worries about our identifying ourselves too much with our individual projects and wellbeing, whereas Heidegger thinks that we have a predisposition to lose sight of our individuality, to blend in with the crowd. "Being-with-one-another dissolves one's own Dasein completely into the kind of Being of 'the Others'. . . . We take pleasure and enjoy ourselves as *they* take pleasure."[179] This conformism is the unfortunate side-effect of, among other factors, the tacit comprehension essential to division I: we are so good at mindlessly doing what one does that we become existentially distracted, taking up tasks and roles casually, spending our time profligately.[180]

Schopenhauer believes that humans naturally think only of themselves, viewing others as competitors for scarce hedonic resources, with every desire and action reinforcing the walls of the self. Where Wittgenstein warns us against willing, Heidegger presses it upon us, echoing Kierkegaard's Judge William's exhortation to make the most fundamental choice—choosing to choose, to make decisions deliberately rather than coasting on the inertia of our community and our past (BT 313-314/268-269). Whereas equipmental breakdowns in division I instigate the problematic switch to disengaged theorizing, division II exploits the way that large-scale collapses, primarily anxiety and the anticipation of death, can awaken us from auto-pilot. Crises individuate us, recalling us from our dispersal into anonymity: "in this distinctive possibility of its own self, it has been wrenched away from the 'they.'"[181] Death gives us the *principium individuationis* that, for Schopenhauer, tragically befalls us upon birth. While division I mounts a revolutionary defense of background unthematic know-how, division II criticizes absentminded flow, calling for just the kind of explicit examination he had defended circumspection from. We must disentangle ourselves from others, willing to be ourselves by intentionally choosing our projects.[182] Heidegger's hell, where "Dasein make no choices, gets carried along,"[183] bears more than a little resemblance to Schopenhauer's nirvana.

Wittgenstein and Heidegger alike see ethical behavior as adverbial rather than as a noun or verb—it's about *how* we act, rather than *what* we do. For Heidegger, there are no existentially special or correct roles; authenticity means deliberately selecting from among those available in one's culture while acknowledging that none has been singled out by God or Nature or some other capitalized, nebulous entity to be our True Calling.[184] This is the culmination of Dasein's first-mentioned feature, that our being is and remains an unsettled issue for us. For Wittgenstein, each concrete occupation represents a selfish and futile preoccupation with happiness instead of the placid acceptance of whatever occurs.[185]

Both thinkers posit a kind of identity of the self with its world. Heidegger establishes this phenomenologically—we are usually absorbed entirely into the world without remainder—and ontologically—the fact that being is phenomena, that is, that which appears or manifests itself, applies to us as well, which means that our worldly actions define us.[186] The call of conscience does pull us out of the unthinking maintenance of our lives, but not *to* anywhere else, for the simple reason that there is nowhere else to go. We discover what kind of beings we are when the content of our lives is temporarily suspended,[187] similar to the way Husserl's bracketing reveals consciousness' noetic acts or Wittgenstein's tautologies illuminate logic; but one of the features we discover is that we are entirely of this world. Attempts to surpass it toward something transcendent, to escape the Cave in order to look upòn real Being, constitute something like Sartre's bad faith, that is, the endeavor to settle the unsettling aspects of our being such as mortality and the lack of metaphysically approved ways of living. In this sense, our mode of being is not just inconspicuous; we actively cover it up, which makes philosophy a battle against the bewitchment of inauthenticity.[188]

Breakdowns show us the formal structure of our selfhood, that we may begin to construct a self appropriate to its true nature, but the materials to do so can only be found in our culture.[189] While there are no "correct" choices, yearning for transcendence is a wrong one, since it conflicts with our very being. Acquiring the appropriate understanding of our finite essence is necessary[190] for us to "become who we are."[191] Whereas traditionally philosophy's focus on presence-at-hand aided our attempts to flee from our true nature, a renewed philosophy can, Heidegger suggests, reverse this trend and help us achieve an authentic existence. Wittgenstein, on the other hand, praises the traditional mindset, suggesting that his own work achieves the ancient dream of transcendence.[192] He sees an identity between self and world—"I am my world"[193]—but this identity is at once more and less than Heidegger's: more in that this "mineness" encompasses the entire world, and less in that a transcendent self in some sense exceeds it.

Their developmental arcs into their later work cross each other.[194] Wittgenstein comes to abandon all transcendence, studying logic and language as fully human phenomena of our "average everydayness." As I will discuss in chapters 2 and 5, he debunks the notion of autonomous reality or logic developing its predetermined essence as we look on, guiding our thought and speech for us. Rather than advising us to relinquish all interference with ethical and logical matters, Wittgenstein now finds language inextricably interwoven with our "complicated form of life" (PI II, i p. 148). It is in the *Philosophical Investigations* that he divests philosophers of any special insight into matters arcane, restricting their teachings to the more humble task of assembling reminders of our pre-reflective understanding of grammar, similar to Heidegger's phenomenological approach in division I of *Being and Time*.

Heidegger, on the other hand, comes to embrace a form of Nietzschean elitism, looking beyond drab everydayness to the towering peaks of language and thought. Instead of humble hammerers, his later work is populated by poets and thinkers, those great few most attuned to being's call, who quiet their own thoughts and actions to let being be through them. Division II's authentic voluntarism becomes villainized as modernity's hubris, the arrogant belief that we determine our own thinking rather than receiving it.[195] Voluntarist action gets beaten into quietist acceptance, a "letting-be." This is not a complete passivity, of course; we make creative rejoinders to and rearrangements of the social and conceptual landscape we find ourselves in but, as I will discuss in chapter 4, even these are ultimately responses. Where early Wittgenstein let fate control our destiny and logic command our thinking, later Heidegger implores us to open ourselves to what being may send.

## Wonder

This disagreement extends to the question of wonder, considered philosophy's starting point since Plato and Aristotle. For Heidegger, stepping outside our everyday absentminded preoccupations functions as what Derrida calls a *pharmakon*, both cure and poison.[196] Whereas disengaging from active involvement has traditionally lead to the unfortunate dominance of presence-at-hand ontology, when cultivated into an attentive, quasi-phenomenological "staying with things" (BW 353)—as Heidegger does in his later work—it yields insight into the nature of being itself.

Near the beginning of *Being and Time*, Heidegger defines phenomenology as the study of what appears or shows itself (BT 58/34) in opposition to the traditional metaphysical focus on what transcends the world of experience—Forms, God, substances, and so on. It does not stay entirely at this level, however, but searches for "something that proximally and for the most part does *not* show itself at all . . . that which remains *hidden* in an egregious sense" (BT 59/35). Heidegger's combination of hermeneutics with phenomenology means that understanding phenomena involves interpretation. While this can never lead us to reject phenomena in favor of something noumenal hidden behind them or something substantial lurking beneath, neither are we forced take things as they initially appear. Conclusions must be borne out by experience, broadly conceived, and this often requires considerable effort and patience.[197] We have already seen three obstacles to accurate description: inconspicuousness, inherited prejudices, and dread-motivated cover-ups. Another cause is our failure to appreciate the "ontological difference": our dealings with individual beings keep our understanding of their modes of being in the taken-for-granted background, so that our ontology remains pre-ontological.

One of the changes that marks Heidegger's *Kehre*—that is, the "turning" from his early to his later work—is his change of emphasis from ways of being to being itself.[198] Metaphysicians have successfully distinguished beings from their way of being—this horse from substantiality, say, or this person from divine createdness—but have failed to investigate how these ways of being come about. The sheer manifestation of entities and their intelligibility, which is how Heidegger comes to define being itself or the truth of being, is now the most inconspicuous phenomenon of all.[199]

As I will discuss in chapters 4 and 5, Heidegger rules out explanations of these most basic facts that there is anything, and that things are intelligible—since any account would presuppose some of the concepts it is meant to explain—but he does believe that we can achieve a kind of experience of it in wonder. When he asks questions such as "why are there beings at all, and why not rather nothing" (BW 110), Heidegger tells us that "if the answer could be given it would consist in a transformation of thinking, not in a propositional statement about a matter at stake."[200] Like authenticity, this marks an adverbial shift, halting ontic dealings that use withdrawn beings in order to help us experience them vividly; we can see why artworks could serve as a model for this kind of philosophical activity. Although all of our experience happens *within* unconcealment, it is only by means of this kind of questioning that we explicitly become aware *of* unconcealment, the utterly simple fact that there *are* beings and that we are open to them. "In astonishment we restrain ourselves. We step back, as it were, from being, from the fact that it is as it is and not otherwise. . . . Thus, astonishment is disposition in which and for which the Being of being unfolds."[201] It is this paradox that explains how Heidegger can be both ontologically democratic—everyone *hears* the voice of being—and elitist—few *harken* to it.

This is why Heidegger values the shocks that break the spell of our ongoing engagement with the world, from the breakdowns of hammers and cultures to artworks and death. The epigraph to *Being and Time* scolds interlocutors *not* for not knowing what being is, but precisely for their sense that they do, for their lack of puzzlement. That book's project is not so much to answer the question of being as to reawaken it and let it provoke us anew. At such moments, the lighting up of the world becomes luminous itself, and the proper response is wonder and gratitude. It's a strange kind of gratitude in that there is no one and nothing to be grateful to, but "thinking" in thematic awareness of this openness becomes a "thanking," the later Heidegger's counterpart to authenticity.

Wittgenstein agrees that wonder is the root of all philosophy. His early description of it comes quite close to Heidegger;[202] in fact, Wittgenstein's sole recorded mention of Heidegger (at a meeting of the Vienna Circle) is to praise him on this topic.

I can readily think what Heidegger means by Being and Dread. Man has the impulse to run up against the limits of language. Think, for example, of the astonishment that anything exists. This astonishment cannot be expressed in the form of a question, and there is also no answer to it. . . . Yet the tendency represented by the running-up against *points to something*. (Murray 1978, 80–81)

While these expressions have no legitimate sense (since they admit no sensible negation, a necessary condition for meaning throughout his career), Wittgenstein finds the feeling they express noble and worthy of deep respect, esteeming religious figures, poets, and composers far higher than the scientists that the logical positivists took as role models.[203] Both Wittgenstein and Heidegger consider explanations and assertions inadequate, even hostile to such ideas, requiring them to deny knowledge in order to make room for wonder. As Kant taught, we are naturally prone to illegitimate metaphysical speculations (Cavell 1995, 133–134).

In his later work, Wittgenstein comes to view positive philosophy as a noxious pest to be prevented from arising when possible, exterminated when necessary. Whereas Heidegger reveres the wondrous questions that cannot be answered ("philosophical questions are in principle never settled as if some day one could set them aside"),[204] Wittgenstein considers these questions to be malformed expressions of inchoate impulses: "we start with a vague mental uneasiness, like that of a child asking 'Why?'. The child's question is not that of a mature person; it expresses puzzlement rather than a request for precise information. So philosophers ask 'Why?' and 'What?' without knowing clearly what their questions are. They are expressing a feeling of mental uneasiness" (LWL 22). Instead of violating logic, his early criterion for pseudo-propositions, now he believes that we ourselves don't really know what these illegitimate questions and statements mean since, once they have strayed beyond their usual circumstances, we lack an agreed-upon way to use them. "In a game in which the rules are indeterminate one *cannot* know who has won and who has lost."[205] For Heidegger, philosophy brings what is best in us to its highest and noblest form;[206] for Wittgenstein, philosophical problems are the artificial results of a peculiar stance he compares to that of children or "savages, primitive people."[207]

Wittgenstein's purpose is therapeutic, dismantling or dis-solving philosophical problems instead of solving them.[208] The only reason to take up these traditional problems is because they keep cropping up, renewing their hold over us. In particular, the queerness that incites wonder is just a side-effect of our philosophical staring, a stupefaction caused by the suspension of our normal knowing our way around. In this sense, Wittgenstein's conception of philosophy remains adverbial: the mood can infect all sorts of phenomena once retrospectively reconceived. "One must remember that all the phenomena that now strike us as so remarkable are the very familiar phenomena that don't surprise us in the least when they happen. They don't strike us as remarkable until we put them in a strange light by philosophizing."[209] Removing a phrase from its ordinary context hardens it into a dead lump incapable of performing its usual job. We then pump all kinds of magical powers into it to revive it. Philosophical theories give the wrong kinds of answers to pseudo-problems, problems born of a self-induced hypnosis.

This makes philosophical problems of no intrinsic worth; we should pay attention to them only to disentangle ourselves from them. "The philosophical concept was derived from the ordinary one through all sorts of misunderstandings, and it strengthens these misunderstandings. It is in no way interesting, except as a warning."[210] Whereas for Heidegger, the fact that mundane phenomena only strike us as strange during wonder represents an essential insight into them, Wittgenstein thinks that it's just an idiosyncrasy of our species that we can hypnotize ourselves by repeating a word until it loses its significance, an odd effect that has inspired centuries of philosophy. Bringing our words back to their normal usage restores our usual tacit mastery of their use, dispelling the illusion of profound enigmas hidden in their depths: "while thinking philosophically we see problems in places where there are none. It is for philosophy to show that there are no problems."[211] Heidegger wants us to see that "at bottom, the ordinary is not ordinary; it is extraordinary,"[212] while Wittgenstein continuously demonstrates that the things philosophers marvel at are nothing marvelous; what Heidegger seeks to ignite, Wittgenstein stamps out.[213] While both critique traditional philosophical theories, for Heidegger "the task is to see the riddle," to let being's questionable mystery endlessly provoke us;[214] for Wittgenstein, both early and late, "the solution of the problem of life is seen in the vanishing of the problem."[215]

As we will see in chapter 5, Wittgenstein often uses deflationary phrases like "this is just how we talk" to demystify phenomena we are tempted to wonder at and seek philosophical explanations for. He even recommends a technique to inoculate ourselves against the wonder that forms the germ of philosophy: when we find ourselves getting excited over, say, how minds can affect and be affected by physical bodies, we should induce in ourselves an overtly artificial case of perplexity over a wholly uninteresting phenomenon. This will demonstrate how easy it is to create this experience, and thus how little it means.[216] In effect, Wittgenstein is trying to disenchant enchantment itself. We should greet the topics that have inspired two and a half millennia of philosophizing with the nonchalant shrug with which we note other idiosyncrasies, like associating colors with particular vowels.[217] Despite their impressive sound and fury, such facts signify nothing—after all, "one can construct an atmosphere to attach to anything" (PI §609)—thus helping us "pass from a piece of disguised nonsense to something that is patent nonsense" (PI §464). For example, philosophers become fixated on the absolute difference between mind and matter, rendering their interaction mysterious and so in need of theoretical explanation. Yet we feel no such compulsion to account for the way a metal antenna "catches" radiowaves from out of insubstantial air and converts them to sound. We are perfectly satisfied with mundane scientific facts in the latter case, but insist that no such fact could possibly explain the mind–body connection. Our comfort with antenna–radio-wave dualism can disarm the parallel issue of mind–body dualism.

We should realize that we have run off the cliff by this point with only pictures and analogies to guide us, leading to bizarre notions that conflict with all sorts of features of the normal usage that we were supposed to be merely extending. The naïveté involved in taking these simple pictures literally creates "a philosophical trouble . . . an obsession, which once removed it seems impossible that it should ever have had power over us. It seems trivial" (AWL 98). Because it was merely a metaphor—I know that thoughts aren't *really* located inside my head—the confusion looks absurd once brought to my conscious attention, thus liberating me from its grip. Having a thought in my head is no more significant than having a song in my heart. We can stop doing philosophy once we see how insubstantial the issues plaguing us are: "the solution of philosophical problems can be compared with a gift in a fairy tale: in the magic castle it appears enchanted and if you look at it outside in daylight it is nothing but an ordinary bit of iron."[218]

Mere confusions, philosophical questions will bother us indefinitely since we can never quite scratch the itch—or rather, since scratching exacerbates the itch. Like the skeptics' goal of *ataraxia*, Wittgenstein seeks the peace of mind that results from putting philosophy down. "The philosophical problems should *completely* disappear. The real discovery is the one that makes me capable of stopping doing philosophy when I want to.—The one that gives philosophy peace, so that it is no longer tormented by questions."[219] This also explains his occasionally lackadaisical approach to assertions: one can use whatever works in the quest for a purely negative result, the way skeptics happily borrow premises from their opponents to perform a *reductio* on them, and then throw away the ladder.

There are some complications to this interpretation, however. Very rarely, Wittgenstein makes more conciliatory comments, such as acknowledging a certain reverence for the pictures that lie at the root of our practices,[220] or conceding that "philosophical mistakes . . . contain so much truth,"[221] which conflicts with his far more common descriptions of them as mere confusions. Loosening these conceptual knots certainly reveals a great deal about grammar and even suggests some general facts about human nature, but that is not the same as the problems containing truth. Similarly, while he frequently claims that his goal is to stop philosophizing and he did steer students away from the discipline, there is at least one recorded comment criticizing those who have achieved this state.[222] It is far from clear what differentiates such shallow thinkers from those who have achieved the peace of mind promised by Wittgenstein's dis-solving method, but these comments are rare exceptions against an extensive and consistent background of opposing claims.

## Summary

Heidegger's early and Wittgenstein's later conception of philosophy both use the understanding tacitly manifest in our mundane interactions to correct the misunderstandings that arise from disengaged contemplation. This understanding—primarily of word-usage for Wittgenstein, and modes of being for Heidegger—is conceived of as a mastery, knowing how to speak or act appropriately. Constantly in use, it remains inconspicuously in the background and vanishes under the theoretical gaze. False problems occur because the understanding that could prevent them resists thematic examination and articulation. Wittgenstein attributes the distorting influence primarily to pictures or metaphors in the lay of the linguistic land on which we build "houses of cards" (PI §118) that should be condemned and torn down. Heidegger sees presence-at-hand as the source of traditional ontology; while legitimate within its limits, philosophy's exclusive focus on it has excluded other, more basic modes of being and understanding.[223]

They view the end of philosophy very differently, however. For Wittgenstein, this end promises the cessation of an activity premised on confusions and trafficking in meaningless conclusions. This entire way of thinking should cease, followed by a peace of mind wholly undisturbed by philosophizing. Heidegger, on the other hand, sees the end of traditional philosophy as opening the way for the different but related art of "thinking." His later approach to thinking embodies the virtues of intensified awareness, gratitude, and wonder—qualities that Wittgenstein's early work prizes, but which he later tries to stamp out as sparks that can at any time reignite philosophy. Heidegger's heavy Teutonic and mystical terms like "holiness" and "destiny" are quite distant from Wittgenstein's later emphasis on the ordinary.

Now that we have seen their general approach to philosophizing as dismantling pictures or theories that lead us astray, let's take a closer look at what they both consider to be the most common and the most virulent offender.

# 2 What Is a Thing?

One says: How can these gestures, this way of holding the hand, this picture, be the wish that such and such were the case? It is nothing more than a hand over a table and there it is, alone and without a *sense*. Like a single bit of scenery from the production of a play, which has been left by itself in a room. It had life only in the play.
—Wittgenstein, *Zettel*, §238

For every experience that I want to consider I must isolate and lift out, break up and destroy the contexture of the experience so that in the end and despite all efforts to the contrary, I have only a heap of things.
—Heidegger, *Towards the Definition of Philosophy*, 64

Chapter 1 explained Wittgenstein's and Heidegger's diagnoses of philosophical confusion as the result of being guided by a picture or understanding of being during reflection, instead of by the tacit understanding that informs pre-reflective acting and speaking. In this chapter, I want to look at the specific picture/conception of being responsible for more befuddlement than any other, what Wittgenstein sometimes calls "meaning-objects" and early Heidegger calls present-at-hand objects.

Wittgenstein's later work is known for its fertility and diversity; one of his goals is to correct philosophy's tendency to fixate on a single notion or kind of example.[1] However, the more I have read and reread these works, the more I have been struck with their focused attack on the idea that "the meaning of each word is an invisible *body*."[2] While the preface of the *Philosophical Investigations* does call the book "an album" or "a number of sketches of landscapes," it adds that they concentrate on the same territory, perhaps like Cézanne's many paintings of Mont Sainte-Victoire: "the same or almost the same points were always being approached afresh from different directions, and new sketches made."[3] If Wittgenstein's return to philosophy was motivated by his realization that his earlier efforts were wrongheaded and if, as I will argue, meaning-objects represent one of the linchpins of that system, then it makes sense that his later work is largely organized around dismantling this idea, as many commentators have noted.[4]

Heidegger considers the tunnel-vision focus on being as constant presence and thus beings as enduring, stable objects to be the greatest obstacle to understanding the world the way we actually experience it. Traditional philosophy is almost entirely organized around "the unexpressed but ontologically dogmatic guiding thesis that what *is* . . . must be *present-at-hand*, and that what does not let itself be Objectively demonstrated as *present-at-hand*, just *is not* at all."[5] He dismantles this prejudice by tracing its origin and showing its limited region of legitimacy.

## Tractarian Object Logic

In the *Tractatus*, the analysis of statements bottoms out in elementary propositions which consist of an organized set of names whose meanings are their referents: simple objects.[6] This is the bedrock on which that book's *explanandum*—language's ability to describe the world—rests. It is here that language gets its meaning because it is here that words get linked to things, the primordial baptism of the world; all other linguistic acts draw their funds from this originary investment of significance. In principle, every sensible statement can be traced back via a semantic apostolic succession to a direct connection with the world: In the beginning was the name, and the name was with its object, and the name's meaning was its object. Wittgenstein describes his early conception of meaning in his transitional period:

the concept of meaning I adopted in my philosophical discussions originates in a primitive philosophy of language. The German word for "meaning" is derived from the German word for "pointing." When Augustine talks about the learning of language he talks about how we attach names to things, or understand the names of things. *Naming* here appears as the foundation, the be all and end all of language.[7]

Importantly, Wittgenstein compares his own early views to the Augustinian conception of meaning that opens *Philosophical Investigations* and which, I believe, remains an orienting landmark throughout the book and his later work in general. This conception is a "particular picture of the essence of human language" (PI §1) that takes its bearings from ostensively defined nouns, rendering language a kind of pointing.

The *Tractatus* identifies meaning with naming because, in the final analysis, language boils down to names. Elementary propositions combine names into structures isomorphic with possible organizations of simple objects into states-of-affairs in the world.[8] The exact nature and identity of these objects is obscure, even to Wittgenstein himself,[9] but I think they resemble Leibniz's monads in a number of ways. Instead of a Lockean substance which is essentially distinct from the accidents it supports, simple objects *are* their "internal properties," that is, the set of states-of-affairs they are capable of entering, also called their form: "if I know an object I also know all its possible occurrences in states of affairs. (Every one of these possibilities must be part of the nature of the object)."[10] While simple objects, lacking complexity, cannot be defined,[11] their essences are shown by their combinatory practices, much as we pick up the sense of logical operations by watching how they operate.[12] Augustine, like the early Wittgenstein, is "thinking first and foremost of *nouns*, and of the remaining words as something that will take care of itself" (PG 56).

Contra Leibniz, Wittgenstein distinguishes an object's *potential* to enter into a certain set of states-of-affairs—its internal properties—from its *actual* occurrence in extant states-of-affairs—its external or material properties. The former are essential and eternal, the latter contingent and mutable; the former unfolds all that can be the case while the latter fills in all that is the case.[13] Material objects, for example, have the internal property of necessarily occupying a specific spatial location, but where a particular object happens to be located at a particular time is a contingent matter.

Once calibrated with its object, a name takes on the linguistic counterpart of the object's internal properties: a name represents or goes proxy for an object in that it can only sensibly occur in propositions that represent states-of-affairs into which its object may enter.[14] The model car that inspired Wittgenstein's theory can represent a real car because it can take on the same spatial relations (above, to the left of, . . .) with the model street and pedestrians as their counterparts.[15] Conversely, if an object cannot enter into a particular state-of-affairs, then its name cannot legitimately occur in propositions describing this state-of-affairs: a piece of music has a certain loudness and pitch, but no color or taste.[16] Linguistic representations serve as their objects' representatives.

This system can be seen as a large-scale expansion of Frege's notion of saturation. In order for a set of words to be a proposition and not just a list of words, Frege argued that some of its contents (subjects, names, arguments) must be saturated or self-sufficient whereas others (predicates, concepts, functions) must be unsaturated, requiring another element in order to form a complete thought.[17] Wittgenstein builds his system around the similar idea that "in a state of affairs objects fit into one another like the links of a chain," which gets reflected in "elementary propositions which consist of names in immediate combination."[18] Instead of Frege's two large classes where any member of one can mate with any member of the other, Wittgenstein's objects couple only with compatible partners in prearranged marriages.[19] Once harmony has been established, language works the same way reality does, forming "all-embracing logic, which mirrors the world" (T 5.511). Thus, "We are looking for the use of a sign, but we look for it as though it were an object *co-existing* with the sign" (BB 5).

This metaphysical-semantic picture requires objects to "contain" or fully anticipate all of their combinatorial possibilities: "if things can occur in states of affairs, this possibility must be in them from the beginning. . . . A new possibility cannot be discovered later."[20] Each object predetermines all of its combinatory possibilities, so the connective potentials of all objects join to map out the totality of all possible states-of-affairs, that is, logical space as a whole.[21] Simple objects have an absolutely determinate sense because both the set of states-of-affairs they are in at any particular time, and the set of possible states-of-affairs they can ever enter, are bivalently fixed: for each state-of-affairs, every object either presently occurs in it or not, and is either capable of occurring in it or not.[22]

This absolute determinacy is then conducted to language through the circuit between names and simple objects, thus fulfilling Frege's stringent requirement for sense.[23] Just as the totality of objects outlines all possible states-of-affairs on the side of the world, so the totality of names delimits all possible elementary propositions on the side of language. As we saw in chapter 1, applying the set of all logical operations to the complete set of possible elementary propositions produces the totality of all meaningful propositions: "suppose that I am given *all* elementary propositions: then I can simply ask what propositions I can construct out of them. And there I have *all* propositions, and *that* fixes their limits."[24] Like Leibniz's elegantly economic deity, Wittgenstein's system gets as much as possible out of as little as possible. In 1913, he wrote Russell excitedly that "one of the consequences of my new ideas will—I think—be that the whole of Logic follows from one Pp only!!,"[25] namely, the general propositional form, "the one and only general primitive sign in logic."[26] This is what allows Wittgenstein to attain his goal, that is, "to draw a limit . . . to the expression of thoughts" from the inside, setting "limits to what cannot be thought by working outwards through what can be thought."[27] Language, reality and thought are limited determinate wholes in lockstep with each other.

As discussed in chapter 1, Wittgenstein's early ethics was deeply indebted to Schopenhauer's ideal of quieting the will in the face of a deterministic universe. Instead of trying to change external circumstances we should resign ourselves to whatever occurs, which alters how we live in the world as a whole rather than any particular features of it—shifting the melody of our lives into a different key rather than altering the notes, so to speak. In a stance that I will call Logical Stoicism, the *Tractatus* applies this idea to logic, the third transcendental subject along with ethics and aesthetics.[28] Just as ethical laws give no instructions concerning specific actions to be done or avoided,[29] so "all the propositions of logic say the same thing, to wit nothing."[30] Rejecting Russell's conception of logic as comprising maximally general laws of reality, Wittgenstein views it as a set of empty tautologies which, saying nothing, show the structure of and relationships among the pieces of the propositions that do say something. It's a little like a foreign currency's equivalency chart: it won't teach you what the money can buy, but rather the internal relationships among the coins and bills, allowing you to make change among them without ever exchanging them for anything external.

This stance assigns the logician the same passive resignation that the good/happy person takes toward worldly events: "logic is not a field in which *we* express what we wish with the help of signs, but rather one in which the nature of the absolutely necessary signs speaks for itself."[31] Wittgenstein repeatedly takes Russell and Frege to task for explicitly defining functions and entities[32] instead of letting the nature of logic speak for itself. Such expositions of logic in everyday language directed at the reader, breaking the text's "fourth wall" so to speak, compromises logic's self-sufficiency and purity: "the rules of logical syntax must go without saying, once we know how each individual sign signifies."[33] Rules contain their consequences and applications, leaving us the job of merely unpacking what's already there. "Logic takes care of itself; all we have to do is to look and see how it does it" (NB 11).

Just as Wittgenstein defines simple objects as sets of possible combinations, so logical operations are ways simpler propositions recursively combine into more complex ones, in other words, a kind of function that cranks out a series when the right kind of inputs are fed into it. The right way to continue such rules—the functions' ranges—must be metaphysically preset for the Tractarian project to succeed, a point Wittgenstein clearly recognizes.

The concept "and so on," symbolized by ". . ." is one of the most important of all and like all the others infinitely fundamental. For it alone justifies us in constructing logic and mathematics "so on" from the fundamental laws and primitive signs. . . .

When the general form of operations is found we have also found the general form of the occurrence of the concept "and so on."[34]

As we saw in chapter 1, an adequate notation lets symbolic operations happen almost by themselves. Because each of these operations anticipates its entire extension, "if we introduced logical signs properly, then we should also have introduced at the same time the sense of all combinations of them."[35] Setting up the meaning of the number two, the starting point of zero, and the operation addition ipso facto circumscribes the range {2, 4, 6, . . .} for the function "+2" as a determinate set. The overarching strategy of the *Tractatus* is to apply this to language: the input of elementary propositions and the ways they can be truth-functionally combined together trace the contours of language. "The syntax of language" draws the limits of the "class of propositions with sense . . . from the inside. The *domain of sense* of a function (that is the totality of values of $x$ regarding which $fx$ has sense) is delimited from the inside by the nature of the function."[36] *We* are not placing limits upon language but discovering where it necessarily ends.

An appropriate symbolism allows all and only legitimate combinations of symbols, the way the physical components of the model of a car accident could enter into the same relationships as the model's referents. "The essence of a propositional sign is very clearly seen if we imagine one composed of spatial objects . . . instead of written signs. Then the spatial arrangement of these things will express the sense of the proposition."[37] As I said earlier, the best model of this would be something like Lego or puzzle pieces where only certain units can interlock with each other, excluding illicit combinations not by laying down laws forbidding them (which would require speaking of that which, he is claiming, cannot be spoken), but by rendering them intrinsically impossible. A currency constructed along these lines would make exchange charts gratuitous by shaping the various coins so that they merge into all and only numerically appropriate compounds: five nickels should snap together to form a quarter, four quarters combine into a jigsaw dollar, and so on. The symbols would tell us how they ought to act by only being able to act properly. Wittgenstein says of the comparison of propositions with reality that "in the case of two lines we can *compare* them in respect of their length without any convention: the comparison is automatic. But in our case the possibility of comparison depends upon the conventions by which we have given meanings to our simples (names and relations)" (NB 111). A proper notation would model the latter on the former, minimizing or even eliminating the role of convention, and thus allowing usage to become virtually automatic. At one point he invokes meaning-bodies to perform this role: "Here one is thinking as if *this* comparison came into one's mind: words fit together in the sentence, i.e., senseless sequences of words may be written down; but the meaning of each word is an invisible *body*, and these meaning-bodies do *not* fit together" (RPPI §42).

As most pre-Kantian epistemologists insisted, any interference on our part in our experience or beliefs—whether by contingent historical or cultural facts, accidental features of our sensory apparatus, or anything else not directly derived from the world—disturbs the mirror of nature, knocking the correspondence between propositions and reality out of whack. Truth requires a passivity in reality's recording device, that the blank paper or soft wax of the mind may take the impression of experience without introducing anything of its own. Russell applies this empiricist stance to logic,[38] a bit like Husserl's categorial intuition which inspired the young Heidegger. Wittgenstein carries epistemological passivity to its logical conclusion in his early work: logic looks after itself as logicians merely look on.

And this is where Wittgenstein's logic meets his sins,[39] where Russell's logical empiricism harmonizes with Schopenhauer's pure will-less witness, where the logician yielding to absolute truth dovetails with the good person resigned to the way things are, conferring simultaneously a kind of omniscience about all that can happen and a kind of invulnerability to all that does. One can only imagine how the young Wittgenstein felt when, after years of tormented searching, all the pieces finally clicked into place, forming a tightly unified system where *simplex sigillum veri*—"simplicity is the sign of truth" (T 5.4541). It must have felt like hearing the voice of God.

### Meaning-Bodies

Recall from chapter 1 that pictures are a principal cause of philosophical confusion by leading us to think about one topic in terms borrowed from a very different subject. Wittgenstein came to see the dominant picture behind what are often called Platonic theories of meaning as the "inclination to think of a meaning-body,"[40] an inclination that leads us to move unwittingly from talking about meanings as they actually operate in our daily lives to talking about them like physical objects. One of the sources of this confusion in the Tractarian system lies in its demand that the set of combinations that a simple object or name can legitimately enter be absolutely determinate. The set of states-of-affairs that actually hold is the real, but the set of all possible states constitutes the space within which the real occurs—the space of sense, reality's "unalterable form."[41] This treats possibility as, in a sense, actual: the space of the possible is already there with all possible possibilities precisely mapped out within it. Alain Badiou calls the *Tractatus* "an ontology of the virtual" (2011, 104).

Wittgenstein describes how this "objectification" works with the "idea idea," that is, the notion that perception occurs via the medium of ideas:

we are tempted to use the grammar which we use for a word designating a physical object—we are tempted to use this grammar for words that designate impressions. In our primitive language most substantives relate to some physical object or other. When then we begin to talk of impressions, we have a temptation to use the same kind of grammar. This produces a puzzle which doesn't look as though it were a grammatical puzzle.[42]

The grammar of physical objects conflicts in all sorts of ways with how we talk about meaning in everyday life, leading to a wide variety of confusions. But instead of giving up this inappropriate conceptual frame, philosophers, mesmerized by their own picture, add more and more epicycles to jerry-rig the recalcitrant data. "A simile that has been absorbed into the forms of our language produces a false appearance, and this disquiets us. 'But *this* isn't how it is!'—we say. 'Yet *this* is how it has to *be*!'"[43]

Taking names as the essence of language, a central feature of the *Tractatus* and the Augustinian conception of language, reinforces this picture. Since the ostensive definition of a noun by pointing to an object seems to present such a clear and compelling exemplar of how language hooks onto the world, it takes over all thought about how language relates to the world. The "What is *x*?" questions that philosophers since Socrates (very much including Heidegger) have been so enamored of feeds this confusion, as the opening of *The Blue Book* explains.

The questions "What is length?," "What is meaning?," "What is the number one?," etc., produce in us a mental cramp. We feel that we can't point to anything in reply to them and yet ought to point to something. (We are up against one of the great sources of philosophical bewilderment: a substantive makes us look for a thing that corresponds to it).[44]

This account of a word's meaning as the thing it stands for may be roughly true for a small portion of language (though things are considerably more complex even here, as we shall see), but philosophers extrapolate it to define language as a whole, a conspicuous example of philosophy's predilection for monomaniacal diets. "The basic evil of Russell's logic, as also of mine in the *Tractatus*, is that what a proposition is is illustrated by a few commonplace examples, and then pre-supposed as understood in full generality."[45]

This noun-besotted theory stumbles over abstract concepts which, unlike chairs, cannot be pointed to. A philosophical craving arises from a question which bothers one and yet seems unanswerable in a straightforward way. "What is a chair?," by comparison with "What is 3?," seems simple. For if one is asked what a chair is one can point to something or give some sort of description; but if asked what the number 3 is, one is at a loss. . . . This question, "What is 3?," arises from a jumble of misunderstandings, one of which is due to our having the word "meaning" in our language. "Meaning" is thought to stand for (1) something to which one can point, or (2) something in the mind.[46]

Like most philosophical pictures, this one results from a misleading analogy, here between "What is *x*?" questions about ordinary physical objects and those concerning abstract concepts. Misled by the isomorphism between these questions, we model words' meanings in general on nouns of easily point-out-able moderate-sized dry goods, in Austin's phrase, and then become puzzled when we cannot point to certain "*x*'s." An implicit disjunctive syllogism arises, much like the one about the mind we saw in chapter 1: if meanings are some kind of thing we can point at, but plainly not physical objects our fingers can indicate, then the kind of thing and the kind of pointing must be queer—mental fingers, perhaps, designating metaphysical objects. Plato explicitly argues that if we can talk intelligibly about Beauty while only seeing beautiful things, then an Idea of Beauty must exist beyond this world, and must be accessed by something other than these crude bodily senses.

Not only does this move solve the mystery of un-point-out-able objects, but it has the added benefit that their new location in a meta-physical or mental sphere confers upon them whatever strange powers one might need in order to satisfy the picture's demands. Processes like understanding, meaning, or thinking "seem to take place in a queer kind of medium, the mind; and the mechanism of the mind, the nature of which, it seems, we don't quite understand, can bring about effects which no material mechanism could" (BB 3). One demand, as we have seen, is for meanings to be completely settled in advance: either the meaning itself lies coiled within simple objects or our understanding has scouted ahead to survey all possible paths, locating the right way in every context. While ordinary objects could never perform such a feat, metaphysics lets our imagination loose to build a more suitable entity out of transcendent materials, the stuff that philosophical dreams are made on. The performance of queer acts is secured by the creation of queer agents.

Wittgenstein hunts down a number of metaphors that inform and sustain this "dream of our language."[47] One is "a most important idea: the idea of possibility as a different kind of reality; and we might call it a shadow of reality."[48] Shadows—falling somewhere between solid physical objects and wisps of nothingness—nicely represent possibilities that are actual but only as possible. "It looks as if a sentence with e.g. the word 'ball' in it already contained the shadow of other uses of this word. That is to say, the *possibility* of forming those other sentences" (Z §138). Simple objects and names fix all possibilities by inhabiting them all in advance, extending shadowy tentacles throughout the whole of conceptual space like electrons following every possible route, as one interpretation of quantum mechanics has it.

Meanings are also imagined as ethereal, often as the conclusion of the now familiar disjunctive syllogism which finds no physical referents for meaningful terms.

Let me remind you here of the queer role which the gaseous and the aethereal play in philosophy,—when we perceive that a substantive is not used as what in general we should call the name of an object, and when therefore we can't help saying to ourselves that it is the name of an aethereal object. . . . When we are embarrassed about the grammar of certain words, and when all we know is that they are not used as names for material objects.[49]

A third model is that of "a *logical* germ, something which had to develop the way it does out of *logical* necessity."[50] Just as an acorn encloses *in nuce* the oak tree it will become, so notions contain their future behavior. Another is "the logical machine—that would be an all-pervading ethereal mechanism.—We must give warning against this picture."[51] The picture of machines, which guided the automatic functioning of an ideal notation in Wittgenstein's early work, sometimes employs spatial containment as a sub-picture, a picture that guides the use of the machine picture: "'the machine's action seems to be in it from the start' means: we are inclined to compare the future movements of the machine in their definiteness to objects which are already lying in a drawer and which we then take out. . . . The movements in question . . . had to be really—in a mysterious sense—already *present*."[52] If its future movements are set, then in a sense they already exist, premonitions of unborn ghosts pre-haunting the machine. Of course, real machines can always malfunction, so we conjure a magical "ideally rigid machine."[53]

When applied to rules, meaning-objects take the form of a predetermined range of outcomes, often modeled on the spatial inclusion of a group of physical objects, "as if the grammar were contained in the sign like a string of pearls in a box and he had only to pull it out. (But this kind of picture is just what is misleading us)."[54] A problem now arises: while all applications of rules or terms must be set from the start, actually employing words and following rules are, as Augustine points out, temporally extended acts in which individual uses come into being and pass away. This disparity between the temporally flowing words and actions on the one hand and the entirely unfolded meaning-object on the other is a typical philosophical worry that, entirely absent from engaged activity, becomes troubling while reflecting on it—the primal scene of philosophical troubles discussed in chapter 1. Wittgenstein pinpoints the responsible picture: "it perplexes us that there is no moment at which the thought of a sentence is completely present. Here we see that we are comparing the thought with a thing that we manufacture and possess as a whole. . . . We are misled by a plausible simile."[55]

One popular solution to this conceptual unease, used by Frege and Plato among many others, is to make the temporal employment of words an accidental appendage to their meaning, which resides outside of time and independently of human knowledge or application.[56] This solution transfers Boethius and Leibniz's reconciliation of divine foreknowledge with human free will into semantics: the essence of meaning-objects is to occupy all relevant sectors of logical space; indeed, like simple objects, I think that they simply *are* the contours they fill in. They cover their entire area simultaneously, like a continent on a map, although for us it unfolds temporally as we travel the land, thus appearing to our linear perspective to be an anticipation that reaches ahead to nail down all future employments. "We expect every idea to have tentacles or affinities, so that it predetermines what will satisfy it" (AWL 85). In line with Logical Stoicism, this picture relieves the logician of the burden and responsibility of making up her mind—similar to Boethius' fatalist resignation, or the way Dasein avoids genuine consideration of her death. Viewing death as a future actuality safely insulates us from it by "a long time," paradoxically disarming it: "one of these days one will die too, in the end; but right now it has nothing to do with us. . . . Death gets passed off as always something 'actual'; its character as a possibility gets concealed."[57]

Whereas in *Being and Time* Dasein is unsettled by death and existential meaninglessness, the anxiety haunting the *Tractatus* concerns the loss of meaning, a semantic nihilism.[58] The meaning-object picture ensures objective truth in all circumstances by changing uncertain future employments into actualities already existing, determined by "a kind of ideal connection that is as it were sketched in advance by Logic so that reality only has to trace it. It is possibility conceived as a shadowy actuality."[59] Wittgenstein detects this picture underlying his predecessors' conversion of functions or rules into sets of preordained outputs for each input, as in set theory's definition of number.

Should we say we have 4 chairs if they are 1-1 correlated to a paradigm class, or if they can be 1-1 correlated? . . . If not correlated materially, Russell and Frege wanted to say that in some ethereal way they are correlated. If the correlation is a drawn line, one feels that before the correlation there was the possibility—like a very thin line which one traces in heavily when one draws, or like a poem muttered quickly when one is asked whether one knows it from memory, which is then traced in heavy lines by reciting it. The possibility of correlation seems to be some sort of correlation. Often its being possible to do something is like doing something similar.[60]

The word "red" for example has the sharp meaning demanded by Frege and the *Tractatus* because all and only red things in the world have already been herded—immaterially—into a group. Categorizing red objects occurs in time, but the set of all red objects already exists, encircled by an ideal line our classification simply traces. The question "Is this object red?" may seem to require a judgment or decision, whereas "Is this a member of the set, Red Objects?" feels like it must always have a definitive, bivalent answer. Colors may have their shades, but membership in a set is a black-or-white matter. Presumably, this applies to any meaningful category whatsoever, so that, say, the set of all liquid that will have passed through my body during my lifetime in some sense exists right now, invisibly outlined blobs of water tumbling and reshaping themselves all over the planet.

Meaning-objects play a similar role in rule-following. Like the set "Red Objects," operations such as "+2" must have a fixed extension in order to meet the Fregean-Tractarian standard of significance, which is achieved by transforming temporally extended serial applications of a function into a fully but mysteriously present series.

Your idea was that that act of meaning the order [+2] had in its own way already traversed all those steps: that when you meant it your mind as it were flew ahead and took all the steps before you physically arrived at this or that one.

Thus you were inclined to use such expressions as: "The steps are *really* already taken, even before I take them in writing or orally or in thought." And it seemed as if they were in some *unique* way predetermined, anticipated—as only the act of meaning can anticipate reality.[61]

The metaphysical idea that the set already exists, in the "joints" of reality as Plato put it, finds its epistemological counterpart in the notion that understanding the rule comprehends the entire set at once. Since the range logically and inexorably follows from the rule, grasping the latter brings the former in its entirety in its wake: "I believe that I perceive something drawn very fine in a segment of a series, a characteristic design, which only needs the addition of 'and so on,' in order to reach to infinity."[62] Running through all applications of a rule instantaneously, under one's mental breath as it were, seems necessary to explain the way we immediately recognize when a series has gone wrong.

Suppose our man got to the number 100 and followed it up by 102. We should then say "I *meant* you to write 101." Now the past tense in the word "to mean" suggests that a particular act of meaning had been performed when the rule was given, though as a matter of fact this expression alludes to no such act.[63]

As usual, retrospection distorts what really happened, in this case creating "this curious superstition, as one might be inclined to call it, that the mental act is capable of crossing a bridge before we've got to it."[64]

This magical anticipation further proves its worth by preventing semantic nihilism: it ensures the existence of an objectively right answer at every step, backing up our correction of "102" the way the gold at Fort Knox used to secure the value of U.S. paper money. Instead of having to decide each step, risking caprice, we merely follow a series that is already there, stretching out like "a visible section of rails invisibly laid out to infinity" (PI §218).

## Focus on Presence-at-Hand

Now that we have examined meaning-objects, the main target of Wittgenstein's later work, we can turn to its counterpart in Heidegger's thought. In line with my general interpretative strategy, Wittgenstein's critique of his own earlier work resembles Heidegger's early analysis of previous philosophy. *Being and Time* distinguishes three irreducible modes of being in order to demonstrate that Dasein's mode of being, which he calls "existence," cannot be understood in terms of the others, presence-at-hand and readiness-to-hand, as has traditionally been done. While Heidegger does discuss the interpretation of Dasein in terms of worldly readiness-to-hand,[65] more important and much more common historically is the misconstrual of Dasein as a present-at-hand substance.

We are strongly tempted to conceive of everything as present-at-hand objects or substances because they are what we find when we stop acting in the world in order to examine it. "In general our understanding of Being is such that every entity is understood in the first instance as present-at-hand. . . . Presence-at-hand has been equated with the meaning of Being in general."[66] As an inherently contemplative endeavor, philosophy naturally conceives of beings as present-at-hand even though this clashes sharply with normal experience. Heidegger grants this mode a restricted validity, but he objects to its ontological monopoly. It rightfully reigns over its own ontological region, but its legitimacy ends at its border.

We endeavor to examine reality as it really is by eliminating all disruptive distractions and prejudices, but this passive beholding is itself a prejudice, one that ironically does precisely what we were trying to avoid. The very attempt to study the subject undisturbed produces a profound transformation in it, making the present-at-hand object the metaphysical model for everything. "The priority which has always been granted to cognitive comportment from ancient times is at the same time associated with the peculiar tendency to define the being of the world in which Dasein is primarily in terms of how it shows itself for a cognitive comportment."[67] We understand ourselves as present-at-hand objects as well—thinking things—which, as self-contained substances, need to establish a cognitive connection to the separate world of things, else skepticism threatens. As in Wittgenstein's analysis, epistemology and metaphysics reinforce each other. Philosophy tries to assume Nagel's view from nowhere or Putnam's God's-eye view to see the way things are independently of any cultural, historical, or anatomical idiosyncrasies, without realizing that these features are essential to our ability to have any view whatsoever. Weaning us off such metaphysical aspirations, reconciling us to what I am calling original finitude, is one of Heidegger and Wittgenstein's central goals.

Heidegger unceasingly insists on the question of being because the way we understand something's being directs all of our thinking about it, much like Wittgenstein's pictures. Present-at-hand ontology has long guided philosophy, determining what kinds of questions we ask, what kinds of answers we accept as legitimate and relevant, and what constitutes a genuine problem—as Heidegger planned to demonstrate in detail in the second part of *Being and Time*.[68] For example, Descartes's "ontological orientation in principle towards Being as constant presence-at-hand" leads to his conception of knowledge as a disinterested beholding and of truth as what remains constant across variations of time, place, and observers.[69] In a slightly modified form of Plato's divided line, true knowledge doesn't change because genuine reality remains the same. Whereas Descartes argues that we must prove our own faculties before we can rely on them to know anything else, such as ontology, Heidegger responds that this very strategy presupposes a particular ontological structure, namely one that posits us as subjects, the world as objects, and knowledge as the primary relationship between them.[70] Since, as Descartes's case shows, the epistemology one finds reasonable rests upon one's ontology, Heidegger returns metaphysics to its traditional position as First Philosophy.

Wittgenstein makes a similar objection to the way a single form of language dominates thought about language as a whole. Augustine's extrapolation of naming as the general model of how words get meaning serves as the *Investigations'* representative of philosophical tunnel-vision.

Augustine, we might say, does describe a system of communication; only not everything that we call language is this system. And one has to say this in many cases where the question arises "Is this an appropriate description or not?" The answer is: "Yes, it is appropriate, but only for this narrowly circumscribed region, not for the whole of what you were claiming to describe." (PI §3)

Among other problems, this "craving for generality" (BB 17) blinds Augustine to the great heterogeneity of kinds of words and speech-acts, just as Heidegger diagnoses traditional philosophy as "dominated by an idea of Being which has been gathered from a definite realm of these entities themselves."[71]

## Explanation through Dismemberment

Beyond this formal similarity between later Wittgenstein and early Heidegger's critique of the exclusive focus on what is actually only one mode of language or of being, they agree substantially in their understanding of the tyrannical paradigm. As I will discuss in chapter 3, the engaged use of words on the one hand, and Dasein's dealing with equipmental totalities on the other, operate within a holistic web of dynamic interconnections. The change-over to disengaged observation desiccates this living network, leaving us with isolated objects and words. Like the traditional view of substances, present-at-hand objects stand in need of nothing else: self-contained, they retain their identity regardless of context. To paraphrase Gertrude Stein, a substance is a substance is a substance. Indeed, it is this constancy across time, place, and observers that makes a substance's primary qualities essential instead of accidental.[72]

Contemplation ceases our active dealings, clogging the dynamic interconnections among tools and between us and our environment, detaching the object of study from its organic context. "For every experience that I want to consider I must isolate and lift out, break up and destroy the contexture of the experience so that in the end and despite all efforts to the contrary, I have only a heap of things."[73] In an early work, Heidegger calls this "explanation through dismemberment," where "the stilled stream of lived experiences now becomes a series of individually intended objects."[74] What had been a part of a living breathing world has now "dwindled to an unrecognizable fragment" (BT 476/424) lying beached, immobilized, once the vital medium of use has receded. Philosophical analysis distorts what it seeks to understand, precisely *by* its attempt to understand it. "It has been cut off from that significance which, as such, constitutes environmentality. . . . It dwindles to the structure of just letting one see what is present-at-hand. . . . Only so does it obtain the possibility of exhibiting something in such a way that we just look at it."[75] The contemplative stance shatters Dasein's holistic being-in-the-world,[76] thereby setting the stage for a number of traditional philosophical views and issues.

Similarly, Wittgenstein's meaning-objects carry their entire meaning with them, allowing them to move to any context without changing. Since words derive their meaning from reaching right out to atomic situations, themselves isolated from everything else,[77] nothing external can affect their meaning. The affirmation or denial of the existence of a state-of-affairs derives its truth value entirely and exclusively from that fact; no matter where I am or what I feel or whatever else holds, the cat is either on the mat or not, making my affirmation simply true or false. Karl-Otto Apel puts the point nicely:

self-sufficient theory of meaning constitution through name-giving, taken out of the pragmatic context of language games bound up with life forms, exactly corresponds to the transition described by Heidegger from contextual world understanding to the deficient mode of simply staring at the present-at-hand. . . . To the Heideggerian limiting case of "de-worlding" (in which what is present-at-hand is simply stared at and so can have no more "meaning" for us) there corresponds, with Wittgenstein, the limiting case in which language "goes on holiday," that is, is no longer bound up with its use in a given life *praxis.*[78]

Heidegger and Wittgenstein both attribute the lion's share of philosophical pseudo-problems to the isolation that results from disengaging from activity in order to study a phenomenon. Such efforts are, as Iain Thomson puts it, "like trying to learn what it is like to ride a bike by staring at a broken bicycle" (2011, 56).

Wittgenstein attributes the very need for a philosophical account of meaning to this contemplative withdrawal. Once engaged speaking or writing has come to a halt, "the dead line on paper" does not seem up to the job of meaning something, demanding "a further dimension" to jolt the detached limb into motion, like Galvani's electrically stimulated frog's leg.[79] Nothing of the same nature such as further sounds or marks can do the trick—if it could, we would just stick with the words in the first place—thus making meaning queer: something gaseous, ethereal, shadowy. These preternatural forces which we ourselves don't understand lead to Frankenstein-like conceptual monstrosities we cannot control.

Meaning-objects play a crucial role in philosophy for Wittgenstein. As discussed in chapter 1, most philosophical confusion occurs when we remove words from the normal contexts in which we know how to use them to the bizarre, uncharted waters that philosophers delight in. Here, like most students studying philosophy for the first time, we have no clear sense of how to continue, forcing us to cling to pictures and analogies that peter out and leave us stranded without our even realizing it. This is why "a philosophical problem has the form: 'I don't know my way about'" (PI §123). The stranger the setting, the greater our disorientation, and hence the more vulnerable we are to the bewitchment of queer theories. "It is only in normal cases that the use of a word is clearly prescribed; we know, are in no doubt, what to say in this or that case. The more abnormal the case, the more doubtful it becomes what we are to say" (PI §142).

The new detail we can now add to this diagnosis is that meaning-objects underwrite the whole procedure. Since words are soldered onto "unalterable and subsistent"[80] objects that contain all of their combinatorial possibilities, they retain the same meaning under all conditions; we can simply use them the way we always have, no matter how far we have strayed from customary circumstances. This faith in words' intrinsic, static meaning that has anticipated all possible applications gives us the confidence to use words in extraordinary situations. "People say to us: 'You understand this expression don't you? Well, I too am using it with the meaning you are familiar with.' . . . This is to treat meaning as a halo that the word carries round with it and retains in any sort of application."[81] This belief in nonreactive verbal transplants functions a kind of *ur*-picture, a picture that authorizes our reliance on pictures generally by reassuring us that changing the context has no significant effect on significance; it is, in pop-psychological parlance, philosophy's "enabler."

Lest one think it a straw man, we find clear expression of this idea in Wittgenstein's early, Fregean analysis of meaning as absolutely sharp: "if the proposition 'The book is on the table' has a clear sense, then I must, whatever *is the case*, be able to say whether the proposition is true or false" (NB 67, emphasis in original). Complementing the conception of meaning as predetermining all possible states-of-affairs is a theory of comprehension according to which I can only be said to understand the proposition "The watch is lying on the table" if I can answer every possible question of the nature of, "'Yes, but if the watch were _____, would you still say it was lying?'"[82] In his later work, Wittgenstein describes the notion he was in thrall to: "the sense of a sentence—one would like to say—may, of course, leave this or that open, but the sentence must nevertheless have *a* definite sense. An indefinite sense—that would really not be a sense *at all*."[83] Meaning is a thoroughly bivalent affair: either the "and so on" attached to every word and rule continues on to infinity, or it has no extension whatsoever.

In the early 1930s, Wittgenstein rejects the idea that extending the same rules/game/meaning to new circumstances is automatic or follows directly from a core meaning, established rules, previous usage, or analogies.[84] A metaphysically preset way to follow rules is just a picture, inspired by the ease with which we usually apply words and rules to somewhat novel circumstances. He comes to believe that the application of an idea to wholly new circumstances, philosophy's bread and butter, is inescapably underdetermined (though this way of putting it can easily mislead, as we will see in chapter 4). "It's no help to us that we find a way of speaking ready-made in our ordinary language, since this language uses each of its words with the most varied meanings, and understanding the use of the word in *one* context does not relieve us from investigating its grammar in another."[85] In what looks like a direct rejoinder to his earlier discussion of the watch lying on the table, Wittgenstein imagines a chair disappearing and reappearing to demonstrate that we have no ready-made response to absolutely *all* unforeseen circumstances—and yet this hardly undermines our understanding of "chair." We neither have nor need such an all-encompassing comprehension, the idea of which is incoherent anyway.[86] Wittgenstein's later work disenchants it: "the expression 'and so on' does not harbor a secret power by which the series is continued without being continued."[87]

Heidegger places the conception of all beings as present-at-hand objects at the root of many traditional pseudo-problems. For one, it creates external-world skepticism by separating self and world, forcing us to rebuild their link as a knowledge-relationship between self-sufficient objects. This is why Heidegger famously retorts to Kant's labeling the absence of a solution to skepticism a scandal, that "the 'scandal of philosophy' is not that this proof has yet to be given, but that *such proofs are expected and attempted again and again*. Such expectations, aims, and demands arise from an ontologically inadequate way of starting with *something* of such a character that independently *of it* and 'outside' *of it* a 'world' is to be proved as present-at-hand."[88] Seeing self and world as present-at-hand objects creates an artificial and, on those terms, insoluble problem. We need to dissolve rather than solve this pseudo-problem by recovering the original holistic unity we will take up in chapter 3.

The problem of other minds is a second artificial problem created by this ontological fore-conception.

The theoretical problematic of understanding the "psychical life of Others" . . . gets taken as that which, primordially and "in the beginning," constitutes Being towards Others and makes it possible at all. This phenomenon, which is none too happily designated as "*empathy*," is then supposed, as it were, to provide the first ontological bridge from one's own subject, which is given proximally as alone, to the other subject, which is proximally quite closed off. (BT 161–162/124)

In normal circumstances, we immediately perceive other people and their states of mind, as we will see in chapter 4. We do not first see a moving body and then infer a mind behind these movements; we talk with friends about things and events around us. Like external-world skepticism, the only problem here is the idea that there is a problem.

Third is the way this conception of self-sufficient present-at-hand objects spreads to our view of language, a topic Heidegger takes up at greater length in his later writings. Once again, this orientation leads to pseudo-problems by obscuring the subject matter's true way of being—the one in and with which we live all the time.

The *logos* has been Interpreted in a way which is ontologically inadequate. . . . The *logos* gets experienced as something present-at-hand and Interpreted as such, while at the same time the entities which it points out have the meaning of presence-at-hand. This meaning of Being is left undifferentiated and uncontrasted with other possibilities of Being.[89]

This approach severs sounds and scratches from their significance (recall that just this kind of isolation of meaningless marks inspires some of Wittgenstein's early thought)[90] in the same the way that the problem of the external world sifts out ideas or sensory data, and the problem of other minds isolates bodily motions and vocalizations as distinct moments in our experience. Detached study breaks off a level of experience that may represent, but can never prove, a reality beyond it—the world as causing sensory data, minds as controlling bodily gyrations, and significance breathing life into the nostrils of mere marks or sounds. And now we face the impossible task of throwing meaning over these bare objects, an artificial problem that calls for artificial solutions like Donald Davidson's notion of radical interpretation.[91]

## Phenomenological Recovery

Having reached similar diagnoses, Heidegger and Wittgenstein recommend the same cure: careful descriptions of our mundane ways of talking or reading or hammering, to remind us of what we already know. Instead of arcane insights into realms beyond, the "facts" these therapies teach are banal, extraordinarily ordinary, inconspicuous features of everyday life which are overlooked precisely because of their ubiquity. Just as Wittgenstein's philosophical theses would be obvious almost to the point of triviality, calling for recollection and description rather than explanation or theorizing,[92] so Heidegger's phenomenological descriptions should prompt a rush of recognition of what we've always known but somehow never knew that we knew. "'The secret judgments of common sense'—that means those unspoken, unknown, and un-understood comportments that underlie all the daily comportments of existence. It is the business of the philosopher to bring these secret (hidden) judgments of common sense to light."[93] Dredging up this "subconscious" know-how that's constantly running in the background of our everyday lives breaks the spell of philosophical illusions.

This solution makes sense given that many received philosophical problems are artificial products of the philosophical attitude. It is only when we have suspended engaged speech to retrospectively reflect upon words, rules, or tools that they fall limp and lifeless to the ground, requiring extraordinary measures to resuscitate them.

What was characteristic was that I said to myself "I wonder what time it is?"—And if this sentence has a particular atmosphere, how am I to separate it from the sentence itself? It would never have occurred to me to think the sentence had such an aura if I had not thought of how one might say it differently—as a quotation, as a joke, as practice in elocution, and so on. And *then* all at once I wanted to say, then all at once it seemed to me, that I must after all have *meant* the words somehow specially; differently, that is, from in those other cases. The picture of the special atmosphere forced itself upon me; I can see it quite clear before me—so long, that is, as I do not look at what my memory tells me really happened.[94]

A given word's potential ambiguity did not attract my notice when I said it but now, retrospectively, it baffles me and threatens the very determinacy of my speech. Since I had no doubts or hesitations while speaking, I *must* have performed an act of meaning to nail down which sense I intended. Although I remember no such act, the queer entities and actions that populate philosophical theories now crowd insistently into my thoughts as ways to fill in the newly discovered gaps.

We only pine for such exotic fare while philosophizing; accurate memories plainly show that no such act or object was present or needed. "But what does using one sentence in contrast with others consist in? Do the others, perhaps, hover before one's mind? *All* of them? And *while* one is saying the one sentence, or before, or afterwards?—No. Even if such an explanation rather tempts us, we need only think for a moment of what actually happens in order to see that we are going astray here."[95] Wittgenstein's linguistic phenomenology reminds us of what actually happens during normal speech: we don't consult mental images or train intentional rays on referents, despite what retrospective reasoning craves. As one commentator writes,

the traditional philosophical way of looking at things gives priority to disengaged contemplation as a source of knowledge about the true nature of things, a contemplation in which such matters as the fact that we are usually actively involved in our world . . . can seem irrelevant. But that philosophical conception of the world, he now argues, is not primary: it is only what we see when we let our eyes wander in a particular way.[96]

Normally none of these queer processes take place, nor do we feel their absence. But, like Heidegger's equipment breakdown, halting the language-game to stare at it distorts our reconstructions of it, often bringing meaning-objects in to do the difficult work. "'It's as if we could grasp the whole use of a word in a flash.'—And that is just what we say we do. That is to say: we sometimes describe what we do in these words. But there is nothing astonishing, nothing queer, about what happens. It becomes queer when we are led to think that the future development must in some way already be present in the act of grasping the use and yet isn't present" (PI §197).

The way out of this labyrinth is to follow the thread of actual usage, to realize that these quandaries are merely grammatical mirages induced by staring at the subject. The spell is broken by reminding us of the difference between actual acts of speech and our later reconstruction of them. The latter attitude is highly susceptible to the pictures that give birth to philosophical systems, while a faithful recollection of the former knocks down these houses of cards. "'For a moment I meant to . . .' That is, I had a particular feeling, an inner experience; and I remember it.—And now, remember *quite precisely*! Then the 'inner experience' of intending seems to vanish again" (PI §645). Although Wittgenstein often dismisses phenomenological or introspective data,[97] these critiques seem to target Williams James's use of introspection which, finding particular feelings attached to words, gives these feelings an essential role in speech.[98] In fact, Wittgenstein frequently appeals to accurate remembering as an antidote to philosophical RRRs, telling readers over and over again, "to repeat: don't think, but look!"[99]

Rejecting the idea of unmediated experience, Heidegger argues for the hermeneutic idea that all encounters with beings are shaped by tacit conceptual frameworks, the fore-structures of understanding.[100] Traditionally, philosophy's "ontological orientation in principle towards Being as constant presence-at-hand" (BT 129/96) structures the way we approach and understand phenomena, filtering out evidence of other modes of being which could undermine its ontological monopoly. Seemingly innocuous ways of setting up the inquiry and the field to be studied are permeated with inconspicuous presuppositions, thus requiring what Heidegger calls a "destruction."[101] This does not connote how to philosophize with a bulldozer, but rather consists in carefully dismantling prejudices that have become so obvious we no longer see them. (Think of Wittgenstein's, "it is like a pair of glasses on our nose through which we see whatever we look at. It never occurs to us to take them off" [PI §103]). For example, in response to the question of which entities should serve as the subject of our study,

one may answer: "Things." But with this obvious answer we have perhaps already missed the pre-phenomenal basis we are seeking. For in addressing these entities as "Things" (res), we have tacitly anticipated their ontological character. When analysis starts with such entities and goes on to inquire about Being, what it meets is Thinghood and Reality. Ontological explication discovers, as it proceeds, such characteristics of Being as substantiality, materiality, extendedness, side-by-sideness, and so forth. But even pre-ontologically, in such Being as this, the entities which we encounter in concern are proximally hidden.[102]

Wittgenstein agrees that "nothing is more difficult than facing concepts *without prejudice*. (And that is the principal difficulty of philosophy),"[103] with grammar-induced pictures substituting for Heidegger's historically inherited ontological frameworks.[104]

We recover from philosophical illness by uncovering the understanding that directs our usual mastery. The phenomenological recollection of what actually occurred helps us resist Rational Reconstructions of it. For one thing, descriptions can dispel philosophy's monomaniacal focus on a single paradigm. Whereas Augustine's naming may apply to certain situations (with qualifications to be discussed below), we need to train our eyes on the

countless different kinds of use of what we call "symbols," "words," "sentences." . . . It is interesting to compare the multiplicity of the tools in language and of the ways they are used, the multiplicity of kinds of word and sentence, with what logicians have said about the structure of language. (Including the author of the *Tractatus Logico-Philosophicus*.) (PI §23)

Similarly, for Heidegger, "the working-out of the question of the meaning of Being in general must be turned away from a one-sided orientation with regard to Being in the sense of Reality. We must demonstrate that Reality is . . . only *one* kind of Being *among* others."[105]

Fortunately, we already know that there are several different ways to be, as our behavior shows. We could never make our way through the world, could not do anything or be anyone, without differentiating among different types of beings—so that, for example, I treat my students differently than I treat my shoes (on good days, at least). The understanding of being that Heidegger incessantly worries about is not some arcane lore to be reached by close argumentation or mountaintop meditation; it is the ability to interact appropriately with the various types of entities that we're constantly interacting with. The question of being is no "matter for soaring speculation about the most general of generalities," but rather *"of all questions, both the most basic and the most concrete,"* because "we always conduct our activities in an understanding of Being."[106] Every action, every inaction, every thought embodies and enacts this understanding. It is because Dasein possesses this understanding of being that Heidegger focuses his inquiry into being on this one being.[107] We need not embark on an arduous journey to far-flung regions in search of esoteric truths; like Dorothy's ruby slippers, we've unwittingly had it all along.

As I will discuss further in chapter 4, Wittgenstein's first point is that speaking generally occurs without mental acts or objects of any kind; *de facto*, nothing does play such a role. The second point is that no mental act or object *could* do what we demand of it; *de jure*, nothing can play such a role. He frequently argues that anything—any picture, mental state, rule, and so on—can be interpreted in indefinitely many ways. We appeal to meaning-objects to nail down all applications, letting reality relieve us of any active role, but "you never get beyond what you've decided yourself; you can always go on in innumerable different ways. . . . You want to make an investigation, but no investigation will do, because there is always freedom to go into another world" (LFM 145).

## Ethics Revisited

This leads us to the topic of motive. We have already seen that one reason our pre-ontological understanding of being and grammar is so easily overlooked is due to its inconspicuousness. Wittgenstein adds the labyrinthine lay of the grammatical land, and Heidegger points to the peer pressure of millennia of philosophers as further reasons. However, like Kant, they both see a curiously tenacious tendency toward philosophical confusion, as well as a resistance to cures. Wittgenstein insists that we must accurately describe "the workings of our language . . . *in despite of* an urge to misunderstand them,"[108] while Heidegger argues that due to Dasein's nature, attempts to accurately describe it *"should capture the Being of this entity, in spite of this entity's own tendency to cover things up."*[109]

I think this commitment to misinterpretation has to do with the notion I am calling Logical Stoicism. Remember that one of the guiding ideas of the Tractarian system is that "the form of a word is the possibility of its occurrence in a proposition. Every such possibility must already be contained in the word. If all words are given to us, then all possible statements are given too."[110] It is this verbal predestination that allows Wittgenstein to draw the limits of language once and for all by preventing anything genuinely new from occurring somewhere down the line: "it is possible . . . to give in advance a description of all 'true' logical propositions. Hence there can never be surprises in logic."[111] This resonates with the ethical feeling of absolute safety since the best way to make one's *theory* invulnerable is to accommodate all possible answers so that it will never be overturned.

According to Logical Determinism, "'all the steps are really already taken' means: I no longer have any choice. The rule, once stamped with a particular meaning, traces the lines along which it is to be followed through the whole of space. . . . When I obey a rule, I do not choose."[112] The idea that logic takes care of itself ensures objective truth, thus staving off semantic nihilism while simultaneously unburdening the logician, whose total immersion into objectivity crowds out all subjectivity. As in Schopenhauer's aesthetic and reflective observation, the "I" gets absorbed into the world like logical operations into their truth-tables, erasing both choices and chooser. Ethically good people resign themselves to fate without trying to meddle; logically pure philosophers crave the "idea that 'something must make us' do what we do,"[113] justifying their use while simultaneously absolving them of responsibility.

This is a form of logical bad faith, an attempt to divest oneself of freedom in order to escape accountability and the uncertainty that haunts all things human. The fact that elementary propositions arrive with their objects already "in immediate combination" (T 4.221) obviates the need for a Kantian transcendental unifier, as discussed in chapter 1, and the way meaning-objects reach throughout logical space pushes out any choice or decision. The true logician lets logic develop its own intrinsic essence, letting logic work through her without interference.

While biography should not take on a load-bearing role in philosophical analysis, it is hard not to think of the nearly universal descriptions of Wittgenstein's personality as deeply uncomfortable in his own skin; guilty over his financial inheritance and the suicide of three of his brothers in the face of an enormously successful, overbearing father; mercilessly flagellating himself over what most would consider minor peccadilloes, and tortured by a sexuality that thrashed between tormenting desires and self-loathing acts.[114] He seems to be a man who would welcome some time off from himself, a quieting of his will and relaxation of the twisted tension that marked so much of his life. And while Westerns are a far cry from Wagner's operas, descriptions of the way Wittgenstein would seek out such undemanding cinematic fare immediately after class, of the way "he sat as far to the front as he could get, leant forward in his seat and was utterly absorbed by the film,"[115] bears more than a passing resemblance to Schopenhauer's view of aesthetic experiences: "when we enter the state of pure contemplation, we are raised for the moment above all willing, above all desires and cares; we are, so to speak, rid of ourselves" (WWRI 390; see also WWR I 195–196). The classic Western scenario of a lone honorable man facing gutless curs in a lawless land admits of as little moral ambiguity as a well-constructed syllogism allows for epistemological vagueness; in both cases, the conclusion is foregone.[116]

The ideal of Tractarian security fell apart when Wittgenstein realized that "we can't smuggle the *use* of the sign into its introduction (the rule is and remains a sign, separated from its application)."[117] If the application of a rule is like a machine, it's still up to us to operate it; we must decide when it's working correctly and when it has malfunctioned, and what to do about it.[118] We cannot consult the core meaning of the word or rule for an authoritative ruling because it has dissolved into a family of overlapping resemblances—nor can we consult unvarnished reality, as we will see in chapter 5. As one writer says of Heidegger's view, "what is disclosed, rather, is an individual freedom and responsibility that cannot be 'delegated.' My interpretation of the world cannot be dictated by the way the world, independently of human interpretation and comportment, really is—for there is no such way. . . . The buck stops with me" (Cooper 2002, 250).

The *Tractatus* ends in silence, pulling its logical ladder up into a cloudless austerity so pure that it suffers no connection to the merely human, not even the link we need in order to reach this perspective. Like Plato's study of the Forms, dwelling amidst this coldly beautiful, crystalline structure lifts us up and purifies us of the squalor and muck we are born of. The *Investigations* on the other hand begins with a child's acquisition of language—an acquisition, moreover, driven by desires. Like Aristotle's democratic *phronêsis*, here we muddle through with jerry-rigged contraptions that get the job done, even if they make a racket and are ugly as hell. If the tool of choice of his earlier book would be a cooled superconductor—frigid frictionless perfection—Wittgenstein's later book prizes duct tape—usually able to get one more use out of the thing. Where the first book ends with a monastic exit from language, purged of all longing and at peace with the world, the second begins with our messy entrance into the human community, starting up the endless negotiations and uncertain compromises that make up the clutter of life. The *Tractatus* culminates with the voice of God reverberating in the silence, while the *Investigations* initiates a cacophonous family argument that threatens to flare up without resolution on any given holiday. The overriding insight of the later work is that we cannot divest the world of the human, that we cannot escape ourselves—whether it be into logic or Hollywood Westerns. As we will discuss in chapter 5, this realization can be terribly disconcerting, bringing on great anxiety, especially in a person of Wittgenstein's character.[119] This is a man whose demands for absolute exactness in building a house for his sister reduced an engineer to tears, who spent a year looking for a company capable of casting with sufficient precision to make the house's radiators, and even raised the ceiling of a large room by three centimeters when the house was nearly finished (Monk 1990, 236–237). Heidegger says of Nietzsche that he, "most quiet and shiest of men, . . . endured the agony of having to scream" (WCT 48). We might say of Wittgenstein, that most anal and obsessive-compulsive of men, that he endured the full embrace of the messiness of a human life in his later work.

Much of our daily lives and the history of philosophy, for Heidegger, consists in the attempt to settle these unsettling features, committing what he calls "fleeing" and "inauthenticity," which gives an ethical motivation to his *Destruktion* of the traditional view of being as constant presence in addition to its ontological one. *Being and Time* uncovers our true essence beneath the disguises we cover it up with, allowing us to become who we are.[120] Along with mortality, one of the unsettling facts about us is that we have not been favored with a special role, a task given us by reality or God whose approval would demonstrate that we're not just muddling through but doing something important—healing the realm with the Grail, say, or restoring balance to the Force, or liberating people from the Matrix, or some other dramatic feat derived from Joseph Campbell.[121] We desperately want to believe that we are not what our drab surroundings say we are, just another mundane person trying to eke out a life. These dull trappings are a disguise, hiding me until I am ready to reclaim my rightful place. Heidegger's existentialism tells us that we are what we do, that the humble preoccupations of our days is precisely the stuff our selves are made of.

### Summary

Both Heidegger and Wittgenstein contrast our unreflective engaged activity with philosophical reflection upon this activity after the fact. The former tacitly knows how to use tools and words but has trouble putting this mastery into words, whereas the latter only recognizes articulate statements of fact. Philosophical reflection suspends activity to focus on self-sufficient entities—meaning-objects or present-at-hand objects—which maintain their meaning independent of context. Philosophers attempt to reconstruct commonplace, fluid interactions in terms of these isolated inert "things," retroactively falsifying what has happened in order to satisfy the demands of a disengaged reason. Being different from what actually occurs during use, however, these lifeless units cannot account for our everyday competence in acting and speaking, thus rendering them mysterious and in need of ever-more magical solutions. Fortunately, we have all the understanding of meaning and being that we need; we just have to recover it by uncovering the reflective notions that have covered it up. Much of Heidegger and the later Wittgenstein's work confronts reason's misguided and impossible demands with our easy performance of mundane actions in order to expose these expectations as inappropriate and unnecessary. It is to this normal experience that we will now turn.

# 3 The Whole Hurly-Burly of Human Actions

Every significant word or symbol must essentially belong to a "system," and . . . the meaning of a word is its "place" in a "grammatical system."
—Wittgenstein, *Philosophical Occasions*, 51

The compound expression "Being-in-the-world" indicates in the very way we have coined it, that it stands for a *unitary* phenomenon. This primary datum must be seen as a whole.
—Heidegger, *Being and Time*, 78/53

Atomism in some form or other has been the default ontology for most of the history of philosophy: objects are what they are because of their own intrinsic nature, gaining only superficial features from whatever relationships they happen to enter into. This metaphysical structure can then secure semantic determinacy: synching words with referents that retain their nature regardless of circumstances makes words' meanings independent of their context. They simply mean what they mean regardless of when, where, or by whom they are employed. Chapter 2 showed how the *Tractatus* bases all language ultimately on the relationship between a name and a simple object which consists of a set of "unalterable" internal properties that subsist "independently of what is the case."[1] This idea is what authorizes the drastic shifts in use that create philosophical confusion, as covered in chapter 1. Similarly, for present-at-hand ontology, "the real entity is what is suited for thus *remaining constant*,"[2] a prejudice that distorts metaphysics and compromises authenticity.

Heidegger and later Wittgenstein embrace holism, according to which an object or word derives its nature and meaning from its place within a network, all other members of which likewise draw their sense from their interrelationships. This framework eliminates atomistic determinacy: if an item's meaning is established by its context, then altering this context changes its meaning—and the greater the change, the sketchier and thinner becomes the item's connection with its earlier sense.[3] Chapter 1 laid out these thinkers' conceptions of philosophy as based on a contrast between normal mastery and disengaged confusion. Chapter 2 showed how atomist theories of meaning and being funded the traditional philosophy that both seek to overturn. In this chapter, we will try to recover the holistic and engaged understanding that defines our behavior primarily and for the most part, but which gets covered up by reflection.

## The Colorful Unraveling of Wittgenstein's Early Atomism

Atomism played an important part in the founding of analytic philosophy. One of the points Russell and Moore emphasized in their rejection of idealism was the doctrine of external relations, that is, the idea that many of an object's properties and relations are contingent and can change without fundamentally altering the entity so that "an isolated truth may be quite true."[4] In the *Tractatus*, each state-of-affairs exists in complete isolation of all others; none is affected by the presence or absence of, or changes within, any other state-of-affairs.[5] Correlatively, each elementary proposition enjoys a truth value independently of the rest of language.[6] While each elementary proposition does presuppose all of logical space, or at least all of its particular region,[7] it only decides a hermetically sealed single point therein, which can be filled in or left blank without regard for anything else.[8] Wittgenstein uses the metaphor of a measuring stick: the way a picture "reaches right out to" reality is that "only the end-points of the graduating lines actually *touch* the object that is to be measured."[9] Words and objects make contact vertically, unaffected by the horizontal matters of other words or objects.

But this account runs into a problem almost immediately. Although Wittgenstein never specifies the nature of simple objects, colored specks occasionally crop up as a likely candidate.[10] Colors, however, are not atomically independent but mutually exclusive; if a point $(x, y)$ is blue, then it cannot simultaneously be red or puce or any other color. This allows us to deduce apparently elementary propositions ("Point $(x, y)$ is not red") from other elementary propositions ("Point $(x, y)$ is blue"), just the kind of inference that logical atomism forbids.[11] Wittgenstein mentions this problem in the *Tractatus* but appears to solve it to his satisfaction by translating color into the speed of particles: the fact that a particle cannot simultaneously have different speeds accounts for chromatic incompatibility.[12] This is hardly helpful, though, since we can now infer that "The light reflected off of point (x, y) is not moving at the speed determined by a wavelength of 620–750 nm" from "The light reflected off of point (x, y) is moving at the speed determined by a wavelength of 450–495 nm," thus reproducing the same problem that particle-speed was supposed to fix. As Parmenides and Spinoza argue, apparently simple positive claims are often disguised aggregates of negations. Recall Wittgenstein's dictum, learned from Russell and Frege's logical analyses that grammatical appearances are not to be trusted.

Upon his return to philosophy, Wittgenstein was struck anew by the color contradiction, which calls for a new solution.[13] In 1929, he says that,

once I wrote, "A proposition is laid against reality like a ruler. Only the end-points of the graduating lines actually touch the object that is to be measured." I now prefer to say that a *system of propositions* is laid against reality like a ruler. . . . It is not the individual graduating lines that are laid against it, but the entire scale. If I know that the object extends to graduating line 10, I also know immediately that it does not extend to graduating lines 11, 12, and so forth. The statements describing for me the length of an object form a system, a system of propositions. Now it is such an entire system of propositions that is compared with reality, not a single proposition.[14]

Some claims about reality that appear to be hermetically sealed and hermeneutically self-sufficient actually presuppose an interconnected system of ideas, loading each individual claim with implications for the other members of its set. Wittgenstein had been so captivated by one aspect of the picture of a ruler—that it can connect two entities by touching a single point on each—that he was blind to another feature—that rulers measure things by having lots of mutually exclusive numbers. He still believes that propositions are held up to reality, but now some of these propositions come in bundles from which they cannot be extricated. Not only would the practice of measuring collapse, or at least be severely truncated, if we could only measure, say, exactly seven inches, but even the number "seven" derives its meaning from its place on the number line.

This holism expands over the next several years until it absorbs all of Wittgenstein's later thought. In 1930, he claims that "a proposition cannot be significant except in a system of propositions."[15] He still clings to determinacy in this transitional period, but a determinacy now spread over an organized whole. This transforms the internal properties that had defined simple objects into "rules of syntax" (LWVC 134) governing restricted systems like "color-space." These interconnected but separable structures then take root in language itself, incorporating all sentences: "it is only in a language that something is a proposition. To understand a proposition is to understand a language."[16] Language evolves into language-games which include not just other propositions, but "the actions into which [language] is woven" (PI §7). Linguistic study can no longer just look at words since the context that defines them encompasses behavior as well. "Here the term 'language-*game*' is meant to bring into prominence the fact that the *speaking* of language is part of an activity, or of a life-form."[17] This holism continues to expand and deepen until "what determines our judgment, our concepts and reactions, is not what *one* man is doing *now*, an individual action, but the whole hurly-burly of human actions, the background against which we see any action."[18]

This marks a drastic change from his early theory of meaning-objects. As David Pears writes, Wittgenstein

realized later that this theory of language greatly underestimated our continuing contribution to the fixity of meaning and so represented the whole enterprise in a way that made it impossible. One of the recurrent themes of *Philosophical Investigations* is that we cannot give a word a meaning merely by giving it a one-off attachment to a thing. What is needed is a sustained contribution from us as we continue to use the word. . . . This distinction [between obeying a rule and disobeying it] must be based on our practice, which cannot be completely anticipated by any self-contained thing. We do not, and cannot, rely on any instant talisman.[19]

Starting from Frege's context principle[20]—that words only have meaning within a sentence—Wittgenstein's holism expands from closed systems of propositions to a meaning-giving background consisting of cultural practices and the basic patterns of behavior that make up ordinary human life.

Without meaning-objects filling up words with a plenum of meaning upon connection, words and propositions must draw their significance from all kinds of "external" circumstances. This undermines philosophy's originary act of studying terms in isolation or transferring them to strange circumstances. Wittgenstein's considered position is not that use *is* meaning, as some statements appear to claim, but rather that words have their usual meaning in their "average everyday" habitat—that is, when used in ordinary circumstances. A word's or a proposition's meaning is its place within a language-game, against the background of human life; detach it from these, and you no longer have the same word or proposition.

A meaning of a word is a kind of employment of it.
   For it is what we learn when the word is incorporated into our language. . . .
   When language-games change, then there is a change in concepts, and with the concepts the meanings of words change.[21]

This idea of a word's meaning as its position within a system replaces the rigid Tractarian link with a meaning-object, fundamentally altering the landscape of Wittgenstein's thought.

## Game-Changer

Frege set up a dichotomy concerning linguistic meaning: signs are either lifeless marks and sounds, an idea that troubled early Wittgenstein,[22] or they represent intrinsically significant referents residing "in Euclidean heaven" (LFM 144) which lend the marks their life. The *Tractatus* takes the latter option: names get their meaning from ostensive definitions tying them to rigid, unchanging meaning-objects. A picture's method of projection—that is, the way we connect the shapes on paper to the things they represent—is so natural to us that it becomes dangerously inconspicuous, as if these shapes referred automatically to their particular subject, without the aid of convention. Picturing seems to take care of itself by being intrinsically, transparently intentional; pictures wear their "aboutness" on their sleeves.

But this is just the kind of picture—a picture of picturing—that stampedes our thought down certain paths, trampling all countervailing evidence. 'Games' come to replace pictures as Wittgenstein's favored model of language partly because games present such a clear and forceful alternative to atomistic meaning. They neatly sidestep Frege's dichotomy: the "meaning" of a queen in chess is neither contained within the piece of carved wood (we can use practically anything as a chess piece), nor does it stand for a metaphysically queer queenly quintessence. Rather, each part of a game derives its sense from its context, its relations to all the other parts, each of which in turn gets fixed by *its* relationships. Isolating a single game-piece for study cannot improve our understanding of the game or the piece, but actually prevents it. No matter how closely you examine the bit of wood or a single move, you cannot grasp its significance without a sense of the other pieces and the game as a whole. It isn't that discovering this quality would be difficult outside the proper circumstances, but that its meaning simply doesn't exist without them. As in Derrida's Saussurean theory of language, all the elements mutually pushing against each other prop up a structure of meaning like an arch, without relying on an external foundation. "The use of a word in such a case is like the use of a piece in a game, and you cannot understand the use of a queen unless you understand the uses of the other pieces. What you do with one sort of piece is intelligible only in terms of what you do with it in relation to what is done with the other pieces."[23]

But the holism doesn't stop there. The physical action of pushing a piece of wood across a checkered board cannot by itself constitute a move in chess, regardless of what mental contents you throw into the mix. "A move in chess doesn't consist simply in moving a piece in such-and-such a way on the board—nor yet in one's thoughts and feelings as one makes the move: but in the circumstances that we call 'playing a game of chess.'"[24] The right kind of setting—a standard practice, the right kinds of actions and statements from the players before, during, and after play, and so on— makes a given movement a chess move; no set of facts, no matter of what nature or how complete, can constitute such a move in the absence of the proper circumstances. As Meredith Williams writes,

Wittgenstein's contextualism is, of course, the other side of the coin to his critique of meaning or intentional content as object. As Wittgenstein emphasizes throughout his later thought, nothing carries its significance within itself. . . . Any candidate for playing the privileged role of setting a standard or fixing meaning or telling us how to continue or anticipating the future plays such a role only in virtue of how we use it. . . . Wittgenstein's contextualism is pervasive.[25]

Without self-sufficient meanings, circumstances play an ineliminable role in linguistic sense: "every significant word or symbol must essentially belong to a 'system,' and . . . the meaning of a word is its 'place' in a 'grammatical system.'"[26]

Since each part of a language-game is holistically interdependent with the other aspects, they cannot retain their meaning outside their normal context. "Understanding $p$ means understanding its system. If $p$ appears to go over from one system into another, then $p$ has, in reality, changed its sense."[27] Change the circumstances surrounding the pushing of chess pieces around a board enough—put the tableau on stage as part of a play, say, or make it the transmission of a coded message between spies—and you fundamentally alter the significance of the "same" motions. Conversely, under the right conditions just about anything can count as chess pieces or moves.[28]

What is the everyday use of this expression in ordinary language? For you learned it from this use. If you now use it contrary to its original use, and think you are still playing the old game with it, that is as if you were to play draughts with chess-pieces and imagine that your game had kept something of the spirit of chess. (Z §448)

Holistic semantics explains why removing words from their customary language-games creates insoluble pseudo-problems, what most of us call philosophy. "Someone who idealizes falsely must talk nonsense—because he uses a mode of speaking that is valid in *one* language-game in another one where it doesn't belong."[29] Besides transferring them to outlandish scenarios of demons and caves, philosophy tries to isolate words and ideas from all context. Philosophers ascend Plato's divided line from various concrete instantiations to a pure, unwavering essence in search of something's absolute form—what it *really* is regardless of what we think or how we use it. We don't want plain old certainty; we want a Cartesian certitude that must be true no matter what, or Kantian acts that are good regardless of whatever else occurs.

It would produce confusion if we were to say: the words of the communiqué—the proposition communicated—have a definite sense, and the giving of it, the "assertion" supplies something additional. As if the sentence, spoken by a gramophone, belonged to pure logic; as if here it had the pure logical sense; as if here we had before us the object which logicians get hold of and consider—while the sentence as asserted, communicated, is what it is in *business*. As one may say: the botanist considers a rose *as a plant*, not as an ornament for a dress or room or as a delicate attention. The sentence, I want to say, has no sense outside of the language-game. This hangs together with its not being a kind of *name*. As though one might say "'I believe . . .'—*that's* how it is" pointing (as it were inwardly) at what gives the sentence its meaning.[30]

It is this "no-matter-what" demand for the unconditional that requires independence from all local conditions. Philosophers want to make absolute statements which remain true come what may, statements with an italicized "*really*," but this only works if words anticipate all possible uses and, contra meaning-holism, retain their meaning in all situations.

For one thing, Wittgenstein reminds us that these "context-free" assertions actually take place within the specialized context of philosophizing by pointing out how incomprehensible such statements would be in mundane circumstances. A bit like Kierkegaard's lunatic who assures others of his sanity by repeatedly crying out a true fact ("The world is round!") every time a rubber ball tied to his coattails whacks him on the bottom,[31] the philosopher believes that truth is truth, and can be uttered with complete legitimacy in any situation. Wittgenstein reminds us of how baffling these statements would be were they baldly stated in the course of normal life. "I am sitting with a philosopher in the garden; he says again and again 'I know that that's a tree,' pointing to a tree that is near us. Someone else arrives and hears this, and I tell him: 'This fellow isn't insane. We are only doing philosophy,'"[32] a rather fine distinction, perhaps, in Wittgenstein's eyes.

Although the philosophical context may assuage doubts of sanity, it usually lacks sufficient agreed-upon usage to sustain sensible discussion. Once the philosophical ascent leaves behind the atmosphere in which our everyday words breathe, their use dissipates, leaving us grasping for wildly inappropriate pictures or analogies that fizzle out even as they seem to yield profound insights. "'But this supposition surely makes good sense!'—Yes; in ordinary circumstances these words and this picture have an application with which we are familiar.—But if we suppose a case in which this application falls away we become as it were conscious for the first time of the nakedness of the words and the picture."[33]

One reason Wittgenstein found Moore's paradox—that is, the problem involved in making statements of the form, "*p* is the case, and I don't believe that *p* is the case"—so interesting is that it brings factors other than simple denotation into interpretation, in this case the speaker, whom Wittgenstein's early work had tried to efface (T 5.542). Such analyses show that "logic isn't as simple as logicians think it is" (von Wright 1977, 177). Tellingly, Russell wrote of Wittgenstein's ideas in 1930 that "as a logician, who likes simplicity, I should wish to think that they are not [true]" (Monk 1990, 546). Once, Wittgenstein was scheduled to give a talk on Descartes's *cogito*, which went unmentioned in his actual remarks. When asked to comment on the supposed subject of his talk, his response was simply to say, "*That's a very peculiar sentence.*"[34] I take Wittgenstein's meaning to be that it lacks the proper circumstances to guide our use of it, "as if 'I know' did not tolerate a metaphysical emphasis" (OC §482).

Wittgenstein wants "to bring words back from their metaphysical to their everyday use,"[35] not because ordinary language enjoys an absolute priority, but because it is there that we know what to do with these words, a meaning that we now know cannot be simply picked up and dropped into new situations. "We learn to use the word 'think' *under particular circumstances*. If the circumstances are different we don't know how to use it."[36] New meanings are born all the time and neither philosophers nor lexicographers have the authority to rule them in or out, the way a grasp of logic and proper propositional forms seemed to offer a privileged perspective in Wittgenstein's early work. This is no conservative version of ordinary language philosophy; Wittgenstein explicitly acknowledges that languages develop and builds openness into philosophical investigation.[37] If someone can show us the way they're using a term and it catches on, Wittgenstein has no objections; how could he?[38] The problem is that philosophy is inherently drawn to situations that muddy meaning, like trying to figure out who won a game of tennis played with an imaginary ball. "The fundamental fact here is that we lay down rules, a technique, for a game, and that then when we follow the rules, things do not turn out as we had assumed. That we are therefore as it were entangled in our own rules."[39] Wittgenstein's method is to rigorously develop the consequences of a fairly straightforward claim: we need to know how we are to apply our words if we are to understand what we're saying. He never objects to words or ideas because they're *wrong*, but because they fall apart in our hands.

Whereas his earlier work had criticized everyday language from the external perspective of pure logic and the structure of reality, now Wittgenstein issues internal challenges, showing us that we have run off the cliff into thin air without realizing it, a method rather like Socrates' *elenchus* or Kierkegaard's indirect communication.

This is how it is with grammar in general. The only thing we can do is *to tabulate rules*. If by questioning I have found out concerning a word that the other person at one time recognizes these rules and, at another time, those rules, I will tell him, In that case you will have to distinguish exactly *how* you use it; *and there is nothing else I wanted to say*.

In my book [the *Tractatus*] I still proceeded dogmatically. . . .

Thus I do not talk of sense and what sense is at all; I remain entirely within grammar. . . .

Thus I simply draw the other person's attention to what he is really doing and refrain from any assertions. Everything is then to go on within grammar. (LWVC 184–186)

Outside their normal home, exotic linguistic notions glitter seductively but have no determinate sense—or rather, they seduce *because* they've lost their sense; returned to their language-game, they become at once sensible and mundane.[40] Bringing words down to earth where we know how to use them clears up philosophical confusion and thereby dispels their charm: "for each one of these sentences I can imagine circumstances that turn it into a move in one of our language-games, and by that it loses everything that is philosophically astonishing."[41]

Wittgenstein's cure moves us "from a piece of disguised nonsense to something that is patent nonsense" (PI §464). Whereas we think we know how to gauge knowledge under the demon's baleful watch, the necessary conceptual traction has sublimed into clouds of imagination. Analogous language-games may lend our ruminations the veneer of respectability, running a meaning-laundering service for counterfeit notions, but Wittgenstein believes that we will willingly drop these topics once we realize that we haven't the slightest idea how to handle them. We don't know how to use them not because they're deep but because they're meaningless. He cites the idea of five o'clock on the sun or a railway station on Mars as examples of "patent nonsense" that clearly demonstrate how little we understand common phenomena when they've been resettled in utterly alien situations.[42] "To the statement 'I feel in my hand that the water is three feet under the ground' we should like to answer: 'I don't know what this *means*.' But the diviner would say: 'Surely you know what it means. You know what "three feet under the ground" means, and you know what

"I feel" means!' But I should answer him: I know what a word means *in certain contexts*" (BB 9). Some commentators have taken Wittgenstein's claim to not posit philosophical theories to mean that he never puts forth any claims at all. My view is that he subscribes to ideas like the holistic conception of meaning but considers the alternative meaning-object view to be incoherent, as we would see if we persevered in analyzing these ideas without the use of pictures that disguise its nonsense.[43] Therapy does not settle these issues by issuing a definitive answer—there can be no answers to meaningless questions, as he had discovered in the *Tractatus*—but by cutting the Gordian knots entangling us.

One application Wittgenstein makes of meaning-holism is to dissolve skepticism. Doubting has a meaning; it cannot be used any which way and remain doubt. Only certain uses succeed in doubting whereas others, as Austin puts it, misfire. "So how does the doubt get expressed? That is: in a language-game, and not merely in certain *phrases*. . . . But this expression of doubt by no means always makes sense, nor does it always have a point. One simply tends to forget that even doubting belongs to a language-game."[44] The point isn't to prohibit certain troublesome uses ad hoc the way Russell's theory of types circumnavigates his own paradox, but to point out that our ability to apply terms like "doubt" or "know" presupposes certain conditions that the skeptical employment tries to do without. Meaningful uses are unable to construct the skeptical scenarios.

When you say "Suppose I believe . . ." you are presupposing the whole grammar of the word "to believe," the ordinary use, of which you are a master.—You are not supposing some state of affairs which, so to speak, a picture presents unambiguously to you, so that you can tack on to this hypothetical use some assertive use other than the ordinary one.—You would not know at all what you were supposing here (that is what, for example, would follow from such a supposition), if you were not already familiar with the use of "believe." (PI II.x p. 164)

The never-ending disagreements among philosophers about what can *really* be known, what *really* exists, and so on, are due to the fact that we're making up our usage as we go along, led on by the ghostly tendrils of pictures and the fading wisps of analogies.

The fact that phrases or ideas must take place within shared language-games undermines both skepticism and its attempted refutations, since both employ ideas (doubt and knowledge respectively) outside the language-games within which they make sense.

So to say "It is meaningless . . ." is to point out that perhaps you are being misled by these words, that they make you imagine a use which they do not have. They do perhaps evoke an idea . . . but the game with the sentence is so arranged that it doesn't have the essential point which makes useful the game with similarly constructed sentences.[45]

I often find that upon first reading Descartes, students tend more toward bewilderment than to the scandalized protests I expect. They're not so much outraged by his skepticism as disoriented by it, wondering not how Descartes could entertain such preposterous ideas or leaping to the defense of common sense, but paralyzed, with no sense of just what the heck all this means. And my job isn't to reveal their Faculty of Critical Thinking, hitherto lying fallow beneath years of lazy credulity; rather, I initiate them into the philosophy game: what kinds of moves are appropriate in which circumstances, what sorts of reactions get encouraged or dismissed, and so on. Even the kind of naïve, spluttering indignation against the Cartesian project from the "noble savage" perspective of common sense is itself a somewhat sophisticated and late-coming move *within* the game that I must coax out of them.

It's true that once we have mastered their meaning, we can reflect upon words outside the surroundings that enabled us originally to grasp them, allowing the words to accrue meanings that have little to do with their primary meaning but which feel like extensions of their sense. Wittgenstein considers this phenomenon to be an insignificant idiosyncrasy whose only significance seems to be the parlor games we can play with it.[46] These feelings are not deep insights, but just the odd epiphenomena of speech—a word's phantom limbs, as it were.

## Private Language

This discussion of holistic meaning gives us a helpful perspective on the so-called Private Language Argument (PLA). The first thing to note about it is that it isn't an argument, at least not in the standard sense of a set of premises entailing a conclusion. *Philosophical Investigations* could be seen as a series of overlapping tectonic plates; Wittgenstein returns to certain topics again and again, breaks off into new but related discussions that often circle back, with few clean breaks between topics. It is one of the ironies of Wittgenstein scholarship that these writings that repeatedly emphasize holistic understanding are often broken up into bits which are then studied on their own. But, if Wittgenstein were made to talk like a philosopher, we wouldn't understand him. Figuring out the relationships among the aphorisms in all of Wittgenstein's writings is difficult, and made more difficult by the multiple editorial hands involved in most of their selection and arrangement. Still, until disproved, we should operate on the assumption that the context of a passage is relevant, which argues against isolating any idea too much from the rest of the text in which it appears. This kind of approach has recently become more common, with scholars often criticizing the standard take on the Private Language Argument as a misunderstanding caused by removing key passages from their context.[47]

In fact, Wittgenstein discusses the idea of a private language many times which come together to form a pattern. First, in line with his standard analysis, he sees most discussions as operating with a picture of a private language without examining what it means or how it works. Our inconspicuous facility with reporting sensations leads us to consider such reports as being intrinsically meaningful, independent of and unaffected by context.

"This form of words seems to mean something but means nothing." That is: We connect a certain image with this expression or we are inclined to use it because it sounds analogous to other expressions and we connect a certain attitude, state of mind etc. with it; but if we then ask ourselves how we are going to use it we find that we have no use for it or a use of a totally different kind from that which we at first vaguely imagined.[48]

Privately seen objects like a carefully covered poker hand form the model, guiding our thoughts about sensations inside of us to which only we have access. No one else can peer over the wall of my body to spy on my mind as it secretly cavorts with mysterious but oh-so-vivid entities, like a princess strolling among peacocks in the inner garden of her castle, forbidden to be looked upon by commoners' eyes (PO 300, 330).

As usual, Wittgenstein does not reject the picture—or the sensations—but unpacks their significance, so that we can recognize how we are using it and where our wires have unwittingly crossed. "*Certainly* all these things happen in you.—And now all I ask is to understand the expression we use.—The picture is there. And I am not disputing its validity in any particular case.—Only I also want to understand the application of the picture" (PI §423). Following out the picture's implications will make its disguised nonsense patent.

The idea of a private language rests upon meaning-objects, which make an appearance right in the middle of what is traditionally considered the *Investigations*' discussion of it: "'but I can (inwardly) undertake to call THIS "pain" in the future.' . . . 'Once you know *what* the word stands for, you understand it, you know its whole use.'"[49] We know what objects and pointing and privacy and reporting all mean, so transferring them from the realm of the physical to the mental should be as simple as the move from pointing at a plant in someone's front yard to pointing at one inside the house when seen through the window.

It seems as though, however the outward circ[umstance]s change, once the word is fastened to a particular personal experience it now retains its meaning; and that therefore I can now use it with sense whatever may happen. . . .

It seems, whatever the circumstances I always know now whether to apply the word or not. It seems, at first it was a move in a special game but then it becomes independent of this game. . . .

But can't the old game lose its point when the circ[umstance]s change, so that the expression ceases to have a meaning, although of course I can still pronounce it.[50]

Tying the word 'pain' to an inner sensation by means of a mental, ostensive definition seems to allow us to cut all ties to external manifestations while retaining full sense. Of course I know what pain is—it's *that* feeling. Then sensation's intrinsic nature can guide all applications without the safety net of intersubjective checks.

The holistic view of meaning of course disputes these allegedly neutral transplants.

When you say "the expression '—' means to you a certain private exp[erience]" you are (indeed) supplementing this statement by imagining a color/ red/ or looking at a red object (which supply the "namely this") but how do you use /make use of/ the expression and the experience you thus connect with it? For what we call the meaning of the word lies in the game we play with it.[51]

The picture of meaning as forging an unbreakable link with a meaning-object through naming funds the intelligibility of a private language, but with counterfeit money.

If words' meanings are their referents, as the *Tractatus* had it, and if only I have access to internal referents, then no one else can understand my statements about them, which raises a dilemma. On the one hand, the more ideas and terms the private language borrows from public ways of talking, the more meaningful and usable it is; I can talk to others about my toothache because everyone knows what a toothache is. Calling the internal object in question a pain or sensation, or just an object, or even just a something, employs words taken from common usage, which must behave the way they do in normal public circumstances if they are to enjoy the same sense.[52] But the closer the private language approaches communicable public talk, the more it loses that absolute privacy that *ex hypothesi* defines it. Satisfying the demand for metaphysical privacy pushes us to abandon the public vocabulary for sensations, stripping away more and more verbiage until we are reduced to "an inarticulate sound."[53] But even a barbaric *yawp* that sings of my untranslatable self, if it is to "mean" my pain in any way at all, must have a place within an appropriate language-game.

Of course, one may try to opt for the latter horn of the dilemma and surrender the use of a private language for communication, retreating to the citadel of a strictly internal usage. Maybe I cannot talk *to you* about my inner sensations, but surely I can muse upon them *to myself* once I have linked words to referents in the dark smithy of the soul. Like the elders teaching baby Augustine the names of all the shiny things he wants by pointing at them and emitting sounds, I show myself the sensation in question—looking up a memory sample kept like fabric swatches in a drawer—and affix a word to it like pinning a label, a conception of language that Quine calls the myth of the museum.[54] This baptism must take place by a mute, internal, ostensive definition since identifying the referent by describing it would use common terms, thereby compromising its absolute privacy. Pinpointing a pain by describing it as "that hurty feeling," for instance, sews intersubjective uses of these words into the sensation which then pull it out into the speakable open. On the other hand, mentally pointing to the object while holding one's mental tongue (as it were) allows a direct face-to-face contact with the entity in question, bypassing all mediation by word or concept.[55] In what appears to be an innocuous extension of the ostensive definitions that form the foundation of Augustine's picture of language, naming by internal acquaintance dispenses with common terms to fashion a direct link between signs and the feelings buried deep within the recesses of my mind by pointing at it inwardly while intoning gravely to myself, "*This* is a Gorignak."

But it is from public language-games that we learned of internal feelings in the first place; they set up what was called in the *Tractatus* the idea's logical space, which develops into grammar in the later works. "Would I know that pain, etc., etc., is something inner if I weren't told so?" (RPPII §643). This isn't just placing a label on a fully fleshed-out object, but the establishment of what *kind* of object it is, which then sets up the appropriate ways to think and talk about it.[56] What seem like simple, immediate encounters with private entities clandestinely rely on this grammar in order to make sense—even to ourselves.

When one says "He gave a name to his sensation" one forgets that a great deal of stage-setting in the language is presupposed if the mere act of naming is to make sense. And when we speak of someone's having given a name to pain, what is presupposed is the existence of the grammar of the word "pain"; it shews the post where the new word is stationed.[57]

Public language-games are not accidental verbal appendages that simply direct our attention to intrinsically meaningful terms; according to Wittgenstein's holism, language-games *constitute* meaning in the sense of creating and sustaining it, albeit inconspicuously. "Suppose someone says he knows something is happening in him. But *what* does he know? The expression 'happening in him' is one he has *learnt*."[58] Rather than Descartes's absolutely primary, incorrigible realm as the source of all intelligibility, protected from all external interloping—what Husserl, a great admirer of Descartes, called our "Sphere of Ownness"—we learn of it the way we learn everything else: socially.

Wittgenstein's holism applies to our selves as well as to our language: society comes first and individuals are born of, and continuously borne by, this context.[59] Even our "insides," so to speak, come from the outside because we only have a sense of these internal contents—how to look for them, their taxonomy, what it makes sense to say about them—via the grammar learned from language-games. This deep structure cannot be neatly severed from public phenomena without taking all sense with it, yet this is precisely what private, ostensive definitions of sensations purport to do. We imagine we have left all communal notions behind upon entering our inner space, having unwittingly smuggled contraband grammar in with us. Private languages are, of necessity, public meaning mules.

## Ostensively Naming Meaning-Objects

The view of language that underlies private languages, the same basic view that informed the *Tractatus* and that has been under consideration since the opening of the *Investigations*, takes names as its paradigm and referents as their meaning, making the way words get connected to their objects of central importance. Immediately after defining a private language, Wittgenstein asks, "how do words *refer* to sensations?"[60] As an essential component of the meaning-object picture of language, Wittgenstein subjects ostensive definitions to sustained, withering criticisms.

This picture imbues ostensive definitions with magical powers. A word's significance derives entirely from the named entity, so that just forging the linguistic connection accomplishes everything. Once words and objects are geared together, reality takes over, turning the wheels with a perfect and complete determinacy. "'Surely it makes sense to say what I see, and how better could I do this than by letting what I see speak for itself!' . . . It seems as though the colour which I see was its own description."[61] Once a dead sign has undergone this semantic transubstantiation by the laying-on of ostensively pointing hands, it can function under any circumstances, including within the privacy of one's own soul. "One could almost imagine that naming was done by a peculiar sacramental act, and that this produced some magic relation between the name and the thing. . . . A primitive philosophy condenses the whole usage of the name into the idea of a relation, which thereby becomes a mysterious relation."[62]

But when meaning-objects go, so too must "superstitions about 'the connexion of meaning,'" since "an ostensive definition is not a magic act."[63] Wittgenstein argues over and over again in his later work that it is circumstances that determine meaning rather than anything intrinsic to the word, referent, or mental act, as the model of games shows so clearly. Just as castling can only take place within a chess game, so giving something a name only works in certain circumstances. Just as playing chess is a public event which consists in observable features rather than thinking you're playing chess or having that old chess-playing feeling, the same applies to naming and talking about entities.

Wittgenstein insists on the distinction between a picture or an object and its use or meaning, which exposes the ineradicable indeterminacy of ostensive definitions: no matter how unambiguous our pointing feels, slippage betwixt finger and object allows endless miscommunication.

How does pointing to its colour differ from pointing to its shape?—We are inclined to say the difference is that we *mean* something different in the two cases. And "meaning" here is to be some sort of process taking place while we point. . . . If on the other hand, we look for two such characteristic mental acts as meaning the colour and meaning the shape, etc., we aren't able to find any. . . . The difference, one might say, does not lie in the act of demonstration, but rather in the surrounding of that act in the use of the language.[64]

The gap between definition and understanding is rarely noticeable because for the most part, we easily and reliably "get the point," literally. This is due neither to rationality nor to exceptional pointing talent, but rather to one of those immensely important, inconspicuous-because-ubiquitous facts about humans, namely, that "pointing is used and understood in a particular way—that people react to it in a particular way. . . . One only has to point to something and say, 'This is so-and-so,' and everyone who has been through a certain preliminary training will react in the same way."[65] This common reaction is essential to communication—if we had no way of drawing someone's attention to a particular object, how could we even begin to teach? But like most skills, adeptness hides the skill itself, giving the impression of a self-evident understanding that anyone would grasp. Because teaching a new noun to a competent speaker rarely presents much of a problem ("See that over there? *That* is a Gorignak"), and misunderstandings can usually be easily corrected ("No, not that; *that*, over *there*"), we don't realize just how much preparation this presupposes. However, as we will see in chapter 4, all of this rests on a complex mixture of expectations and reactions that humans get from their nature and their socialization. Like Heidegger, Wittgenstein lights up this inconspicuous ability through its breakdown, where attempts to point to a specific aspect or thing to those who lack our training or our natural reactions to this training fail, as we will see in greater detail in chapter 5.[66]

It is precisely because we don't notice this process going on in the background, silently filling in the spaces of the severely abbreviated meaning-giving acts we usually get by with, that we think we can dispense with it in private circumstances. But this turns out to be a prime example of philosophical confusion, by jettisoning the very features that give the act of naming sense,[67] thereby reducing it to an empty ceremony, like one's left hand selling something to the right hand, an example that crops up in the middle of the *Investigations'* private language discussion.[68] It is not a matter of physical or metaphysical impossibility—that conjures up the image of our straining to do something that is beyond our power, though it may be within the scope of God's power—but rather something that makes no sense. We don't really know what it would look like if we succeeded.

The great difficulty here is not to represent the matter as if it were a matter of inability. As if there really were an object, from which I derive its description, but I were unable to shew it to anyone.—And the best that I can propose is that we should yield to the temptation to use this picture, but then investigate how the *application* of the picture goes. (PI §374)

Transferring the notion of buying and selling from the interpersonal to the intrapersonal moves it from the familiar contexts where we know how to do it, to a context in which it *cannot* have the same meaning, and where the deck is stacked against giving it any real meaning. We might go through the standard motions of possession exchange—the right hand hands the thing over to the left, who then writes out a receipt—like children pretending to do adult tasks they don't quite grasp. You can do these things, certainly; but do they mean anything if nothing follows from them—if, for instance, the left hand cannot take the right hand to court for underhanded dealings? Such paradoxical contortions of supposedly self-sufficient meanings removed from their language-games reminds me of a particularly unsuccessful superhero in a movie I once saw who could turn completely invisible—as long as no one was looking at him.

The moral of the lesson here is that "'to give a sensation a name' means nothing unless I know already in what sort of a game this name is to be used" (PO 241). A private language gives the *impression* of ostensive definition, but with neither the surroundings nor the effects that would give the act any content.[69] Shorn of their context, we have nothing but the sign-language of these semantic phantom limbs which can say anything precisely because they say nothing. If, on the other hand, we give a real function to our sensation such as indicating a rise in blood pressure, then all significance immediately shifts from the private referent, which is supposed to be the name's meaning according to this picture, to the observable event. As long as I continue to correctly anticipate the rise, what I "actually feel" becomes a freely spinning wheel with no impact on the mechanism.[70] Despite an almost irresistible urge to say it and *really mean it*, to insist in italics that I *really do* have a sensation purified of everything external, if we think of the relationship between absolutely private sensations and names on the model of object and designation, the game falls apart; the object, the thing that the whole process was designed to get a conceptual grip on, ends up dropping out as irrelevant.[71] Ostensive definitions, in such circumstances, are only ostensible definitions.

Despite appearing counterintuitive, this conclusion directly follows from the way the issue has been set up. If we expel the referent from language-games in order to privatize it, then quite obviously the games no longer include it—so how could it play any role in them? As Hegel objects to Kant's treatment of noumena, just asserting their existence requires a comprehension of what this means, thus bringing them back into the field of language-games, an argument echoed in the preface to the *Tractatus*.[72] This is why Wittgenstein frequently says that samples used to illustrate a word are not extra-linguistic chunks of brute reality, but pieces within the language-game—pieces that play the role: "sample of X."[73] Either we must pass over the private matters in silence, complete silence, or even the minimal assertion of its existence or its privacy ipso facto publicizes it.

Wittgenstein is perfectly happy to admit the difference between having a certain feeling and not; we just have to understand what this really consists in, which means how we actually apply these terms.[74] The possibility of pretense seduces us here. Deception appears to cleanly separate sensations from their manifestations: disproportionately impressed by the fact that we can hide a feeling, stoically repressing all signs of pain until everyone has left us before collapsing, groaning, into a chair, we are tempted to base our entire understanding on these exceptions rather than what does and, Wittgenstein argues, must happen most of the time.

Taken to its logical conclusion, the divorce between a phenomenon and its manifestation leads to metaphysical deception, that is, the possibility of either never showing the pain one feels or never feeling the pain one shows.

There were cases in which we should say that the person sees green [where] I see red. Now the question suggests itself: if this can be so at all, why should it [not] be always the case? It seems, if once we have admitted that it can happen under peculiar circumstances, that it may always happen. But then it is clear that the very idea of seeing red loses its use if we can never know if the other does not see something utterly different.[75]

This thought experiment breaks what I will call the Rules-Exception Ratio Law: while perhaps every rule has exceptions, they cannot become so common as to overtake the customary usage without undermining the game as a whole.[76] An exception may prove the rule (a saying that doesn't mean what most people take it to mean, incidentally—"prove" originally meant "test" rather than "demonstrate;" why would contradictory evidence strengthen an idea?), but a mass of exceptions disproves it, unraveling its very sense. Were people *usually* to hide all signs of being in pain, or to exclaim "Now I see it!" only to find themselves incapable of continuing a series, then the meaning of pain or understanding a series would fundamentally change, possibly even die out owing to the difficulties that would plague teaching and employing them.

In order for us to make sense of it, lying must have a rough set of normal—if imperfect and occasionally absent—indications and surroundings.[77] Even pretense, the perennial counterexample, requires the presence of at least some of a wide range of typical features (a motivation, a victim, appropriate "theory-of-mind" assumptions about disparity in knowledge) and behaviors (shifty eyes, mannered reassurances or forced casualness, significant changes once the victim is out of range such as a relaxation of tense self-monitoring, sly cackling over the victim's credulity, admiration of one's own skills, shoulders slumping in guilt) just for our imagination to gain purchase on the possibility. As Austin so wittily puts it, "'You cannot fool all of the people all of the time' is 'analytic'" (Austin 1979, 113 n.1). Someone who *never* breaks character, well, simply has that character.[78] Teaching the concept of pretending (and pain and internal monologues and so on) must be able to count on some indicative features, or how could it ever get off the ground? "But what does it mean to say that all behaviour *might* always be pretence? Has experience taught us this? How else can we be instructed about pretence? No, it is a remark about the concept 'pretence.' But then this concept would be unusable, for pretending would have no criteria in behaviour."[79] We only learn and continue to use these words meaningfully if they have typical manifestations which indicate appropriate applications, with of course a great deal of variation and exceptions.

In the case of private languages, even though we can have all sorts of local disconnects between sensations and outward manifestations, a total uncoupling would render the terms meaningless. Ultimately, "we would have no use for these words if their application was severed from the criteria of behaviour. . . . The point of the game depends upon what *usually* happens."[80] As I will discuss in chapter 4, these criteria can often justify claims to know another's feelings, undermining the supposed asymmetry that underwrites absolute privacy.

As Wittgenstein repeatedly emphasizes, this is not behaviorism. He is not denying that anything relevant is going on inside us in favor of defining internal sensations entirely in terms of outward behavior. The lesson is rather that "we must not look for 'toothache' as something independent of behaviour. We cannot say: 'Here is toothache, and here is behaviour—and we can put them together in any way we please.'"[81] Sensations and typical behavior are intrinsically connected and certain ways of putting them together renders the whole thing incomprehensible. We don't notice this because, under the spell of the picture of words linked directly with extra-linguistic objects, we prop up our talk with bits borrowed from the normal grammar—just enough to let language get a grip on shadowy quasi-things. Dualism allows the possibility of any sensations in any body regardless of behavior, but Wittgenstein insists that we can only coherently attribute pain to something that evinces roughly recognizable pain-behavior in roughly relevant circumstances. Like a chess move, without the right kind of surroundings to make sense of it, our concepts cannot "get a foothold."[82]

This reading shows how the *Investigations* is unified by its target, namely, Augustine's proto-Tractarian conception of language: once names have been attached to internal referents, the meaning-object's surfeit of significance courses up the connection to charge up the name, making private discourse unproblematic. Indeed, given the disengaged contemplator's predilection for isolating the subject of study, the solitary landscape of the mind represents a particularly perspicacious environment in which to observe the naming process in its essence, sterilized of distractions like intersubjective learning and communication. Private sensations not only impress us with their vivacity; they also appear to be examples of objects whose rules could not have been taught to us socially, leaving internal naming as the only possible origin of our talk about them. The moral of the Beetle in a Box argument clearly shows that Wittgenstein's attack on the idea of private languages is another application of his overall argument against the meaning-object picture of language: "if we construe the grammar of the expression of sensation on the model of 'object and designation' the object drops out of consideration as irrelevant."[83]

## The Point

The standard view has the PLA resting on verificationism: the objection is that the private linguist cannot reliably verify the recurrence of the same sensation, since all he has to go on is his feeling that the present instance is of the same type as the previous one. Without an external check on my reidentification of the Gorignak, I cannot satisfactorily determine whether I have applied the term correctly or not, that is, whether this entity here now is a token of the same type as the one previously so baptized. My attempts to evaluate the consistency of my own applications cannot suffice because, being at the same level as the acts of identification themselves, they provide no justification of these acts; on my own, I'm just buying multiple copies of a given newspaper to check the headlines of the first (PI §265). Without such an external check, then, the difference between merely believing I am following a rule correctly and actually doing so collapses, taking the very notion of a rule, and that of language in general, with it.[84]

Some commentators have denied that this argument appears in Wittgenstein's discussion of PLA at all, but I find it expressed too clearly in too many texts to dismiss it entirely. However, as has been pointed out, this kind of verificationism clashes with many of his other ideas, in particular his frequent claims that we neither have nor need justification to carry out many rule-governed activities perfectly well, a claim that, in fact, often appears within his discussions of private language. For example: "'but when I in my own case distinguish between, say, pretending that I have pain and really having pain, surely I must make this distinction on some grounds!' Oddly enough—no!—I do distinguish but not on any *grounds*."[85] As we shall see in chapter 4, Wittgenstein believes that every interpretation must bottom out in some unjustifiable immediate reaction in order to escape the infinite regress of interpretive rule-following,[86] so demanding an overt justification for the correct recognition of sensations even to be conceivable seems odd. I believe that Wittgenstein uses verification to indicate the purposelessness rather than the intrinsic incoherence of private language-games, as clearly stated here: "you have to remind yourself of the use to get out of the rut in which all these expressions tend to keep you. The whole point of investigating the 'verification,' e.g., is to stress the importance of the use as opposed to that of the picture" (PO 453).

The attack on private languages primarily focuses on the emptiness of private ostensive definitions: no matter what it feels like, no matter the vivid pictures it conjures, it actually accomplishes nothing.[87] Idiolectically naming an inner sensation is an empty ceremony, like the puerile commercial transaction between one's hands, which has been purified of the features and context that give it sense.

The objection that private naming accomplishes nothing—that it has and, in its strict form, can have no use—leads us to another well-known component of Wittgenstein's later thought, namely, the connection between meaning and use. We saw above that his holism expands until it includes the behavior and regular practices surrounding our talk. These interconnected complexes of acts and speech are not random combinations but organized wholes, which tend to be teleologically oriented or goal-driven. "The game, one would like to say, has not only rules but also a *point*."[88] A game's point organizes and informs its components, illuminates its structures, distinguishes between its essential and inessential features depending on how they affect and effect the goal, and so forth.[89] One reason why removing words from their context disrupts our sense of how to use them is that this transfer often leaves behind the original goal, without which the various threads of the activity separate and fall apart. Wittgenstein describes his reaction to a typical philosophical statement like this: "we are at a loss not knowing what reasonings, what actions, go with this expression. Moreover we believe that he made up a sentence analogous to sentences used in certain lang[uage] games not noticing that he took the *point* away."[90]

The primary change that effects this beheading of the pragmatic is the paradigmatic initiating gesture of philosophy, as discussed in chapter 1: the thinker's withdrawal from practical tasks to brood upon words or ideas separated from their normal contexts. "The question 'What is . . .' doesn't refer to a particular—practical—case, but we ask it sitting at our desks" (PO 173). Philosophy's treasured contemplative solitude severs these teleological ties, kidnapping phrases from their homes to interrogate them, not realizing how unreliable forced confessions are: "in philosophy language *idles*. No one asks how it is used."[91] Instead of mundane busywork distracting us from fixing our steady gaze upon the shining essence of reality, Wittgenstein's holism suggests that practical circumstances are essential components of meaning; this is one reason he coined the term "language-game." "What interests us is: How does the word 'I' get used in a *language-game*? For the proposition is a paradox only when we abstract from its use."[92]

Wittgenstein's well-known command to examine how a word is "actually used . . . in the language which is its original home"[93] issues from the need to "let the use *teach* you the meaning."[94] Confusions arise because when we philosophize "we are guided not by practical purposes in forming our sentences" (PO 189), so a return to the guidance of practical purposes will help disperse the clouds of abstruse reasoning. "If I had to say what is the main mistake made by philosophers of the present generation, including Moore, I would say that it is that when language is looked at, what is looked at is a form of words and not the use made of the form of words" (LC 2). Philosophical problems do not arise in ordinary life precisely because there we use language rather than stopping to study it.[95] Besides Wittgenstein's qualification ("for a *large* class of cases—though not for all"), G. E. M. Anscombe's rendering of the oft-quoted section 43 of the *Investigations* distorts his sentence by translating *erklären* as "define" rather than "explain" or "clarify."[96] Although a word's meaning cannot be simply equated with its use, which would be the kind of debatable theory Wittgenstein says he isn't proposing, we can only investigate its meaning from how it is used and what it is used for, just as we can only understand chess by watching it being played rather than staring at the queen under a microscope.

Once again, the model of games frames the issue helpfully since removing the goal of checkmate from the game of chess leaves a meaningless series of pieces being pushed around a board. We cannot understand why a player chose one move rather than another, indeed we cannot really understand her move itself, except in light of the overall purpose of winning.[97] Wittgenstein also frequently compares words to tools. One point of this comparison is that similar appearances conceal multifarious and heterogeneous uses.[98] Another point is that it would be very difficult to grasp what a screwdriver is without seeing it in use, actually screwing in screws: a tool is, in Heidegger's parlance, an "in-order-to" that can only be understood teleologically. "You must think about the purpose of words."[99]

When reinstated in their usual context where we can watch them do an honest day's work, the fog surrounding these phrases dissipates, leaving philosophically uninteresting but perfectly understandable speech.

"I know that that's a tree." Why does it strike me as if I did not understand the sentence? though it is after all an extremely simple sentence of the most ordinary kind? It is as if I could not focus my mind on any meaning. Simply because I don't look for the focus where the meaning is. As soon as I think of an everyday use of the sentence instead of a philosophical one, its meaning becomes clear and ordinary.[100]

It isn't that a word's use *is* its meaning, but that a word actively plays its role in its language-game while being used, and *this* is its meaning: "the meaning of a word is its place in the symbolism, and its place will be shown by the way in which it is used."[101] We must look at words at work because that is when their holistic integration into language-games circulates meaning through them; philosophy rips them out of this sustaining network, to find only pale inert objects. Although this focus on the practical situation can look like pragmatism, I do not think this is right. Wittgenstein frequently argues that the uses we put language to cannot be reduced to achieving practical goals, as we will see in chapter 5.

## Heidegger's Early Holism

I have spent a good bit of time on Wittgenstein in this chapter because these issues—private language, ostensive naming, meaning as use—form some of the central topics of his later work and receive a great deal of attention in the secondary literature. We saw in chapter 2 that it is the move from the inconspicuous mastery of speaking in holistic contexts to the atomistic isolation of ideas or words that gives rise to philosophy; and conversely, the restoration of sense comes from returning us to the meaningful circumstances of our everyday lives. This dynamic, along with various forms of holism, are at the heart of Heidegger's work from the beginning to the end of his career.

Like Kierkegaard and Nietzsche, Heidegger's early work accepts the existentialist depiction of Dasein as a herd animal, naturally tending toward conformity. We are porous creatures, whose "interior" is continuous with "external" forces like societal norms and ontological prejudices we unthinkingly absorb.[102] The canonical understanding of being going back to the Greeks, which forms our taken-for-granted background understanding of being, is constant presence: that which remains the same and best withstands the ravages of time *is* to the highest degree. This theory has its origin in the breakdown dynamic: while operating smoothly, ready-to-hand tools dissolve inconspicuously into their circuits of use, but stopping to study them stiffens them into present-at-hand objects that just sit there. The very act of formulating an ontology loads the dice toward one particular form of being by filtering out everything but self-sufficient static substances, thus inclining metaphysicians to take presence-at-hand as the paradigm of being. Husserl, still in the grip of these ideas, enshrined the methodological suspension of activity in his *epochê*, condemning his analysis in Heidegger's eyes to disproportionately emphasize the contemplation of objects.[103]

Like Wittgenstein's pictures, this understanding of being locks our thought onto a particular path, treating all potential counterevidence as insignificant exceptions or as ultimately reducible to presence-at-hand. Heidegger's *Destruktion* of the tradition is meant to take apart these prejudices, freeing us to phenomenologically discover other modes of being, especially those that inconspicuously permeate our daily existence. Just as disenchanting unnatural pictures returns us to our tacit understanding of how to apply words in mundane situations, so the dismantling of present-at-hand ontology reminds us of our pre-ontological understanding of these everyday ways of being.

Beyond their formal agreement on the contrast between tacit mastery and theoretical comprehension, and their therapeutic preference for the former, Heidegger and Wittgenstein also characterize the content of these kinds of understandings similarly. Wittgenstein's meaning-objects' anticipation of all future applications keeps meaning static when isolated or transplanted into bizarre contexts, thereby anchoring both atomistic metaphysics and semantics. The main target of Heidegger's early work is philosophy's exclusive focus on presence-at-hand, on that which

> *is* in the authentic sense. Such entities are those *which always are what they are*. Accordingly, that which can be shown to have the character of something that *constantly remains* . . . makes up the real Being of those entities of the world which get experienced. That which enduringly remains, really *is*. . . . Being is equated with constant presence-at-hand.[104]

These self-sufficient objects are what remains once we have switched from engaged use to detached observation. They serve science well, but that only demonstrates their pragmatic utility, not that they represent the deepest level of reality.

This understanding of being, of which substance ontology is a prominent example, leads to an atomistic conception of entities where individual beings are first and foremost, while properties and relationships take place on the basis of a static substantial core. Relationships are essentially secondary, accidental to the related things' true natures. Starting with present-at-hand objects prevents the holistic interdetermination of beings since they are what they are independently of all relationships. If a change in context appears to alter an object significantly—the shape of a melting piece of wax, say, or different people's aesthetic evaluations of a painting—then either this entity ranks low on the ontological spectrum or we are mistaken as to its true nature.

Like Wittgenstein's admission that Augustine's naming picture corresponds to a small subregion of language, Heidegger concedes a limited validity to presence-at-hand, rejecting only its traditional monopoly. We spend far more of our lives using tools and speaking with people than studying objects. Where Wittgenstein loosens the hold of this dominant picture of meaning-objects by stressing the profound differences between objects and meanings, likening it to the heterogeneity among "a railway train, a railway accident, and a railway law," *Being and Time* lays out "a genealogy of the different possible ways of Being"[105] in order to highlight the inconspicuous and neglected modes of existence and readiness-to-hand.

In his construction of these neglected ways of being, Heidegger attributes to them two features that Wittgenstein also singles out as essential to language-games as opposed to meaning-objects, namely, holism and teleology. First, Heidegger repeatedly insists upon the central tenet of holism which I will call the Primacy of the Whole.[106] According to this principle, the whole precedes its parts, both phenomenologically and logically; that is, we experience the totality first and individual items emerge out of it, while parts derive their meaning from their relations to other parts and to all of them as a whole. Second, Heidegger argues that we can only understand tools or Dasein in light of their particular goals. Both of these characteristics are absent from present-at-hand objects, which is why an ontology based on that mode of being distorts our lives so drastically. Let's see how Heidegger applies this principle to three important topics: equipment, being-in-the-world, and Dasein's relationship to society.

## All the Equipment in the World

Whereas Wittgenstein began philosophizing in thrall to an ideal, Heidegger's grounding in Husserl's phenomenology, Kierkegaard's existentialism, and Aristotle's method of starting with common opinions kept him firmly rooted in the concrete from the start. He insists that the study of Dasein must avoid the traditional focus on some unusual state or capacity as indicative of our essential nature or highest ability, the perennial favorite being disengaged contemplation. To avoid prejudicing his analysis, Heidegger examines Dasein "as it is *proximally and for the most part—in its average everydayness.*"[107]

In keeping with this principle, our analysis of reality must begin not with Forms or God as the entities that best embody a presupposed definition of being, but rather with "an ontological Interpretation of those entities within-the-*environment* which we encounter as closest to us."[108] Instead of starting with transcendent beings as the paradigm of what it means to be and then working our way down to lesser versions, let's look at the humble, mundane entities we encounter and deal with all the time. Because we live out our lives by using entities around us to accomplish goals (reading books, eating food, driving cars), the vast majority of entities we encounter are equipment with the mode of being Heidegger calls "readiness-to-hand."

The understanding of the analysis is possible only by placing ourselves in the specific natural kind of preoccupation with the world in which we constantly move. We do not actually have to make this displacement but need only to make explicit the kind of comportment in which we constantly move everyday, and which, for the reasons stated, is at first the least visible of all. (HCT 186)

We are always already in this situation which is, for that reason, inconspicuous, so we need to pay attention while remaining in the midst of ongoing activities, watching ourselves out of the corner of our mental eye or "*overhearing*" ourselves (BCAP 30).

One of the defining features we discover from seeing how tools act in normal life activities is that they are fully integrated into a network of complementary equipment: an *Umwelt* or "environment." Just as Wittgenstein's chess piece gets its meaning from the game, so pens can only be what they are within a larger circuit of paper, desks, books, erasers, ink, lamps, and so on. "All equipment is what it is and the way it is only within a particular context. This context is determined by a totality of involvements."[109] Note that this is not a contingent fact that happens to be true of certain tools, what Heidegger calls an "ontic" fact about particular entities; this is an "ontological" fact about readiness-to-hand. A tool's interconnections are built into it from the beginning rather than accruing to it upon being placed in relation to other tools, so much so that even talking about an individual piece of equipment is misleading; they are "*not substances but functions*" (HCT 200). Only out of the whole can single items appear as distinct items, an individuation that culminates in present-at-hand objects when stared at. "In the 'in-order-to' as a structure there lies an *assignment* or *reference* of something to something. . . . Equipment—in accordance with its equipmentality—always is *in terms of* its belonging to other equipment. . . . Out of this the 'arrangement' emerges, and it is in this that any 'individual' item of equipment shows itself."[110] An almost Neo-Platonic emphasis on the primordiality of unity and the derivative fallenness of division runs throughout Heidegger's early work.[111]

Since tools get their meaning from their place within an equipmental totality, pulling them out for isolated study freezes and thus kills their dynamic significance. Removed from the circulation of "in-order-to" relations, a pen's penness expires like a fish out of water or Aristotle's amputated hand or a Coke bottle in the day-to-day life of a pretechnological African tribe (as in *The Gods Must Be Crazy*). This process, which Heidegger sometimes calls "deworlding," characterizes theoretical observation when the entity under examination "has been cut off from that significance which, as such, constitutes environmentality. The 'as' gets pushed back into the uniform plane of that which is merely present-at-hand. It dwindles to the structure of just letting one see what is present-at-hand."[112] This kind of disengaged scrutiny "when we merely stare at something" has long been prized as our best access to true reality,[113] but Heidegger argues that it covers over the more primordial and common web of significance we move in most of the time, which is what he is trying to return us to.[114] This distortive ontology "arises from a characteristic exemplary approach to the world which prompts us to assume in the first instance that a thing is as it is present in an isolated perception of it."[115]

Schopenhauer, one of the main influences on the *Tractatus*, presents an account of the experienced world (representations or Kantian phenomena) similar to Heidegger's description of our everyday environment as teleologically organized into "concatenations" of linked causal relations. Like the holistic groups of intertwined equipment, Schopenhauer holds that we understand beings entirely in terms of relations, although this demonstrates the fatal flaw of mundane familiarity for him. Genuine knowledge can only be heard once we have silenced the will's concerns and emotions' subjective coloring, when "we ourselves have also stepped out of relations, and have thereby become the pure subject of knowing. . . . This state is conditioned from outside by our remaining wholly foreign to, and detached from, the scene to be contemplated, and not being at all actively involved in it" (WWRII 372).

Although philosophers favor disengaged observation because it sifts subjective projections out of objective reality, Heidegger believes that it strips away the most pervasive and important features of the world we live in. Just as Wittgenstein says that this move induces a temporary, artificial ignorance in philosophers, making them "forget" the ways they automatically navigate word usage in daily life, so Heidegger considers the change-over from competent use to staring to be in many ways an epistemological loss: "when we merely stare at something, our just-having-it-before-us lies before us *as a failure to understand it any* more. This grasping which is free of the 'as,' is a privation of the kind of seeing in which one *merely* understands. It is not more primordial than that kind of seeing, but is derived from it."[116] The disengaged perspective isn't exactly wrong, but it covers over our normal rich understanding with a diluted, derivative knowledge of inert objects. When the living breathing world we normally live in deflates, the know-how Heidegger calls "circumspection" goes along with it, leaving us to a blank confrontation with things. To sum up this first point, tools are intrinsically holistic and our understanding of them must take their equipmental context into account, which is precisely what the study of isolated objects filters out in the name of achieving a better understanding of the world.

The second point is that equipment's interconnected assignments result from their teleological organization. It is the very nature of equipment to point beyond itself, both toward the other members of its use-family and toward the goal of the activity, its "in-order-to."[117] We can only understand a particular tool in light of its context which is structured by its purpose. A pen isn't a pen due to its "intrinsic" features (a squid contains and emits ink, but it isn't a pen), but because it is an "in-order-to-write"; it occupies a place within an activity loop which gives it sense by linking it to a purpose.

This characteristic has implications for our understanding of time, a topic very important to Heidegger. Whereas substances are what they are due to their present state, with each moment apparently a completely self-contained now-moment, Heidegger sees that the three tenses are inextricably interconnected, flowing into and drawing each other out. The future becomes the privileged tense because, among other reasons, it is only in terms of its projected function that we can understand a tool. We see the now by the light reflecting off of its relevant goals; now-slices are meaningless without the way they press into the future. Fixing your eyes on this squiggle of ink makes sense in the context of your project of finishing the sentence, which progresses toward the chapter and the entire book (I hope), as Augustine pointed out. I understand your action of getting up to go to the door by viewing it as steps taken in-order-to leave the room, which is why Heidegger says that "when I go toward the door of the lecture hall, I am already there, and I could not go to it at all if I were not such that I am there."[118]

Although Wittgenstein was not interested in offering theories of the nature of time, he does employ a similar point to help move us from atomistic meaning-objects to holistic contexts. He conducts a thought experiment which isolates a thin slice of an activity from its temporal context of what happens before and after: "could someone have a feeling of ardent love or hope for the space of one second—*no matter what* preceded or followed this second?—What is happening now has significance—in these surroundings. The surroundings give it its importance. And the word 'hope' refers to a phenomenon of human life."[119] Although we're strongly attracted to the picture of, say, love as entirely a matter of internal feelings, Wittgenstein's *reductio* inserts this feeling between utterly incongruous precedents and consequents. This argument against instantaneous significance helps disenchant understanding as a purely mental state, as in a person who has memorized the rules of chess and mentally consults them at each point, but constantly makes illegal moves.

Heidegger's holism is teleological, and his teleology is holistic. A tool's immediate uses lead to more distant and overarching projects that culminate in Dasein's for-the-sake-of-which, the way all lines of longitude meet at the poles, and it is this that pulls tools together. This capstone is a broad role or self-conception (or a small set of them) that we use to define ourselves in an (ultimately vain) attempt to settle the unsettling issue of our being (BT 116–117/84). An in-order-to is not a mere means to a goal, but rather constitutes that aim in an ongoing, dynamic way. In other words, it isn't that you must spend quality time with your children *in order to* be a good parent, but that spending quality time with your children is part of what being a good parent *is*. Using certain circuits of tools *is* performing the act in question, acts which, in turn, *are* being one's for-the-sake-of-which. It is not something one achieves, but rather something one enacts. Collectively, these chains of equipment dangling from for-the-sake-of-which's make up the world—or technically, "the worldhood of the world"—which leads us to our next point.

### Being-in-the-World

First, one of the most important facts about Dasein's mode of being, "existence," is its deep holism, a point Heidegger never tires of making. Existence's initial gloss as "being-in-the-world" already introduces this idea: "The compound expression 'Being-in-the-world' indicates in the very way we have coined it, that it stands for a *unitary* phenomenon. This primary datum must be seen as a whole."[120] While we have to study its aspects sequentially, we need to constantly keep in mind that existence can only be, and can only be understood, as an integrated whole. In line with the Primacy of the Whole, the integrated totality precedes the parts; this totality could never be constructed from the separated parts, whereas we can make sense of the pieces as precipitates.[121] One of Heidegger's early works' guiding hermeneutic principles is what I call the Humpty-Dumpty Thesis: if we break a primordial unity into discrete items, we cannot build the initial unified phenomenon by putting them back together.[122] No matter how tightly we press them together, the cracks will show. The right strategy is thus to preserve the phenomenon in its initial totality.

As we have seen, both Heidegger and Wittgenstein see traditional pseudo-problems as the result of distortive preconceptions. Precisely where we believe we have avoided all presuppositions—as in Descartes's method-ological doubt or Husserl's phenomenological reduction—is where a num-ber of profound assumptions sneak in since it is only on the basis of these assumptions that such methods appear as desirable and achievable. "This is not a convenient evasion of a problem. The question rather is whether this so-called problem which is ostensibly being evaded is really a problem at all" (HCT 216). Whereas the Cartesian perspective characterizes Heidegger as naïvely starting with ontology before critically inspecting the episte-mological access that would allow us to conduct an ontological inquiry successfully, Heidegger responds that the demand to make epistemology First Philosophy rests on an entire system of ontological claims which have slipped by, unnoticed, smuggling substantial ontological baggage into the supposedly innocuous epistemological preparation. "In its very *approach to the problem*, with the isolation of sense data as the elements to be explained or eliminated as unclear residues alien to consciousness, the all-determin-ing *step into the theoretical* has already been taken."[123] Recall Wittgenstein: "the first step is the one that altogether escapes notice. . . . (The decisive movement in the conjuring trick has been made, and it was the very one that we thought quite innocent)" (PI §308). The question of being must precede all other questions because the mode of being we take as our para-digm will organize the ways we think about and investigate everything else.

Many pseudo-problems result from the holism-blindness of disengaged observation, forcing us to piece various phenomena together in ways that always come too late. For instance, the question about how our minds gain access to reality only makes sense within a particular ontological picture of reality and of our nature, our knowing faculties, and our relationship to the world. Asking how we make contact with the world presupposes that we are initially, in some sense, not in contact with it, which in turn implies a certain way of understanding ourselves, the world, and what kind of rela-tionship such entities can have.

To take our orientation from this "between" would still be misleading. For with such an orientation we would also be covertly assuming the entities between which this "between," as such, "is," and we would be doing so in a way which is ontologically vague. The "between" is already conceived as the result of the *convenientia* of two things that are present-at-hand. But to assume these beforehand always *splits* the phenomenon asunder, and there is no prospect of putting it together again from the fragments. . . . What is decisive for ontology is to prevent the splitting of the phenomenon—in other words, to hold its positive phenomenal content secure.[124]

The fact that external-world skepticism rests on an ontology which has been largely given a pass constitutes the true scandal of philosophy. The

Humpty-Dumpty Thesis strikes here: "after the primordial phenomenon of Being-in-the-world has been shattered, the isolated subject is all that remains, and this becomes the basis on which it gets joined together with a 'world'" (BT 250/206). Attempts to put these pieces together start with, well, pieces—and this prevents true holism in advance.

To correct this mistake-engendering mistake, our examination must preserve the original holism between Dasein and world, which requires terms and concepts untainted by presence-at-hand assumptions. This is why Heidegger invents a new class of terms for Dasein, and why he chose the term Dasein itself (BT 70/44). Like tools, Dasein is intrinsically related to other entities in Heidegger's adaptation of intentionality. "It is not the case that man 'is' and then has, by way of an extra, a relationship-of-Being towards the 'world'. . . . Dasein is never 'proximally' an entity which is, so to speak, free from Being-in, but which sometimes has the inclination to take up a 'relationship' towards the world."[125] Conceiving of ourselves and the world as present-at-hand renders external-world skepticism insoluble; appreciating the modes of being of existence and readiness-to-hand, on the other hand, renders the problem of the external world neither external nor problematic. Conceiving of all being as presence-at-hand simultaneously creates the problem and hides the solution.[126]

Pure psychology's "one-sided" treatments [of the psycho-physical] are possible only on the basis of the concrete wholeness of the human being. . . . The [notion of the] "pure psychic" has arisen without the slightest regard for the ontology of the whole human being . . .—rather, from the beginning, since the time of Descartes, it has come out of *epistemological* concerns.[127]

Heidegger's phenomenological descriptions of the inconspicuous unity of Dasein and world show us that we've had the answer all along, like Wittgenstein's story of the man who needs to be turned around in order to realize that he isn't actually locked in a room. "With such presuppositions [of an external world], Dasein always comes 'too late'; for in so far as it does this presupposing as an entity . . . it is, *as an entity*, already in a world" (BT 249/206).

Second, our intertwinement with the world is due to Dasein's teleological orientation. Dasein exists by pursuing a role by means of using relevant equipment and, conversely, equipment can only be equipment if Dasein employs it.[128] The two form an indissoluble whole: Being-in-the-world. Dasein

*finds itself* primarily and constantly *in things* because, tending them, distressed by them, it always in some way or other rests in things. Each of us is what he pursues and cares for. In everyday terms, we understand ourselves and our existence by way of the activities we pursue and the things we take care of. We understand ourselves by starting from them because the Dasein finds itself primarily in things.[129]

We are always already melded with the world because we are constantly meddling with it. Just as Wittgenstein's language-games are integrated into practices and social behavior, so Dasein can only be what it is by incorporating and being incorporated into the world.

This comes out most explicitly in the discussion of Dasein's way of "being-in." The profound differences among ontological modes require distinct vocabularies and concepts for each, in order to avoid the kind of crossed wires that Wittgenstein also attacks. In this case, the danger is modeling our relation to the world on the picture of spatial inclusion, as discussed in chapter 1. We cannot be in the world the way a fly is in a bottle, that is, as one present-at-hand object located within another in a contingent spatial relationship—precisely the picture that "becomes the 'evident' point of departure for problems of epistemology" (BT 86/59).

The world that we daily live in is made up of holistic chains of equipment, and we are "in" it the way one is in love or in a band or in a mood: we are involved with the world by being a certain kind of person (a father, a professor) through engaging in the relevant activities (tucking into bed, teaching) with the pertinent equipment (stuffed animals, chalkboards). We don't become a certain kind of person simply by thinking that we are or from an internal state of mind, no more than these alone could confer the status of chess move on the mere act of pushing a piece of wood. To the waiter who tells himself that even though he waits tables he is *really* a writer, he just has not yet had the chance to express the masterpiece locked within him—we want to say, as Sartre does, "writers write," understood as ontology rather than as career advice.

Of course, just performing certain actions alone does not make me who I am; in order to be me, I need the right kinds of relations with things and others, which often requires specific contexts. Without the institution of higher learning in our society, I could not be a college professor, even if I met with young people several times a week, told them to read books and write papers, and so forth. Without gearing into the institution of a college and interacting appropriately with students, colleagues, and classrooms I simply am not a professor.[130] We weave our selves into and out of the social skein of the world.

Thus, we are "in" the world by pursuing goals and projecting roles within relevant equipmental circuits, all of which ultimately rests on the fact that we *care* what happens to us. Unlike a rock that is fundamentally apathetic to its fate—and thus incapable of hopes, fears, and aspirations—it matters to me whether my projects flourish or founder. Even suicide, as Wittgenstein pointed out in his Schopenhauer phase, is a form of caring about what happens to me: death is preferable to the pain of living.[131] This is why Heidegger argues that "care" is the meaning of Being-in-the-world in its unity, where "meaning" denotes the conditions of something's possibility and intelligibility.[132] Dasein's holistic unity, both in its own structure and in its union with the world, must be understood teleologically. Our very selfhood is understood in terms of our wordly pursuit of a selfhood. This is one reason why Heidegger prioritizes the future tense: we can only understand the present and the past in light of our pressing forward into projects. Whatever we actually are is a function of our possibilities, an anticipatory echo of the self we are trying to be.[133]

**The Who**

After covering "being-in" and "worldhood," *Being and Time* turns to who it is that is in-the-world, refusing the self-evidence of subjectivity as loaded with presuppositions. We must keep our ontology open to accommodate phenomenological findings that do not fit traditional categories. It is very easy to slip into presupposing the self's way of being—to fail to examine the *sum* in Descartes's *cogito ergo sum*, as Heidegger believes most philosophers have.[134] Heidegger's phenomenology restores our pre-ontological familiarity with phenomena that are rendered invisible by the assumption that anything real must be a kind of thing. Take the social "one" or "they" (*das Man*), for example: "if we 'see' it ontico-ontologically with an unprejudiced eye, it reveals itself as the 'Realest subject' of everydayness. And even if it is not accessible like a stone that is present-at-hand, this is not in the least decisive as to its kind of Being."[135] Of paramount importance is to avoid the "ontological perversion of making Dasein something present-at-hand" (BT 293/250), a view that begins with the self-identical, self-sufficient subject and then moves on to its relationship to others.

In fact, Heidegger finds that, although Dasein is defined as in-each-case-mine,[136] "proximally and for the most part, Dasein *is not itself.*"[137] Instead of consciously choosing our goals which make up our self, we generally drift along, doing what "one" does, "dispersed into the 'they.'"[138] Rather than actively leading our lives, "Dasein, as a they-self, gets 'lived.'"[139] Drawing on Kierkegaard's (and perhaps Nietzsche's) analyses of societal pressures to conform to norms and bring everything down to the lowest common denominator,[140] Heidegger emphasizes our natural inclination to unquestioningly take our cues from peers instead of "choosing to choose a kind of

Being-one's-Self" (BT 314/270). This tendency, called "falling," is the dark existentialist underbelly of our automatic knowing-how to wend our way through the world: our competence lulls us to sleep.

Our porous nature means that the Primacy of the Whole plays the same role for society as it does for equipment:

Dasein *first of all* does *not* live in its own and nearest. First of all and everyday, one's own world and own Dasein are precisely the farthest. What is first is precisely the world in which one is with one another. It is out of this world that one can first more or less genuinely grow into his own world. (HCT 246)

A substantial self could not be-in a world the way we are, nor could a water-tight ego have anything but accidental relations with others. But "with the rejection of this approach and the uncovering of Being-in-the-world, there can be no question of an isolation of the I" (HCT 238), whether from the world or from society. Demonstrating that Dasein is not a substance or a subject[141] clears the way for an analysis of Dasein that will show that "the problem of *empathy* is just as absurd as the question of the reality of the external world."[142]

Like equipment's referentiality, being-with others is an intrinsic, defining feature of Dasein rather than an external relationship acquired upon encountering others. "Dasein in itself is essentially Being-with."[143] And the Humpty-Dumpty Thesis applies here too: we cannot account for our sociality "by somehow 'explaining' it as what results from taking the Being-present-at-hand-together of several subjects and then fitting them together."[144] We will discuss this primordial sociality in greater detail in chapter 4.

Proximally and for the most part, we encounter others in two ways. First, through the impersonal character of equipment: the shoes I buy were not created specifically for me, but for any feet my size.[145] Equipment tends to be anonymous, ready for anyone's hand, which is why tools have appropriate, standard uses—this is how one hammers, and while there's room for individual styles, past a certain degree of idiosyncrasy, it becomes questionable whether what you are doing still counts as hammering. Second, the worldly roles that are open to me, the for-the-sake-of-which's, get laid out by the society I live in (HCT 244–246). These too are impersonal in that, as academic philosophy's job market readily shows, plenty of other people could teach the courses I teach and sit through the meetings that I do in my role as a professor. Ironically, I can only make my self my own—can only take "ownership" of my life, to play with one of the meanings in *eigentlich*—by means of intrinsically anonymous tools and roles that could be filled by others.[146] Thus, the world I grow up in and into is essentially a with-world; I must live in a shared world for a long time before I can even

conceive of a private one. "Because Dasein's Being is Being-with, its understanding of Being already implies the understanding of Others. . . . Knowing
oneself is grounded in Being-with."[147] Like Wittgenstein (and Hegel), Heidegger adheres to a social anthropology: we are inherently social creatures
rather than self-contained, self-sufficient subjects. If I am not automatically
and strictly myself, neither are "others" truly and wholly other or separated
from me, as Levinas objects. Division II of *Being and Time* recoils from this
"horizontal" holism with society, from the way we start off "dispersed into
the 'they'" (BT 167/129). There, authenticity demands Dasein to "pull itself
together from the dispersion"[148] in favor of a "vertical" holism which inte-
grates all of one's projects into a coherent self, like Kierkegaard's "purity
of heart."[149] Where God's mysterious, transcendent commandments lift
us out of our social bonds into the frosty isolation of the individual for
Kierkegaard, the anticipation of "non-relational" death performs this feat
for Heidegger. As we all must die our own deaths, so should we live our
own lives, not apart from social relations but still, in some important sense,
distinct from them.

Since the meaning of Dasein is care, all of her features must be interpreted in terms of caring about herself, which occurs in her projects and
their tools.[150] Heidegger calls our teleological striving "ec-static," that is,
"standing-outside" ourselves interacting with tools and others rather than
closed up within the shell of a substance. This is his more practice-oriented
version of intentionality. "In clarifying Being-in-the-world we have shown
that a bare subject without a world never 'is' proximally, nor is it ever
given. And so in the end an isolated 'I' without Others is just as far from
being proximally given."[151] Our inside is always already punctured and permeated by the outside. In order to retreat from the world and others to an
inner sanctum, a "primordial" sphere of ownness, I need ideas acquired
in learning the basic understandings I soak up in becoming socialized as a
full-fledged Dasein.

The fact that care defines us fits the idea I am calling original finitude.
Perhaps a god can be truly self-sufficient, in need of nothing else to be, a
divine narcissist like Aristotle's god; but we begin from a lack. It is because
we forget that we pull pens and paper into our worldly activities, because
we hunger that pies call out to us, because we are lonely and lusty that we
couple and it is because we will die that we strive to create something that
will last. It is not our overflowing Being that, like Nietzsche's Zarathus-
tra, radiates brilliance from sheer joy at our abundance of power and self;
rather it is need, hunger, want, and death that drive us "out." We are closer
to Aristophanes' half-people—forever searching for something missing, so

destitute that we do not even know what we are missing—than we are to a Neo-Platonic god's resplendent effulgence.

## The Later Heidegger's Holism

With criminal brevity, I want to point to three forms of holism in Heidegger's later work, since this is such an important theme for him. First and most importantly, the early notion of Dasein as being-in-the-world develops into a relationship between man and being that I have elsewhere called Mutual Interdependence.[152] Neither can be without the other since man's essential feature is to let being come to presence (understood very broadly) while being's essential feature is to present itself to man. In a late interview, Heidegger goes so far as to say that "the fundamental idea of my thinking is exactly that Being, relative to the manifestation of Being, *needs* man and, conversely, man is only man in so far as he stands within the manifestation of Being. . . . One cannot pose a question about Being without posing a question about the essence of man."[153] The two are so entwined that neither can be or be understood except in relation to the other; each is defined relative to each other. Of course, stating this fundamental relationship runs into the same problem that Heidegger's early work encountered in laying out the facets of being-in-the-world sequentially: even saying that they are inextricably connected starts with two separate entities and then attributes a relationship to them.[154] Similar to the *Tractatus*'s transcendent truths that must be shown since stating them turns them into nonsense, asserting the unity between Being and man unintentionally divides them.[155] In keeping with the Primacy of the Whole, it is the relationship that is primary and the *relata* must be understood from it.

Second, Heidegger's later work analyzes the history of being in terms of epochs organized around their own metaphysical systems; this history determines for the people of that time what it means 'to be,' which then shapes all other views, similar to the way presence-at-hand structures detached thinking about beings in the early work. "Metaphysics grounds an age in that, through a particular interpretation of beings and through a particular comprehension of truth, it provides that age with the ground of its essential shape. This ground comprehensively governs all decisions distinctive of the age."[156] This core idea ramifies across all dimensions of a culture's lives and thoughts for that era. Ethically, it lays out what kinds of lives we can and should lead, somewhat like *Being and Time*'s for-the-sake-of-which's.[157] Only Greeks can be tragic heroes, only Medievals pure-hearted saints, and only moderns comfort-seeking gadget-users. Epistemologically, an interlocking system of beliefs and attitudes sets the general range of ideas that we can entertain and possibly believe, our "live options" in James's term. This idea is very important to *On Certainty*, where Wittgenstein argues at length that "my convictions do form a system, a structure."[158] Ideas that fit neatly into the present system are far easier to assimilate and more likely to be accepted, while incongruous ideas face an uphill battle for acceptance, overcoming knee-jerk rejection or outright incomprehension. As Heidegger says in a proto-Kuhnian analysis of Newton's law of inertia, while "we consider it self-evident. . . . During the preceding fifteen hundred years it was not only unknown, but Nature and Being in general were experienced in such a way that it would have been senseless."[159]

Finally, a number of Heidegger's most important later phenomenological descriptions are holistic. For instance, an artwork's earth and world are locked in a codependent "strife" in which they are only understandable from their interaction (BW 174). Similarly, his analysis of buildings posits a kind of environmental Gestalt gathered together by successful buildings rather than a preexisting landscape onto which a structure is dropped.[160] Perhaps the most holistic phenomenon, although also the one I can make the least sense of, is the fourfold: "by a *primal* oneness the four—earth and sky, divinities and mortals—belong together in one."[161] Like the aspects of being-in-the-world, although we can only describe one at a time, we must keep reminding ourselves that with each one, "we are already thinking of the other three along with it, but we give no thought to the simple oneness of the four" (BW 351).

## Summary

In the previous chapter, we examined meaning-objects and present-at-hand objects, the semantic and ontological targets of Wittgenstein's and Heidegger's respective attacks. These are the self-contained, isolatable, inert building blocks whose relationships are essentially secondary to their intrinsic natures. This chapter discussed their alternatives views, which are defined by holism and teleology. Words, beliefs, actions, tools, and persons are the way they are in and through their interactions with other persons, words, ideas, behaviors, and tools that are thoroughly informed by goals, albeit not necessarily practical or explicitly chosen ones. With this conception of things, words, and people in hand, we will next look at the conception of thinking these two thinkers propose as fitting this model. In other words, if this is what meaning is like, then what must the grasp of such meaning be like?

# 4  What Is Called Thinking?

In philosophy, one is constantly tempted to invent a mythology of symbolism or of psychology, instead of simply saying what we know.

—Wittgenstein, *Philosophical Grammar*, 56

We can learn thinking only if we radically unlearn what thinking has been traditionally.

—Heidegger, *What Is Called Thinking?*, 8

We began this study by examining Wittgenstein's and Heidegger's projects as therapeutic treatments of the pseudo-problems that strike us when we disengage from normal, ongoing activity. We then devoted a chapter to each of the perspectives or stances that frame their thought—the theoretical notion of static, discrete meaning and being, in chapter 2; the dynamic and holistic processes we actually live in, in chapter 3. Now I want to turn to the conceptions of thinking that correlate with these respective views.

The theoretical view pictures thought as the explicit and articulate, or at least fully articulable, thematic consideration of ideas. The recognized founder of this idea, Plato, argues that one does not know something unless one can express this knowledge and give reasons for it. Lacking this, even successful practitioners of an art or skill can have a knack, but not true understanding.[1] Thought must passively mirror its object, and since the highest form of reality does not change, neither does the highest form of truth. Familiarity with the dancing shadows of this world can never amount to more than *doxa*, so we should lift our gaze to the unchanging, either to the Forms or God, which prepares us for a heavenly afterlife, or to the fixed and quantifiable qualities of things, which give us the power to scientifically secure earthly delights.

Since human nature and our relationship to the world are often characterized as primarily epistemic, and since epistemology generally intertwines with metaphysics (think of Plato's divided line), the implications of this conception of thinking ramify across many topics. A faulty conception of thinking is instrumental in creating pseudo-problems and unsolvable aporiai—skepticism about the external world, other minds, rule-following, and so on. Along with overhauling the nature of meaning, the world, and our relationship to them, Wittgenstein and Heidegger also construct highly innovative accounts of thought to fit their new conceptions of these, in the hope that a more accurate account of thought may prevent these pseudo-problems from arising in the first place.

## Wittgenstein's Pictorial Underdetermination

Wittgenstein pointedly ignores the nature of human thinking in his early work. He defines thoughts, along with propositions, as the mirror of reality, leaving it to psychology to explain how people are able to access them.[2] In fact, as Frege's anti-psychologism demands, Logical Stoicism makes human comprehension not just a tangent, but a non-issue. A proper notation liberates thinking from thinkers; once they have been aligned, states-of-affairs control propositions and thoughts in perfect synchrony. Logic allows us to fade into the pure will-less spectator who needs not act or decide anything, preferably even barred from interfering in the rigid symbolic machinery.

However, like the incompatibility between elementary propositions about color discussed in chapter 3, this idea runs into problems from the start. Immediately after introducing the logical syntax that automatically prevents nonsense, Wittgenstein concedes that "in order to recognize a symbol by its sign we must observe how it is used with a sense. A sign does not determine a logical form unless it is taken together with its logico-syntactical employment."[3] Ideal symbols may govern their own use, but the written or spoken signs by which we handle them don't; we must see signs in action to figure out which symbols they denote. This apparently minor concession lets the confounding complexity of everyday language seep back into logic's pristine clarity.[4] Where Frege found himself forced to rely upon metaphors and the earthy connotations of German[5] to construct a purely denotational symbolic order, the *Tractatus* must have recourse to ordinary language to teach us "self-sufficient" logic.

Wittgenstein's later work "stick[s] to the subjects of our every-day thinking" (PI §106), resisting getting "dazzled by the ideal" (PI §100) by "talking about the spatial and temporal phenomenon of language" (PI §107). Now he turns to the conditions for the possibility of language as spoken by living breathing humans, foregrounding the question of how we learn and use language. Ultimately, he is pursuing the same question as before—how do we succeed in meaning anything?—but whereas he had earlier focused on the autonomous operations of the crystalline clockwork of meaning, now the emphasis is on the "we" who are doing the meaning.[6] And on the "we" who are philosophizing about linguistics acts as well, to keep us on our guard against beguiling pictures.

Perhaps the most seductive picture of a person thinking about something is that of an image of a subject matter on display in her private mental gallery for her introspective inspection. When her mind's eye is fixed upon this mental image, we can say that she is thinking about it—or at least we would be able to say this were we able to open up her head and plot her mental gaze.[7] This gaze can resolve the problems that beset dead signs, such as ambiguous terms: the image occupying her mental field of vision decides which kind of "bank" her words meant.

But as the later Wittgenstein never tires of demonstrating, pictures underdetermine how we understand and use them. Whereas Logical Stoicism sought rules that apply themselves with absolute determinacy, his very first classes upon returning to philosophy emphasize the fact that "you can't give any picture which can't be misinterpreted."[8] Rather than intrinsic intelligibility, it is our fluency in our culture's pictorial idiom that enables unproblematic communication, but as with Dasein's knowing-how to use a tool, our adroitness at filtering out potential misunderstandings covers its own tracks. We see only the standard meaning which seems to be the sole possible interpretation, largely because it is the only one that strikes us.[9] Automatically following rules in standard ways makes it feel as though the application were contained within the rule and apparent on its face, ruling out all other interpretations as palpably absurd. Under normal circumstances, these countless alternatives remain dormant because our constant handling has worn them away, but when viewed "from the outside," with our normal facility bracketed, endless alternate interpretations suddenly pop up with no metaphysically decisive way to pick out the right one.[10] Let us call this the Thesis of Inescapable Ambiguity.

As with the incompatible color points, the earlier Wittgenstein was aware of this problem but considered it tractable. In the late 1920s, however, it metastasized and helped bring about the systemic failure of the entire Tractarian structure, which is why he spends so much time showing how various possible solutions to this problem fail. For instance, one might add a second step—something like an interpretation or projection of the picture—to filter out the clamoring mass of interpretations allowed by the picture on its own, a solution he had considered in his early work.[11] But this just passes the explanatory burden from the picture to the act of interpretation, which now faces the same problems. A picture that shows how the picture in question relates to reality[12] sets off an infinite regress since *it* would then need a picture to tell us how to read it; this is one reason why the *Tractatus* forbids the picturing of pictorial form itself.[13] Cutting off this regress by immediately grasping the second picture, on the other hand, invites the question, why not just do so from the start?[14]

Another strategy is to employ mental pictures to clear matters up. While physical snapshots allow for multiple readings, a picture developed in the stuff the mind is made of dispels all cloudiness. "It seems to be a super-picture. It seems, with thought, that there is no doubt whatever. With a picture, it still depends on the method of projection, whereas here it seems that you get rid of the projecting relation, and are absolutely certain that this is thought of that."[15] A super-picture painted in ethereal mind goo has super-intentionality, letting it do what no actual picture can—unequivocally indicate its subject. After all, we puzzle over the subject of our thoughts even less than over photographic images, which can be blurry or faded. But this solution enjoys the advantages of theft over honest toil: mental pictures are simply declared to require no interpretation thanks to their interiority, without any account of how cerebral citizenship confers this amazing power. This is argument by stipulation, supported not by reasons but by picture-induced intuitions. Whenever we feel the temptation to enlist the queer or "occult" powers of the mental arena in service of a theory, Wittgenstein suggests that we substitute a physical picture for the mental one.[16]

The failure of these attempted solutions seems to leave us at the mercy of Inescapable Ambiguity: any picture, regardless of medium or apparent legibility, underdetermines its interpretation. The same goes for ostensive definitions: just pointing at something and saying "This is *x*" cannot by itself convey which aspect of the thing one is naming or under what description or in what context, and so forth.[17] And for rules: it is "possible to derive anything from anything according to some rule or other—nay, according to *any* rule with a suitable interpretation."[18] Inescapable Ambiguity leads to what I will call the Interpretation Aporia: the limitless ways we *could* take a picture or rule make the fact that we *do* take it a particular way, and generally the same way as everyone else, baffling. No matter how self-evident its standard application appears, it can always be carried out otherwise by someone sincerely trying to follow it correctly,[19] as Saul Kripke and Nelson Goodman argue. Examples and past applications are finite, after all, whereas rules extend indefinitely, which means that in principle rules apply to more than has been or can be definitively settled in advance. And now it looks as if we have lost precisely what we were trying to secure, namely, how meaningful language is possible: "how am I supposed to follow a sign-post, if whatever I do is a way of following it?"[20]

These discussions can induce dread-drenched premonitions of semantic nihilism, the feeling that we stand on the vertiginous precipice of verbal anarchy.[21] This anxiety motivates philosophers to retroactively add something to the moment of speech or rule-following that can undergird our communal agreement, laying down guard rails that keep us from the abyss. In other words, the Rational Retrospective Reconstruction (RRR) of speech fills in the void uncovered by disengaged analysis with meaning-objects.

We are extraordinarily affected by the way in which we do in fact react to a sign. The result is that certain ideas stand to us for certain uses because that is how we usually apply them. We therefore think that those ideas have that most usual use *in* them, though they could perfectly well be imagined to have another use.[22]

As usual, Wittgenstein contrasts mundane situations where things go smoothly with philosophy's retrospective anxiety and dissatisfaction with the plain facts. Although I followed an order "'automatically,'" when I am "asked to give the reason" I reach for "a justification *post hoc*" (BB 14). Staring at signs renders them, in McDowell's phrase, "normatively inert,"[23] calling for queer explanations of its normal potency. If, as Wordsworth says, poetry is "emotion recollected in tranquility," Wittgenstein views philosophical confusions as engaged competence recollected—badly—in contemplation. Hindsight is 20/20, but only because its theories act "like a pair of glasses on our nose through which we see whatever we look at" (PI §103). The detached examination of, say, automatically following an arrow from its feathers to its point reveals other ways of following it (from point to feathers or vertically), thus demanding that something weed out the bad ones.

One solution is to retroactively insert mental acts at the moment of understanding to correlate with the meaning-objects. Obviously, we didn't hit on the right interpretation by chance, so we must have been thinking of it—unconsciously, perhaps, or very quietly. Along with ambiguous words or phrases, other linguistic events that must be accounted for are continuing one's line of thought after an interruption—which evokes an image of the interrupted sentence lying coiled up in the back of one's cranium, ready to continue spooling out where it left off[24]—or being surprised—which suggests that we must have been expecting something *else* if what did happen surprised us.[25]

Wittgenstein lays out this vision of semantic nihilism not because it represents the true state of things we had been blissfully, if irresponsibly, unaware of, but in order to demonstrate that (a) it results from a particular conception of thinking, (b) it is absurd and obviously contradicted by daily experience, which means that (c) we need to revise that conception. In a negative image of transcendental inquiry, this view of thinking is a condition for the *im*possibility of language: if such difficulties did truly plague understanding, we would never be able comprehend signs or follow rules or talk to each other. Since we plainly do, something is amiss with this account.

As commentators continue to instruct Kripke's interpretation, Wittgenstein's discussion is a *reductio* of traditional conceptions of thinking.[26] He is not bringing to light a profound discovery that exposes a heretofore unknown vulnerability of understanding, but charting a particularly virulent distortion introduced by philosophical contemplation. The philosopher's bafflement before suddenly mute or excessively permissive signs is an artificial product of the characteristic philosophical behaviors discussed in chapter 1: stopping ongoing usage and staring.

It is felt to be a difficulty that a rule should be given in signs which do not themselves contain their use [that is, which are not meaning-objects], so that a gap exists between a rule and its application. But this is not a problem but a mental cramp. That this is so appears on asking when this problem strikes one. It is never when we lay down the rule or apply the rule. We are only troubled when we look at a rule in a particularly queer way. The characteristic thing about all philosophical problems is that they arise in a peculiar way. As a way out, I can only give you examples, which if you think about them you will find the cramp relaxes.

In ordinary life one is never troubled by a gap between the sign and its application. To relieve the mental cramp it is not enough to get rid of it; you must also see why you had it. (AWL 90)

Wittgenstein's account of philosophy does explain why we fall prey to this semantic illusion: detaching a phenomenon from absorbed activity drains it of the meaning that flows through it while knitted into its language-game. It is this shriveled, barren husk of meaning that seems strikingly incapable of generating vibrant communication. Instead of a profound discovery about language or meaning or thought, however, this is just an odd fact about us, like the way repeating a word over and over again ("noodle, noodle, noodle . . .") reduces it to a thick senseless sound.[27] It offers no secret insight into the profound workings of anything, except the folly of philosophy. "It may easily look as if every doubt merely *revealed* an existing gap in the foundations. . . . The sign-post is in order—if, under normal circumstances, it fulfills its purpose" (PI §87).

To paraphrase Heidegger,[28] the most astonishing fact about the way we follow rules is how little it astonishes us. Although there are indefinitely more possible interpretations than we think of, people generally do in fact follow them the same way; we have to for many important practices to be possible.[29] It is one of those extremely general, inconspicuous facts that humans tend to take pictures, signs, and rules similarly. Wittgenstein has shown that the traditional cognitivist account of thought, far from explaining this, renders it inexplicable by igniting an exponential explosion of alternate interpretations. His job now is to account for our virtually universal agreement without resorting to "a mythological description of the use of a rule" (PI §221).

## Un-Thinking

The traditional conception of thinking as consisting of conscious, rational acts is the source of the Interpretation Aporia and its Inescapable Ambiguity, not their solution. The futility of the neutral observer's search for the "right" interpretation amid a sea of alternatives represents a *reductio* of the idea that we are actually faced with such an array from which we must choose. At the root of this line of thought is the idea that what we are doing in these situations is interpreting.

It can be seen that there is a misunderstanding here from the mere fact that in the course of our argument we give one interpretation after another; as if each one contented us at least for a moment, until we thought of yet another standing behind it. What this shews is that there is a way of grasping a rule which is *not* an *interpretation*, but which is exhibited in what we call "obeying the rule" and "going against it" in actual cases.[30]

The intellectualist theory depicts thought as shining a spotlight on its object, mentally turning it over and examining its facets as one does in contemplation. This brilliant attentive stare evaporates meaning's life-blood, leaving behind a hard inert object which, admitting of multiple interpretations, requires us to interpret it. And now we are locked into the line of thought that leads to the rule-following paradox. Avoiding this paradox will require a different picture of thought itself, one which places far less importance on, well, thinking.

One of the ongoing targets of Wittgenstein's later work "is a kind of general disease of thinking which always looks for (and finds) what would be called a mental state from which all our acts spring as from a reservoir."[31] Whereas most philosophers focus on our lamentably rare moments of explicit analysis as the ideal essence of thinking that we ought to aspire to, Wittgenstein selects immediate reactions as his paradigm cases. The kinds of actions that best exemplify normal understanding are automatic, unthinking responses, like calling for help or immediately obeying an order or saying something as an aside during a conversation or casually identifying a color. These are "way[s] of grasping a rule which [are] *not* an *interpretation,*" moments when we react "without thinking. But *entirely* without thinking? Without *reflecting.*"[32] The interlocutor's shocked question here betrays his assumption that action can only take place on the basis of thinking: screaming for help presupposes that I understand the meaning of the word "help," that I know that I am in danger, that sounds travels, that others have minds and ears, and so on. This line of thought resembles Wittgenstein's early view that the implicit understanding of the rules of sign-application (T 4.002) must rest upon the possibility of a complete analysis which unpacks all implications, in the absence of which one cannot be said to understand.[33] Every statement and every act depends on countless beliefs in the absence of which it makes no sense. Wittgenstein is not rejecting this traditional picture for its opposite—a zombie-like mindlessness or Lucretian seizures—as his interlocutor fears; he wants to get past the entire framework that makes both the traditional notion and its antithesis appear sensible. His examples are meant to relax our mental cramp, to "remove the temptation to think that there '*must* be' what is called a mental process of thinking, hoping, wishing, believing, etc., independent of the process of expressing a thought, a hope, a wish, etc."[34]

Once again, it is the tacit classification of the phenomena—the preparatory conjurer's trick—that lays the ground for problems. A careful examination the way we use words like "know" or "understand" quickly shows that the circumstances surrounding these notions are far more important than anything that happens in the mind. In keeping with his understanding of philosophy, Wittgenstein does not present this claim as new information he has gleaned from specialized research, but rather as a matter of refamiliarizing us with the way we use these words in our everyday lives.

But don't think of understanding as a "mental process" at all.—For *that* is the way of speaking that is confusing you. Rather ask yourself: in what kind of case, under what circumstances do we say "Now I can go on," if the formula has occurred to us?

That way of speaking is what prevents us from seeing the facts without prejudice. . . . So let us not think we *must* find a specific mental process, because the verb "to understand" is there and because one says: Understanding is an activity of the mind.[35]

He is not denying the existence of inner phenomena but trying to change how we think of them—or better, restoring our normal understanding of them.

In Wittgenstein's later analysis of thinking, context trumps inner events. When someone grasps a rule by catching on to a pattern of numbers, for example, we're tempted to (RRR) place the formula before his mental eye as that which enables him to continue the series correctly, the way you might dial a phone number by reading it off a piece of paper or transcribe a quotation. *This*, we want to say, is what understanding really is. But Wittgenstein dismantles this tempting line of reasoning, arguing that "various things may have happened; for example . . . he says nothing at all and simply continues the series."[36] Let's look at three arguments for this view.

## (1) Phenomenological Absence

Disengaged philosophical contemplation neutralizes meaningful signs, thus divorcing internal meaning from external marking. Active verbs mislead us into positing a distinct activity of meaning the signs: I didn't just mouth those words, I *meant* what I said; I *meant* a river bank rather than a financial bank. The mind breathes significance into a lifeless sign's nostrils, as God inflated Adam's body with a soul.[37] But this is a Retrospective Reconstruction built according to the specs imposed by a picture's blue-prints.

Examine expressions like "having an idea in one's mind," "analysing the idea before one's mind." In order not to be misled by them see what really happens. . . . To say that we are trying to express the idea which is before our mind is to use a metaphor, one which very naturally suggests itself; and which is all right so long as it doesn't mislead us when we are philosophizing. For when we recall what really happens in such cases we find a great variety of processes.[38]

Wittgenstein is not denouncing the pictures or metaphors, but warning us to handle them cautiously lest they take over.

We imagine the thinker of our thoughts as carrying on an incessantly droning inner commentary on what we're doing, like a disembodied mouth in a Beckett play or an overbearing sports announcer or a bad DVD commentary. Wittgenstein breaks this spell by a phenomenological reminder of what actually happened.

All this will become clearer if we consider what it is that really happens when we say a thing and mean what we say.—Let us ask ourselves: If we say to someone "I should be delighted to see you" and mean it, does a conscious process run alongside these words, a process which could itself be translated into spoken words? This will hardly ever be the case.[39]

For the most part we respond to what J. J. Gibson calls "solicitations" from the environment with little to no conscious thought. We don't interpret; we react, letting our feet find their footing without any supervision from an inner homunculus. Wittgenstein doesn't deny that explicit thinking ever happens, of course, but he does deny that it always does or that it must happen for understanding to take place. "If I say, 'Talk to me and observe yourself,' you find nothing at all. You say there *must* be something—but there is only the 'must.'"[40] We insist on finding inner events alongside outward behavior only because disengaged contemplation demands it.

Although Wittgenstein often dismisses the relevance of introspective experience for his grammatical investigations,[41] introspection's failure to find anything where theories require mental acts is a good reason to doubt their supposed necessity. If we can understand without distinct mental acts, then understanding cannot be identified with nor can it require such acts. He uses this argument to deflate a number of mental phenomena, such as remembering, recognition, and expectation;[42] in each case, the negative results of introspection undermines reliance upon the introspectable. Wittgenstein's anxious interlocutor often raises the specter of semantic nihilism: if we aren't *meaning* our words, then aren't they meaningless, especially since the lifeless linguistic leftovers served up to theorizing seem so inadequate? But notice that such worries never arise during normal life.[43] These paltry tokens generally get the job done admirably, revealing our anxiety to be the product of philosophical analysis, not its stimulus. We know that we don't have to keep pumping our words full of meaning to keep them from collapsing into mere sounds for the very good reason that we don't do this.

One attraction of the metaphor of games is the fact that, once we know how to play, we can simply move the tokens around the board, alternately absorbed or distracted. If a problem arises, we can disengage from absorbed play to consult the rules as to a move's legality, but we must beware of retroactively putting these thoughts in our minds at the time we made the move. Mastery enables skillful players to simply see good moves and make them without a detour through the conscious mind. Hubert Dreyfus, who has done a great deal of philosophical and empirical work on this topic largely inspired by Heidegger and Wittgenstein, sometimes cites grandmasters' skill in speed chess, which is played so quickly that it precludes pondering.[44] Unreflectively reacting fits Wittgenstein's conception of understanding as know-how since skills, once mastered, require little cognizant supervision. "This understanding, the knowledge of the language, isn't a conscious state that accompanies the sentences. . . . It's much more like the understanding or mastery of a calculus, something like the *ability* to multiply."[45] As Meredith Williams writes,

ordinary competence also is non-theoretical and non-reflective. . . . The attempt to model such basic competence upon the basis of theory construction and use is going to distort the character of this competence. . . . This basic competence, which embodies both understanding of the world one lives in and understanding of language, is not a way of interpreting the world but a way of acting and judging non-reflectively in accord with others.[46]

Proficiency allows our supposed mental homunculus to delegate his work to "muscle memory" as long as nothing extraordinary or problematic happens.

Although absorbed competence is most apparent in physical activities, Wittgenstein also attributes it to activities we usually classify as mental. It isn't just hammering or walking that neither has nor needs express attention; as paradoxical as it sounds, most thinking is similarly thoughtless. Whereas syllogistic reasoning has long served as a paradigm of the highest form of thought, Wittgenstein puts it back into its everyday circumstances.

Imagine a procedure in which someone who is pushing a wheelbarrow comes to realize that he must clean the axle of the wheel when the wheelbarrow gets too difficult to push. I don't mean that he says to himself: "Whenever the wheelbarrow can't be pushed . . . ," but he simply *acts* in this way. And he happens to shout to someone else: "The wheelbarrow won't push; clean the axle," or again: "This wheelbarrow won't push. So the axle needs cleaning." Now this is an inference. Not a logical one, of course.[47]

Wittgenstein notes the absence of a universal conditional premise ("Whenever . . ."), indeed of all mental monologue ("I don't mean that he says to himself . . ."); the reasoning lies in the actions rather than in thoughts accompanying the actions, thereby eliminating the imagined "jump from *knowing* to doing."[48] Certainly, the "ideas" guiding his behavior can be retrospectively constructed and expressed; but if they are, this is an accidental addition brought on by circumstances (". . . he happens to shout to someone else"). The primary level is simply the person acting.

When Heidegger describes our average everyday behavior, he finds the same phenomenon. The philosophical priority of knowledge insists that it must underlie all action,[49] which means that, in order to use the hammer, I must first know that this object is a hammer, understand the concept of hammering, know what kind of materials are suitable for hammering, and so on. Furthermore, if our fundamental relationships are cognitive, we must subject these beliefs to epistemological stress-tests like Socratic *elenchus* or

Cartesian doubt; only those that pass the tribunal of reason deserve our trust. This picture of us first and foremost as knowers and the world as an object of knowledge is what frames philosophical discourse.[50]

For our ontological ails, Heidegger prescribes his usual panacea of phenomenological descriptions of the involved beings' modes of being. Although his constant insistence on such an esoteric-sounding procedure may sound forced—even a committed Heideggerian like myself must concede that his chronic invocations of being can approach self-parody, a kind of metaphysical Tourette's syndrome—the claim actually makes perfect sense. What kind of entity something is determines how it does and can act, what kinds of relationships or properties it can have, and so forth.[51] Since all questions ultimately boil down to the way various beings are and can be, "philosophy is universal phenomenological ontology."[52] We possess a pre-ontological (that is, unthematic or noncognitive) understanding of the being of these entities (as attested by our ability to interact appropriately with them), so we just need to focus our attention on what we already know but "forget" during intellectual examination, the process Wittgenstein calls "assembling reminders" (PI §127). In the present case, a proper account of the self's interactions with the world comes from studying what kinds of entities self and world are.

Heidegger argues that knowing is not basic but "founded upon Being-in-the-world."[53] Theorizing can only take place on the basis of years of more practical interactions with equipment and others, making skeptical questions about their reality a kind of performative contradiction. Our immersion in them is a condition for the possibility of questioning their reality; our ability to ask the question contains the answer.[54] Like Wittgenstein, Heidegger thinks that the real question is why we find this question urgent or even coherent in the first place, which he explains by citing our misunderstanding of the modes of being involved. Whereas Dasein lives holistically intertwined with equipment and others, a walking refutation of skepticism, philosophers see things through the ontological lens of self-sufficient substances whose relationships to anything else can only be accidental, as we saw in chapters 2 and 3.

What we find when we look at our average everydayness with an open mind is that Dasein is first and for the most part an engaged actor in the world, a user of tools rather than a detached theoretician. Philosophical examination almost inevitably misses this inconspicuous way of being-in-the-world, which shows that what appears most obvious to thematic attention should not be granted automatic jurisdiction.

The explicitness and the awareness of the modes of being and their ontological foundation in the course of being do not decide on what belongs to the phenomenal
composition of a structure of being. . . . Explicitness and awareness do not decide
on these matters. Rather, the very lack of explicitness in traversing this course . . .
is characteristic of all concerned being-in-the-world, inasmuch as we define it as
*absorption* in the world.[55]

While Husserl's notion of truth as the intuition that fulfills our expectation focuses on maximal explicitness, in Heidegger's hands phenomenology becomes an unprecedented tool for circumventing philosophy's theory
prejudice. Dismantling the overly conspicuous present-at-hand objects,
Heidegger unearths the far more common and important inconspicuous
features which had been previously covered up.

Heidegger prioritizes holistic and teleological equipment, as we saw in
chapter 3. Equipment is engaged by "circumspection," an absorbed, unthematic know-how which represents a distinct epistemological mode that
cannot be reduced to explicit thought. Correlatively, equipment is irreducible to present-at-hand objects.

Equipment can genuinely show itself only in dealings cut to its own measure (hammering with a hammer, for example); but in such dealings an entity of this kind
is not *grasped* thematically as an occurring Thing, nor is the equipment-structure
known as such even in the using. The hammering does not simply have knowledge
about the hammer's character as equipment, but it has appropriated this equipment
in a way which could not possibly be more suitable.[56]

Its fullest actualization occurs not in scrutinizing beliefs or cogitation, but
in what psychologist Mihaly Csikszentmihalyi calls flow, where our skills
match a task's demands and self-awareness fades out. Heidegger isn't just
making the empirical observation that we don't think much—philosophers
have always said this, even citing this lack as the reason philosophers need
to sting sleepers awake. He is making the deeper point that this nonthink-
ing engagement is a distinct and legitimate form of mental activity: "the
non-objectivity of the immediately given world is not nothing; it is a positive phenomenal character belonging to the presence of the environing
world" (HCT 198).

Heidegger and Wittgenstein are not so much disputing the claim that
circumspection is a weak, thin form of knowledge as the idea that it is a
form of knowledge at all, at least as traditionally conceived. Circumspection is fundamentally different from theoretical knowledge and cannot be
reduced to a form of it; it is, in the terminology, non-epistemic. Heidegger
agrees with Wittgenstein when he asks, "why should the language-game

rest on some kind of knowledge?" (OC §477), and again when he answers that "the end is not an ungrounded presupposition: it is an ungrounded way of acting."[57] This way of dealing with the world is embodied in suitable actions rather than in assertions of facts, which is why, like Wittgenstein's example of how a clarinet sounds, it can be so hard to articulate.[58] The aim of Heidegger's early project is to know that which isn't knowledge by paying attention to what withdraws from attention, and so discover "a basic phenomenal trait of the worldhood of the environing world: *presence in the manner of inconspicuousness*, its presence precisely on the basis of not yet being apprehended and nevertheless having discovered primarily, permitting encounter" (HCT 197).

According to the *pharmakon* logic of *Being and Time*, some of the ideas put forward in division I are partially undone in division II. While the study of our average everydayness in division I emphasizes the background circumspection informing our daily activities, the voluntarism of division II deplores this.[59] Common practices exert an undertow of conformity, drawing us down to what one does for no other reason than that that is the sort of thing that is done. Authenticity consists in choosing to choose, thus fighting the inertia of banality with a practical version of spotlight consciousness. We need to be jolted awake from "the oblivious passing of our lives" in order to engage in our lives vigorously.[60] For existentialists, the unexamined life is barely lived. Heidegger's antihumanist later work overcomes this early voluntarism, offering the most coherent account of free will that I know of, as I will briefly discuss below.

### (2)   Underdetermination and Infinite Regress

The first argument states that, phenomenologically, mental acts do not accompany all speech or intelligent behavior; the second argument claims that even if they did, it would solve nothing because any explanatory entity or process would be vulnerable to the same objections that faced the sign in the first place. For example, we might supplement the physical arrow with a mental arrow telling us to read the physical arrow from feathers to point rather than point to feathers, but this immediately raises the problem of correctly following the mental or meta-arrow. While this example may seem too crude to tempt anyone, Wittgenstein argues that all supplementary instruction suffers from the same flaw: "isn't every explanation of how he should follow the arrow in the position of another arrow?"[61] More sophisticated means—verbal directions, diagrams, gestures, anything you can think of— must itself be comprehended, which reinstates the initial interpretive difficulties. No mental event or content can by itself account for understanding since it underdetermines our use of it; since it could be followed in endless directions, it merely pushes the question of comprehension back a step.[62]

This strategy launches an infinite regress of steps since, *ex hypothesi*, no sign by itself can actually tell us what to do with. Like the Third Man argument, installing an additional mental step to reach across "the unbridgeable gulf between rule and application"[63] gives birth to Hydra-headed needs: we must now fill the gap between hearing an order and grasping what we are to do—and the one between grasping it and following it—and all the pullulating lacunae that follow. When ordered to select a red object, for example, it seems that you would have to imagine the color red to compare an apple with, thus making sure that you've selected correctly. But did you first have to imagine a sample of red in order to make sure that you correctly imagined the red you compared with the apple?[64] And then what about that color sample? We avoid this infinite regress of interpretations because intellectual processing ends at a spade-turning moment of noninterpreting reaction. "Adopt whatever model or scheme you may, it will have a bottom level, and there will be no such thing as an interpretation of that."[65] Since the problem results from the idea that we are interpreting, the solution—famously if obscurely suggested in section 201 of the *Philosophical Investigations*—is that we usually follow rules without interpreting them. This thesis receives additional support from the first argument, above, which showed our mundane activities going on without the aid of interpretive ruminations.

Heidegger's work on interpretation places him at the center of twentieth-century hermeneutics, as the link between Dilthey and Gadamer.[66] He rejects what he sees as Husserl's naïve belief in intuition as the direct perception of essences independently of all historical or cultural influences.[67] Attempts to bracket one's culture and knowledge-base in order to uncover objective reality are futile, and usually lead to an uncritical acceptance of these prejudices.[68] Heidegger argues that interpretation is ubiquitous: we always approach objects of perception and thought from what he calls the fore-structures of understanding that shape where we look, what we find, and what we make of what we find.

But it is easy to misinterpret his views here by turning interpretation into a distinct act which accompanies bare perceptions. Heidegger defines interpretation as explicitly "laying out" (*aus-legen*) the holistic network that circumspection lives within. Interpretation articulates an entity's aspects and relations so that we can thematically survey them, thus facilitating repairs or creating the opening for a phenomenological understanding of modes of being.[69] This is an act of some degree of explicit examination and the more detached it is, the more it forces its object onto its conceptual Procrustean bed. Perhaps Heidegger's fundamental criticism of Husserl is that the very method he uses to be faithful "to the things themselves" actually betrays them. Bracketing our ongoing engaged behavior in order to study it as "the natural attitude" ipso facto renders our attitude unnatural.[70] By making belief in the world theoretical, the *epoché* surreptitiously produces that which it simultaneously brackets.

Once a breakdown has shattered the inconspicuous absorbed flow of circumspection, our thematic attention changes a tool's mode of being to, at its most extreme, a mere present-at-hand object limply sitting there, its referential connections of significance cut. This is where interpretation arises. "Being-in-the-world is now modified to a state of solely *looking*, a mere looking which *interprets*."[71] Like Wittgenstein's contemplative rule-follower staring at an arrow, Heidegger's theoretician must interpret because he faces insignificant faceless things. As the situation that presents itself to the philosophical gaze, it forms ontology and epistemology in its image, often defining perception as a two-step process of taking in dumb sensory data which then need to be interpreted, like Wittgenstein's dead marks.[72] This picture then gets retroactively read into all encounters; how else could I have cognitively moved from a mere lump of wood and metal, which is what is really there after all, to a useful hammer unless "some world-stuff which is proximally present-at-hand in itself were 'given subjective colouring' in this way"?[73]

This appears to expose a previously hidden multiplicity of ways to see the object (the Interpretation Aporia), which then provokes the retrospective insertion of interpretation in order to nail down our previous ease. Besides being phenomenologically false or unfaithful to experience, objective observation creates the gaps that skepticism lives in: people become bodies in motion, the world a set of inert objects, words scratches or noises, all of which require a discrete moment of interpretation which, alas!, can never be fully justified.[74] Thus are born projects like Quine and Davidson's radical translation and interpretation, which make an anthropologist's first encounter with an isolated tribe the perspicuously presented truth of all linguistic exchanges.[75]

### (3)   Outward Criteria

Wittgenstein has shown that for understanding to take place, anything *can*—and nothing particular *must*—come into one's mind. He is quite happy to acknowledge that feelings, images, or explicit thoughts sometimes accompany acts of comprehension—just as he admits the difference between actually having pain and pretending to be in pain.[76] His point is that the inner phenomena don't have the role we are tempted to give them when reflecting. This is a grammatical argument, in his sense of grammar: "meaning is not a process which accompanies a word. For no *process* could have the consequences of meaning."[77] If we compare the way we use these terms with the inner events that press themselves upon us in contemplation, we will see that these tempting events cannot do the job the demanded of them.

Take the example of telling someone to follow a rule, say, repeatedly adding two. It isn't that when we teach this procedure to her we don't know what we want her to do, but that this knowledge shouldn't be modeled on the picture of a mind encompassing the range of the function "Add two" in its gaze, even though our reflexive correction of a wrong answer makes it appear as if we were comparing the series coming out of her mouth with a written list.

"When I teach someone the formation of the series . . . I surely mean him to write . . . at the hundredth place."—Quite right; you mean it. And evidently without necessarily even thinking of it. This shews you how different the grammar of the verb "to mean" is from that of "to think." And nothing is more wrong-headed than calling meaning a mental activity![78]

The interlocutor here argues that since we know that 1,002 should follow 1,000 when we issue the order "Add two," a sequence not explicitly considered at the time the order was issued, something queer must be plugging us into the entire series. Wittgenstein reverses the polarity of the argument. We know what should follow 1,000 and the humble cogitative actions we find do not consciously anticipate every step—so understanding the rule must enable us to correct immediately *without* explicit thoughts.

The mirage of the meaning-object's containment of all future applications shimmers into existence here to supplement the woefully underpowered act of comprehension.

"In a *queer* way, the use itself is in some sense present."—But of course it is, "in *some* sense"! Really the only thing wrong with what you say is the expression "in a queer way." The rest is all right; and the sentence only seems queer when one imagines a different language-game for it from the one in which we actually use it. . . .

"It's as if we could grasp the whole use of a word in a flash."—And that is just what we say we do. That is to say: we sometimes describe what we do in these words. But there is nothing astonishing, nothing queer, about what happens. It becomes queer when we are led to think that the future development must in some way already be present in the act of grasping the use and yet isn't present. (PI §§195, 197)

Instead of attributing mythical powers and imaginary actions to thinking, we ought to distinguish the grammar of knowing how and explicitly thinking which, despite some superficial similarities, operate very differently. As we saw earlier, knowing how to do something like adding two is not like knowing that, nor is it holding an image before the mind's eye. "The word 'know' doesn't denote a state of consciousness. That is: the grammar of the word 'know' isn't the grammar of a 'state of consciousness.'"[79] The fact that we use these terms very differently in normal discourse shows that we fully appreciate the distinction; Wittgenstein is but reminding us of our inconspicuous grasp of it.

The philosophical account of understanding places a fully formed and comprehensive meaning-object in our minds, like Athena crouching in Zeus' head, thereby making our understanding wholly independent of outward expression.[80] This picture of private understanding is buttressed by possibilities that seem to cleave understanding from external manifestations, possibilities like feigning ignorance while gazing upon a picture or formula in the private interior of my mind. As he did with pain, Wittgenstein argues against understanding and expression coming apart so neatly by taking these possibilities seriously and exploring their consequences.

If one says that knowing the ABC is a state of the mind, one is thinking of a state of a mental apparatus (perhaps of the brain) by means of which we explain the *manifestations* of that knowledge. . . . But there ought to be two different criteria for such a state: a knowledge of the construction of the [mental] apparatus, quite apart from what it does.[81]

We need some way of talking about someone's comprehension that makes no reference to external manifestations whatsoever if we are to actually use this idea, and this turns out to be far trickier than the picture implies.

The only way we could have learned the concept "understanding" in the first place is through behavior, thus intertwining the grammar of knowledge with a public ability from the beginning. "Private" mental events could only have significance if "experience shewed that there was a connexion between thinking of the formula—saying it, writing it down—and actually continuing the series,"[82] which compromises the posited division. The rare occasions on which demonstrating or evaluating understanding miscarry disproportionately impress us and, like broken-down presence-at-hand, become the model on which we base our theories of understanding.

While there certainly are times when knowledge does not out, this is a perfect example of the Rules-Exception Ratio Law: it is not just that determining whether another person understood something would be difficult were such occasions commonplace, but that the whole idea of understanding would lose coherence and become unusable. Were most masteries of technique lodged deep in the recesses of the mind, wholly divorced from actions, then correctly performing the action in question would become irrelevant; a fully isolated comprehension could accompany any behavior whatever. Ultimately, someone could consistently misidentify the pieces, make only illegal moves, attempt to eat her opponent's king, and so on—and yet understand chess perfectly as long as she had the right "internal" experiences.[83]

Isolating understanding from manifestation also drives us into the private language dilemma. On the one hand, detaching thoughts completely from all external behavior makes comprehension incomprehensible. Like the private-linguist's pain, we cannot identify and describe this kind of mental entity without some use of public terms, which compromises its wordless, worldless solitude. Respecting its absolute privacy, however, comes at the cost of classifying it as comprehension, or as anything—just as the private-linguist's use of the term "sensation" drags it into the public light.

If you say he sees a private picture before him, which he is describing, you have still made an assumption about what he has before him. And that means that you can describe it or do describe it more closely. If you admit that you haven't any notion what kind of thing it might be that he has before him—then what leads you into saying, in spite of that, that he has something before him?[84]

Ineffably isolated entities fall out of explanations like a gear whose turning leaves the larger mechanism unaffected, or the beetle permanently shielded from all other eyes. This is how I understand the line, "an 'inner process' stands in need of outward criteria,"[85] where the scare quotes indicate that, once equipped with the needed links to the "outside," we can no longer call the process "inner" in the strict sense the philosopher wants, a point that Heidegger makes as well.

Despite the importance we place on it during reflection, Wittgenstein argues that we actually care very little about what goes on in another's mind when assessing their understanding. If a person never goes on in the right way, her assurance that nevertheless she is having a distinctive experience of understanding or a picture or rule in mind won't convince us of her comprehension. Conversely, if she can perform the tasks in question competently, it doesn't particularly matter what, if anything, is going on in her head. "Does something happen when I understand this word, intend this or that?—Does nothing happen?—That is not the point; but rather:

why should what happens within you interest me? (His soul may boil or freeze, turn red or blue: what do I care?)"[86]

One of the main conclusions of Wittgenstein's later holism is that, as Putnam famously put it, meanings just ain't in the head—or to modify it slightly, meanings ain't *just* in the head. Wittgenstein insists that we examine thought in its broader holistic context,[87] asking questions like, When do we use these terms? Under what circumstances do we recognize or refuse to recognize someone's understanding? "When he understood the principle, then possibly he had a special experience . . . but for us it is *the circumstances* under which he had such an experience that justify him in saying in such a case that he understands."[88] Our actual use gives the lie to the emphasis on supposed inner processes that lack all outward criteria. Meaning and understanding are spread across a motley group of characteristic actions, expressions, and contexts rather than being concentrated in any one essential factor. "Reading is connected with certain experiences: but *with* these experiences in certain cases I would not say I read, and in others *without* them I *would* say I read."[89] No mental event can trump a significant accumulation of contextual cues of either the presence or absence of understanding. In the vast majority of cases, appropriate behavior constitutes, not indicates, understanding.

Wittgenstein's arguments against an essential but ineffable comprehension that hides behind the closed doors of the mind resonate with Heidegger's critique of traditional metaphysics, and of Kant in particular. Kant takes phenomena to be the objects of scientific knowledge that are all that is or can be of epistemic concern to us. Were angels to whisper to us of the inner workings of reality in-itself, we should stop up our ears like Odysseus against the Sirens (PFM 101/353). The desire to follow this disastrous metaphysical call is built into our nature, so that we can never decisively quit metaphysics—we have to be tied to the mast. For Kant, we can't kick the habit once and for all; the best we can be is a recovering metaphysician. This picture of metaphysics' seductiveness obviously resonates with Wittgenstein's thought, both early and late.

Phenomenology, as the name suggests, focuses on phenomena as reality, dismissing noumena as not just irrelevant but incoherent. Kant writes that noumena can be nothing to us, though they could be something to a different kind of intelligence; they are also the source of phenomena, whatever that means, making it hard not to see the scientific study of phenomena he recommends as settling for second best. Phenomenology, on the other hand, only admits into its ontology that which we can become aware of: "*intuition* means: simple apprehension of what is itself bodily found just as it shows itself. . . . Intuition in the phenomenological sense implies no special capacity, no exceptional way of transposing oneself into otherwise closed domains and depths of the world."[90] Anything we talk about must be accessible to us in some way just for us to be able to talk about it, which rules out things cut off in principle from manifestation, whether they be noumenally transcendent or internally immanent.

This allows us to align the antimetaphysical tactics employed by both philosophers. Compare Wittgenstein's discussion of language—"a sentence has not got its sense 'behind' it; it has it in the calculus in which it is used"[91]—with Heidegger's ontology—"one cannot ask for something behind the phenomenon at all, since what the phenomenon gives is precisely that something in itself."[92] Their focus on the manifest fits their methodological emphases on description rather than explanation: we need not look behind or beneath anything since "nothing is hidden."[93] We must adjust our conceptual focus from the metaphysical to the inconspicuous, which is hidden only because it is so very unhidden.

## The Perceptual Model of Thought

The upshot of these discussions is that we need not have anything in mind—no explicit thoughts of rules, patterns, pictures—to know how to do something. The kinds of processes philosophers typically build their reconstructions of are not necessary for comprehension; they do not always, or even often occur during comprehension; nor could they satisfactorily explain it if they did. To briefly recap the preceding arguments: (1) The fact that intelligent speech and action take place in the absence of vigilant consciousness demonstrates that it is not needed, dispelling our compulsion to retroactively implant it. (2) Any reasons I could cite to justify the way I follow a rule would be equally open to various interpretations, triggering an infinite regress of interpretations. (3) Making understanding an entirely interior affair has absurd consequences which conflict with our normal use of the idea of understanding. Having shown the incoherence of traditional accounts of thought, we can now turn to the proposed alternative, which begins with a careful description of what actually happens in normal circumstances.

Wittgenstein and Heidegger are constantly bringing us back to everyday phenomena in order to preempt the erection of explanatory structures that produce more smoke than light. The explanatory compulsion gives rise to many of the problems both thinkers want to extinguish, so the best thing to do is to put it out before it ignites, which turns out to be rather challenging:

"*not* to explain, but to *accept* the psychological phenomenon—that is what is difficult."[94] One of the reasons these minimalist accounts don't satisfy is how threadbare they are. In general, we follow rules "*blindly*" (PI §219), "*without reasons*" (PI §211), or "*mechanically* . . . without *reflection*" (RFM 422). This doesn't mean unintelligently, but with a form of intelligence that doesn't look like what we expect thinking to be. "It is no act of insight, intuition, which makes us use the rule as we do at the particular point of the series. . . . There is an idea that 'something must make us' do what we do. . . . *We need have no reason to follow the rule as we do*. The chain of reasons has an end."[95] This idea shocks philosophers' demands that something must account for our comprehension, especially when the explanatory agent has taken on the luster of the miraculous against the backdrop of the Interpretation Aporia. The Logical Stoic's compulsion to be compelled so that meaning may be shielded from whim and absurdity calls for something to compel us, but unprejudiced examination finds us for the most part unreflectively acting without considering and winnowing out a clamoring crowd of alternative interpretations.

Like Ryle, Wittgenstein often considers the appropriate use of words in the right circumstances to *be* understanding, rather than indications of the real action going on in the mind: "what went on when I suddenly understood him? . . . I did not now have further to grasp a *sense* (something *outside* the sentence, hence something ethereal) but the familiar sound of English words perfectly suffices me."[96] This conforms to the metaphor of games, since understanding chess simply is the consistent and correct manipulation of the pieces in the right circumstances, which does not need, and often does not have, explicit thought. "When I think in language, there aren't 'meanings' going through my mind in addition to the verbal expressions: the language is itself the vehicle of thought."[97] Heidegger also ridicules the idea of language as "a mere means of expression that can be taken off and exchanged like a garment, without that which has come to language being touched by it" (PM 298; see also WCT 129). Our disappointment with these humble facts and the philosophical impulse to connect them with a transcendent source of Truth feed each other, resulting in manifestly absurd constructions. Manifest, that is, if we follow out their consequences.

Heidegger also emphasizes how little higher-order cogitation occurs in our mundane life. We generally go about our daily occupations on autopilot, with conscious thoughts or intentional control of our actions rarely surfacing. The first full exposition of being-in-the-world in *Being and Time* defines it as "a non-thematic circumspective absorption in references or assignments constitutive for the readiness-to-hand of a totality of equipment. . . . In this familiarity Dasein can lose itself in what it encounters within-the-world and be fascinated by it."[98] Primarily and for the most part, we glide along trails worn by habit, solicited and guided by familiar environments and ongoing, often repetitive projects. While Heidegger does condemn this perfunctory way of living as "fallenness,"[99] especially in division II, he presents it as a far more accurate account of thinking than is enshrined in the tradition.

The fundamental mistake for Wittgenstein is the idea that we interpret a rule or picture; this is what creates the Interpretation Aporia at the heart of skepticism. Similarly, Heidegger criticizes previous philosophers for taking theoretical knowledge as our defining essence and our basic relationship to the world. This attitude produces an agglutination of inert objects that cannot account for our normal experience. Both thinkers propose a more accurate picture of what we are and do, which I will call the Perceptual Model of Thinking. This model places understanding closer to perception than to running through a syllogism in one's mind. Rather than weighing the pros and cons of an array of options confronting us, we simply see what is to be done in a given situation. This conception bears more than a passing resemblance to Aristotle's *phronêsis*, as I will take up at the end of this chapter.

Phenomenology strongly rejects the two-step empiricist theory of perception as a passive reception of color patches or sonic blasts which then get synthesized or interpreted as representations of external objects in "the old mythology of an intellect which glues and rigs together the world's matter with its own forms" (HCT 70). This view only accepts universally accessible, constant aspects—primary qualities—as real, while characterizing all else as subjective projections; all we *really* see is a hunk of wood and metal, but we trowel mushy features like ugly or useful onto this bare perceptual matter. Distinguishing an inert base from the livelier accidents we stick into it like toothpicks in cubes of cheese rests on the assumption that sterile objects are at the foundation of all things, that is, present-at-hand substance ontology.

This empiricist analysis has it exactly backward. The richly meaningful is the *first* layer of experience, whereas seeing it as merely data requires a discrete and rather sophisticated act of abstraction. "What we 'first' hear is never noises or complexes of sounds, but the creaking wagon, the motorcycle. We hear the column on the march, the north wind, the woodpecker tapping, the fire crackling. It requires a very artificial and complicated frame of mind to 'hear' a 'pure noise.'"[100] We don't infuse gray stuff with significance but immediately grasp a meaningful *world*, as Heidegger repeatedly

lectures Husserl under the mask of Descartes. Bare perception and its interpretation only come apart in detached contemplation.

In pure experience there is no "founding" interconnection, as if I first of all see inter-
secting brown surfaces which then reveal themselves to me as a box, then as a desk,
then as an academic lecturing desk, a lectern, so that I attached lecternhood to the
box like a label. All that is simply bad and misguided interpretation, diversion from
a pure seeing into the experience. I see the lectern in one fell swoop, so to speak, and
not in isolation, but as adjusted a bit too high for me. I see—and immediately so—a
book lying upon it as annoying to me. . . . The meaningful is primary and immediately given to me without any mental detours across thing-oriented apprehension.[101]

My surrounding world makes sense to me and *makes* sense *for* me, arranging the holistic world from and within which I, my tools, and my life have
their meaning.

Now it is true that perceptions can vary across observers depending on
background, knowledge, taste, and so forth—Heidegger's "fore-structures"
of understanding. This variability traditionally downgrades such features
from real to merely subjective—if something is really there, it should appear
the same to everyone—but this argument only works on the assumption
that constancy correlates with reality. This assumption, which has guided
virtually all philosophy since Parmenides, is based on the comfort and utility that unwavering knowledge offers. As Nietzsche points out, scholars
tend to like quiet consistent surroundings as conducive to their favorite
activities, but they project this personal preference onto the cosmos. It is
simply a non sequitur to move from useful to real. Moreover, the idea that
the unchanging is most real is continuously contradicted by virtually all
of our experience—all except, that is, a contemplative staring that tries to
make its subject hold still. Along with skillful know-how, Heidegger wants
to rehabilitate the lively flux which makes up our lives, to integrate time
back into being. "It is precisely when we see the 'world' unsteadily and fit-
fully in accordance with our moods, that the ready-to-hand shows itself in
its specific worldhood, which is never the same from day to day. By looking
at the world theoretically, we have already dimmed it down to the uniformity of what is purely present-at-hand."[102] We live out our lives inside
Plato's Cave, as it were, naming and predicting flickering shadows for a living, and we should not necessarily grant the sun-bedazzled philosopher the
authority to tell us what is really real.[103]

Wittgenstein also rejects the two-step theory because perception often
leaps immediately to comprehension, with rare daylight between the two.[104]
Like Heidegger, Wittgenstein blames isolation as the reason they occasionally come apart: "'purely acoustical' is a description that applies when you

can reproduce exactly what you've heard, leaving all other relations out of it."[105] Both were impressed by Gestalt psychology, with Wittgenstein saying that "it is—contrary to Köhler—precisely a *meaning* that I see,"[106] the criticism of one of the founders of Gestalt psychology here appearing to be that he is not sufficiently "Gestalt." Interestingly, Heidegger suggests a similar point when he praises Husserl for explaining "the meaning of any genuine philosophical empiricism" (BT 490n.x). I take this to mean that the empiricists weren't empiricist enough because they viewed experience through an assumed theory of perception, whereas phenomenology's perception of meaning more faithfully captures what we actually experience, as I will discuss below. But regardless, Wittgenstein and Köhler were alike impressed with Goethe, who wrote that "I have ideas without knowing it, and even *see them with my eyes.*"[107]

Now I don't want to simplify Wittgenstein's views on this topic, which occupied his thoughts for several of his final years; he told Drury that the subject was "hard as granite."[108] His analysis, as usual, is nuanced, patiently teasing apart the "tangled"[109] grammatical strands of seeing, seeing-as, thinking, and interpreting, following out the ways they overlap and interconnect. One of Wittgenstein's main points is that seeing-as—for example, seeing this piece of metal as a fork—only arises with the possibility of seeing it differently, what he calls the noticing or dawning of an aspect.[110] As with rule-following, considering other possible ways of taking a thing—as a weapon or a chunk of metal or a particularly bad portrait of Ethel Merman—makes our original, unthematic use of it to eat a salad retroactively appear like an act of seeing it *as* a fork. In one sense this is perfectly true, but the danger is that we tend to assimilate this seeing-as to interpretation, a kind of thinking,[111] which then pulls us into the Interpretation Aporia.

The first thing to jump to my eye in this picture is: there are two hexagons.

Now I look at them and ask myself: "Do I really see them *as* hexagons?"—and for the whole time they are before my eyes? (Assuming that they have not changed their aspect in that time.)—And I should like to reply: "I am not thinking of them as hexagons the whole time." . . .

Of course I might also have seen the picture first as something different, and then have said to myself "Oh, it's two hexagons!" So the aspect would have altered. And does this prove that I in fact *saw* it as something definite? . . .

A *concept* forces itself on one. (This is what you must not forget.)[112]

In general, Wittgenstein resists applying "seeing-as" to our normal, unthinking encounters because it brings in too much epistemic machinery.[113] The urge to enlist these conceptual structures only strikes us after alternate aspects have appeared, hence Wittgenstein's fascination with the duck-rabbit figure. A shape that can continuously undergo aspect-change offers a controlled environment within which to conduct this philosophical experiment. "Only through the phenomenon of change of aspect does the aspect seem to be detached from the rest of the seeing. It is as if, after the experience of change of aspect, one could say 'So there was an aspect there!'"[114] Like Heidegger's breakdown of tools, the very idea that thought is involved in these actions is an RRR which only arises when things have been disturbed: "if everything goes normally, no one thinks of the inner event which accompanies speech."[115] Modeling this now-necessary process on explicit thought consummates the confusion, expanding a drop of grammar into a whole cloud of philosophy.

The aspect of perception that Wittgenstein and Heidegger appeal to is its immediacy: we don't think or infer that that is a book; we see it. Even saying that we see it *as* a book says too much, because it implies that we *might* have seen it differently, starting the whole Rube Goldberg contraption going. We obey commands, we see beautiful pictures, we glance at an arrow and go left—all without interpreting. In another allusion to Augustine's philosophical befuddlement over time, Wittgenstein writes, "if someone asks me 'What time is it?' there is no inner process of laborious interpretation; I simply react to what I see and hear. If someone whips out a knife at me, I do not say 'I interpret that as a threat'" (PG 47). Moreover, these immediate reactions are not the primitive stirrings of an early stage of our development that we have now outgrown, but characterize how we behave all the time, as we saw above with Wittgenstein's example of reasoning about the wheelbarrow. As one commentator puts it, "what is striking is not only that one's first learning of words is an outgrowth of unthinking, instinctive behavior, but that something of the same kind permeates and surrounds all human acting and all use of language, even at sophisticated levels."[116] The response of "10" to follow the series "2, 4, 6, 8, . . ." resembles my leg's jump when the doctor hits my knee more than it does a conscious consideration of various possibilities.

Retrospective justification lays out a series of steps that lead to a given conclusion, but we often act "without reasons" (PI §211); we simply leap right to the conclusion, striding through the space of reason in seven-league boots. We might later come up with a plausible path to this conclusion, but this should not be read back into the moment of action. Like the Third Man problem, any steps introduced to bridge the steps of an argument create new gaps. And when the rule is extremely simple, any *explanans* will be more complex than the *explanandum*, leaving communication or instruction to devolve into spluttering "But how can you not see *that!*"

Coming to rest on this lowest explicable, spade-turning ground is only a flaw on the Socratic assumption that all knowledge must be articulable and defensible—an assumption that creates the problems we have seen. "To use a word without a justification does not mean to use it without right."[117]

Wittgenstein's distinction between *seeing* the fork and, after alternatives arise, interpreting it *as* a fork, has a direct parallel in Heidegger's distinction between the existential-hermeneutical "as" and the apophantical "as." The former is simply lived—we take the hammer as a hammer by taking it in hand and hammering.

> In concernful circumspection there are no such assertions "at first." But such circumspection has of course its specific ways of interpreting, and these, as compared with the "theoretical judgment" just mentioned, may take some such form as "The hammer is too heavy," or rather just "Too heavy!," "Hand me the other hammer!" Interpretation is carried out primordially not in a theoretical statement but in an action of circumspective concern—laying aside the unsuitable tool.[118]

We could reconstruct this as reasoning but, as with Wittgenstein's wheelbarrow, it is enacted "still wholly wrapped up in concernful understanding" (BT 201/158), that is, without reflection or articulation. If the hammerer speaks, she need do no more than mention the relevant quality or even just grunt and cast her tool aside. Compare this with Wittgenstein's discussion of the same scenario of a worker silently selecting and using tools, which concludes that "thinking is not an accompaniment of the work, any more than of thoughtful speech" (Z §§100–101). Heidegger's apophantical "as," on the other hand, arises when hammering has stopped and the present-at-hand object now has the quality of weight.

Heidegger derives his Perceptual Model of Thinking from categorial intuition, one of Husserl's few ideas he consistently praised, which means the direct perception of allegedly abstract and subjectively projected concepts.[119] Where Brentano introduced Heidegger to Aristotle's question of being, Husserl's method showed him how to approach it by placing being in the realm of the perceptible. We find the three modes of being out there in the world, inconspicuous but observable.

> When we analyze this as-structured comportment of sense-making, we see that, in it, something is always already understood. What is understood therein is the thing's "what-as." . . . This what-as, in the light of which I understand and which I already have from the outset (although unthematically), is, nonetheless, not understood thematically in this "having-from-the-outset." Rather, I *live* in the understanding of writing, illuminating, entering-and-exiting, and the like. More precisely, as existing—whether in speaking, entering/exiting, or understanding—I am an act of intelligently dealing-with.[120]

For Heidegger, we don't infer that that thing is a book; we pick it and read it. We don't stitch together adumbrations or patches of color into a representation of a chair; we see a yellow chair, even the *being*-yellow of the chair. Wittgenstein makes the same point with the same example, with an echo of the color exclusivity problem: "I do not see red: rather, I see *that the azalea is red*. In this sense I also see that it is not blue. It is not that a conclusion is drawn consequential upon what is seen: no—the conclusion is known immediately as part of the seeing."[121]

Not only is this perceptive reasoning legitimate, it solves the three problems that beset the notion of reasoning all the way down. (1) Immediate responses to solicitations mesh perfectly with the phenomenological absence of explicit thought, as well as with Wittgenstein's models of tools, games, and know-how, and with Heidegger's analysis of our absorbed use of tools and circumspection. "The man who makes the move in chess according to rule sees something different from the man who does not. Similarly, the man who understands a word sees more in it than the man who does not. . . . It is not a matter of interpretation; we *see* something different" (LWL 51). (2) Perceiving the right way to follow the rule halts the infinite regress, connecting the perception directly to the act, thus avoiding the detour through the quicksand of explicit thought. "If . . . you realize that the chain of *actual* reasons has a beginning, you will no longer be revolted by the idea of a case in which there is *no* reason for the way you obey the order."[122] For Heidegger, the fact that we are always already involved in our world means that questions of correctly establishing our relationship to the world always come too late. (3) Since understanding flows through actions rather than through the mind, as traditionally conceived, the notion of private understanding falls away. "We refer by the phrase 'understanding a word' not necessarily to that which happens while we are saying or hearing it, but to the whole environment of the event of saying it" (BB 157).

### Autonomy, the Self, and Receptivity

The Perceptual Model of Thinking has consequences for a number of topics. Philosophers have traditionally considered reason to be the key to autonomy: as the defining essence and highest aspect of the self, we gain control over our selves by rationally directing our behavior. Rather than the epitome of spontaneity, however, Heidegger and Wittgenstein draw our attention to the passivity of these moments of seeing patterns and reaching conclusions.[123] I do not choose to believe that the series continues "10, 12,

14, . . ." nor did I decide to continue this series by way of sober rationality rather than a whimsical guess. I simply do what comes naturally, going with the mental flow. "I should have said: *This is how it strikes me.* When I obey a rule, I do not choose."[124] At the bottom of all interpretation and articulation lie perceptions, solicitations to continue a pattern in a certain way.

As I have discussed in detail elsewhere,[125] Heidegger's later work replaces his early voluntarism with a heavy emphasis on our passivity, both in thought and action. We think the thoughts the world provokes; we do what most appeals to us. Not only is the model of intentionally choosing what to do generally phenomenologically inaccurate, it leads to aporiai. I decided to eat the ice cream rather than the spinach because I care more about taste than health—but did I choose this preference? And if so, on what criteria? Either these meta-criteria were themselves chosen, leading to an infinite regress, or they simply appeared to me to be the right way to go about my business, making me a passive recipient of the criteria that were supposed to constitute my active choice. Taken to its end, this leads to Sartre's notion of an original project which, accepting nothing as given, becomes either Lucretius's swerve or Buridan's ass.[126]

We escape this problem by constructing a more accurate account of thinking and acting as responses within a continuous circuit of activity, the dynamic circulation of being-in-the-world. Our experience is more an autonomic stream of activity than a series of consciously controlled steps. Except when something has knocked us out of alignment and broken the spell, little conscious intentional attention occurs in my mental life. Wittgenstein is recorded as calling the pronoun "I" misleading. In an allusion to *Tractatus* 5.631–5.6331, "he said that 'Just as no [physical] eye is involved in seeing, so no Ego is involved in thinking or in having toothache'; and he quoted, with apparent approval, Lichtenberg's saying 'Instead of "I think" we ought to say "It thinks"' ('it' being used, as he said, as 'Es' is used in 'Es blitzet' [it rains]."[127] Heidegger would similarly amend the deceptive grammar which posits a doer for every deed: "simple inspection does not discover anything like an 'I.' What I see is just that 'it lives.'"[128] Like Wittgenstein's eye which is not *in* the visual field but *is* the visual field, so Dasein "*is* itself the clearing."[129] The retroactive imposition of a self is due to the presupposition that actions must be performed by an agent, itself suggested by the prominent presence of the self during thematic examination. Heidegger's antihumanism is more of a positive doctrine, whereas Wittgenstein is primarily trying to avoid philosophical confusions, but they arrive at the same idea by describing the same phenomena.

Wittgenstein primarily applies this idea to language. For example, he analyzes the process of searching for a word as a matter of responding rather than deciding.

How do I find the "right" word? How do I choose among words? Without doubt it is sometimes as if I were comparing them by fine differences of smell: *That* is too . . . , *that* is too . . . ,—*this* is the right one.—But I do not always have to make judgments, give explanations; often I might only say: "It simply isn't right yet." I am dissatisfied, I go on looking. At last a word comes: "*That's* it!" *Sometimes* I can say why. This is simply what searching, this is what finding, is like here.[130]

This homely description makes the same point as Heidegger's brilliant, if rather portentous, later discussions of language. Although "speaking and hearing are customarily set in opposition to one another," really "speech, taken on its own, is hearing. It is listening to the language we speak. . . . It is language that speaks."[131] We express ourselves by selecting the appropriate terms by means of how they strike us, attending to them in way that Heidegger compares to listening. This reaches its apex with poets, who discover the *mot juste* through an acute sensitivity to connotations, sound, and other subtle features, like hitting different phrases with a tuning fork.[132]

The same kind of receptive response characterizes abstract thinking, which has its own habits and ruts that carry us along well-worn trains of thought.

In the course of a scientific investigation we say all kinds of things. . . . It isn't as though everything we say has a conscious purpose; our tongues just keep going. Our thoughts run in established routines, we pass automatically from one thought to another according to the techniques we have learned. And now comes the time for us to survey what we have said. (CV 65)

Despite the tempting retrospective picture of freely and consciously deciding, deliberate acts of will are largely absent from our daily activity. "In many cases of voluntary speech I don't feel an effort, much that I say voluntarily is not premeditated, and I don't know of any acts of intention preceding it."[133] In a strange way, Wittgenstein has turned his early Schopenhauerian quest inside out: he had first sought to disconnect himself from the worldly self caught up in a web of will, only to find out that we coast along rather will-lessly, under the guidance of habit, most of the time.

Heidegger also inverts his early project, from encouraging a self-conscious choice of the roles and equipmental webs we had merely drifted into to praising *Gelassenheit* or "releasement" of the will. Whereas Dasein had, in *Being and Time*, rarely exercised his will though he should do so in a heroically anxious moment of claiming and making his self, in the later writings modern technological man is constantly willing but should let things be.[134] Furthermore, the greatest among us are not Nietzsche's *Über-menschen* who will to will or Kierkegaard's knights of faith who choose to choose in fear and trembling, but thinkers, the poets of being. They are the ones who listen most carefully to the call of being, and this is what enables them to put their epoch's understanding into words.[135]

Heidegger's position on free will in his later works resembles soft determinism. We choose among the pertinent options, but they must present themselves as more or less desirable if there is to be a reason why we choose as we do, and this reason is something we cannot have chosen on pain of infinite regress.

The inclination, that is, various directions of being inclined, are the presuppositions for the possibility of the decision of a faculty. If it could not and did not have to decide for one inclination or the other, that is, for what it has a propensity to, decision would not be decision, but a mere explosion of an act out of emptiness into emptiness, pure chance, but never self-determination, that is, freedom. (STF 148–149; see also STF 154–155)

Riding the inertia of one's past and personality has traditionally been understood to compromise freedom, but here it represents the necessary condition of free choice.

A freedom entirely unburdened by anything unchosen ends up as a spasm; it is only when the things of the world variously pull and push me that I can make a decision instead of flipping a coin. Rather than resenting these inclinations as external coercions, we should welcome them as enabling free actions. "Freedom is to be free and open for being claimed by something. This claim is then the ground of action, the motive. I cannot exist at all without constantly responding to this or that address in a thematic or unthematic way; otherwise I could not take so much as a single step, nor cast a glance at something."[136] We employ such a distorted conception of freedom because we base our conception of choice on relatively rare moments of an explicit weighing of options, rather than on the vast majority of inconspicuous cases in which we distractedly reach out for the chocolate while continuing a conversation or put our wallet in our pocket as we leave the house. Choice becomes the detached evaluation of alternatives in a breakdown state, when I have been taken out of the immediacy of the moment or when no option particularly appeals to me.

This logical argument is backed up by phenomenological descriptions. I don't choose chocolate ice cream over vanilla by weighing their pros and cons with solemn neutrality. Chocolate draws me toward it, seduces and entices me with its dark rich yumminess, whereas vanilla is just vanilla, withdrawing from the primal scene of flavor selection as a not requiring consideration. Not only do things present themselves with qualities like beautiful or within reach, as *Being and Time* notes; they also show up as "obviously preferable," or "really should be eaten." We don't project "appetizing" onto inert food-stuffs. Rather, as that great phenomenologist Chuck Jones renders it, pies cooling on window sills send out tantalizing tendrils of scent that pull us toward them by our nostrils.

Like Wittgenstein, Heidegger also applies this receptivity implicit in the Perceptual Model of Thinking to abstract thought: "to think is before all else to listen, to let ourselves be told something."[137] While the title of his book, *Was Heisst Denken*, can be translated as *What Is Called Thinking?* it can also be rendered *What Calls Upon or For Thinking?* which better indicates the receptivity he wants to emphasize. Being's sendings make thinking possible at all, and guide its particular manifestations. In general, we only think about the things and details that attract our attention. "We will have to rely on Being, and on how Being strikes our thinking, to ascertain from it what features essentially occur."[138] In logic, we do not decide what can and should be negated; propositions present themselves to us as negatable. "Whatever has been seen can be demonstrated only by being seen and seen again. What has been seen can never be proved by adducing reasons and counter-reasons. Such a procedure overlooks what is decisive—the looking."[139] This is Heidegger's version of Husserl's "principle of all principles," namely, that *"Immediate 'seeing,'* not merely sensuous, experiential seeing, but *seeing in the universal sense as an originally presentive consciousness of any kind* whatever, is the ultimate legitimizing source of all rational assertions" (1982, §19/36). Even the basic impulse to explain and understand is something that befalls us rather than being chosen: "we are constantly addressed by, summoned to attend to, grounds and reason."[140] Thus, the Gibsonian machinery of environmental affordances and solicitations should be expanded from just perception to making decisions and thinking. We dwell among intellectual solicitations while thinking just as much as in physical or perceptual ones when acting.[141]

### Non-Epistemic Belief

For Heidegger, the understanding of something's way of being occurs in our pre-predicative use of it. As necessarily preceding theoretical knowledge, circumspection is non-epistemic, meaning that it cannot be parsed in terms of "belief" or "knowledge." "I cannot adequately define the concept of understanding if, in trying to make the definition, I look solely to specific types of cognitive comportment."[142] A careful description of our everyday behavior during smooth interaction shows the absence of this epistemic machinery. Here he differs from Husserl who defines our "natural attitude" or basic stance in terms of belief, especially the belief in the existence of the world. For Heidegger,

> nothing exists in our relationship to the world which provides a basis for the phenomenon of belief in the world. I have not yet been able to find this phenomenon of belief. Rather, the peculiar thing is just that the world is "there" *before* all belief. The world is never experienced as something which is believed any more than it is guaranteed by knowledge. Inherent in the being of the world is that its existence *needs no guarantee in regard to a subject.* . . . Any purported belief in it is a theoretically motivated misunderstanding. This is not a convenient evasion of a problem. The question rather is whether this so-called problem which is ostensibly being evaded is really a problem at all.[143]

It's not, of course, that we *don't* believe in the world, but rather that belief is an inappropriate way of cashing out our usual being-in-the-world. Wittgenstein gives an uncannily similar assessment of the foundational framework within which all of our actions and thoughts take place, but which itself does not belong in the arena of reasoning, justification, and belief: "the language-game . . . is not based on grounds. It is not reasonable (or unreasonable). It is there—like our life."[144]

There are two good reasons why we are under no obligation to demonstrate the validity of our belief in the external world: first, as discussed above, because the world is not external; and second, because we don't believe in it. Not because we're skeptical, but because our relationship takes place at a much deeper level, so that to approach it in epistemic terms is to commit a category mistake. Any proof or defense

> always comes "too late." . . . "Earlier" than any presupposition which Dasein makes, or any of its ways of behaving, is the "*a priori*" character of its state of Being as one whose kind of Being is care. To *have faith* in the Reality of the "external world," whether rightly or wrongly; to "*prove*" this Reality for it, whether adequately or inadequately; to *presuppose* it, whether explicitly or not—attempts such as these . . . presuppose a subject which is proximally *worldless* or unsure of its world, and which must, at bottom, first assure itself of a world.[145]

There are two arguments here. Phenomenologically, we find no apparatus of belief; the demand that some such scaffolding must be there supporting our actions is an unmotivated assumption based on the model of theoretical knowledge rather than circumspection. Logically, engaged being-in-the-world is the necessary prerequisite for even raising such a question, since we need to have mastered a way of thinking and speaking from years of interacting with things and people just to be capable of thinking of these matters. G. H. von Wright puts it nicely in discussing Wittgenstein: "the problem of the existence of the external world, one could say, *is* in fact solved before it *can be* raised."[146] Compare with Heidegger: "the question of whether there is a world at all and whether its Being can be proved, makes no sense if it is raised by Dasein as Being-in-the-world; and who else would raise it?" (BT 246–247/202).

Hubert Dreyfus has conducted empirical studies of the stages of skill-acquisition which strongly support Wittgenstein and Heidegger's ideas in this regard.[147] At first, a student recites rules to herself and carries out actions with intentional control, generally resulting in graceless and poor performance. With practice, conscious control relaxes and trained reactions take over. Ironically, the kind of explicit consideration that philosophy has always privileged as the highest form of ratiocination often proves a hindrance, not just in physical activities but also in "mental" acts such as language-comprehension or chess-playing. Wittgenstein occasionally cites animals as examples of living beings that are capable of intentional, sophisticated actions and beliefs unfettered by the cogitation we demand in ourselves.

When a cat lies in wait by a mouse-hole—do I assume that it is thinking about the mouse?

When a robber waits for his victim—is it part of this, for him to be thinking of that person? Must he be considering this and that as he waits? Compare one who is doing such a thing for the first time, with one who has already done it countless times.[148]

As Wittgenstein suggests here, Dreyfus's contrast between actions taken while learning a skill and actions taken once that skill has been mastered differentiates the cases where we must think from those where habit can take over.

## Something Animal

Although Wittgenstein and Heidegger generally work at weaning us off the hunger for explanations, as we will see in more detail in chapter 5, they do offer something of an explanation of how we achieve understanding. This account, however, is largely in terms of nonrational factors and pays careful attention of the intrinsic limits of all explanation. The first move, as we have seen, is the negative point that a purely rational being, awash in possible interpretations, could not achieve the understanding that four-year-old children effortlessly have; hence this cannot be the correct account of understanding—at least not ours. The next step is to give a positive description of how four-year-old children, not to mention philosophers, do accomplish this understanding.

The point that has emerged is that anything—rules, ostensive definitions, formulae, pictures, examples—can be followed in diverse ways, which undermines their ability to convey or evince understanding on their own. "Whatever goes on in his mind at a particular moment does not guarantee that he will apply the word in a certain way in three minutes' time."[149] Unlike self-applying meaning-objects, ideas or rules must be taken the right way for them to do their work. The Interpretation Aporia—the proliferation of readings that beset the disengaged intellect—shows that this theoretical faculty cannot be the fundamental source of understanding. This should not be understood as revealing a serious defect that threatens semantic nihilism, but as a *reductio* that shows that we usually operate quite differently. "The most important thing is: The rule is not needed. Nothing is lacking. We do calculate according to a rule, and that is enough. This is how one calculates. Calculating is this. What we learn at school, for example. Forget this transcendent certainty which is connected with your concept of spirit" (OC §§46–47). The point is not, as Kripke has it, that "the *entire* idea of meaning vanishes into thin air,"[150] but merely that *one* specific idea vanishes. We must now look for a better one.

And we will look for it in the place "where all ladders start," in Yeats' phrase—"in the foul rag and bone shop of the heart." Wittgenstein's later and Heidegger's early work constantly work at removing temptations toward the transcendent, that we may make peace with the human. One of the ways this comes out in Wittgenstein's thought is in his peculiar brand of naturalism. Although a staunch anti-naturalist in some ways (one possible reason for the plunge in his philosophical stock in Quine's wake), he actually emphasizes our animal nature, and does so precisely where it is least expected and least welcome: in the heart of thought.[151] Thinking is the aspect of ourselves that philosophers typically deify, plugging it into a transcendent reality that infuses our minds with something higher, more divine, like lightning racing down Benjamin Franklin's kite string. As part of what I am calling original finitude, Wittgenstein mounts an extended campaign to bring this faculty back within the sublunary sphere, helping us quit our addiction to quintessence. He repeatedly portrays thinking as "a human activity" (RFM 331) or "just a phenomenon of human life" (RFM 351), by offering "remarks on the natural history of man."[152]

Decoupled from metaphysical guarantees, thoughts threaten to spin freely, raising the specter of semantic nihilism. Like Nietzsche's mourners of God, we swing from the extreme of absolute determination of meaning and objectivity to the absence of any determination of meaning whatever. If there are no meaning-objects, we fear, everything grammatical is permitted. Wittgenstein charts a middle path that replaces metaphysical determination with naturalistic.

"Then according to you everybody could continue the series as he likes; and so infer *any*how!" In that case we shan't call it "continuing the series" and also presumably not "inference." And thinking and inferring (like counting) is of course bounded for us, not by an arbitrary definition, but by natural limits corresponding to the body of what can be called the role of thinking and inferring in our life. . . . It is for us an essential part of 'thinking' that—in talking, writing, etc.—he makes *this sort* of transition. (RFM 80)

Meanings do not descend from the Forms, but arise out of cultural habits and a human nature whose contours set parameters for our speech and acts.

The clearest discussion of this topic appears in Wittgenstein's final work, *On Certainty*—a masterpiece that, along with portions of his *Remarks on the Foundations of Mathematics*, stands shoulder-to-shoulder with the *Tractatus* and *Investigations*. Beneath reason and language lies a much more basic level which enables us to learn and use these "higher" abilities. Instead of little gods, Wittgenstein wants "to regard man here as an animal; as a primitive being to which one grants instinct but not ratiocination. As a creature in a primitive state. Any logic good enough for a primitive means of communication needs no apology from us. . . . Language did not emerge from some kind of ratiocination."[153] His argument here has two steps that resemble deconstruction. First, he reverses the traditional privilege given to ratiocination over primitive instinct. Whereas philosophers have generally denigrated animal instincts, forcing them to kneel before the tribunal of reason, Wittgenstein assigns them an essential role in the formation of a rational, linguistic being. Basic reactions need not be ashamed before their more civilized, better-educated relations, especially since the latter are actually the former's progeny.

The second, deeper point is to undermine the instinct–reason distinction itself. We need to rid ourselves of the Platonic picture of the "human" as a combination of divine knower and unthinking brute—an immortal soul tied to a dying animal, to invoke Yeats again. While it is true that the higher level depends on the lower one, and that the lower outperforms the higher in certain areas (instincts have street smarts, say, rather than book smarts), the division itself needs to be rethought from the ground up. We need to get past the depiction of reason as shuffling off this shoddy mortal realm to touch something pure and good. It's time we grow up philosophically, and put away childish ideas. Wittgenstein insists that all of our aspects must be conceived in light of our animality—especially the usually exempted reason.

Heidegger's reticence to make Dasein and animals continuous is well known, and has been criticized.[154] But he does offer a two-step argument quite similar to Wittgenstein's, casting engaged use in the role of the epistemologically lower faculty which is traditionally neglected in favor of a higher, disengaged contemplation. First, Heidegger reverses this traditional priority of contemplation, making absorbed interaction primary in at least three respects: (1) chronologically, because one can only think abstractly after many years of concrete dealings in the world; (2) logically, because he defines detached reflection as a dimming down of our engaged being-in-the-world; and (3) qualitatively, because contemplation shears off the rich meaningfulness of our world. Respectively, these make theoretical knowledge founded, derivative, and privative. Such knowledge does uncover genuine aspects of reality—after all, phenomenological ontology defines reality as what appears and these features certainly appear to reason's gaze—but it is an impoverished set of features, the inert lumps left over after the theoretical gaze has evaporated all living significance.[155]

Heidegger's second step, while not repudiating the first, makes this first step more nuanced by blurring the division between unthinking acting and unacting thinking. Even the purest form of contemplation has components that run on auto-pilot, like a scientist's absentminded adjustment of her microscope while staring intently at the slide. Thinking also has a mood, a concern, an *Umwelt*—all the scorned, "subjective" features of everyday understanding—however much it lives in denial of these features.[156] The fact that use has its own kind of intelligence, "circumspection," shows the circumspection–reflection distinction to be far messier than initially appeared.

## Training

The topic of instruction is no tangent to these questions. The particular circumstances in which one learns a specific rule may be irrelevant to its truth, but learning how to follow rules in general is essential to being a rational agent. Absent myths of prenatal recollection or divine illumination, the question of how an infant becomes a person who can be spoken with and understood is both a pressing question and a promising topic for shedding light on rationality, making accusations of the genetic fallacy a misunderstanding. "Am I doing child psychology?—I am making a connexion between the concept of teaching and the concept of meaning."[157] The most basic level of instruction teaches people how to carry on doing the same, that is, how to recognize the same sameness as the rest of us, which forms the ground for all further learning and rule-following and keeps the Interpretation Aporia from getting off the ground.

Meaning-objects fit the intellectualist conception of learning: all members of a rule's range issue directly from a core idea, so we encompass the former in grasping the latter. In a Leibnizian fashion, "$2*X$" is pregnant with the set $\{2, 4, 6, \ldots\}$, so learning the former brings the latter in its wake. Teaching then consists in telling the formula to the student, whose comprehension occurs in a sudden "aha" moment of catching sight of this idea. Examples may aid in directing the student toward it, the way Plato allows physical objects to help turn us toward the Forms, but they can do no more than assist.[158]

"Once he has seen the right thing, seen the one of infinitely many references which I am trying to push him towards—once he has got hold of it, he will continue the series right without further ado. I grant that he can only guess (intuitively guess) the reference that I mean—but once he has managed that the game is won." But this "right thing" that I mean does not exist. The comparison is wrong. There is no such thing here as, so to say, a wheel that he is to catch hold of, the right machine which, once chosen, will carry him on automatically.[159]

In the wake of the rejection of meaning-objects, we must rethink education; we can no longer conceive of teaching as the transfer of a core lump of 'meaning' from teacher to student, like an egg-and-spoon race.

As we have seen, at the most basic level any supplementary devices used to guide the way we take a teacher's lessons are themselves vulnerable to misunderstanding and so require the very kind of know-how we are trying to impart. The intellectualist conception of thinking cheats. It sidesteps the infinite regress of instruction by retroactively furnishing the prerational learner with rationality, the way baby Augustine has fully-formed intellectual abilities and categories of objects at his disposal, lacking only the linguistic labels (PI §32). This ignores the problem rather than solving it because it leaves the *acquisition* of these basic abilities unexplained; it simply declares the *explanandum* to be the *explanans*.

The words "right" and "wrong" are used when giving instruction in proceeding according to a rule. The word "right" makes the pupil go on, the word "wrong" holds him back. Now could one explain these words to a pupil by saying instead: "this agrees with the rule—that not"? Well yes, if he has a concept of agreement. But what if this has yet to be formed? (The point is how he reacts to the word "agree.")

One does not learn to obey a rule by first learning the use of the word "agreement."

Rather, one learns the meaning of "agreement" by learning to follow a rule.

If you want to understand what it means "to follow a rule," you have already to be able to follow a rule.[160]

We must find a non-epistemic level beneath learning to enable learning; for Wittgenstein, it is training that stops the cognitivist infinite regress of teaching the rules we need to learn rules. "To what extent can the function of language be described? If someone is not master of a language, I may bring him to a mastery of it by training. Someone who is master of it, I may remind of the kind of training, or I may describe it; for a particular purpose; thus already using a technique of the language. To what extent can the function of a rule be described? Someone who is master of none, I can only train" (RFM 333). All higher-level teaching takes root in soil prepared by training, or the student would not know how to take the lessons.

We are habituated to react to orders or pictures or pointing in certain ways through a process much closer to Pavlovian conditioning than to discoursing in the Platonic Academy. "The child learns this language from the grown-ups by being trained to its use. I am using the word 'trained' in a way strictly analogous to that in which we talk of an animal being trained to do certain things. It is done by means of example, reward, punishment, and suchlike."[161] Conditioning bypasses reflection before it can lock us onto an infinite regress or plunge us into a sea of interpretations, thus preventing the Interpretation Aporia. "These misunderstandings only immensely rarely arise—although my words might have been taken either way. This is because we have all been trained from childhood to use such phrases . . . in one way rather than another."[162] Children acquire these techniques as a side-effect of the interactions by which they become socialized. They pick up, and ultimately use, these skills with little or no conscious attention,[163] which explains the difficulty in laying them out explicitly when the need arises, as we saw in chapter 1.

From its beginning, *Philosophical Investigations* insists that teaching a child to talk "is not explanation, but training."[164] Explanations only work if the child reliably reacts in certain ways: finding certain similarities relevant and others not, looking at what ostensive definitions point to, reading pictures and taking rules certain ways, and so on. Once these tendencies are in place, the student can learn more sophisticated rules and can do so in more explicit ways, just as ostensive definitions are a perfectly good way to learn new words after one has mastered the skill of looking at what is being pointed out and associating it with a word.[165] To use Heidegger's well-known phrase, we are "always already" rationalized since the ability to reflect on such matters presupposes ideas we could not have acquired by reasoning. The more explicit instances of learning retroactively cover over the foundational training they presuppose, making it hard to even imagine not knowing how to continue a very simple series or to look at what's being pointed out; witness Augustine's implausible account of his baby thoughts as fully mature awareness of the world merely suffering from a lack of vocabulary. One of the purposes of Wittgenstein's appeals to strange tribes is to overcome the oppressive obviousness of our ways of thinking by showing that other ways of taking rules or pictures are always possible.[166]

This view of initial and initiating training fits the conception of understanding as a skill rather than the entertainment of explicit ideas: "when I say to the child, '106 is not analogous' or 'Surely 106 is not analogous.' I am training him to use the word 'analogous.' . . . I try to give him an idea of how I'm going to use 'analogous.' It is part of a skill."[167] Another congruent part of this picture is the deflationary account of rule-following in which little to nothing occurs in one's mind while acting: "a rule is best described as being like a garden path in which you are trained to walk, and which is convenient. You are taught arithmetic by a process of training, and this becomes one of the paths in which you walk. You are not compelled to do so, but you just do it" (AWL 155). Note that Wittgenstein compares arithmetic—a perennial paradigm of transcendent and explicit knowledge from Plato to Russell—to walking—a clear example of autonomic action. Whereas Russell spent years founding mathematics in pure logic, Wittgenstein plants it in animalistic conditioning.

With the loss of meaning-objects that encapsulate their applications, the use of examples becomes for Wittgenstein what Derrida calls a necessary detour—that is, the kind of thing we actually need even though we insist that it is accidental, a disposable ladder. Wittgenstein sometimes makes the relatively weak claim that learning entirely by examples is possible and, if it results in students correctly following rules, is as good as any other form of learning, especially the more overt kinds we tend to focus on.[168] At other times, he makes the stronger claim that rules can *only* be grasped via examples since there is nothing beyond or behind or underneath such examples—at least nothing that can do what we want it to do. Although I may feel that my examples are merely indications of something deeper, something more essential, it's examples all the way down. "If a person has not yet got the *concepts*, I shall teach him to use the words by means of *examples* and by *practice*.—And when I do this I do not communicate less to him than I know myself."[169] In one of his rare engagements with the canon, Wittgenstein says that "when Socrates asks for the meaning of a word and people give him examples of how that word is used, he isn't satisfied but wants a unique definition. Now if someone shows me how a word is used and its different meanings, that is just the sort of answer I want."[170]

Heidegger, especially in his later works, argues that we live in the same world and are able to talk intelligibly to each other due to being "attuned" to the same understanding of being. It is only once a fundamental way of experiencing and thinking about the world is in place that we are able to pick out and discuss individual items. This is why he frequently claims that truth as correspondence depends on the deeper form of truth as unconcealment. "Inquiry and investigation here and everywhere require the prior grant of whatever it is they approach and pursue with their queries. Every posing of every question takes place within the very grant of what is put in question."[171] It is an epoch's clearing that performs the "stage-setting" that Wittgenstein thinks is needed to make ostensive definitions successful. Wittgenstein agrees on the Tractarian concept being rejected: "the whole point of this emphasis upon technique is to help us to get rid of the common impression that language is like a mirror, and that whenever a sentence has meaning, there is something, a proposition, corresponding to it" (Conv 23–24; see also Sluga and Stern 1996, 428).

## Form of Life

Wittgenstein takes one more step in his inquiry into the conditions for the possibility of thought and speech. We only react to orders and rules appropriately on the basis of training but, we can now add, this training can only instill these reactions in certain kinds of beings. Necessary to successful conditioning is a conditionable human nature which reliably reacts in certain ways rather than others. One of his favorite examples is the way dogs easily take to tasks that cats simply will not or cannot; this is due to a disparity in natures, not intelligence or vigor in training. "Acts of encouragement will be of various kinds, and many such acts will only be possible if the pupil responds, and responds in a particular way. . . . Imagine . . . that you tried to teach a cat to retrieve."[172] Without the right kind of instinctive reactions, no amount of instruction can succeed; with them, a single gesture may suffice. Certain instinctive orientations—a sensitivity to other people's reactions and a desire to please and fit in with others—are needed if training is to find purchase upon our souls. This stops the infinite regress of education: we cannot and need not be conditioned to be conditionable; we are born that way and, were we not, we could not become so—at least not through training or teaching. In sum, we must possess a certain "form of life" in order to be socialized, even humanized; training cannot create *ex nihilo*, but can only cultivate. Our apparently "spontaneous expression[s]" actually arise on the basis of two factors: "by nature and by a particular training" (PI §441) where the latter presupposes the former. This represents for Wittgenstein the "pinch of salt" that Frege reluctantly admitted he needed from the reader.

Human nature serves as the ultimate given, not in the sense of being an absolute foundation but rather as the last step open to examination; as the Hintikkas put it, it serves as "the highest court of semantical appeal."[173] If someone lacking this nature cannot see the point of a very simple series, we have nothing to fall back on besides the "Oh, Come On Now!" Argument or the "But Can't You See?" Objection. This pressure may be pedagogically effective on a recalcitrant student who shares our form of life, but it can do nothing for a true outsider. Without the requisite critical mass of agreement communication halts, and the only option left is ostracism.[174]

We say a man has learnt to use such words, only when he behaves like a normal human being. . . . Having been taught, the child must use the word in a normal way. There will be exceptions, but the centre of reference is ordinary human life, and the further we go from ordinary human life the less meaning we can give such expressions. . . . The use of the psychological expressions presupposes a great conformity to ordinary conduct.[175]

In an application of the Rules-Exception Ratio Law, if he does not even come up to the level of disagreeing with us, we can only brand him a lunatic and refuse him membership in our community of rationality.[176] He cannot enter our space of reasons because he cannot figure out how to open the door.

The history of AI supports this assessment, as Dreyfus has been arguing for decades. The first strategy to encode intelligence constructed a computer mind along cognitivist guidelines, taking explicit articulate thought and knowledge of facts as its paradigm. The computer scientists, much taken with "the program of Frege and of Whitehead and Russell for formalizing logic,"[177] accessed the mental processes people use to solve problems by studying "the protocols that human subjects produced while thinking aloud during the performance of a problem-solving task" (Haugeland 1997, 94). In light of Wittgenstein and Heidegger's analyses, we can see that this approach is precisely the wrong way to go about it because it forces the tacit skills actually used through the strainer of explicit thought when the test subjects stopped what they were doing to reflect upon what they were doing. The whole procedure unwittingly created Artificial Stupidity.

Furthermore, Dreyfus argues that since science views all knowledge in terms of an explicit awareness of facts, it misses the tacit skills that orient humans, as well as what Heidegger calls "care," that is, one's investment in the outcome.[178] These experiments, both thought and real, expose the reams of know-how we silently take for granted, demonstrating how thoroughly communication and comprehension implicitly depend on our agreement in "form of life" and "judgments."[179] Wittgenstein often makes the point by imagining what a Martian (PI p. 46n.) or a member of a deeply different tribe might make of our pictures, signs or practices, as we will see in chapter 5. One well-known cognitive science project filled a computer to the brim with facts about common human situations (like celebrating a birthday or dining in a restaurant), which the computer was to use to understand a brief story set in a given scenario. This proved to be a smashing failure, and a very instructive one; it highlighted all that is tacitly assumed, the limitless mass of facts that aren't in a story but, we might say, under it or just outside its edges, which give it an intelligible form.[180] Some computer scientists tried to plug up these holes with the only form of knowledge their presuppositions acknowledge: more facts. But it turns out that one needs more than facts to understand; one needs a world.

In the absence of meaning-objects, socializing molds beings with our form of life into rational agents who react in standard ways. This equips us with hermeneutic blinders, a basic sense of relevance (notably lacking in computers) that filters out the Interpretation Aporia's swarm of possible interpretations. Colin McGinn describes this well:

what should be opposed is not the very idea of future determination, either for meaning or for dispositions, but rather mythical conceptions of what this determination consists in—notably the idea that in some queer way the future manifestations are *already present* in the meaning or disposition but in a shadowy form. Wittgenstein's fundamental thesis, as I have interpreted him—that meaning rests ultimately upon the bedrock of our natural propensities—can be seen as a position which avoids the normative anarchy of the creative thesis while not falling into the trap of making meaning magically *contain* all of future and counterfactual use.[181]

Wittgenstein does not reject the notion of shared meaning or determinate answers, but transfers their source from the conscious acknowledgment of truths to the way our natural reactions get shaped by training. Pure reason falters, dizzied by the countless interpretations every situation admits but, as Hume says, nature is too strong for that to happen. A rule prompts a particular continuation as a conditioned response in beings who have our form of life and have been subjected to our training. Despite our philosophical hang-ups, such unthinking reactions do not irresponsibly make unproven assumptions; they are rather the non-epistemic foundation on which language-games are built, including the games of legitimating. They are the ground beneath the space of reason. After all, "why should the language-game rest on some kind of knowledge?" (OC §477).

## The Solution of Other Minds

Heidegger explicitly endorses a social self. He shares Wittgenstein's "enduring hostility to the idea of an individuated, substantive self. Insofar as the belief in such a self is most easily associated with Descartes, we can call Wittgenstein's position an anti-Cartesianism."[182] Heidegger's diagnosis of skepticism toward the external world and runs parallel to his analysis of skepticism toward other minds.

The theoretical problematic of understanding the "psychical life of Others" . . . gets taken as that which, primordially and "in the beginning," constitutes Being towards Others and makes it possible at all. This phenomenon, which is none too happily designated as "empathy," is then supposed, as it were, to provide the first ontological bridge from one's own subject, which is given proximally as alone, to the other subject, which is proximally quite closed off.[183]

Appealing to a sense of empathy based on an argument from analogy to justify our beliefs that other bodies are inhabited by minds only appears sensible within the present-at-hand framework which depicts us as self-enclosed minds who need to build bridges to other minds.

As with training, empirical exposure to the behavior of humanoid bodies could never reveal the significance of others to a being who is "mind-blind," such as a computer. One would need to be able to pick out this group of entities as deserving special attention, and then view their actions and noises as meaningful just to amass and interpret the evidence that supposedly sets the argument from analogy in motion. As Wittgenstein demands, "how could I even have come by the idea of another's experience if there is no possibility of any evidence for it?" (BB 46). Two sealed-off subjects trying to make contact cannot amount to more than "a solipsism en deux,"[184] certainly not the robust community we live in.

The cure here is the same one used for skepticism about the external world. Long before any belief or assumption about the matter can be formed, we are with others. Heidegger's social Primacy of the Whole short-circuits the idea of *establishing* contact with others.

It is not the case that on the one hand there are first individual subjects which at any given time have their own world; and that the task would then arise of putting together, by virtue of some sort of an arrangement, the various particular worlds of the individuals and of agreeing how one would have a common world. This is how philosophers imagine these things when they ask about the constitution of the intersubjective world. We say instead that the first thing that is given is the common world—the Anyone—, the world in which Dasein is absorbed such that it has not yet come to itself. (HCT 246)

We are always already among others from the start, as a feature of our nature rather than due to the accidental fact of exposure to humans. Dasein's Being-with is primordial, which means that one cannot be Dasein without it: along with the world, an essential relatedness to others fundamentally belongs our way of being.[185] This emotional orientation of caring about others opens us to this category of beings, forming something like a "fore-feeling" for the experience.[186]

Emotions play a positive role in general for Heidegger, who makes care the "meaning" of being-in-the-world, that is, that which makes it understandable as a whole.[187] All the ways we are in-the-world, including epistemological ones, grow out of this simple fact that what happens to us matters to us: it is in trying to make a good life for ourselves that we pursue the projects that unfurl the world's equipment and link us to others. Thus, care not only shapes the way we experience the world; it is what enables us to experience it at all.[188] In order to be able to think, in order to be a Dasein at all, I must be-in-the-world, which means pursuing certain goals or roles by means of their constituent equipmental chains. Once I have accumulated a critical mass of these, I can then take up the goal of objective observation which retroactively interprets all of these relationships as secondary superficial forms of thought. Ultimately, the two cannot be cleanly separated: "man is not a rational creature who . . . in addition to thinking and willing is equipped with feelings; . . . rather, the state of feeling is original, although in such a way that thinking and willing belong together with it."[189] We cannot be purified of our emotional side because it isn't a side; mood "determines us through and through."[190] It reveals features of the world invisible to cold calculation: "the possibilities of disclosure which belong to cognition reach far too short a way compared with the primordial disclosure belonging to moods."[191] In line with his definition of truth as unconcealment, what moods reveal is perfectly valid.

Heidegger applies the Perceptual Model of Thinking to our relations with others. We do not encounter others as moving mannequins onto which an act of interpretation or inference projects personhood. As with tools, it takes a radical change in stance to see others as mere bodies which might or might not trail immaterial minds behind them like balloons on strings, but we are vulnerable to such a view because our ability to read other people is ubiquitous and inconspicuous. Normally, another's "being-there-with in the environing world is wholly immediate, inconspicuous, obvious, similar to the character of the presence of world-things";[192] it only shows up as problematically opaque during reflection or communication breakdowns. It is then that we find Davidson's question—how can I *really* know what this person means or even that they mean anything when all I have to go on are these raw noises and movements?—urgent, troubling. Once we reach this point, the fix is in: we have bought into the bewitching picture. Phenomenology allows us to reach back before this ontological misstep to recover our originary, interlaced involvement with others.

Instead of hermetically sealed selves bumping into others, we are first one of the crowd, doing what "one" (*das Man*) does or following what "They" say ought to be done.[193] Dasein is usually porous: the flow of going about our daily business draws no firm boundaries between self, environment, and others.[194] We pick up our society's ways of doing things, its tacit norms, through a kind of osmosis, especially as we learn how to be a member of our society during childhood, intensely worried about standing out as different. Rather than a self-sufficient agent who is always actively deciding, it is more accurate to say that for the most part "Dasein as being-with *is lived* by the co-Dasein of others and the world which concerns it in this or that way."[195] In general, Heidegger suggests, we don't *lead* our lives; we follow. We experience our distinct identity as a later development which arises out of uncomfortable instances when one doesn't mesh smoothly with others. It is when we stand out from the crowd—misinterpreting the phrase, "fancy dress party," say—that we become "self-conscious," moments that gradually accrete into a self-consciousness that philosophers retroactively slip into all experience.

Just as Wittgenstein's form of life with its agreement with others grounds the training which endows us with reason, so Heidegger's being-with opens Dasein to the meaningful shared world, and the world to Dasein. It is because we are primordially determined by this predisposition to treat others as special and, in some way, care about them and what they think of us that we respond to the intersubjective pressures that socialize us into mature persons. Taking pride in one's originality and having disdain for what others think is, essentially, secondary, requiring the mastery of all sorts of impersonal phenomena. Where Wittgenstein emphasizes animalistic training, Heidegger focuses on peer-pressure, what he calls "distantiality."[196] Our desire not to stand out from the crowd, not to be abnormal pressures us to imitate and seek approval (this idea points backwards to Nietzsche and ahead to Foucault). This impulse is what drives our socialization: in our attempts to fit in, we absorb the way "one" behaves, especially the proper use of equipment to accomplish goals and take on roles. This impulse teleologically interprets the world for us, which forms the basis for thought and communication. All Dasein are, by definition, engaged in roles that are derived from their communities and that largely define them.[197] In order to be a self at all, we need a community to provide a repertoire of roles, as well as the equipment and institutions necessary for their practice—for example, the colleges, students, and seminar rooms that allow me to be a professor. As Wittgenstein's "private"-linguists can only introspect with public tools, so for Heidegger "knowing oneself is grounded in Being-with."[198]

A *pharmakon* logic structures Heidegger's early analysis of being-with. Although this prepares the ground for and pushes us toward inauthenticity, we *have* to want to fit in, we have to desire positive feedback and dislike the negative if socialization is to take root. Low-functioning people who lack a "theory of mind" or computers will have tremendous difficulty acquiring social skills, no matter how intelligent they may be in a more abstract sense. Long before we are capable of intellectually reflecting on whether these others' bodies have minds we crave their approval; before we can rail against the untruth of the crowd, we dread standing out from it. Being outstanding can become a point of pride later on, but we must first not want to stand out just to be educable, if we are to be able even to think of the goal of individualism. Heidegger's early analysis of sociality has a Kierkegaardian moment of horror at the leveling influence of the crowd, but he begins from a Hegelian recognition of our necessarily social starting point.

Wittgenstein also rejects the argument from analogy, in favor of the perception of others. No bare observation of bodily motion followed by an investigation and inference as to its cause takes place, not even a silent or lightning-fast process lurking in the background.

That statement "I believe he feels what I feel in such circumstances" does not yet exist here: The interpretation, that is, that I see something in myself which I surmise in him.

For in reality that is a rough interpretation. In general I do not surmise fear in him—I *see* it. I do not feel that I am deducing the probable existence of something inside from something outside; rather it is as if the human face were in a way translucent and that I were seeing it not in reflected light but rather in its own.[199]

It is important that, in rejecting an *inference* from analogy, Wittgenstein is not replacing it with an *assumption* that other bodies are animated by minds. That would simply demote us from quick reasoners to bad ones. Instead, he wants to toss out the whole epistemic framework of belief, inference, and evidence as inapplicable.

While suspending belief in other minds is possible in very unusual circumstances,[200] this does not retroactively show that we have been *believing* in other minds all along, just like something's changing aspects doesn't reveal a previous seeing-as. This category simply does not apply to these reactions.

"I believe that he is suffering."—Do I also *believe* that he isn't an automaton? It would go against the grain to use the word in both connexions. (Or is it like this: I believe that he is suffering, but am certain that he is not an automaton? Nonsense!). . . . My attitude towards him is an attitude towards a soul. I am not of the *opinion* that he has a soul.[201]

The conceptual framework forces us into dichotomies like classifying our belief as either a justified inference or a mere assumption, but Wittgenstein wants to change the entire approach to the subject.[202] As Stanley Cavell writes, for Wittgenstein "our relation to the world as a whole, or to others in general, is not one of knowing, where knowing construes itself as being certain. So it is also true that we do not *fail* to know such things."[203]

Wittgenstein makes a basic, almost biological orientation toward others the necessary foundation for further, more intellectual interactions. "Being sure that someone is in pain, doubting whether he is, and so on, are so many natural, instinctive, kinds of behaviour towards other human beings, and our language is merely an auxiliary to, and further extension of, this relation. Our language-game is an extension of primitive behaviour. (For our *language-game* is behaviour.) (Instinct)."[204] Immediate reactions are both logically and chronologically primary in the sense "that this sort of behaviour is *pre-linguistic*: that a language-game is based *on it*, that it is the prototype of a way of thinking and not the result of thought."[205] A prerational sensitivity to others is a necessary condition for our ability to respond to conditioning, and thus to develop into rational speakers who may in time come to raise doubts about other minds. Hence animalistic reacting to others undergirds not just particular language-games like pain-attribution, but rationality and language-speaking as a whole, making the self intrinsically social. When Wittgenstein says that trust must come before suspicion, he means this not just as a matter of chronological fact but of logical necessity.[206] We aren't deceiving ourselves or missing something essential by ignoring all divergent interpretations: "a doubt is not necessary even when it is possible."[207] It is just this natural conformity to the norm that enables us to think and use language at all. The (at least initially) unexamined life is the only one we *can* live. Today, the scientific support for this view is considerable, as emphasized by those who work in cognitive science, the nexus where phenomenology, computer science, and neuroscience meet.[208]

This entire line of thought is encapsulated beautifully in a passage from *Remarks on the Foundations of Mathematics*, which deserves to be quoted in full:

"I know how I have to go" means: I am in no doubt how I have to go. [Here we see everyday confident competence with no consideration of alternative interpretations.]

"How can one follow a rule?" That is what I should like to ask. [The philosophical inquiry arises.]

But how does it come about that I want to ask that, when after all I find no kind of difficulty in following a rule? [Here philosophical puzzlement is contrasted with everyday facility.]

Here we obviously misunderstand the facts that lie before our eyes. [Philosophy misconstrues inconspicuous facts.]

How can the word "Slab" indicate what I have to do, when after all I can bring any action into accord with any interpretation?

How can I follow a rule, when after all whatever I do can be interpreted as following it? [This is the Interpretation Aporia.]

What must I know, in order to be able to obey the order? Is there some *knowledge*, which makes the rule followable only in *this* way? Sometimes I must *know* something, *sometimes* I must *interpret* the rule before I apply it. [The cognitivist account of knowledge guiding our action does occasionally apply.]

Now, *how* was it possible for the rule to have been given an interpretation during instruction, an interpretation which reaches as far as to any arbitrary step?

And if this step was not named in the explanation, how then *can* we agree about what has to happen at this step, since after all whatever happens can be brought into accord with the rule and the examples? [The apparent gap between instruction about a rule and its indefinite extension rears its head.]

Thus, you say, nothing definite has been said about these steps. [Semantic nihilism seems to follow.]

Interpretation comes to an end.[209]

The wonderfully concise final line shows Wittgenstein's rejection of the cognitivist view of understanding as interpretation. Instead of revealing important facts about comprehension, it creates artificial problems such as endless alternatives and infinite regresses. Although conscious thinking certainly occurs, it is not and cannot be the final word in understanding, precisely because it never allows a final word. Interpretation all the way down would prevent understanding the way infinitely divisible time keeps Achilles from catching up to the tortoise. We need something that takes over after interpretation ends and before it begins.

### Phronêsis

Heidegger likes to say that the history of philosophy is dynamic, continually reorganizing and reinitiating new concerns and old questions; this is why his student Gadamer compares reading a text to having a conversation.[210] If Heidegger and Wittgenstein are in fact the twentieth century's greatest and most influential thinkers, and if they agree on many central topics, then a new canonical constellation should organize itself around other figures who have given insightful treatments of the same topics. I thus want to briefly present Aristotle as a predecessor of their views on thinking, while chapter 5 will discuss Hume.

Heidegger and Wittgenstein want to put to rest the traditional concentration on the disengaged intellect that explicitly deliberates about arguments and knows facts. Instead, they see thinking as largely tacit, deeply formed and informed by "irrational" influences such as emotions and upbringing which, rather than being unfortunate and corrupting interferences, are essential to thought. Both argue that we must start with certain inborn nonrational orientations, especially toward others, for any more sophisticated education to take hold.

Aristotle's notion of *phronêsis* anticipates many of these ideas. Heidegger's tremendous admiration for Aristotle pervades his early work; he tellingly translates *phronêsis* with his own "circumspection" in an early work.[211] Heidegger also grants Aristotle the honorary title of "phenomenologist" a couple of millennia *avant la lettre*.[212] In contrast with Socrates' claim that to know the good is to do it and Plato's demand for articulate and defensible definitions to underwrite competence, Aristotle argues that much expertise cannot be expressed with any degree of exactness, nor can it be learned by memorizing a definition or objective formula.[213] Instead, it is a know-how that is learned by doing, in concrete circumstances, and by following the right models. This is precisely how Wittgenstein—who, you will recall, disagrees with Socrates' notion of definitions—describes many cases of learning, with examples and tips carrying the epistemological weight traditionally attributed to formulae.

Is there such a thing as "expert judgment" about the genuineness of expressions of feeling?—Even here, there are those whose judgment is "better" and those whose judgment is "worse." . . .

Can one learn this knowledge? Yes; some can. Not, however, by taking a course in it, but through *"experience."*—Can someone else be a man's teacher in this? Certainly. From time to time he gives him the right *tip.*—This is what "learning" and "teaching" are like here.—What one acquires here is not a technique; one learns correct judgments. There are also rules, but they do not form a system, and only experienced people can apply them right. Unlike calculating-rules.

What is most difficult here is to put this indefiniteness, correctly and unfalsified, into words.[214]

Compare Wittgenstein's final sentence here with the warning Aristotle issues at the beginning of the *Nicomachean Ethics*: "our discussion will be adequate if its degree of clarity fits the subject-matter; for we should not seek the same degree of exactness in all sorts of arguments alike."[215] Think also of Heidegger's defense of "vague" and "subjective" measurements of space like "as long as it takes to smoke a pipe" (BT 140/105) against Descartes's mathematics.

*Phronêsis* operates in specific circumstances which cannot be anticipated by universal rules. No matter how clear the rule, we always apply it to particulars, which is a matter of seeing the right thing to do relative to the particular situation and actors. Thus, Aristotle follows what I am calling the Perceptual Model of Thinking: "but how far and how much we must deviate to be blamed is not easy to define in an account; for nothing perceptible is easily defined, and [since] these [circumstances of virtuous and vicious action] are particulars, the judgment about them depends on perception."[216] He even calls *phronêsis* the "eye of the soul" (NE 1144a30). Seeing what to do in a situation does not stand in need of further justification, nor could it receive any—at least none that would persuade one who is lacking in *phronêsis*. This is Aristotle's spade-turning, regress-ending bedrock; he defines being educated as knowing when an explicit proof is needed and when it is not, a comment quoted approvingly at the end of one of Heidegger's last essays.[217] Aristotle's epistemology follows the same pattern as Wittgenstein's arguments: deductive reasoning must be based upon an immediate, perceptive grasp of ideas which cannot be justified deductively without an infinite regress.[218]

We are social animals who must begin with an inborn orientation to pleasure and pain; it is this that instruction builds on and refines.[219] "Arguments and teaching surely do not influence everyone, but the soul of the student needs to have been prepared by habits for enjoying and hating finely, like ground that is to nourish seed. . . . Hence we must already in some way have a character suitable for virtue, fond of what is fine and objecting to what is shameful."[220] Socialization is necessary to become a mature rational human, and this socialization requires a nonrational foundation in feelings and perception. Aristotle emphasizes our natural potential to behave in certain ways which gets actualized by the right upbringing, in parallel to Wittgenstein's form of life which enables training and Heidegger's being-with that prepares the ground for socialization. "The virtues arise in us neither by nature nor against nature. Rather, we are by nature able to acquire them, and reach our complete perfection through habit."[221] As one commentator puts it, "the molding of desire begins in early childhood by exploiting a natural inclination to find pleasure in being praised and pain in being blamed. . . . Habituation of character is thus made possible by the political nature of the human being before the rational nature is developed" (Burger 2008, 53). Epistemological virtues are inextricable from ethical virtues, desires, and emotions.[222] Repeated actions habituate us, developing a character that guides us through most actions without explicit deliberation.[223]

While there is a Platonic strain in Aristotle's prioritization of the perfectly unchanging, transcendent *meta-physis*, both in the world and within ourselves,[224] much of his work focuses on what happens primarily and for the most part, on what the many say—that is, on average everyday phenomena.

The truth, however, in questions about action is judged from what we do and how we live, since these are what control [the answers to such questions]. Hence we ought to examine what has been said by applying it to what we do and how we live; and if it harmonizes with what we do, we should accept it, but if it conflicts we should count it [mere] words.[225]

Like Wittgenstein's returning words to their normal use and Heidegger's phenomenological descriptions, the phenomena as we find them usually and for the most part are the prima facie authority. Aristotle recommends experience in order to impart what Wittgenstein calls a perspicuous overview of what we all know instead of philosophy's preference for an unmixed diet.

Lack of experience diminishes our power of taking a comprehensive view of the admitted facts. Hence those who dwell in intimate association with nature and its phenomena grow more and more able to formulate, as the foundations of their theories, principles such as to admit of a wide and coherent development: while those whom devotion to abstract discussions has rendered unobservant of the facts are too ready to dogmatize on the basis of a few observations. (*On Generation and Corruption* 316a5–9)

## Summary

We are now in a position to see how much Heidegger and Wittgenstein agree on this topic. First, much of our behavior neither has nor needs articulate thought. It gets by perfectly well with tacit know-how, and taking thematic knowledge to be the only kind of knowledge creates insoluble problems *for* thematic knowledge. Second, we generally acquire the skills to act appropriately through socialization rather than explicit teaching. No one sits a young Dasein on their knee and explains the facts about the beings and the be's, nor can this understanding be captured in formulae or facts. Instead we acquire it unconsciously, soaking it up as we respond to the endless bits of feedback we're continuously receiving as to how well we're performing Dasein-ish activities. Third, socialization only works on beings with a certain kind of being or form of life. We must be open to and especially attentive to others, emotionally invested in their views of us for these processes to take hold. Together, these ideas explain how we easily navigate a world with qualitative features when detached reason finds nothing of the kind, and how we consistently follow rules in standard ways when reflection presents us with endless alternatives. This view has profound implications for what kind of foundation philosophy can build, which is what we will now take up.

# 5   The Essence of Ground

The difficult thing here is not, to dig down to the ground; no, it is to recognize the ground that lies before us as the ground. For the ground keeps on giving us the illusory image of a greater depth, and when we seek to reach this, we keep on finding ourselves on the old level. Our disease is one of wanting to explain.

—Wittgenstein, *Remarks on the Foundations of Mathematics*, 333

Being is intrinsically groundlike, what gives ground, presences as the ground, has the character of ground. Precisely because it is groundlike, groundgiving, it cannot need a ground. The groundlike is groundless, what grounds, what presences as basis does not need the ground; that is, it is without something to which it could go back as something outside of it, there is no longer any back, no behind itself, but pure presencing itself.

—Heidegger, *Schelling's Treatise on the Essence of Human Freedom*, 170–171

As we have seen, Wittgenstein and Heidegger challenge a number of the assumptions and aspirations that have guided philosophy since its inception. One of these, foundationalism, is the attempt to trace all knowledge back to a source or set of claims that, as necessarily true, secure the truth of all that is derived from them. Just as a valid argument produces only true conclusions from true premises, so a properly built system insulates the circulation of truth throughout its entirety. As Descartes argues, if we don't know that we know what we think we know, then we may not know it after all.

The problem, which has been with us nearly as long as philosophy itself, is that a base–superstructure organization requires an ultimate level which itself has no justifying foundation underneath it. Absent the troubled notion of self-justifying beliefs, we have either a bottom level hovering over the abyss or, as they say, it's turtles all the way down. Wittgenstein and Heidegger accept the first horn of this perennial dilemma. Stopping at an unjustified level only seems worrisome to a mindset conditioned by foundationalism to expect a transcendent ground which, more than being right, *cannot* be wrong, an idea which is incompatible with finite creatures like us. Freed from this incoherent demand, we can accept the grounding afforded by human nature and cultural norms as both all that is possible and all that is needed. Once we are weaned off millennia-old cravings for the transcendent, we can learn to live with the human.

## The Rise and Fall of Wittgenstein's Foundationalism

Wittgenstein's early work, like most early analytic philosophy, is solidly foundationalist, although he leaves the identity of simple objects—the Tractarian system's basic elements—undetermined except for the properties needed for language to work. Absolute determinacy of meaning requires language to bottom out in elementary propositions that directly correlate to states-of-affairs, and it is on the foundation of this language–reality isomorphism that the Tractarian edifice is built. Metaphysical atomism determines the nature of any language that could represent it, making logic metaphysically necessary.[1] The absence of such a foundation seems to make the whole edifice of knowledge and societal practices sway vertiginously, threatening to collapse into epistemological nihilism with neither right nor wrong.[2] Much of traditional philosophy is dedicated to building a bulwark against this possibility, propping up knowledge with all manner of metaphysical flying buttresses.

A transcendental inquiry lends its conclusion an appealing finality: as long as the given phenomenon remains in effect, so must its necessary conditions. Just as Kant repeatedly claims that he has captured the mind's transcendental structure once and for all, so the early Wittgenstein swears that logic is fully settled, reassuring the reader that "there can *never* be surprises in logic."[3] With all possible propositional permutations anticipated, logic leaves nothing for us to do beyond crafting an apposite sign-language.

We have said that some things are arbitrary in the symbols that we use and that some things are not. In logic, it is only the latter that express: but that means that logic is not a field in which *we* express what we wish with the help of signs, but rather one in which the nature of the absolutely necessary signs speaks for itself.[4]

Logic proper deals with the absolutely necessary, where we cannot meddle and nothing is arbitrary. The logician is a metaphysical stenographer, not a novelist.

As discussed in chapter 1, Wittgenstein comes to see this project of grounding our beliefs and practices as an attempt to compensate for the way disengaged consideration renders our unreflective understanding incomprehensible. In chapter 2, we saw how dead, detached signs get resuscitated through the magic of meaning-objects. However, the idea that all future steps are already laid out with God, who sees from above the rule's entire development while we trudge on at ground-level, is just a picture, "a mythological description of the use of a rule" (PI §221) that neither solves nor illuminates anything.

"The position of all primes must somehow be predetermined. We work them out only successively, but they are all already determined. God, as it were, knows them all. And yet for all that it seems possible that they are not determined by a law."—Always this picture of the meaning of a word as a full box which is given us with its contents packed in it all ready for us to investigate.—What *do* we know about the prime numbers? How is the concept of them given to us at all? Don't we ourselves make the decisions about them? And how odd that we assume that there must have been decisions taken about them that we haven't taken ourselves! . . . We are tricked by the image of an "infinite extension" as an analogue to the familiar "finite" extension.[5]

Meaning-objects depict an infinite extension as an extraordinarily long finite extension which exists as fully determinate, independently of our calculations—an actualized "and so on . . . "—rather than the mundane instruction that we are not to stop at any particular point.

This picture seems explanatorily attractive but it loses coherence when pressed. What would it matter to us if the rest of the extension did exist beyond the horizon of the human? That which exceeds our awareness can for that very reason have no impact on our practices: "Nothing would follow from it, nothing be explained by it. It would not tie in with anything in my life" (OC §117). Wittgenstein's later focus on mundane rather than idealized language[6] only acknowledges that which can affect our usage in some way; the *deus ex machina* picture has no significance since it neither does nor could do so.

In fact, this picture is worse than useless: it creates new problems. "In thinking about the technique of expansion, which we have learnt, we use the false picture of a completed expansion . . . and this forces us to ask unanswerable questions."[7] This is not due to a commitment to verificationism on Wittgenstein's part, but the simple requirement that we know what we're doing with the concepts we use. The metaphysical picture of infinite extensions lies outside agreed-upon rules or trained intuitions, and thus falls apart in our hands if we try to use it. "This picture *seems* to determine what we have to do, what to look for, and how—but it does not do so, just because we do not know how it is to be applied."[8] It would be like you and I agreeing to play a game of "Calvinball" without agreeing on how it is to be played. We would both make up rules as we go along—you set up a chess board in under thirty seconds and I knock it down with a cat eating a banana, both of us declaring victory. There would be no answer as to who had won because we weren't really playing a game.

Wittgenstein wants to change the entire way we think about philosophical foundations. One of the recurrent themes of his later work is that our reasons for following a rule a certain way peter out. We may be able defend our actions for a step or two, albeit in terms that could only help someone with at least the capacity to follow the original rule, but "my reasons [*Gründe*] will soon give out. And then I shall act, without reasons [*Gründe*]."[9] Foundationalism considers unjustifiable bedrocks to be a fatal flaw; anything built upon an unlegitimated foundation is thereby illegitimate. But Wittgenstein argues that cessation is built into the notion of justification— "justification by experience comes to an end. If it did not it would not be justification"[10]—and in particular, breaking off at a point that is not an indubitable or self-justifying reason, but an immediate reaction.

"All the steps are really already taken" means: I no longer have any choice. The rule, once stamped with a particular meaning, traces the lines along which it is to be followed through the whole of space.—But if something this sort really were the case, how would it help?

No; my description only made sense if it was to be understood symbolically.—I should have said: *This is how it strikes me.*

When I obey a rule, I do not choose.

I obey the rule *blindly.*[11]

Meaning-objects are conjured to explain the way we follow rules competently without hesitation or mistakes—"it gives expression to the fact that we look to the rule for instruction and *do something*, without appealing to anything else for guidance"[12]—but in a misleading, obfuscating way. We must look at how the practices of reasoning and justifying actually occur in everyday life.

Wittgenstein's point is twofold. First, metaphysical explanations of our rule-following competence do not do what we want them to do—namely, ground our practices in something intrinsically meaningful or self-interpreting. Second, we do not need such a grounding because our form of life, conditioned by socialization, secures for us what metaphysical entities could not. The emperor has neither clothes, nor need of them.

## Arbitrary

Wittgenstein finds it difficult to express his thoughts on the necessity of logic, what he calls "the hardness of the logical must" (PI §437). The terms "arbitrary" and "decision" give him particular trouble since his analysis makes them applicable to our language-games in one way but inapplicable in another. "Then is there something arbitrary about this system [of primary colors]? Yes and no. It is akin both to what is arbitrary and to what is non-arbitrary."[13] As unhelpful as this sounds, I think it is exactly right; let's prise these two aspects apart.

The primary way our language-games are arbitrary is that we cannot justify them in the most natural, obvious way, namely, by grounding them in reality. We want to say that, for example, we pick these colors to be primary because they really are primary; that's the way things themselves are and our taxonomy of the world mirrors its inherent articulation, letting us "carve at the joints." But in his later work Wittgenstein emphatically and repeatedly rejects this notion, often using the word "arbitrary" to denote this rejection: "the rules must be laid down arbitrarily, that is, are not to be read off from reality like a description. For when I say that the rules are arbitrary, I mean that they are not determined by reality in the way the description of reality is. And that means: it is nonsense to say that they agree with reality."[14] The point isn't that we can never know whether our beliefs match up with the world itself, nor that we in fact know that they do not. Rather, Wittgenstein is making the kind of move often made by great philosophers: he is rejecting the conceptual framework within which the comparison makes sense at all.

Experience radically underdetermines what we make of it. Without meaning-objects anticipating their own proper use, the same set of facts can give rise to multiple classifications or sets of rules, even to different takes on what counts as a fact. The bizarre behavior Wittgenstein likes to imagine often shows how people could apply rules or interpret experience or continue patterns in all sorts of ways; this exposes our behavior as being one possibility among many. Like Foucault's invocation of Borges' fantastic Chinese taxonomy, Wittgenstein argues that "the value of such games is that they destroy prejudices; they show that 'it need not always be this way.'"[15] Our classifications don't mirror the way things are, not because they're wrong but because there is no Way Things Are; "there is no absolute similarity" since "everything is analogous to everything else,"[16] nor is there absolute simplicity[17] or exactness (PI §88). The overpowering self-evidence of our way of doing things is due to our familiarity with it, rather than its fit with the world.

We cannot justify our language-games by appealing to Reality Itself because it is only through some game or other that we access reality in order to determine its significance. "I cannot use language to get outside language. . . . Grammatical conventions cannot be justified by describing what is represented. Any such description already presupposes the grammatical rules."[18] Without self-classifying meaning-objects, the world does not tell us how to describe it. We can of course compare various particular claims to the world, but only on the basis of some description, which cannot simply be read off of the world but requires "a great deal of stage-setting."[19] As Quine argues, there are no "objectively" crucial experiments since results get their significance from a context of beliefs and practices that are not presently in question, and supposedly irrefutable evidence can always be given *ad hoc* interpretations. Ruining Logical Stoicism's aspiration to intellective passivity, even a proof "needs our acceptance of it as such (if 'proof' is to mean what it means)."[20]

Like the private-linguist's pain, in order to point to an example of something that escapes our grammar, we would need to describe and understand the anomaly at least enough to refer to it, which shows that our grammar *can* capture it.[21] Whereas earlier he had allowed the unspeakably transcendent to be shown instead of said, he now sees any kind of indication—such as ostensive definitions or internally "pointing" at a sensation—as already caught up in an intelligible game if it is to succeed at all. The attempt to cite deeply countervailing evidence thus faces a dilemma: either the topic fits into our grammar, which eliminates its status as a genuine counterexample, or it doesn't, in which case we must pass over it in complete silence, without even whistling about it.[22] This commits Wittgenstein to a linguistic anti-realism: "the connection between 'language and reality' is made by definitions of words, and these belong to grammar, so that language remains self-contained and autonomous."[23] All attempts to get completely outside our language-games must themselves be moves within a game to be able to make sense.

This point easily slides into the Kantian claim that our thoughts cannot reach the world in-itself, so that we are missing something essential, even *the* essential. Wittgenstein wants to avoid this trap, circling the idea warily. "We have a colour system as we have a number system. Do the systems reside in *our* nature or in the nature of things? How are we to put it?—*Not* in the nature of numbers or colours" (Z §357). The former horn opts for a Kantian idealism where we project features onto things-in-themselves, whereas the latter implies a metaphysical realism where the world determines what we make of it. But both "this assertion, or its opposite is a misfiring attempt to express what can't be expressed like that" (OC §37). This description treats getting beyond language to reality-in-itself as an intelligible possibility that happens to be denied to us, whereas Wittgenstein wants to argue that it is incoherence rather than inability that keeps us from talking about that which transcends our talk.

> The great difficulty here is not to represent the matter as if it were a matter of inability. As if there really were an object, from which I derive its description, but I were unable to shew it to anyone.—And the best that I can propose is that we should yield to the temptation to use this picture, but then investigate how the *application* of the picture goes.[24]

This is an excellent statement of what I am calling original finitude. Kantian finitude depends on what it excludes, defining our limitation as the negative image of what lies beyond our ken, while Wittgenstein wants escape this conceptual framework altogether. As Cavell puts it, "the reason we cannot say what the thing is in itself is not that there is something we do not in fact know, but that we have deprived ourselves of the conditions for saying anything in particular" (1979, 239).

This illuminates Wittgenstein's cryptic equation of grammar with metaphysics: "*essence* is expressed in grammar. . . . Grammar tells what kind of object anything is."[25] While this may sound like a perverse retreat from the study of reality to mere semantics,[26] I think he is trying to undermine this very distinction. What we think of as questions about phenomena are best treated as questions about how a word or concept is to be used, because that is how things show up for us. "Grammar is not accountable to any reality. It is grammatical rules that determine meaning (constitute it) and so they themselves are not answerable to any meaning and to that extent are arbitrary."[27] It isn't that language operates in lockstep with reality so that we can read features of the world off our ways of speaking about it, as the Tractarian mirror strategy has it. Justifying claims by laying them side-by-side with reality can only compare them with reality as we speak of it, making any such attempt either trivial or emptily circular: "we cannot leave our logical world to consider it from the outside."[28] A similar line of reasoning backs up Heidegger's phenomenological ontology: beings are what and how they appear to us, so studying experience *is* studying reality.[29] Whereas *Being and Time* treats language as a secondary layer that lays upon our practical engagement and takes on its contours, Heidegger's later work comes closer to Wittgenstein's position in making experience linguistic all the way down. I will return to this in the conclusion.

While we can make perfectly good sense of ordinary comparisons between assertions and things asserted, this can only take place within a game which itself isn't the kind of thing that is capable of dis/agreement with reality. Wittgenstein often invokes the difference between deciding upon a unit of measurement and taking measurements with this unit, or that between the rules of a game and moves made within it. The categories of right and wrong only apply within a system of measurement or game, and not to the system or game itself; a chess move can be illegitimate, but it makes no sense to say that chess itself is wrong. "We can draw the distinction between hypothesis and grammatical rule by means of the words 'true' and 'false' on the one hand, and 'practical' and 'impractical' on the other. . . . A rule is not true or false."[30] I will call this argument that we cannot judge the rules of a game or the framework of a discussion by criteria applicable within it the Framework Argument.

### Decision

Wittgenstein's early conception of meaning and his commitment to Logical Stoicism drove him to rid the arena of truth and logic of all human interference, which required that the states-of-affairs asserted or denied by a proposition be completely delineated, as we saw with the questions concerning whether the book was still on the table under all possible circumstances. He gave up this dream when he recognized our ineliminable role in applying the rules. No matter how assiduously we strive to passively obey a rule, we still need to make the *phronetic* judgment call as to whether *this* state-of-affairs counts as an instance of the rule: "if calculating looks to us like the action of a machine, it is *the human being* doing the calculation that is the machine."[31]

We feel that all possibilities are settled in advance because we rarely step outside the normal circumstances where our footing is so sure we imagine it to be perfect.[32] Wittgenstein spends considerable time constructing scenarios that throw our intuitions out of whack and leave us uncertain about what to say. This doesn't expose a disturbing, problematic gap in our everyday usage, but rather shows that we get along fine without the propositional omniscience he had previously found necessary.[33]

Without meaning-objects' applications coiled up, as it were, within words or the mind like a retractable measuring tape, Wittgenstein now sees each application as metaphysically unguaranteed by past instances. "We must not suppose that with the rule we have given the infinite extension of its application. Every new step in a calculation *is a fresh step.* . . . It is not in the nature of 23 and 18 to give 414 when multiplied, nor even in the nature of the rules. We do it that way, that is all."[34] No matter how clearly the world seems to take us by the hand and lead us, it is always up to us to recognize its authority and interpret its commands; neither past usage nor reality forces us to go on in one particular way. We will never get to the other side of the ellipsis of "and so on . . ."—not because of our all-too-human limitations, but because there is no other side; that's the point of an ellipsis.

Since the notion of infinite extensions occurs paradigmatically in mathematics,[35] Wittgenstein spends a great deal of time on this subject, originally planning part II of the *Philosophical Investigations* to focus on it.[36] Just as linguistic meaning occurs in our use of it, so mathematics only exists in our calculations, which means that "there is nothing there for a higher intelligence to know—except what future generations will do. We know as much as God does in mathematics."[37] Mathematics and grammar are inventions, not discoveries.[38] As Simon Glendinning writes, each new application of a rule "is ungrounded or structurally abyssal. That is, it is logically prior to a determined rationality (or irrationality)."[39]

Without timeless mathematical truths, the notion that humanity has always followed a rule incorrectly is simply incoherent: how we follow it *is* the right way. *"The point is that we all make the SAME use of it.* To know its meaning is to use it *in the same way* as other people do. 'In the right way' means nothing."[40] This seems to entail the worrying possibility that if everyone began, say, adding differently—getting "6" from "2 + 3," for example—then that "wrong" practice would become "right" (LFM 290–291), but this concern hasn't followed the argument all the way out. If we see this "new" way as maintaining the same rule of addition we have always used, then it isn't new at all. If no one (except a few cranks) judges a change to have occurred then we have no ground to say that a change has occurred.[41] It isn't so much that our notion of green may turn out to be grue as that, if we all "change" from green to grue without noticing it then no change has taken place—and scare quotes proliferate. If a tree changes color in the forest and no one realizes it, then who exactly is claiming that it changed? We imagine God sadly shaking his head at our chromatic apostasy, but the only way for this picture have an effect would be for Him to make His displeasure known—which would mean, in turn, that someone *did* notice. Alluding to the most famous modern discussion of skepticism, Wittgenstein asks: "is no demon deceiving us at present? Well, if he is, it doesn't matter. What the eye doesn't see the heart doesn't grieve over."[42] A deception, carried out perfectly, becomes truth.

Another problem with the picture of reality justifying our grammatical distinctions is that we don't first hit on the notion "primary color" and then look around to see what satisfies this notion. A little like simple objects, a category's meaning is largely constituted by the particulars we group under it.

One is tempted to justify rules of grammar by sentences like "But there are really four primary colours." And if we say that the rules of grammar are arbitrary, that is directed against the possibility of this justification. Yet can't it after all be said that the grammar of colour words characterizes the world as it actually is? . . . Doesn't grammar put the primary colours together because there is a kind of similarity between them? . . . Of which in that case I can say: "Yes, that is the way we look at things" or "We just do want to form this sort of picture." For if I say "there is a particular similarity among the primary colours"—whence do I derive the idea of this similarity? Just as the idea 'primary colour' is nothing else but 'blue or red or green or yellow' is not the idea of that similarity too given simply by the four colours?[43]

The type is an abstraction from the tokens, so the addition of a new element isn't a *discovery* about the class but a change in its meaning.

Since it is not set out in advance how we are to extend a language-game to new cases, each application of a rule requires something like a new decision.

If I am given a general (variable) rule, I must recognize each time afresh that this rule may be applied *here* too (that it holds for *this* case too). No act of foresight can absolve me from this act of *insight*. Since the form in which the rule is applied is in fact a new one at every step. But it is not a matter of an act of *insight*, but of an act of *decision*.[44]

It resembles a decision in that it is up to us to determine how the precedents relate to the present situation—is this another instance of the same thing, or just something with a merely accidental resemblance to the other members of the class? Other applications are always possible and could be considered as continuing to do the same thing given the right conditions. "You never get beyond what you've decided yourself; you can always go on in innumerable ways" (LFM 145). This marks the death of Logical Stoicism.

Of course, it is *not* like a decision in the sense of making a selection from a choice of options. "It is no act of insight, intuition, which makes us use the rule as we do at the particular point of the series. It would be less confusing to call it an act of decision, though this too is misleading, for nothing like an act of decision must take place, but possibly just an act of writing or speaking."[45] Adding two and two allows me no leeway for creative choices; the answer feels forced out of me. This is what Descartes means when he says that he simply cannot doubt that two and three make five while focusing on it. However, like the eavesdropping "primitive people" (PI §194), we misinterpret this feeling of coercion, our automatic response, and universal agreement, by invoking meaning-objects as the cause all of these phenomena. "There is an idea that 'something must make us' do what we do" (BB 143). It is in a sense decided for us, but not by reality strong-arming us. The "flimsy" (LFM 244) support on which our knowledge and practices rest is our natural tendency to respond in certain ways once we've been trained. "What is it that compels me?—the expression of the rule?—Yes, once I have been educated in this way."[46]

Sometimes Wittgenstein appears to distinguish between what we say and what the truth is, implying an objective truth that exceeds humanity's grasp. When read carefully, however, these passages actually say that the *meaning* of mathematical or logical facts is not that people have agreed to these conventions. The meaning of "2 + 2 = 4" is not "We as a society collectively stipulate '4' as the sum of '2 + 2,'" and neither is it "Competent adders always reach '4.'" No, it means that 4 *is* the sum of 2 + 2. Nevertheless, for "2 + 2 = 4" to be true, people must consistently get the same answer. "The proposition *is grounded in* a technique. And, if you like, also in the physical and psychological facts that make the technique *possible*. But it doesn't follow that its sense is to express these conditions."[47] Agreement and its conditions undergird these practices, enabling them to take place, even though there's not a trace of these ideas in the meaning of the statements.

The highest, most secure forms of knowledge seem to require especially strong metaphysical support; mathematics in particular must be plugged into the structure of reality to explain its long epistemological privilege. Wittgenstein's account of these facts is that that we have given this status to these forms by depositing paradigmatic examples in an "archive," turning them from empirical claims into rules, from measured lengths to measuring rulers, up to the ruler that rules over all other rulers, the Parisian standard-meter rod. Their indubitability is the result of our refusal to let anything count as rendering them dubious. "Isn't the question this: 'What if you had to change your opinion even on these most fundamental things?' And to that the answer seems to me to be: 'You don't *have* to change it. That is just what their being "fundamental" is.'"[48] Wittgenstein sometimes calls such ideas a priori (even "synthetic a priori"[49]) because we don't allow empirical evidence overturn them. These propositions, including many of Moore's "certain" truths, have changed from claims to be tested to criteria of competence. Were someone to get an answer other than 144 from multiplying 12 × 12, this would not signal the world-historical discovery that the answer we've been accepting all these years has been wrong; it would be a sign that she hadn't yet learned how to multiply, and we would simply revoke her license to multiply until she gained competence, as demonstrated, *inter alia*, by getting 144. What we see as the world's resistance here is actually our refusal to countenance any countervailing evidence, an artifact of the glasses we see through rather than a fact about the seen.

## Reason

This line of thought becomes especially significant, and startling, when Wittgenstein applies it to reason, treating it as one particular game instead of the overarching sovereign over all games, rendering it arbitrary in the sense described above. "'Reason' only applies within a system of rules. . . . It is nonsense to ask for reasons for the whole system of thought. You cannot give justification for the rules."[50] We want there to be an *ur*-game written into the very fabric of reality that timelessly, serenely presides over all games—but there is no such thing. Chapter 1 saw Wittgenstein expand what counts as a proposition from one narrow type to include the tremendous variety we actually use; he similarly opens up logic and reasoning as a whole. Although we want access to absolute laws so as to reassure ourselves that we're thinking the right way, "there are all sorts of different ways in which we could do logic or mathematics."[51] A reason functions as a reason if we treat it as one; no Reason in-itself transcends our practice to judge all other reasoning. Like game rules or measurement units, the deepest laws governing our thinking have no ultimate foundation apart from human nature as it is formed by societal training. "Here too we cannot give any foundation (except a biological or historical one or something of the kind); all we can do is to establish the agreement, or disagreement between the rules for certain words, and say that these words are used with these rules" (PG 304).

Wittgenstein is well aware of how disappointing his efforts "to replace wild conjectures and explanations by [a] quiet weighing of linguistic facts" (Z §447) will be to his readers. Particularly distressing is the fact that it removes rationality's absolute authority to adjudicate arguments. Our knowledge will indeed look like "very proud and magnificent palaces built only on sand and mud," in Descartes's words.[52]

There will be cases where we will differ, and where it won't be a question at all of more or less knowledge, so that we can come together. . . . We would take sides, and that goes so far that there would really be great differences between us, which might come out in Mr. Lewy saying: "Wittgenstein is trying to undermine reason," and this wouldn't be false. This is actually where such questions rise. (LC 63–64)

The questions arise when incommensurable ways of thinking collide. Each takes her own statement or system to be correct, to be in harmony with Reason itself, branding all dissidents as irrational. But as Sextus Empiricus pointed out long ago, no party can claim a privileged or neutral perspective without relying on a particular way of thinking to legitimate their way of thinking, which thus compromises their alleged neutrality.

While he sometimes hesitates about how to express it, Wittgenstein repeatedly emphasizes the contingency of our ways of thinking and behaving. "Don't think that our concepts are the only possible or reasonable ones: if you imagine quite different facts from those with which we are continually surrounded, then concepts different from ours will appear natural to you."[53] He shies away from speculating about how concepts would change under specific conditions,[54] but he does discuss radically different language-games,[55] insisting on their significance: "one of the most important methods I use is to imagine a historical development for our ideas different from what actually occurred."[56]

He singles out the law of non-contradiction as a leading candidate for an essential element of all rational thought, what appears to be "a fundamental law governing all thinkable language-games."[57] Contradictions can present practical difficulties, certainly: we don't know how to follow conflicting instructions for example,[58] but this can usually be fixed by creating a new rule to adjudicate such conflicts.[59] Wittgenstein focuses on the role of contradictions in theoretical logic, especially the idea that arguments and whole systems founder upon them, which makes the eradication of possible contradictions crucial. He had firsthand experience with the logician's dread of hidden contradictions. Russell's discovery of an implicit paradox in set theory brought Frege to despair, and Gödel did roughly the same for Russell.[60] While logicians feel compelled to painstakingly search their work in order to prevent such a catastrophe, Wittgenstein dismisses such paradox-hunts as a "profitless" game akin to "thumb-catching."[61]

The idea of a hidden contradiction only makes sense within a system whose implications have already been laid out somehow. While it may be working beautifully now, any system may be rotting from within. Looking back from the moment when we discover its flaw, all of our present work will appear to be undermined.[62] But for the later Wittgenstein, logic does not take care of itself, nor can it force conclusions or actions upon us. Whether we reach a contradiction depends not on the rules themselves as if they contain their extension, but on how we apply them. A set of rules no more "contains" an unknown contradiction than the completed infinite expansion of the Pi sequence already has "7777" within it.[63] There is no fact about how to apply the rules until we apply them, hence there cannot be any undiscovered contradictions lurking amid a set of rules or propositions. Contradictions are as contradictions do.

It is the superstition of meaning-objects that makes us think that reason forces us to take certain unwelcome steps. To the objection that anything can be deduced from contradictions, Wittgenstein blithely replies: "well then, don't draw any conclusions from a contradiction; make that a rule."[64] No Logic Police will crash through the windows and put bags over our heads if we decide not to draw conclusions from contradictions. Just add an asterisk. This would have offended his early austerity, but it suits his later embrace of the messiness of human affairs perfectly. In particular, charting virgin epistemological territory allows us a degree of freedom as to how to go on, making it much more like a decision than discovery.

If you say, "The mere fact that a proof *could* be found is a fact about the mathematical world," you're comparing the mathematician to a man who has found out something about a realm of entities, the physics of mathematical entities. . . .

Professor Hardy says, "Goldbach's theorem is either true or false."—We simply say the road hasn't been built yet. At present you have the right to say either; you have a right to *postulate* that it's true or that it's false.—If you look at it this way, the whole idea of mathematics as the physics of the mathematical entities breaks down. For which road you build is not determined by the physics of mathematical entities but by totally different considerations. . . .

Why we should build a certain road isn't because the mathematics says that the road goes there—because the road isn't built until mathematics says it goes there. What determines it is partly practical considerations and partly analogies in the present system of mathematics.[65]

Both early and late, Wittgenstein rejects Russell's realist view of logic as supremely general scientific laws, though for different reasons: the *Tractatus* treats logical theorems as empty tautologies, while the later work considers them a human product.

Wittgenstein does not shy away from applying this view to the deepest rules of thinking, those that seem fundamental to any kind of reasoning: "the laws of logic, for example, excluded middle and contradiction, are arbitrary. This statement is a bit repulsive but nevertheless true."[66] He even entertains the possibility of a "new logic of contradictions,"[67] rather like Riemann and Lobachevsky's alternate geometries that start from non-Euclidean axioms. Human nature and cultural training impose some parameters on which options can be 'live ones' for us, but few intuitions survive the thin air of these abstruse heights to guide us here.

Let's imagine that a contradiction were discovered in the logical foundation for mathematics. What would actually happen? While it is dangerous to speculate, it seems likely that the only results would be a few superficial stories on news sites, and some anxiety for a handful of experts in mathematical logic, with a flurry of technical papers going back and forth among them. Meanwhile, the rest of us would continue to get by, cheating on our taxes, tallying bananas, or whatever mundane tasks we do with numbers. Mathematics needs no industrial-strength legitimation from logic, nor can it be seriously undermined by esoteric conundrums; if it helps you count your bananas, what more do you want? As Wittgenstein puts it, in a phrase that betrays his fondness for Western movies, "why hanker after logic?"[68] The old line about one philosopher's *modus ponens* being another's *modus tollens* applies here: "if a contradiction were now actually found in arithmetic—that would only prove that an arithmetic with *such* a contradiction in it could render very good service."[69]

Wittgenstein pushes the argument one step further, to claim that the very existence of a contradiction depends on our recognition of it.

Suppose among the rules there were two that contradicted each other, but I had such a bad memory that I never noticed this and always forgot one of these two rules or obeyed alternately the one and then the other. Even then I would say, Everything is all right. After all, the rules are instructions for playing the game, and as long as I can play, they must be all right. It is only when I *notice* that they contradict each other that they cease to be all right, and that manifests itself only in this: that I cannot apply them any more. For the logical product of the two rules is a contradiction, and a contradiction no longer tells me what to do. Thus the conflict appears only when I notice it. There was no problem as long as I was able to play the game.[70]

A contradiction is not an objective fact like a structural flaw in a bridge that can present an unknown danger. It is we who apply the rules, and if we do so unproblematically, then there is no problem, none besides "the superstitious dread and veneration by mathematicians in face of contradiction" (RFM 122). The only thing we have to fear about contradictions is the fear of contradiction itself.

## Heidegger's Early Anti-Foundationalism

Heidegger's phenomenological approach leads him to study phenomena as they appear to us, with a principled refusal of any pretense to a God's-eye view. His commitment to hermeneutics means that some laborious interpretive work is occasionally required to fully appreciate phenomena, but this can never appeal to anything outside experience. Ontologically, this commitment to strict immanence focuses us on our daily surroundings: "what is ready-to-hand in the environment is certainly not present-at-hand for an eternal observer exempt from Dasein: but it is encountered in Dasein's circumspectively concernful everydayness" (BT 140–141/160). Epistemologically, this draws attention to the way "truth become[s] phenomenally explicit" (BT 260/217). We can only talk about 'being' and 'truth' in relation to Dasein since we have, by definition, no access to anything inaccessible to Dasein, which leads to an anti-realism similar to Wittgenstein's: "*'there is' truth only in so far as Dasein is and so long as Dasein is. Entities are uncovered only when Dasein is; and only as long as Dasein is, are they disclosed. Newton's laws, the principle of contradiction, any truth whatever—these are true only as long as Dasein is*" (BT 269/226). This raises specters of relativism and subjectivity—worries that "*because the kind of Being that is essential to truth is of the character of Dasein, all truth is relative to Dasein's Being*"[71]—but Heidegger assures us that this does not mean that truth is up to our discretion. According to the Perceptual Model of Thinking, we see things a certain way rather than deliberately deciding how they are.

Despite Husserl's Cartesian foundationalism, Heidegger believes that phenomenology, correctly practiced, rebukes the very idea. Adapting Kierkegaard's ideas, especially in *Concluding Unscientific Postscript*, Heidegger argues that we are inextricably in-the-world, with all higher-order thought presupposing holistic involvements with the world and with other Dasein. We are always already underway and, like Neurath's boat, we cannot bracket or doubt everything in order to start over under the strict guidance of reason. "The ideal possibility of absolute knowledge is but a dream. As historiological knowledge, philosophy not only *can* not, but also *must* not, entertain any such dream."[72] The notion of starting entirely afresh free of all prejudices, achieving a pure, unmediated confrontation with reality represents one of philosophy's oldest prejudices. According to Heidegger's hermeneuticism, understanding necessarily takes place on the basis of preconceptions or "fore-understandings"; the "view from nowhere" simply makes no sense.

This everyday way in which things have been interpreted is one into which Dasein has grown in the first instance, with never a possibility of extrication. In it, out of it, and against it, all genuine understanding, interpreting, and communicating, all re-discovering and appropriating anew, are performed. In no case is a Dasein, untouched and unseduced by this way in which things have been interpreted, set

before the open country of a "world-in-itself" so that it just beholds what it encounters. . . . The "they" prescribes one's state-for-mind, and determines what and how
one "sees."[73]

The very attempt to escape all preconceptions only makes sense on the basis
a bundle of assumptions: "all philosophical discussion, even the most radical attempt to begin all over again, is pervaded by traditional concepts."[74]

Heidegger credits Kant's first *Critique* with teaching him the finitude of
understanding, in particular the idea that we need a sense of relevance, a
way to sift out the significant in order to inquire or even have coherent
experience. This is unavoidable, so "what is decisive is not to get out of
the circle but to come into it in the right way."[75] Instead of preventing
learning, as Meno's paradox has it, a certain kind of circularity *enables* it.
Inquiry starts from a pre-understanding of an entity's being in the form of
a tacit knowing-how to deal with that sort of thing. This initial orientation enables us to examine these beings, exploring the ontological region
to map it in greater detail, which then guides further research, and so on.
The vicious circle turns out to be a virtuous spiral, revising and improving
understanding with every turn. The investigation of being is benignly or
graciously circular, but this does mean that we can never evaluate our ways
of thinking as "correct" or "justified": foundationalism is eliminated.[76]

Just as Wittgenstein plants "giving grounds" in an "ungrounded way
of acting" rather than in beliefs,[77] so Heidegger defines our primary relationship to others and to the world in non-epistemic terms. Dasein "is in
a particular but primarily non-cognitive and not merely cognitive mode
of being. . . . Knowing understood as apprehending has sense only on the
basis of an *already-being-involved-with*. This already-being-involved-with, in
which knowing as such can first 'live,' is not first 'produced' directly by a
cognitive performance."[78] We are always already oriented through a non-
epistemic engagement we have been socialized into rather than a set of
propositional claims we have examined and assented to.[79]

As non-epistemic, these relationships need no justification, or better,
attempts to justify them commit a category mistake. Categories such as
'proven' or 'certain' only make sense within an epistemic framework of
theoretical thought, distorting matters when applied to other situations.

And yet it appears that we also cannot rid ourselves of the repeated objection that
in environmental experience the reality of the external world is *presupposed*. . . . In
environmental experience there is *no theoretical positing* at all. The "it worlds" is not
established theoretically, but is experienced as "worlding." . . . (Epistemology knows
only posits, and sees everything as posit and presup*position*.) . . . When epistemology thus sees and so "posits" environmental experience, then it destroys it in its

meaning and takes it as such (as something destroyed) into a theoretical context. . . .
Only when I move in the sphere of posits can the talk of presuppositions have any
meaning. *Environmental experience itself neither makes presuppositions, nor does it let
itself be labeled as a presupposition. It is not even presuppositionless*, for presupposition
and presuppositionlessness have any meaning only in the theoretical.[80]

Breakdowns shift us into a cognitive framework which interprets everything in terms of explicit claims and seeks to ferret out all presuppositions.
But our immediate experience of the world is so different from this that
even calling it "presuppositionless" distorts the matter by still using the
same constellation of concepts. As Wittgenstein writes, "one cannot make
experiments if there are not some things that one does not doubt. But that
does not mean that one takes certain presuppositions on trust."[81] I can trust
you to pay back what you owe me, but a two-year-old cannot trust his parents to teach him the correct words for things instead of playing a long,
cruel joke on him: both doubt and trust presuppose a cognitive frame of
reference which is precisely what the child is in the process of acquiring.[82]

Heidegger's early work does flirt with a kind of foundationalism in its
notion of authenticity. We are authentically ourselves when we own up to
our choices and live in a manner that is appropriate to our way of being.
Fundamental moods like anxiety and the anticipation of death sift this
ahistorical, universal structure[83] out from the particular projects and equipment that preoccupy us[84] so that we can choose to be ourselves consciously
and explicitly.[85] While no specific choice corresponds to our nature, a certain *way* of choosing does: making our decisions in the anxious awareness
that there are no right answers. The problem is that the acknowledgment
that there is no right answer *is* the right answer, due to the fact that it is
what fits the nature of our existence.

Much of Heidegger's early work tries to balance projection (which correlates with choice) against thrownness (the unchosen) without letting
either dominate. Moods teach us that our thrownness into a particular time
and culture inescapably forms and preforms us.[86] We have always already
absorbed certain ways of thinking from the fore-structures we were born
into, and part of authenticity is accepting this limitation, accepting our
beginning. But the balance is upset when the anticipation of death in a
sense overcomes thrownness, or at least removes its sting. While our culture is not up to us, in 'repetition' we hand our tradition down to ourselves,
almost a retroactive self-creation similar to Nietzsche's *amor fati*.

Dasein make no choices, gets carried along by the nobody, and thus ensnares itself
in inauthenticity. This process can be reversed only if Dasein specifically brings itself

back to itself from its lostness in the "they." . . . "Making up" for not choosing signifies *choosing to make this choice*—deciding for a potentiality-for-Being, and making this decision from one's own Self.[87]

Authentically breaking free of unreflective conformity smacks of voluntarism, tipping the balance to projection over thrownness when we project our very thrownness, choosing our unchosen situatedness. In reconciling ourselves to our ontological structure which has been determined once and for all, and in anxiety's bracketing of our ongoing occupations so that we may explicitly decide about them, authenticity compromises the early Heidegger's general rejection of foundationalism.

## Thrown from Being Itself into the Truth of Being

If his early work is ambiguous on the issue, Heidegger's *Kehre* decisively turns away from foundationalism. Dasein's apparently universal and permanent existential structure becomes man's essence, which is simply to be open to being.[88] To be a "man," a technical term here, comes to mean being aware of things understandingly, which varies considerably. Heidegger still rejects the idea of interpretation-free facts, but the fore-understandings have now been made historical. In an apparent reference to Kant's ahistorical structure, he now says that "grounding time-space does not design an empty table of categories. Rather . . . thinking is historical in its very core."[89] Heidegger's "existentialia"—that is, Dasein's ways of existing—were partially modeled on Kant, leading to a (rare) self-criticism that his early work had not sufficiently appreciated the significance of history.[90] Playing on *Being and Time*'s term for Dasein's way of being, Heidegger now says that "the ek-sistence of man is historical as such,"[91] which calls for a profound revision of his early project.

What is fundamental in fundamental ontology is incompatible with any building on it. Instead, after the meaning of Being had been clarified, the whole analytic of Dasein was to be more originally repeated in a completely different way. Thus, since the foundation of fundamental ontology is no foundation upon which something could be built, no *fundamentum inconcussum*, but rather a *fundamentum concussum* . . . whereas the word "foundation" contradicts the preliminary character of the analytic, the term "fundamental ontology" was dropped.[92]

The dream of fundamental ontology is over, dissipated in the flow of history.

For the late Heidegger, instead of *Being and Time*'s single set of modes of beings (readiness-to-hand, presence-at-hand, existence), anchored in the nature of Dasein, each epoch (pre-Socratic, ancient, medieval, modern, and contemporary) has its own understanding of being which determines its "beingness," or how all beings are in that age, including what he now calls "man."[93] Heidegger occasionally compares these understandings to the a priori because they are prior to and enable experience.[94] As we saw with the virtuous spiral, we cannot first gather neutral observations of the world from which to derive categories, since a particular way of understanding must always already orient the experiences our investigations start from. The ontological is father to the ontic.[95]

Heidegger now calls these understandings "sendings" from being, which I take to mean that they are not results of our conscious choice or transcendental faculties. This is what is sometimes called his "anti-humanism." In abandoning his early Kantian framework, Heidegger shifts the priority from the future to the past, letting thrownness swallow up projection: we receive our essential openness and our particular way of being open and have no control over them. "That Being itself and how Being itself concerns our thinking does not depend upon our thinking alone. That Being itself, and the manner in which Being itself, strikes a particular thinking, lets such thinking spring forth in springing from Being itself in such a way as to respond to Being as such."[96] It could not come from us in principle since our ways of thinking about how we should think depend on the contemporary understanding of being. To alter Kant, the order and regularity we see in reality, being introduces.

An understanding of being determines how people in a given age understand and interact with everything, though for the most part unthematically; like Dasein's understanding of being, the temporary ubiquity of an epoch's understanding renders it inconspicuous to those inhabiting it.[97] Each new epoch "bestow[s] on [man] the foundation of a new essence. This need displaces man into the beginning of a foundation of his essence. I say advisedly *a* foundation for we can never say that it is the absolute one."[98] What strikes one age as nonsense is common sense to others, so the transhistorical essence of man can have little content.[99] The great achievement of metaphysicians is to put their epoch's understanding into words;[100] their great failing is to stop there, and not ask why or how this particular way of seeing things came about.[101] Metaphysicians ascend from beings to their "beingness," that is, what it means "to be" at that age. For example, medievals defined being as having been created by God; anything that claims to exist must meet this criterion, and this idea determines how we think about all other philosophical questions. Metaphysically, the closer something comes to God, the more it is; ethically, the right thing to do is to carry out God's commandments and try to be a holy, god-fearing person, and so on. But we now need to move up another level, largely absent from Heidegger's early thought, from beingness to being itself or the truth of being, which is the bestowal or giving of particular forms of beingness. While this is nothing outside or beyond being's historical manifestations, neither is it exhausted by any particular instantiation.

Studying the history of philosophy helps us resist our tendency to take our own way of thinking as the obvious truth, similar to the way inauthentic Dasein took her own culture's values for granted in *Being and Time*. "What did we seek from this 'historical reflection'? To obtain a *distance* from what we take as self-evident, from what lies all too close to us."[102] Other understandings show us that our way of thinking is *one* way rather than *the* way. "Everything which we are inclined to regard as a 'necessary element of the culture' can one day pass away. So, for example, the 'objectifying' knowledge of physics rests upon the historical destining disclosure of Being."[103] We may not be able to step outside our epochal understanding, but neither should we inhabit it thoughtlessly. This leads to an epochal relativism because evaluative criteria only exist within particular understandings of being. The only way an era can be wrong is by claiming to be permanently, universally right.[104]

Our thrownness into an understanding of being eliminates at once the possibility of absolute justification, since we must use that understanding in any attempt to ground it, and the need for such reassurances. The fact that, from the perspective of the history of being, no individual understanding can claim superiority over others does not make them neutral candidates from which we choose the way we select our entrée from a menu. We are thrown into our understanding, which necessarily exerts a greater influence on us than do the dead options of earlier periods. A deep appreciation of thrownness takes both absolute foundationalism and relativism off the table at a stroke. First, epochal understandings of being, temporary as they may be, do in fact organize our thinking authoritatively. Although we may achieve some intellectual distance from our own epoch's understanding while contemplating alternatives, we will easily slip back unreflectively into it. Second, the absence of absolute truth changes "true for us" into truth, full stop.

We have determined truth as the manifestness of beings, by virtue of which we are fitted and bound in that which is. We have disavowed an absolute truth. That does not mean, however, that we advocate the thesis of an only relative truth; relativity is merely arbitrariness. The rejection of the standpoint of the absolute truth means, at the same time, the rejection of all relations between absolute and relative. If one cannot speak in this sense of an absolute truth, neither can one speak of relative truth.[105]

This is the idea I am calling "groundless grounds:" while they lack absolute grounding themselves, they nevertheless provide us with all the ground we need. Wittgenstein also indicates the difficulty of formulating the point: "one would rather say 'it rests on nothing'; but this gives a feeling of insecurity."[106]

With beings, man, and an overall Hegelian pattern of epochs[107] ruled out as ways to legitimate a particular understanding of being, we might be tempted to have being endow them with a seal of approval. After all, *"Being is akin to grounds, it is ground-like."*[108] Were being to say, "Let there be beings" and declare them good, then the way things are would be right and just. Heidegger calls this attempt to use being, often represented in a particular entity like God or substance, "ontotheology," and he considers it a profound mistake since being is the ultimate groundless ground. It gives us ways to understand and live, but no form of legitimizing can apply to it.

Being . . . offers us a reliance whose reliability cannot be surpassed anywhere. And yet Being offers us no ground and no basis—as beings do—to which we can turn, on which we can build, and to which we can cling. Being is the rejection of the role of such grounding: it renounces all grounding, is abyssal [*ab-gründig*].[109]

In making this point, Heidegger and Wittgenstein are both trying to escape the traditional, inappropriate conceptual framework: being is "both groundless and abyssless" (CPC 130) for Heidegger, while Wittgenstein says that "you can't in fact call language or grammar unsupported because there is no question of its being supported."[110]

Heidegger's tripartite theory of being which distinguishes between beings, beingness, and being itself accords with the Framework Argument: "Being 'is' in essence: ground/reason. Therefore being can never first have a ground/reason which would supposedly ground it. Accordingly, ground/reason is missing from being. Ground/reason remains at a remove from being. Being 'is' the abyss [*abgrund*] in the sense of such a remaining-apart of reason from being. To the extent that being as such grounds, it remains groundless."[111] Like Wittgenstein's form of life, that which determines our thinking and acting cannot itself be grounded in anything deeper. "The groundlike is groundless, what grounds, what presences as basis does not need the ground; that is, it is without something to which it could go back as something outside of it, there is no longer any back, no behind itself but pure presencing itself: the primordial."[112] All attempts to justify it already depend on a particular understanding to justify the source of that understanding, placing being "beyond explanation, for all explanation here necessarily falls short and comes too late, since it could only move within, and would have to appeal to, something that was first encountered as unconcealed in the displacement."[113]

Although tracing our understanding back to being may look like an explanation, these claims are meant to close off investigation. Instead of accounting for why we have these concepts, Heidegger's statements wall them off from explication, bringing us face to face with their unyielding, spade-turning resistance to comprehension. Like Silenus's rose that "blooms because it blooms" (PR 42–43), the claim that being sends epochal clearings adds no new information; we cannot investigate it as a causal relationship or survey past being's behavior to construct a predictive pattern.[114] Heidegger likes tautologies because, unlike explanations that reduce the phenomenon in question to something else, such as defining heat as motion, tautologies force attention onto the phenomenon, the whole phenomenon, and nothing but the phenomenon. "Language is not this and that, is not also something else besides itself. Language is language. Statements of this kind have the property that they say nothing and yet bind thinking to its subject matter with supreme conclusiveness."[115]

This applies above all to being as the event of beings manifesting themselves to us according to a certain conception of beingness, what Heidegger often names with some permutation of *"Ereignis,"* "event" or "appropriation."

We can only name it, because it will deign no discussion. For it is the place that encompasses all locales and time-play-spaces. . . . Propriating dispenses the open space of the clearing into which what is present can enter for a while. . . . What the propriating yields through the saying is never the effect of a cause, nor the consequence of a reason. . . . What propriates is propriation itself—and nothing besides. . . . There is nothing else to which propriation reverts, nothing in terms of which it might even be explained. Propriation is not an outcome or a result of something else; it is the bestowal whose giving reaches out in order to grant for the first time something like a "There is."[116]

Like "The rose blooms because it blooms," the claim that "being sends us our understandings" only looks like a causal explanation. This strategy resonates with one of Wittgenstein's favorite rhetorical devices. Whereas his early texts used tautologies to indicate the borders of intelligible thought,[117] he comes to prefer the stressed indicative to indicate the spade-turning moment: "the danger here, I believe, is one of giving a justification of our procedure where there is no such thing as a justification and we ought simply to have said: *that's how we do it*."[118] For Heidegger, "The 'because'

withers away in the play [of being's sendings]. The play is without 'why'"
(PR 113), while Wittgenstein writes, "Why do I not satisfy myself that I
have two feet when I want to get up from a chair? There is no why. I simply
don't. This is how I act" (OC §148).

Heidegger credits Kant with this insight: "in attempting to lay the ground
for Metaphysics, Kant was pressed in a way that makes the proper foundation into an abyss."[119] Kant places our transcendental faculties beyond the
realm of the explicable or justifiable since, as the Framework Argument
has it, any explanation of our forms and categories must employ them,
and so cannot offer a genuinely independent explanation or justification of
them.[120] The transcendental faculties are the foundation of all knowledge,
but an abyssal foundation or groundless ground since they themselves lack
ultimate justification. Our deepest essence is, "in the ultimate sense, accidental" (KPM 203), but this is original finitude in the sense that it has no
coherent contrast. Any necessity presupposes a particular form of reasoning, which is precisely what is at issue. No matter how far you take attempts
to justify it, the question of legitimacy will always reemerge on the far side
of each justificatory step.

## Alternate Language-Games

Heidegger sees philosophy—indeed, virtually everything we do—as intrinsically involved in a dialog with the past.[121] His early work requires the preparatory step of dismantling traditional views in order to see phenomena
afresh,[122] whereas in the later work being itself transpires historically.[123] He
wants to uncover "the origin of our basic ontological concepts by an investigation in which their 'birth certificate' is displayed" (BT 44/22). Only Hegel
rivals him for emphasizing the history of philosophy, whereas I'm not sure
anyone compares with Wittgenstein's disdain for it. He once exclaimed
in conversation, "here I am, a one-time professor of philosophy who has
never read a word of Aristotle!"[124] (One hesitates to imagine how Heidegger
might have reacted to this admission.) Cavell considers them paradigms of
the contrasting myths of having read everything and having read nothing
(Cavell 1995, 124). While Wittgenstein became increasingly sensitive to the
way language changes over time,[125] he never seriously studied its history.
What matters are the problems that bedevil us. These may have a long heritage—some which are buried deep within our grammar keep arising[126]—but
they can just as easily be of recent origin, emerging from new vocabularies
or newly forged connections among language-games.[127]

Despite this difference, we can bring the two into dialog by aligning Heidegger's epochal sendings with Wittgenstein's strange tribes.[128] The aim of both approaches is to show us that our own way of understanding and interacting with the world is not inevitable or simply the way things are, but rather just one possibility.[129]

Wittgenstein depicts heterogeneous language-games by describing people who behave in jarringly confounding ways. Even identifying their practice as a weird version of what we do is problematic since, as discussed above, the meaning of a word or practice is tied up with its applications. Were a culture to consider purple, red, and gold the primary colors, we would be unsure whether to call their scheme an alternate set of primary colors or a different understanding of the idea of primary color, since the meaning of the class is intertwined with its membership. As divergence from our way of doing things increases, the distinction between "They're doing the same thing as us, just in a really strange fashion" and "They're doing something different," or "We must be mistranslating their words," blurs, as Quine and Davidson argue.[130]

While he acknowledges the difficulty involved in identifying profoundly different language-games, Wittgenstein does not dismiss the possibility. As Bernard Williams writes, "other ways of seeing the world are not imaginatively inaccessible to us; on the contrary, it is one of Wittgenstein's aims to encourage such imagination."[131] Since the range of terms is not fixed in advance, identifications are largely up to the way various connections and analogies strike our trained reactions.[132] Indeed, Wittgenstein cites incommensurable language-games that we actually encounter, such as the difference between a religious outlook and a scientific one.[133] In addition to a few general facts about reality,[134] our interests and needs largely determine what we make of experience,[135] so we conceive alien language-games by imagining different general features of the world[136] or human nature or interests.[137]

This idea may strike many as far-fetched; recall Frege's branding illogical beings as suffering from "a hitherto unknown kind of insanity" (quoted at RFM 95). Since we rarely notice these inconspicuous facts, we seldom consider the potential consequences or even the possibility of their being different than they are. Our form of life and language-games seem so self-evident that they don't show up *as* a form at all; how else *could* one count or sell goods? We all begin from a default setting of unhesitating fidelity to our practices as simply the way to do things, with significantly diverging ones appearing manifestly absurd. "Reason—I feel like saying—presents itself to us as the gauge *par excellence* against which everything that we do, all our language games, measure and judge themselves. . . . We are used, as it were, to 'dismissing' [other patterns] as irrational, as corresponding to a low state of intelligence, etc."[138] Sir James Frazer's *Golden Bough* epitomizes this ethnocentrism for Wittgenstein, whom he found profoundly wrong-headed, even offensive.[139]

As we saw in chapter 4, the fundamental mistake lies in treating language-games as epistemic, that is, as based on beliefs which can be isolated and captured in assertions to be objectively assessed and directly compared with opposing claims. Just as our understanding of words exists in our skillful use of them rather than in definitions, so our deepest convictions are embodied in our behavior, in our reactions and interactions. Our world-view is reflexive rather than reflective, pragmatic rather than epistemic. Belief is not merely the adherence to a list of propositions, which would reduce culture-clashes to "*p* versus ~*p*" to be settled by deciding which is true.[140] According to Wittgenstein's holism, beliefs get their significance from their role within an overall context that encompasses actions, statements, emotions, and training, so we cannot simply extract propositions from diverse forms of life and lay them side-by-side. When a person who believes in the biblical miracles argues with someone who only credits scientific facts, the two are not disagreeing but speaking past each other—an adaptation of the earlier notion of the happy and unhappy men's different worlds.[141] The understanding we get from our world-picture is not and cannot be captured in a set of theses; it is a kind of orientation, a way of knowing one's way around not just one's physical environment but also the cultural medium we breathe in, what Heidegger calls being competent at living a certain kind of life. "Religious belief could only be something like a passionate commitment to a system of reference. Hence, although it's *belief*, it's really a way of living."[142] Beliefs thus resemble Kuhn's paradigmatic examples that model the proper practice of science, imparting not so much facts as a style of practice to the rising generation—just the aspects Joseph Rouse uses to connect Heidegger to Wittgenstein.[143]

Some passages in *On Certainty*, the book in which Wittgenstein most fully addresses this topic, seem to treat Moore's indubitable claims as an epistemic foundation for other claims, beliefs, or actions: I must believe, for example, that the earth has been around for a long time in order to undertake geological analysis, or I must believe that this is a chair if my sitting on it is to be a reasonable action.[144] However, I find this interpretation misleading and inconsistent with other parts of the book. Rather than providing a justificatory basis, it's better to just say that these "assumptions" never come up. Doubting them would topple huge swaths of our daily beliefs and practices, but not because they gave these actions a needed logical support. No, if these ideas become dubious we lose our grip on how to make knowledge claims or go about our daily activities in general.

> What is in question here is a kind of knowing one's way about. Now it would be wrong for me to say "I believe that it's a chair" because that would express my readiness for my statement to be tested. While "I know that it . . ." implies *bewilderment* if what I said was not confirmed.

> My "mental state," the "knowing," gives me no guarantee of what will happen. But it consists in this, that I should not understand where a doubt could get a foothold nor where a further test was possible. . . .

> Now I would like to regard this certainty, not as something akin to hastiness or superficiality, but as a form of life.[145]

Rather than finding that the possibility of dreaming undermines all empirically based knowledge claims, Wittgenstein is siding with Descartes's initial reaction that genuinely entertaining such possibilities is akin to madness.

We never explicitly learned our world-view but swallowed it down in the process of socialization. This is part of his holism, misleadingly put in terms of propositions here: "when we first begin to *believe* anything, what we believe is not a single proposition, it is a whole system of propositions. (Light dawns gradually over the whole)."[146] No one ever told me that my knowledge of my inner feelings is infallible; I just picked up a sense of its peculiar status from the way years of conversing with people gradually shaped my use.[147] In Heidegger's terms, "one" (*das Man*) doesn't question such things. Moore did discover an intriguing type of belief, but he misinterpreted its status. The role these beliefs play is altogether different from knowledge, rather than comprising extremely secure bits of knowledge.

There can be no foundation or universal standard of appraisal once reason has been made into an intra-game set of rules. As with Heidegger's epochal understandings, the ways we test beliefs are internal to particular games, and so incapable of standing outside to judge them. It is only within some framework or other that claims to knowledge make sense, rendering the notion of Knowledge Itself incoherent (OC §§140–144). Where both Moore and his skeptical opponent treat all propositions as epistemic and hence as subject to tests of truth and responsible belief,[148] disagreeing only on the results, Wittgenstein believes that parts of the web of belief have been removed from verification.

Similar to the distinction between the rules of a game and moves within that game, Wittgenstein distinguishes between grounds and what gets grounded. "If the true is what is grounded, then the ground is not *true*, nor yet false."[149] As that which determines what counts as true or false, the ground is not itself open to such appraisal, according to the Framework Argument. The fact that we absorbed this picture during our socialization and never tested its veracity makes us irresponsible reasoners, according to Socrates or Descartes; to allow any unsterilized claims into our belief system is to court the contagion of error. For Wittgenstein, the non-critical incorporation of beliefs is a necessary part of becoming an epistemic agent; accepting certain things without investigation is part of what makes investigation possible.[150] Like Neurath's boat, which can only be repaired underway, the vast majority of our beliefs must remain stable in order for us to be able to examine any particular belief.[151] As what determines rationality itself, "it is not based on grounds. It is not reasonable (or unreasonable). It is there—like our life."[152]

## The Principle of Reason

As we saw in chapter 4, Heidegger models thinking on responding to solicitations rather than on how we usually think of thematic deliberation. Explicit examination of ideas is very rare and derivative of the unthinking reactions that guide most of our behavior most of the time. Moreover, at the bottom of all thought lies a direct perception and response to the way ideas strike us, which is what prevents an infinite regress.

Like Wittgenstein, Heidegger applies this analysis to fundamental laws of logic. Neither thinker is challenging logic per se, but rather "the reigning and never-challenged doctrine of 'logic,'"[153] that is, its dominance over all thought. Heidegger praises Aristotle for recognizing that proofs are only appropriate in certain situations[154] since different topics call for different approaches: "'logic' and 'the logical' are simply not *the* ways to define thinking without further ado, as if nothing else were possible."[155] Where Wittgenstein primarily discusses the Law of Non-Contradiction, Heidegger focuses on the Principle of Reason,[156] the idea that everything that is has a reason for being rather than not being, and for being the way it is rather than some other way. This principle is integral to reasoning because the very act of investigating operates on the assumption that there are reasons to be found.

Heidegger shifts the inquiry from particular questions to the fact of questioning, asking "why then the 'why'?"[157] That is, why do we ask these questions? What reason do we have for believing that everything has a reason? The Perceptual Model of Thinking suggests that beings present themselves as "worthy of questioning," a more literal translation of Heidegger's term *fragwürdig* than the more common "questionable": this better captures the way in which topics evoke curiosity, drawing us in for a closer look.[158] Instead of a spontaneous act of pure rationality which deigns to turn one's countenance upon things, our investigations respond to solicitations from the world: we explain things because things call out to be explained, and in the ways they strike us as appropriate. Beings provoke investigation the way pies demand to be eaten, or chairs beckon us to take a load off, forming the inconspicuous background against which our practices of investigating reasons make sense. Wittgenstein writes that,

all testing, all confirmation and disconfirmation of a hypothesis takes place already within a system. And this system is not a more or less arbitrary and doubtful point of departure for all our arguments: no, it belongs to the essence of what we call an argument. The system is not so much the point of departure, as the element in which arguments have their life.[159]

Using a similar image, Heidegger calls science's adherence to the Principle of Reason "the element within which its cognition moves, as does the fish in water and the bird in air. Science responds to the demand. . . . Otherwise, it couldn't be what it is."[160]

Leibniz's greatness as a metaphysician lies in formulating this inconspicuous Principle of Reason,[161] but like all metaphysicians, he stops there without asking why this principle rules our thought. Had he taken this next step, he would have realized that the principle's demand that everything have a reason "immediately propels us into groundlessness" (PR 13) since following the principle all the way requires a reason for the principle itself.[162] But there can be no reason why everything must have a reason without already assuming the principle itself, and without a particular conception of what counts as a reason. The demand for grounds is an axiom we do and must "assume" without reflection or grounds (another translation of *Grund* in the German version of the Principle of Reason, "*Der Satz vom Grund*"), rather like Einstein's saying, "The *most incomprehensible* thing about the world is that it is at all comprehensible."

We find ourselves in a peculiar situation with respect to the laws of thought. For whenever we attempt to call the principles of thinking to mind, they inevitably become a theme of our thinking—and its laws. Behind us, in back of us as it were, the laws of thought lie ever ready and guide every step of our thinking about them. This directive is immediately evident and appears to check every attempt to properly think the laws of thought in a single move.[163]

Being grounds our interactions with beings by "sending" us a way to think about them but, as that which determines what counts as a ground within that epoch, it cannot itself be grounded. According to the Framework Argument, "man in his very nature belongs to that-which-regions, that is, he is released to it. Not occasionally, but—how shall we say it—prior to everything. The prior, of which we really can not think . . . because the nature of thinking begins here."[164]

This groundlessness would make thought viciously circular were we trying to enter it from outside—if, that is, starting from an epistemological veil of ignorance, we were to try justifying the principle of seeking reasons. Fortunately, being has "graced" us by "throwing" us into this circle from the beginning. We are always already underway in questioning, so we don't need an impossible rational baptism into rationality, just as training uses already present aspects of human nature for Wittgenstein. Arguing in exactly the opposite direction as Kant, it is our irremediable heteronomy that enables us to think and act, which is why the later Heidegger talks so much of trust in and gratitude to being: "The things for which we owe thanks are not things we have from ourselves. They are given to us" (WCT 142). Thrownness is a gift that enables, not an existential burden that compromises.[165] Playing with *Es gibt*, the German expression for "There is" which literally says "It gives," the fact that "there is" anything is a "given," both epistemologically and graciously. "I cannot exist at all without constantly responding to this or that address in a thematic or unthematic way; otherwise I could not take so much as a single step, nor cast a glance at something."[166] This idea gives rise to some of Heidegger's more anthropomorphic talk of gratitude and generosity, but he believes that the gift is actually more wondrous for having no explanatory agent. While the abyss beneath all grounds can provoke anxiety, "close by essential anxiety as the horror of the abyss dwells awe,"[167] rather like the argument given by some atheist biologists that evolution's occurring *without* divine instigation is more wondrous that with it.

Heidegger summarizes these ideas in *The Principle of Reason*:

Insofar as being essentially comes to be as ground/reason, it has no ground/reason. However this is not because it founds itself, but because every foundation—even and especially self-founded ones—remain inappropriate to being as ground/reason. . . . Being *qua* being remains ground-less. . . . But do we not fall into the fathomless with this leap? Yes and no. Yes—insofar as being can no longer be given a basis in the sense of beings and explained in terms of beings. No—insofar as being is now finally to be thought *qua* being. As what is to be thought, it becomes, from out of its truth, what gives a measure. The manner in which thinking thinks must conform to this measure. But it is not possible for us to seize upon this measure and what it offers through a computing and gauging. For us it remains that which is immeasurable.[168] However, so little does the leap allow thinking to fall into the fathomless in the sense of the complete void that in fact it first allows thinking to respond to being *qua* being, that is, to the truth of being.[169]

We must at least initially conform to what shows up as reasonable in the time and culture which give us the grounds to think and discover truths, which may ultimately allow the possibility of different ways of thinking. This is not a choice but a matter of finding ourselves magnetically oriented toward asking certain kinds of questions and accepting certain kinds of answers, which is why Heidegger defines thinking as responding. "What is a telling ground for something is not anything *I* decide,"[170] writes Wittgenstein.

Heidegger describes epochal change in a startlingly Kuhnian way: modern technology "is due to a revolution in leading concepts which has been going on for the past several centuries, and by which man is placed in a different world. . . . From this arises a completely new relation of man to the world and his place in it."[171] This by no means renders revolutions impossible, but it does take them out of the arena of control and rationality. Since the very conception of reason is at stake, there is no neutral position from which to evaluate incommensurable versions of it. Wittgenstein speaks of "conversion," "persuasion" or "combat"[172] among language-games, while Heidegger calls such epochal changes "leaps" that have been "sent" from being. We may be called upon to make creative responses, but we cannot instigate a change on our own—which is at least part of what Heidegger means by his famous comment, "Only a god can save us now." If we knew what to expect, as Derrida often argues, then the new understanding of being would not be a genuinely different way of thinking: "in waiting we leave open what we are waiting for."[173]

This is the paradox at the heart of our epoch: our drive toward autonomously determining ourselves is itself assigned to us; the injunction that we not rely on any ideas that we merely find rather than actively create is itself merely found to be important. We *find* this project reasonable and desirable, we don't *decide* that it is; earlier epochs would have found the same project incomprehensible or hubristic or mad. Thus, while Heidegger cannot label any understanding wrong, he does find an internal inconsistency in technology. We take ourselves to be completely in control of our thought and our machinery, but we cannot control, nor could we have created, this vast project of taking control of ourselves and nature.

For nature could never appear as a store of energy as it is now represented if atomic energy were not elicited, that is, set up by thought. . . . However, that physics has succeeded in framing nature in this manner is a meta-physical incident. . . . Such thoughts do not first come to be by way of mortal thinking. Rather our mortal thinking is always summoned by that thought to correspond to it or to renounce it. We human beings do not come upon thoughts; thoughts rather come to us mortals.[174]

We have been given the modern crusade to refuse all givens.

The culprit is the basic problem of metaphysics: "we forget to ask: What is the ground that enabled modern technology to discover and set free new energies in nature?"[175] "Forgetting" about being lets us take the credit for our actions and thoughts all the way down, fostering an illusion of absolute mastery which then gets reinforced by our technological might. With a subtle nudge, however, this image of total mastery inverts into an acknowledgment of our utter dependence, both on being-sent this technological way of thinking and on nature's cooperation. This is how I understand Heidegger's use of Hölderlin's line that "Where the danger is, however, there grows / that which saves as well" (using Thomson's translation 2011, 58n31) and also his praise for Aristotle's four causes, which place the craftsman/technician as the efficient cause within a network of other needed factors: this corrects modernity's exclusive focus on the efficient cause for the sake of greater predictive and manipulative power.[176] Wittgenstein uses a favorite Heideggerian metaphor to make a similar point: "you cannot draw the seed up out of the earth. All you can do is give it warmth and moisture and light; then it must grow" (CV 42).

This abyss (*Ab-grund*) can disturb: we demand responsible reasoning behind our actions and beliefs, but this requirement itself can have no reason. Wittgenstein's interlocutors worry about cognitive nihilism—"but what becomes of logic now? Its rigour seems to be giving way here"[177]—but this anxiety is based on a misunderstanding. At the end of all justifying must, as a conceptual necessity, lie acceptance; no matter what we put in our foundation, we still have to accept it as grounding. "At the foundation of well-founded belief lies belief that is not founded" or, to modify the translation slightly, "at the ground-level (*Grunde*) of well-grounded (*begründeten*) belief lies ungrounded (*unbegründete*) belief."[178] Thus Wittgenstein's objection to Moore isn't that he has a *bad* answer to skepticism, but that he answers the skeptic at all, like Heidegger's criticism of the "scandal" of continued attempts to prove the existence of the external world. As soon as we start justifying our thinking, we've given the game to the skeptic because this demand can never be met in the absolute sense toward which she will always push us. Moore (inadvertently) shows how our thinking doesn't stop at analytic truths or self-justifying intuitive perceptions of Forms or God or Logic, but at apparently contingent facts like my name or that I am presently in the United States—facts that have been withdrawn from further inquiry. For Heidegger, beliefs bottom out in very basic conceptions of what makes a being a being: that God created all things for our good, that everything has a reason which we can use to manipulate natural forces, and so on. These pictures set the framework within which the people of a given era live their lives and think their thoughts. While ultimately groundless, they give us all the ground we can have or need.

Lacking supra-game criteria, reasons and truths become relative, either to particular language-games or epochal understandings: "a *reason* can only be given *within* a game. The links of the chain of reasons come to an end, at the boundary of the game" (PG 97). Although Truth has been taken off the table, particular truths within smoothly functioning games remain perfectly serviceable. Semantic nihilism only worries us when we spurn such humble fare as unworthy imitators of true Truth—a symptom of metaphysics-withdrawal.

"But is there then no objective truth? Isn't it true, or false, that someone has been on the moon?" If we are thinking within our system, then it is certain that no one has ever been on the moon. Not merely is nothing of the sort ever seriously reported to us by reasonable people, but our whole system of physics forbids us to believe it. For this demands answers to the questions "How did he overcome the force of gravity?" "How could he live without an atmosphere?" and a thousand others which could not be answered. But suppose that instead of all these answers we met the reply: "We don't know *how* one gets to the moon, but those who get there know at once that they are there; and even you can't explain everything." We should feel ourselves intellectually very distant from someone who said this.[179]

As some commentators have noted,[180] Wittgenstein is here playing two perspectives against each other. From an uncritical position within our system, it is as true as true gets that—to change Wittgenstein's outdated example—I am writing in English or that this cup is gray. We misconstrue the nature of knowledge, however, if we take this to mean that anyone must admit this no matter what or be guilty of irrationality or betrayal of their own deep nature or a conflict with reality. "And here the strange thing is that when I am quite certain of how the words are used, have no doubt about it, I can still give no *grounds* for my way of going on" (OC §307).

Metaphysics attempts to escape one's worldview or form of life in order to latch onto something that transcends all perspectives, something that can rule on and rule over all individual views; but the entities posited as transcending all systems, such as Truth or Reality in-itself or God are, like Hegel's thing-in-itself-for-us, posited by and only function within systems. These systems or games can be incommensurable, with no possibility of a common measurement or neutral judge, a Great Umpire in the Sky. "Somebody may reply like a rational person and yet not be playing our game."[181] We should say no more than that their behavior is just not what makes sense to us: "there's only one thing that can be wrong with the meaning of a word, and that is that it is unnatural . . . unnatural for *us*. . . . We just don't go on in that way."[182] While we cannot take up a wholly external point of view, we can inhabit ours critically, without the illusions of metaphysical grounding.

This incommensurability also means that we cannot get the players of strange language-games to start acting normally (that is, as we do) simply by reasoning with them, since the very thing we're trying to teach them is our way of reasoning. Just as a child isn't rationalized through arguments— were she susceptible to arguments, she would already be rational—but through training, so bringing others to think as we do happens through nonrational means.

Supposing we met people who did not regard [the propositions of physics] as a telling reason. Now, how do we imagine this? Instead of the physicist, they consult an oracle. (And for that we consider them primitive.) Is it wrong for them to consult an oracle and be guided by it?—If we call this "wrong" aren't we using our language-game as a base from which to *combat* theirs?

And are we right or wrong to combat it? Of course there are all sorts of slogans which will be used to support our proceedings.

Where two principles really do meet which cannot be reconciled with one another, then each man declares the other a fool and heretic.

I said I would "combat" the other man,—but wouldn't I give him *reasons*? Certainly; but how far do they go? At the end of reasons comes *persuasion*. (Think what happens when missionaries convert natives).[183]

The converted may very well look back on their conversion as a shedding of superstition and an acquisition of rationality (or conversely, as escaping a coldly materialistic viewpoint to accept God's loving embrace). Indeed, accepting such a meta-narrative of "progress" is part of what it means to be fully converted. But the converted will only acknowledge the decisive data or arguments as relevant and obviously true in retrospect. We must first compel her to start thinking like us before she will find our reasons for thinking like us compelling, "brainwashing" her into rationality. At a "meta" level, all argumentation is ad hoc.

While there are elements of pragmatism in the later Wittgenstein (and in the early Heidegger), he accepts no neutral or universally shared desiderata, the successful acquisition of which could offer a neutral way to evaluate various methods for attaining this desideratum. Frazer sees a rain dance as a primitive attempt to manipulate nature to get what one wants. On such a reading, this ritual is simply dumb science: the natives are doing the same kind of thing as our scientists—just very, very badly. Wittgenstein argues that what counts as a good, as well as what counts as successful and appropriate ways to achieve goods, are all internal considerations. Sometimes we justify our practices by their success, certainly, especially since these practices are often teleologically organized; the point of chess—checkmate—highlights which aspects are essential to the game and which are accidental.[184] But it is still up to us to determine what the point is, and what counts as successfully achieving it. Shooting an enemy in the back may get the job done, but without honor; whether such a deed should be cause for pride or shame, whether it counts as success or failure depends on the culture's overall worldview. Heidegger makes the same point: "the truth of a principle can in general never be demonstrated by success. For the *interpretation* of a success *as* a success is, after all, accomplished with the help of the presupposed but unfounded principle."[185]

Furthermore, many of our actions have no purpose. It's simply not true that everything we do is organized around achieving practical ends.

We can now see why we should call those who have a different logic contradicting ours mad. The madness would be like this: (a) The people would do something which we'd call talking or writing. (b) There would be a close analogy between our talking and theirs, etc. (c) Then we would suddenly see an entire discrepancy between what we do and what they do—in such a way that the whole point of what they are doing seems to be lost, so that we would say, "What the hell's the point of doing this?"

But is there a *point* in everything we do? What is the point of our brushing our hair the way we do? Or when watching the coronation of a king, one might ask, "What is the point of all this?" If you wish to give the point, you might tell the history of it.

What was the point of imitating gothic? It isn't clear in all that we do, what the point is.—But in the case of the people distributing the sticks [in a way that made no apparent sense], we would be struck by the pointlessness. . . . Then what is wrong? They do this. And they get along all right. What more do you want?[186]

Many things we do are neither based on epistemic beliefs nor aimed at practical goals. No, we do some things because that's how we were brought up; that's just what one does.

Burning in effigy. Kissing the picture of one's beloved. That is *obviously not* based on the belief that it will have some specific effect on the object which the picture represents. It aims at satisfaction and achieves it. Or rather: it *aims* at nothing at all; we just behave this way and then we feel satisfied.[187]

Wittgenstein finds this kind of behavior so common that "one could almost say that man is a ceremonial animal,"[188] which undermines the evaluation of games from the supposedly straightforward standpoint of success.

Wittgenstein's views here are close to a number of continental thinkers influenced by Heidegger who, while not denouncing reason, eye it suspiciously. Foucault worries about the power given to Officers of Rationality such as psychiatrists' authority to lock up the mad or pronounce forms of sexuality abnormal. Lyotard adopts the notion of language-games to denounce the way one game's judgments obscure other games' unique features (the "*differend*") during the supposedly innocent preliminary step of getting all disputing parties to speak the same language.[189] And Levinas's central point is that reason, by its very nature, assimilates otherness to the same, both epistemologically and ethically. These views are often called "post-colonial" since they resist an intellectual "imperialism" that resembles missionaries forcing indigenous people to wear proper clothes and worship real gods (in this context, Wittgenstein's parenthetical aside about missionaries is very suggestive).

Particular claims get their justification from their particular language-game, which in turn depends upon a form of life and the cultural upbringing of those who share it. This historical complex, in turn, is not justified or grounded, nor can it be. It cannot be true or false, rational or irrational, both because it is not epistemic and because it determines what truth or rationality are. Besides, justification must come to an end somewhere, inevitably leaving the last step unjustified. It is here that Wittgenstein's pointing statements come in: "*this* is how we think. *This* is how we act. *This* is how we talk about it."[190] "Why do we do this sort of thing? This is the sort of thing we do do."[191] PI §217 explicitly connects the moment when we can only say, "This is simply what I do" to the point at which "I have exhausted the justifications [*Gründe*]." Like Heidegger's tautologies, these apparently empty statements battle philosophy's drive to explain where there can be no explanation. "The difficult thing here is not, to dig down to the ground; no, it is to recognize the ground that lies before us as the ground. . . . Our disease is one of wanting to explain."[192] Wittgenstein considered "everything is what it is, and not another thing" for the epigraph to *Philosophical Investigations*.[193]

The demand for grounds creates an infinite regress since any reason cited must itself be grounded, so Wittgenstein prefers to stop the chain before it gets started: "why do you demand explanations? If they are given you, you will once more be facing a terminus. They cannot get you any further than you are at present."[194] In 1916, he praised prescientific cultures for recognizing, far more fully than do our scientific cultures, the necessary end of explanation.[195] While seeking reasons or explanations makes perfect sense within a game—indeed, it's an important part of many games—we cannot do this for the game as a whole.

*What* counts as a reason for an assumption can be given *a priori* and determines a calculus, a system of transitions. But if we are asked now for a reason for the calculus itself, we see that there is none. . . .

   "Surely the rules of grammar by which we act and operate are not arbitrary!" Very well; why then does a man think in the way he does, why does he go through these activities of thought? (This question of course asks for reasons, not for causes.) Well, reasons can be given within the calculus, and at the very end one is tempted to say "it just is very probably, that things will behave in this case as they always have"—or something similar. A turn of phrase which masks the beginning of the chain of reasons. (The creator as the explanation at the beginning of the world).[196]

Although our worldview fully grounds our beliefs, it itself cannot be grounded. Heidegger makes the same point: "here questioning already counts as knowing, because no matter how essential and decisive an answer might be, the answer cannot be other than the penultimate step in the long series of steps of a questioning founded in itself."[197]

## An Ethics of Explanatory Restraint

Wittgenstein's and Heidegger's fight against philosophy's drive to explain goes hand in hand with their method of reminding us of hyper-obvious facts about mundane existence, rather unimpressive stuff compared with the grandiose metaphysical systems of lore. Their conclusions don't sate the philosophical appetite but frustrate it, which turns out to be quite tenacious. The history of philosophy is a graveyard full of bygone tales of intellectual manifest destiny, whose ghosts cannot easily be exorcised by saying, "this is what we do." "It is so difficult to find the *beginning*. Or, better: it is difficult to begin at the beginning. And not try to go further back."[198]

   Humility is not a word that typically leaps to mind when discussing Heidegger, but his early work does concentrate on the mundane features of everyday life, albeit with an air of pageantry that Wittgenstein was constitutionally averse to. An important part of Heidegger's later work is the chastising of reason's pride. We must acknowledge the ineradicably mysterious way our understanding befalls us with a grateful awe that some have called mystical.

The origin of the principles of thinking, the place of the thinking that posits them, the essence, that is, essential presencing of this place and its locality—all that remains in the dark for us. This darkness is perhaps always in play, in all thinking. Human beings cannot avoid it. Rather, they must learn to recognize the dark as the ineluctable and to keep at a distance those prejudices which destroy the lofty sway of the dark. . . . The dark is rather the secret mystery of what is light. . . . It is hard to keep the dark pure and clear, to preserve it from admixture with a brightness that does not belong to it.[199]

He finds such efforts at illumination not just futile, but something like sacrilegious, insofar as sacrilege is still possible after the death of God.

Heidegger's later work develops an ethics of explanatory restraint. Whereas *Being and Time* retains a version of Kantian autonomy—Dasein's call of conscience comes from herself because the self represents "the sole authority which a free existing can have"[200]—his later work reverses this, arguing that only something beyond us can be truly commanding. Comprehending a phenomenon is a form of mastering it—transparently so in the way science leads to technology—which filters out whatever does not aid our getting what we want as irrelevant or subjective.[201] Like Wittgenstein's take on Frazer, Heidegger says that the gods flee when we regard them as superstitious accounts of natural phenomena that are better captured by science. The more we understand, the more control we have and the less obligated to anything outside ourselves we feel, leading eventually to nihilism. "Beings *are*, yet they remain abandoned by Being and left to themselves, so as to be mere objects of our contrivance. All goals beyond men and peoples are gone."[202] A universe drained of all significance beyond the efficient achievement of our desires is a universe which cannot sustain a good human life, a meaningful existence. This is what he means when he says that "no one dies for mere values," or, in regards to philosophical explanation, "before the *causa sui*, man can neither fall to his knees in awe nor can he play music and dance before this god."[203] Even those committed to a hard-nosed scientific worldview cast their project as a noble quest to conquer barbarous superstition and cleanse humanity of a dark curse from ages past; witness Richard Dawkins.

Just as Wittgenstein praised primitive belief in the gods over modern science because the latter fosters the illusion of complete grounding, so Heidegger welcomes the Principle of Reason's revelation of the abyss beneath our feet. It "is, as the supreme fundamental principle, something underivable, the sort of thing which puts a check on thinking" (PR 45). This check instills wonder and gratitude, restraining our attempts to organize all of reality around maximizing the satisfaction of our desires: "everything depends on our inhering in this clearing that is propriated by Being itself— never made or conjured by ourselves. We must overcome the compulsion to lay our hands on everything" (N III:181). Ultimately, both Wittgenstein's basic human reactions and Heidegger's sendings of being escape rational justification or evaluation. Both want to rethink the matter outside the traditional categories. Just as Wittgenstein calls our form of life or language "akin both to what is arbitrary and to what is non-arbitrary" (Z §358), so Heidegger says that "one cannot inquire into the 'correctness' of a projecting-open at all—and certainly not into the correctness of *that* projecting-open through which on the whole the clearing as such is grounded. . . . Is then the projecting-open pure caprice? No, it is the utmost necessity, but of course not a necessity in the sense of a logical conclusion" (CP 229–230/§204). They are the source of all reasoning, and hence cannot be rational or irrational themselves: "the grounds that essentially determine humans as having a *Geschick* ["destiny"] stem from the essence of grounds. Therefore these grounds are abysmal" (PR 37).

We must appreciate both parts of the phrase, "groundless grounds."[204] On the one hand, these understandings of Being do in fact ground an age. They constitute the deepest level of intelligibility we can access, and they determine and support the thought and action of an epoch. These ways of understanding constitute a ground by allowing us to experience anything, and by shaping how we experience almost everything.[205] On the other hand, these grounds are themselves groundless. They cannot be justified or legitimated because they are the source of our ways of justification and legitimation. Explanations of why any particular understanding replaced its predecessor necessarily use criteria derived from a specific understanding, and so are inextricably partial and partisan. Histories of thought seem condemned to be either relativist or Whig. As Heidegger puts it at one point, "*ab*-ground is ab-*ground*" (CP 265/§242); the abyss serves as a ground for mortals to stand and walk upon.

## Hume

At the end of chapter 4, I showed how Aristotle's notion of *phronêsis* anticipated many of Heidegger and Wittgenstein's views on thinking. In particular, *phronêsis* acknowledges its dependence—becoming skilled requires factors such as a good upbringing and society—and its limitations—there are times when argumentation falters, especially when trying to convince someone who lacks those prerequisites. Of course, one shining hope for Aristotle is the apprehension of eternal truths by *nôus*, a divine or semidivine part of us that transcends the human. This apprehension would be a grounding or grounded ground—ultimately, lines of argument would come

to rest in that which is necessarily true, that which can be no other way—
an idea quite distant from Heidegger's and Wittgenstein's stopping points
which are, metaphysically speaking, contingent. We may find other ways
of thinking closed or unnatural to us, at present, but we cannot rule them
out as Wrong.

If we want to find a sophisticated discussion of contingency in the canon,
the figure to turn to is David Hume, a philosopher Heidegger seems never
to have come across in his constant readings of the history of philosophy,
despite Hume's importance to Kant, an essential thinker for Heidegger.[206]
There are plenty of points of close agreement between Hume and Wittgenstein's early work: the fact–value distinction that renders ethics "transcendental" for Wittgenstein, subjective for Hume;[207] the atomistic rejection of
necessary causality in the natural world,[208] especially concerning the connection between our will and our actions,[209] which thus classifies induction
as psychological;[210] the rejection of the subject as the unified or unifying
thinker of our thoughts;[211] the division of legitimate statements into contingent descriptions of the world and necessary but empty propositions;[212] and
the subsequent division between sensible claims and nonsense, although
Wittgenstein's passing over the latter in silence is a bit more restrained
than Hume's proposed torching of libraries.[213] Furthermore, these points
of agreement take place within similar overall projects. Indeed, we could
seamlessly transplant Hume's description of his undertaking in the *Enquiry
into Human Understanding* into the *Tractatus*'s preface with but a single substitution. Hume writes that "the only method of freeing learning, at once,
from these abstruse questions [of metaphysics], is to enquire seriously into
the nature of human understanding"—read "language" for Wittgenstein—
"and show, from an exact analysis of its powers and capacity, that it is by
no means fitted for such remote and abstruse subjects" (HE 12).

We find deeper connections with Humean ideas in Wittgenstein's later
work, as well as in Heidegger's early thought. Hume builds his philosophy
around the contrast between "common life" in which we're talking with our
friends or playing backgammon at the local pub, and the strange thoughts
that steal in upon us in the dusty solitude of our study—a division that parallels Wittgenstein's and Heidegger's etiology of philosophical confusion.
Hume focuses on "ideas, which, in common life and to a careless view,
are very clear and intelligible, but when they pass through the scrutiny of
the profound sciences . . . afford principles, which seem full of absurdity
and contradiction."[214] The cessation of normal activity leads to the atomistic events that breed bizarre theories, the way Heidegger's present-at-hand
objects direct distorted metaphysics and Wittgenstein's meaning-objects

mangle our thoughts about language. Instead of illuminating how we think, disengagement renders our usual experiences of causal links, equipment, other people, and language mystifying; this in turn leads to either a skeptical abandonment of these ideas or the construction of baroque metaphysical theories to underwrite them.

The contrast between the vulgar, thoughtless many and the learned few has been around in philosophy since Parmenides, but Hume's innovation is that he sides with the vulgar. The fact that normally we don't bother about the validity of our expectation that striking a match will ignite it is not a sign of irresponsible carelessness but a kind of wisdom that is greater than that achieved by "false philosophy"—that is, the metaphysics that reaches its absurdly logical conclusion in the carelessness of Pyrrho, the Mr. Magoo of ancient Greece. Thankfully, our "form of life" saves us from such a fate. We humans simply cannot keep up such an abstemious epistemology, no matter our resolve.[215] Hume explains our "average everyday" thoughts and actions by appealing not to rational justification, but to features "kneaded into our frame," reactions "inseparable from our make and constitution."[216]

Hume anticipates the Perceptual Model of Thinking with his analysis of our immediate, unreflective connection with others, which allows a communication of feeling that stands in no need of intellectual inference or interference; all three agree that we directly perceive others' feelings. Indeed, Hume bases his entire ethics on "fellow-feeling," that is, our spontaneous pleasure in seeing others' happiness: "others enter into the same humour, and catch the sentiment, by a contagion or natural sympathy."[217] The fact that another's joy seeps into my state of mind both lays the ground for morality and short-circuits solipsism before it can get started. Compare Wittgenstein:

But can't I imagine that the people around me are automata, lack consciousness, even though they behave in the same way as usual?—If I imagine it now—alone in my room—I see people with fixed looks (as in a trance) going about their business—the idea is perhaps a little uncanny. But just try to keep hold of this idea in the midst of your ordinary intercourse with others, in the street, say! Say to yourself, for example: "The children over there are mere automata; all their liveliness is mere automatism." And you will either find these words becoming quite meaningless; or you will produce in yourselves some kind of uncanny feeling.[218]

And Heidegger:

because Dasein, for its own part, cannot first be subjected to proof, the necessity of truth cannot be proved either. It has no more been demonstrated that there ever has "been" an "actual" sceptic (though this is what has at bottom been believed in the refutations of skepticism, in spite of what these undertake to do) than it has been demonstrated that there are any "eternal truths." (BT 271–272/229)

Like Wittgenstein's form of life and Heidegger's being-with, Hume argues that, were we to lack fellow-feeling, we would not be able to learn moral truths by reason alone. "If morality had naturally no influence on human passions and actions, 'twere in vain to take such pains to inculcate it; and nothing wou'd be more fruitless than that multitude of rules and precepts, with which all moralists abound."[219]

Another basic feature of human nature that Hume focuses on is 'custom' or 'habit,' that is, our tendency to expect like effects from like causes after repeated exposure to their consistent spatial contiguity and temporal succession. Seeing matches getting struck and then burst into flame many times creates the automatic expectation of flame upon seeing a match getting struck. This is not a matter of ratiocination or evaluation of evidence, since "custom operates before we have time for reflexion."[220] This instinct must prime us to react in certain ways if we are to perceive causal relations, much less rise to the abstract level of scientifically analyzing them. Reasoning cannot forge this link; any attempt to connect cause and effect rationally founders on circular reasoning by relying on past instances to prove that we can rely on past instances to predict future ones. But Hume's point is precisely that this lack of justification does not undermine its legitimacy. Not only *will* instinct overcome all cool reasoning, but it should and, indeed, *must* if we are to survive. Rather than exposing flaws in common life in order to inspire us to surpass such shaky ideas for higher truths, philosophy undermines itself, leaving us back where we started, but chastened, willing to accept our daily thoughts and acts.

Hume's analysis of causality runs parallel to Wittgenstein's discussion of rule-following, as has been noted by a number of commentators.[221] What we imagine to be there—a secret power necessarily connecting cause and effect, or inherent moral qualities, or a substantial self, or a rule's complete application—is not.[222] Nothing in the statement or thought of a rule, or in the structure of reality contains its future applications, and yet we rarely disagree about how to go on due to our nature and training. Whereas Wittgenstein talks of tribes, Martians, and aspect-blind people who, bereft of our form of life, are unable to read arrows or pictures the right way, and Heidegger invokes earlier epochs when our common sense would have been nonsense, Hume constructs the thought experiment of Adam, a man with fully formed rational and sensory faculties but unmarked by experience.[223] No matter how intelligently or thoroughly he investigates the world around him, neither pure thought nor isolated empirical data can foretell effects from causes, consigning him to a blooming buzzing whirlwind of events that will soon "put an end to [his] miserable existence" (HE 160). A parallel argument applies to ethics: a person lacking sympathy or fellow-feeling would be rendered "mind-blind," incapable of discerning the slightest hint of moral goodness or badness in the world (HE 235). All three thinkers argue that people relying entirely on reason—philosophical Vulcans, if you will—would not be perfected versions of humans but intellectual cripples, unable to accomplish the simple tasks we effortlessly do everyday. Hence, we mistake the nature of reason and the role it plays in most of our behavior.

Instead, all three turn to nonrational features which are inborn or acquired through socialization. Heidegger depicts the entrance into the social, linguistic space of *das Man* as enabled by a built-in being-with and motivated by a yearning for identity and acceptance. For Wittgenstein, it is our form of life—our propensity to react in similar ways to similar stimuli—combined with years of largely tacit training that allows people to follow most rules without effort, disagreement or reflection. Hume credits custom or habit and fellow-feeling as the factors that enable us to draw, respectively, scientific and ethical conclusions from experience.[224] He pounds home the point that this is no cool examination of the steps of a syllogism with assent withheld until definitive results are in hand. He says over and over that "the supposition, *that the future resembles the past*, is not founded on arguments of any kind," "*that belief is more properly an act of the sensitive, than of the cogitative part of our natures.*"[225] Rather than recoiling in horror at the rational nihilism that seems to follow from these ideas, we should make peace with the fact that, while nothing metaphysical undergirds our applications, our smashing success in acting harmoniously the vast majority of the time shows that nothing of the sort is needed. Groundless grounds are all we have ever had, which proves their adequacy.

The first part of Hume's argument reverses the traditional priority of reason, making it the slave of passion (HT 415). The second undermines the reason–passion distinction itself by claiming that "reason is nothing but a wonderful and unintelligible instinct in our souls."[226] One of his arguments for this places reflexive unreflective reactions within abstract thinking, thus anticipating the Perceptual Model of Thinking and the idea of intellectual solicitations.

Thus all probable reasoning is nothing but a species of sensation. 'Tis not solely in poetry and music, we must follow our taste and sentiment, but likewise in philosophy. When I am convinc'd of any principle, 'tis only an idea which strikes more strongly upon me. When I give the preference to one set of arguments above another, I do nothing but decide from my feeling concerning the superiority of their influence.[227]

Now this is all bound up with a rather obsolete faculty psychology and hydraulic conception of belief, but the view of reason as at least partially a matter of nonrational reactions is revolutionary, and it is shared by all three philosophers: "belief consists merely in a certain feeling or sentiment; in something, that depends not on the will, but must arise from certain determinate causes and principles, of which we are not masters" (HT 624). It is just this conception of thinking as response that Heidegger deploys to overcome our age's notion of autonomy and Wittgenstein uses to escape the Interpretation Aporia.

Hume realizes how unorthodox and shocking this view is: "men will scarce ever be persuaded, that effects of such consequence can flow from principles, which are seemingly so inconsiderable, and that the far greatest part of our reasonings, with all our actions and passions, can be deriv'd from nothing but custom and habit" (HT 118). Downgrading humans from just beneath angels to barely above animals outrages most philosophical self-conceptions, but no one ever accused Hume of shying from a fight. While Heidegger clings to a sharp (albeit occasionally softened) division between Dasein and animals, Wittgenstein agrees with Hume on their continuity, even citing causal "inferences" as a shared trait. "The squirrel does not infer by induction that it is going to need stores next winter as well. And no more do we need a law of induction to justify our actions or our predictions."[228] For Hume, reasoning "is not directed by any such relations or comparisons of ideas, as are the proper objects of our intellectual faculties. Though the instinct be different, yet still it is an instinct, which teaches a man to avoid the fire; as much as that, which teaches a bird, with such exactness, the art of its incubation."[229] Wittgenstein discusses Hume's central topic in a very similar way.

The character of the belief in the uniformity of nature can perhaps be seen most clearly in the case in which we fear what we expect. Nothing could induce me to put my hand into a flame—although after all it is *only in the past* that I have burnt myself. . . .

"Why do you believe that you will burn yourself on the hot-plate?"—Have you reasons for this belief; and do you need reasons?[230]

As we have seen, Wittgenstein chooses immediate reactions like recoiling from flame as paradigms of thinking over the more traditional candidates like mathematics or logic.

Hume also employs an infinite-regress argument to prove that cogitation alone cannot achieve answers. Indulging our "sifting humor" (HE 32) indefinitely can only end in ruin, precisely because it never ends. The demand for reasons cannot be sated since it can—and indeed must, if it is live up to its own conception of responsibility—present the demand for a further reason to each new reason that is adduced. Reason is the four-year-old child who, to every answer given, repeats "Why?" As any parent knows, the only way to stop this line of inquiry is to distract the child, since this endless questioning cannot be satisfied on its own terms. Foundational beliefs won't do the trick, since an unappeasable reason will need to scrutinize the reasons for accepting those beliefs as foundational, thereby prolonging the regress.

We must make peace with our all-too-human limitations and accept the fact that we have to stop at unjustified instincts so deeply entrenched in us that any attempt to justify them must perforce rely upon them.[231] In other words, one "cannot defend his reason by reason" (HT 187). Every inquiry stops at a bedrock of basic principles and brute facts that cannot themselves be accounted for.

Hence we may discover the reason why no philosopher, who is rational and modest, has ever pretended to assign the ultimate cause of any natural operation. . . . The utmost effort of human reason is to reduce the principles, productive of natural phenomena, to a greater simplicity, and to resolve the many particular effects into a few general causes. . . . But as to the causes of these general causes, we should in vain attempt their discovery; nor shall we ever be able to satisfy ourselves, by any particular explication of them. These ultimate springs and principles are totally shut up from human curiosity and enquiry. . . . Thus the observation of human blindness and weakness is the result of all philosophy. (HE 30–31)

Hume happily applies this principle to his own work. Custom on the epistemological side, and fellow-feeling on the ethical side, represent his inquiry's highest or deepest levels, which resist further explanation or justification.

It is needless to push our researches so far as to ask, why we have humanity or a fellow-feeling with others. It is sufficient, that this is experienced to be a principle in human nature. We must stop somewhere in our examination of causes; and there are, in every science, some general principles, beyond which we cannot hope to find any principle more general.[232]

Bottoming out at groundless grounds is no flaw or limitation, since the alternative philosophy dreams of is incoherent. Uncovering these boundaries indicates that we have done all that can be done concerning the matter, that we have found the point where spades are turned.

It also fulfills the promise of ancient skepticism: it pacifies our restless questioning.

When we see, that we have arrived at the utmost extent of human reason, we sit down contented; tho' we be perfectly satisfied in the main of our ignorance and perceive that we can give no reason for our most general and most refined principles, beside our experience of their reality. . . . And as this impossibility of making any farther progress is enough to satisfy the reader, so the writer may derive a more delicate satisfaction from the free confession of his ignorance, and from his prudence in avoiding that error, into which so many have fallen, of imposing their conjectures and hypotheses on the world for the most certain principles. When this mutual contentment and satisfaction can be obtained betwixt the master and scholar, I know not what more we can require of our philosophy.[233]

Hume emphasizes this goal a number of times:

these are therefore the principles of union or cohesion among our simple ideas. . . . Its effects are every where conspicuous; but as to its causes, they are mostly unknown, and must be resolv'd into *original* qualities of human nature, which I pretend not to explain. Nothing is more requisite for a true philosopher, than to restrain the intemperate desire of searching into causes, and having establish'd any doctrine upon a sufficient number of experiments, rest contented with that.[234]

Another way to put the idea would be, "the real discovery is the one that makes me capable of stopping doing philosophy when I want to.—The one that gives philosophy peace, so that it is no longer tormented by questions which bring *itself* in question" (PI §133). Or Heidegger's insistence that we preserve the mystery of being's sendings by not interrogating their causes or reasons.[235]

The infinite regress of justification constitutes a problem only if one demands reasons for everything. Since this demand cannot in principle be satisfied, "the understanding, when it acts alone, and according to its more general principles, entirely subverts itself."[236] It is from this self-undermining perspective that "any interpretation still hangs in the air along with what it interprets, and cannot give it any support" (PI §198), and the universal demand for reasons "immediately propels us into groundlessness" (PR 13). While we tend to credit reason with everything important, following out the ideal of pure rationality shows that reason cannot deliver on its promises, that fully rational creatures would lack features that are indispensable to our material, social, and even intellectual lives. The fully examined life cannot survive. Wittgenstein performs a *reductio* on purely rational rule-following, not by flatly denying it but by giving it every chance to develop its line of reasoning and then showing how each attempt fails. Heidegger demonstrates that the Principle of Reason, another formulation of reason unbound, implodes by claiming that everything is explicable and justifiable—except for this principle itself. Hume uses these aporiai as a *reductio* to chasten reason and return us to a more modest (if less innocent) common sense. "Reason first appears in possession of the throne, prescribing laws, and imposing maxims, with an absolute sway and authority. Her enemy, therefore, is oblig'd to take shelter under her protection, and [make] use of rational arguments to prove the fallaciousness and imbecility of reason."[237]

Rather than searching for a self-authenticating idea or fact, we must find the "way of grasping a rule which is *not* an *interpretation* . . . in actual cases" (PI §201). Or rather than finding it, we need to *return* to it, since this is how we act all the time. "I don't reason. The picture of the rule makes it clear how the picture of the series is to be continued. . . . Whence this certainty? But why do I ask that question? Is it not enough that this certainty exists? . . . Language just is a phenomenon of human life."[238] Just as Wittgenstein and Heidegger "remind" us of what we already know in our normal engaged state, so Hume wants to return us to common life where these troubling doubts simply fall away:

Since reason is incapable of dispelling these clouds, nature herself suffices to that purpose, and cures me of this philosophical melancholy and delirium, either by relaxing this bent of mind, or by some avocation, and lively impression of my senses, which obliterate all these chimeras. I dine, I play a game of back-gammon, I converse, and am merry with my friends; and when after three or four hour's amusement, I wou'd return to these speculations, they appear so cold, and strain'd, and ridiculous, that I cannot find in my heart to enter into them any farther.[239]

Wittgenstein disenchants the mesmerizing charms of philosophy, while Heidegger's phenomenological descriptions show how artificial and distortive philosophical metaphysics is by reminding us of what our ongoing life is really like. All three want to return us to what we *already* know in our usual comings and goings, by exposing reason's limitations—its finitude, its dependence on factors that escape rational analysis or legitimation.

The stopping points of inquiry often mark the starting points of behavior. These are the "always already" present features of our thoughts and actions, what must be in place for us to learn particular facts, what "we must take for granted in all our reasonings" (HT 187). And Heidegger and Wittgenstein, like Hume before them, fix upon the reality of the external world as one such point. They all agree that this reality cannot be proven, and that it need not be, since our relationship to it is not epistemic. Heidegger says that, "nothing exists in our relationship to the world which provides a basis for the phenomenon of belief in the world. I have not yet been able to find this phenomenon of belief. Rather, the peculiar thing is just that the world is 'there' *before* all belief" (HCT 215–216). For Wittgenstein, certain facts are "fused into the foundations of our language-game. . . . The language-game . . . is not based on grounds. It is not reasonable (or unreasonable). It is there—like our life" (OC §§558–559). And for Hume "it seems evident, that men are carried by a natural instinct or prepossession, to repose faith in their senses; and that, without any reasoning, or even almost before the use of reason, we always suppose an external universe."[240] This stance is not an irresponsible judgment that we ought to either ground or discard as Descartes has it, but an automatic reaction that is hardwired into us. "Nature, by an absolute and uncontroulable necessity has determin'd us to judge as well as to breathe and feel," which is why any external-world skepticism can only momentarily daze us.[241] Certain forms of 'assent' are simply features of our thrownness, not of our decision. We don't employ these because we have satisfied ourselves of their legitimacy. No, as Hume puts it, "we assent to our faculties, and employ our reason only because we cannot help it" (HT 657).

There are also, of course, clear points of disagreement—places where Hume entertains notions which are firmly rejected by Heidegger and Wittgenstein, indeed by most twentieth-century philosophy. For example, the veil of ideas, that is, the notion that we are in immediate contact only with ideas or representations of objects and never with the objects themselves;[242] or the fact–value distinction, which withdraws values like beauty or goodness from the world and places them in the mind as mere subjective projections—both ideas directly targeted by phenomenology.

But a deep, fundamental idea guides Wittgenstein's and Heidegger's thinking no less than Hume's: "be a philosopher; but, amidst all your philosophy, be still a man" (HE 9). We have inherited philosophies built for gods, and the task that falls to us, we who live amid their ruins, is to develop a philosophy that is proper to humans. This is why all three focus on common life or average everydayness: "we must stick to the subjects of our every-day thinking";[243] "we must therefore glean up our experiments in this science from a cautious observation of human life, and take them as they appear in the common course of the world" (HT xix); "[the world and being-in-the-world] are to be considered within the horizon of average everydayness—the kind of Being which is *closest* to Dasein."[244] Unquenchable doubts and questions spring up when we look beyond the phenomena to something transcendent to explain them, so we must work at maintaining immanence from the beginning.

If the material world rests upon a similar ideal world, this ideal world must rest upon some other, and so on without end. It were better, therefore, never to look beyond the present material world. . . . When you go one step beyond the mundane system, you only excite an inquisitive humor which it is impossible ever to satisfy. . . . The first step which we make leads us on forever. It were, therefore, wise in us to limit all our inquiries to the present world, without looking farther. No satisfaction can ever be attained by these speculations which so far exceed the narrow bounds of human understanding. (Hume 1998, 31–32)

Just as for Wittgenstein metaphysics places familiar words and concepts into contexts where we cannot rely on our usual understanding, so Hume sees metaphysics as transcending our experience of common life but, of necessity, employing concepts that were developed there.

We are got into fairy land, long ere we have reached the last steps of our theory; and *there* we have no reason to trust our common methods of argument, or to think that our usual analogies and probabilities have any authority. Our line is too short to fathom such immense abysses. . . . This fancied experience has no authority when we thus apply it to subjects that lie entirely out of the sphere of experience.[245]

Ultimately, all of Hume's thought aims to "show the whimsical condition of mankind, who must act and reason and believe; though they are not able, by their most diligent enquiry, to satisfy themselves concerning the foundation of these operations, or to remove the objections, which may be raised against them."[246] In other words, our instinct-guided reasoning is a *groundless ground*: it enables us to think successfully (as we measure success) but admits of no justification itself. The point of philosophy is not to teach us esoteric lessons about the transcendent meaning of reality, but to know when it is time to stop seeking such lessons.

## Summary

Heidegger and Wittgenstein seek to change the way we think about justification. Both argue that we receive our ways of thinking and cannot control them. Both employ infinite-regress arguments—attempts at justifying our ideas either go on forever or come to a halt in something which is itself not justified—and circular reasoning—attempts to justify our basic ways of thinking must use these very ways of thinking, and so can provide no independent legitimation. This encourages a kind of humility, especially in contrast with ancient orientations to the divine and modern quests for radical autonomy. Both philosophers emphasize our dependence on society, nature, and our own human nature—a dependence we never outgrow.

# Conclusion: Original Finitude

Let us be human.

—Wittgenstein, *Culture and Value*, 30

It is precisely a question of becoming certain of this finitude in order to hold oneself in it.

—Heidegger, *Kant and the Problem of Metaphysics*, 152

Like all great philosophers, Wittgenstein and Heidegger discuss a wide range of topics; I have surveyed those I consider to be central to their work and of greatest interest. One topic at the foundation of much of their thought is the idea of limits or finitude. Wittgenstein's early work plots the limitations of what we can think and speak. Focusing on language rather than thought, and on what language can say while leaving what it can't unspoken, helps Wittgenstein avoid the trap of transgressing these limits in the act of tracing them. Language limns the contours of cognition, entailing the entirety of logic and mirroring the structure of reality. By setting the limits to all possible language, logic implicitly contains a mystical sketch of the world as a limited whole, allowing Wittgenstein to have his ineffable cake and eff it too.

As we have seen, definitively determining language's limits requires positing a fixed, singular essence. The entire universe of sensible discourse must implicitly lie coiled up in the Tractarian trinity of elements (the general form of all propositions, the set of all elementary propositions, and the set of all logical operations that combine elementary propositions into more complex ones) if we are "to view the world sub specie aeterni . . . to view it as a whole—a limited whole" (T 6.45). This kind of conclusion would satisfy philosophy's oldest dream of reaching absolute knowledge, truths that can never be overturned. As Wittgenstein later writes of his early bewitchment, "there seemed to pertain to logic a peculiar depth—a universal significance.

. . . For logical investigation explores the nature of all things. It seeks to see to the bottom of things."[1] In the *Tractatus*, he describes it like this: "that utterly simple thing, which we have to formulate here, is not a likeness of the truth, but the truth itself in its entirety" (T 5.5563).

Despite his strategy, the attempt to fix our limitations once and for all commits epistemological hubris by requiring us to rise above our empirical situation and look upon the world and language from the outside. Only a transcendent perspective would offer a view of all possible propositional permutations. This search for a definitive knowledge that allows us to glimpse the innermost, crystalline structure of logic, language, existence, and thought all at once—this desire to peel back the skin of the world to take the measure of its organs and bones—this is philosophy's origin and, from one perspective, its original sin. More than any specific ideas or arguments, Wittgenstein's later work aims to correct the frame of mind that inspires such a project.

The *Tractatus* lives in the gap between the pure, ideal structure of language and its contingent, particular instantiations. These temporal instantiations of language, while sensible, are draped in confusing, accidental forms, and Wittgenstein's early project is to use logical analysis to strip all the misleading garb off language's true body. When he drops this crucial distinction, it alters his project profoundly. For the later Wittgenstein, we must try to see things the way they are, stopping our ears to philosophy's siren song of how they ought to be or even how they must be, regardless of overwhelming experiential evidence. Philosophers have been mesmerized by the ideal, and under its spell have propped up retrospective reconstructions of the real that filter out all countermanding evidence as illusory or accidental. If we *know* that language must have certain properties, "then this investigation will perhaps be superfluous. But first we must learn to understand what it is that opposes such an examination of details in philosophy."[2] For philosophy, the perfect is the enemy of the ordinary. If I may invoke one more myth, it was Epimetheus—literally, "hindsight" or "afterthought"—who was responsible for Pandora opening her box and unleashing a swarm of horrors upon the human race. While this myth depicts the final spirit released from Pandora's box, Hope, as the one solace in our sufferings, it is precisely the metaphysical hope for ultimate truth—our willingness to continue an impossible search for perfection despite endless failures and conflicts with experience—that is perhaps the greatest curse of them all.

Wittgenstein's quasi-phenomenological orders—"don't think, but look!" (PI §66)—are meant to combat these preconceived expectations created by our search for Truth. What we actually find when we "look" are overlapping similarities rather than singular essences, rough approximations which cannot be cashed out in precise certitudes, hazy clouds of ceteris paribus conditions swirling round rules and definitions. We come looking for a wizard but find only a shabby confidence man handing out degrees and hot air, an allegory that nicely fits Wittgenstein's view of education. These disheveled accounts disappoint—Wittgenstein had already anticipated the worry about logic's use of "such peculiar crotchets and contrivances" in the *Tractatus*, but assured us that they "are all connected with one another in an infinitely fine network" (T 5.511)—and may instill semantic angst.

"But still, it isn't a game, if there is some vagueness *in the rules.*"—But *does* this prevent its being a game?—"Perhaps you'll call it a game, but at any rate it certainly isn't a complete game." This means: it has impurities, and what I am interested in at present is the pure article.—But I want to say: we misunderstand the role of the ideal in our language. That is to say: we should indeed call it a game, only we are dazzled by the ideal and therefore fail to see the actual use of the word "game" clearly.

We want to say that there can't be any vagueness in logic. The idea now absorbs us, that the ideal *"must"* be found in reality. (PI §§100–101)

The logical forms *must* exist, or so we have been told, or so we tell ourselves. If we do not find them, it must be because they lie hidden within the deepest linguistic depths. We must redouble our efforts, digging further and discarding all superficial details (like actual usage) to uncover their subterranean foundation, the true ground that forms the metaphysically stable basis for all that rests upon it.

When we believe that we must find that order, must find the ideal, in our actual language, we become dissatisfied with what are ordinarily called "propositions," "words," "signs." . . . Here it is difficult as it were to keep our heads up,—to see that we must stick to the subjects of our every-day thinking, and not go astray and imagine that we have to describe extreme subtleties.[3]

This contrast between flawless ideality and messy reality, the demands of the pure 'ought' endlessly let down by the ragged "is," gave birth to philosophy and now sustains and haunts it—or rather, sustains it *by* haunting it. The ideal, often fleshed out in theological pictures, props up the metaphysical aspirations that seduce us from our actual state.

A picture is conjured up which seems to fix the sense *unambiguously*. The actual use, compared with that suggested by the picture, seems like something muddied. . . . The form of expression we use seems to have been designed for a god, who knows what we cannot know; he sees the whole of each of those infinite series.

In the actual use of expressions we make detours, we go by side roads. We see the straight highway before us, but of course we cannot use it, because it is permanently closed.[4]

God looks upon the completed infinity, while we plod through one step at a time, leaning on crutches and cobbled together contrivances like "and so on" or ". . ." or "etc.," and so on. The sets really do exist in their totality, we are assured, but our heads are too small to encompass them, our vantage-point too low for us to see more than a few steps ahead—just enough to keep trudging on. We may only be able to gesture at the correct way to follow a rule, but it exists—it has to exist if there are to be correct and incorrect acts of following it.

Wittgenstein wants to help us face the knotted squalor of the real, to force our heavenward gaze down to the detritus of practice. In order to indicate our finitude without drawing a border beyond which we cannot go, we need the idea of 'original finitude,' in which our finitude is not demarcated by a shared boundary with the infinite. Without an invidious contrast with the ideal, the ordinary ceases to be a second-best we must settle for; cut free from a spurious transcendence, human affairs can quit losing a rigged game. Traditional philosophy has been "designed for a god," and has produced picture after picture that is fundamentally unfit for our use. Considering the role Wittgenstein accords instinct and natural reactions in thought, one commentator writes that metaphysics constitutes "a denial of the animal in favor of the godlike."[5]

Apart from its distortion of actual practice, Wittgenstein argues that our notion of the 'ideal' is fundamentally incoherent. Like many other philosophical ideas, the 'ideal' is a picture that simply falls apart under examination.

Here it happens that our thinking plays us a queer trick. We want, that is, to quote the law of excluded middle. . . . "In the decimal expansion of $\pi$ either the group '7777' occurs, or it does not—there is no third possibility." That is to say: "God sees—but we don't know." But what does that mean?—We use a picture; the picture of a visible series which one person sees the whole of and another not. The law of excluded middle says here: It must either look like this, or like that. So it really—and this is a truism—says nothing at all, but gives us a picture. And the problem ought now to be: does reality accord with the picture or not? And this picture *seems* to determine what we have to do, what to look for, and how—but it does not do so, just because we do not know how it is to be applied.[6]

While we find this picture compelling, it does not and cannot inform our practice: whatever God sees or doesn't see can be of no consequence to how we mortals conduct our business, a prayer wheel whose turning leaves the machine unaffected. And note that Wittgenstein calls his characterization of this *as* a picture "a truism": no one could disagree with the claim that it's merely a picture once they've considered the matter, even though many brilliant thinkers have regarded it quite differently. This is why I think it is wrong to say that Wittgenstein's later work cannot make positive claims since he professes to utter only truisms. A careful examination of actual practice—just the kind of *Realphilosophie* that philosophical habits discourage—is necessary to grasp Wittgenstein's point. How could he leave everything *entirely* as it is if he is trying to clear up confusions? He leaves our concrete behavior as it is but changes how we think of it by reminding us of how it transpires, reminders that "everyone would agree" with once we have been disabused of the distortions of the ideal.[7]

Wittgenstein sometimes turns the theological picture inside out. The certitude of mathematics, for instance, invites Platonic realism but, as a human construct, it is exhausted by the way we conduct it. "I want to say: Even God can determine something mathematical only by mathematics. Even for him the mere rule of expansion cannot decide anything that it does not decide for us."[8] It makes no more sense to say that we have always calculated incorrectly than that we have always moved pawns illegitimately: these are inventions rather than discoveries, and this rules out the possibility of collective mistakes. Just as Heidegger says that Newton's laws were neither true nor false before they were discovered and written out,[9] so Wittgenstein argues that new mathematical questions lack answers until we decide them.[10]

*On Certainty* applies this analysis to epistemology. The quest for absolute certitude is an excellent example of the philosophical aspiration to transcend the human sphere, the kind of quest expressed in italics and capital letters. We want to know not just whether a claim is warranted or widely believed or well-tested—no, we want to *Know* whether it *Really* captures *Reality*, and not just reality it appears to us or how we are inclined or even forced to view it, but as it *Really Is*. The context in which a claim is made, in particular whether we are or could ever be in a position to verify it, is irrelevant to its Truth. But of course, this isn't at all how we actually use the word "know" since we take fallibility into account all the time.[11]

In its language-game [a claim to know something apparent, like that one is sitting in a chair] is not presumptuous. There, it has no higher position than, simply, the human language-game. For there it has its restricted application.

But as soon as I say this sentence outside its context, it appears in a false light. For then it is as if I wanted to insist that there are things that I *know*. God himself can't say anything to me about them.[12]

In normal contexts, claims of knowledge make perfect sense and we use them easily: I ask, "Do you know the time?" and you respond, "Certainly, it's five o'clock." But when normal circumstances have been artificially suspended, philosophers think they've isolated the sublimed essence of knowledge—the real stuff, purified of all the dross of mundane use. Heidegger also focuses on this process; philosophy, he says, has "been guided by the predominance of an empty and thereby fantastic idea of certainty and evidence. . . . Care about a specific, absolute knowledge, taken purely as an idea, predominates over every question about the matters" (IPR 33). And it is precisely this appeal to the decontextualized sublime that Wittgenstein wants to shut down. He "would like to reserve the expression 'I know' for the cases in which it is used in normal linguistic exchange" because "it is as if 'I know' did not tolerate a metaphysical emphasis."[13] Were we able to connect words directly to bits of reality which contain their entire significance, then context would be irrelevant; we would simply be right or wrong about the complete extension of "$\pi$" or the presence of sensation "S" or the correct application of a given rule.

But absent meaning-objects, reality cannot be called on to substantiate our claims independently of our practices of gathering and evaluating evidence. "Correspondence to reality" is merely a way of saying that something is true, a compliment we pay to our best beliefs, as Rorty liked to say, but one that never gets outside our practices. "Well, if everything speaks for an hypothesis and nothing against it—is it then certainly true? One may designate it as such.—But does it certainly agree with reality, with the facts?—With this question you are already going round in a circle."[14] Nor can mental contents do the trick since practices of knowing trump any internal feelings or ideas.[15] John McDowell captures this idea beautifully:

> now if we are simply and normally immersed in our practices, we do not wonder how their relation to the world would look from outside them, and feel the need for a solid foundation discernible from an external point of view. So we would be protected against the vertigo if we could stop supposing that the relation to reality of some area of our thought and language needs to be contemplated from a standpoint independent of that anchoring in our human life that makes the thoughts what they are for us. . . . This realism chafes at the fallibility and inconclusiveness of all our ways of finding out how things are, and purports to confer a sense on "But is it *really* so?" in which the question does not call for a maximally careful assessment by our lights, but is asked from a perspective transcending the limitations of our cognitive powers.[16]

We can appeal to nothing beyond these practices because any such appeal thereby incorporates the evidence into our language-games, thus compromising its desired independence from our practices. For the possibility of making mistakes to operate, we need a way of comparing our beliefs to a reality that is, at least in principle, accessible to comparisons. "'But I can still imagine someone making all these connexions, and none of them corresponding with reality. Why shouldn't I be in a similar case?' If I imagine such a person I also imagine a reality, a world that surrounds him; and I imagine him as thinking (and speaking) in contradiction to this world."[17] The sense of wonder created by philosophy is merely the giddy dizziness one gets from being spun around to the point of disorientation; thankfully, it fades as we regain our bearings.[18]

Heidegger begins with the sense of finitude that Wittgenstein fought so hard to achieve. Heidegger understands the basic lesson of the first *Critique*—a book that both men admired—to be that "finitude is not some property that is merely attached to us, but is *our fundamental way of being*. If we wish to become what we are, we cannot abandon this finitude or deceive ourselves about it, but must safeguard it."[19] This safeguarding informs all of Heidegger's thought, beginning with metaphysics.

Phenomenology's basic method is to bracket questions about how reality "really is" beyond possible experience in order to describe it as we experience it. Since we by definition lack access to whatever transcends our grasp, we have no business making claims about it, and should commit ourselves instead to radical immanence: "our investigation . . . asks about Being itself in so far as Being enters into the intelligibility of Dasein."[20] Kant broke the hold that the picture of capturing reality as it really is has had on metaphysics since its inception, but he retained the notion of this reality itself. Irrelevant for our purposes it may be, yet its very existence casts aspersions on our world, sicklied over now with the pallor of the "merely."[21] Heidegger's phenomenology eliminates transcendent reality entirely from the philosophical horizon: we are only concerned with and can only make sense of a world we can be concerned with and make sense of.[22] Anything beyond this is not merely idle but incoherent speculation. Wittgenstein considers metaphysical realism to be a witching picture that is suggested by grammar; Heidegger blames it, rather, on a particular conception of what it means to be that has been passed down through generations of metaphysicians, starting with Plato's divorcing empirical appearing from the really real.

Phenomenology gives up the dream of Reality Itself, and it does so without "settling" for a metaphysical second-best. Without a contrast, the world we live in stops being "merely" our experience to become the only reality that merits the name.[23] Since, as we just saw with Wittgenstein, metaphysical realism is often organized around theological notions (think of Kant's connection between noumena and intellectual intuition), Heidegger occasionally links his phenomenological ontology to the "death of God."

Along with the assumption of an absolute intuition . . . the concept of a thing in itself also dies away. But things do not thereby vanish into phantoms and images—phantoms and images which we produce for ourselves. For appearances are the things themselves, and they are the things that they are without these things having to be thought as things in themselves on the basis of an untenable concept of being and on the basis of the assumption of a representing God.[24]

The point here, like the final step of Nietzsche's "How the 'True World' Finally Became a Fable," is that the death of the noumenal brings about a conceptual transformation in what had been defined in contrast to the noumenal—namely, the world and life.

However, then there is really no absolute truth! Of course not. It is time that we cure ourselves of the consternation over this and finally take seriously that we are for the time being still human beings and no gods. . . . From the fact that there is no absolute truth for us, however, we may not infer that there is in general no truth for us. . . . What for us is true in this sense of truth is quite enough for a human life.[25]

Heidegger agrees with Wittgenstein that "I know" does not tolerate a metaphysical sense, but knowledge and truth and right survive the end of metaphysics.

Authenticity represents a groundless ground in ethics. To adapt Yeats's famous words, "the best" for Heidegger lack one specific conviction—the conviction that there is a center, that it holds, and that somewhere the divine falconer is calling us back, even if we have strayed too far to hear his call. Yet it is the absence of this conviction that calls forth another, very different conviction—a far more precarious but no less passionate commitment, one that is ever unsure of itself: a commitment to live in the ever-widening gyre. We have traded Yeats' "center" for Kierkegaard's "70,000 fathoms of water." The only revelation at hand is the Kafkaesque one that there is no assurance of a revelation; that if a revelation comes we may not understand it aright or even recognize its coming; and that we will never know—even after its appearance—whether what is coming toward us is a healing god or a rough beast. What Yeats mourns as the dying embers of belief Heidegger accepts as our essential situation: we are too late, to bring in his later phrasing, for the gods and too early for another beginning.

In this situation, Wittgenstein and Heidegger want to create a positive notion of finitude, one that doesn't live on infinitude's leavings, a mere shadow cast by Plato's sun of Goodness and Being. They want to examine our limitedness without thereby transgressing our limitations, without peeking over to see that nothing lies beyond this world's horizon—not even nothing. They aspire to a metaphysical humility that doesn't even say that "*from a God's-Eye View there is no God's-Eye View.*"[26] "A judge might even say 'That is the truth—so far as a human being can know it.' But what would this rider achieve?" (OC § 607). According to their anti-realism, nothing beyond our ways of talking and acting can determine or justify these ways, at least not non-circularly. A bit like the *Tractatus*'s equation of thoroughgoing solipsism with realism—since a completely consistent solipsism deprives one of the intellectual resources to contrast one's own experience with anything beyond it, draining all content from the idea that it's *my* experience by removing the ability to make sense of a contrast—so our ways of talking about reality exhaust it insofar as we can talk about.

Phenomenology, as explained in the article Husserl partially co-authored with Heidegger for the 1927 *Encyclopaedia Britannica*, makes a similar move.

In the systematic work of phenomenology . . . the old traditional ambiguous antitheses of the philosophical standpoint are resolved—by themselves. . . . *Subjectivism* can only be overcome by the most all-embracing and consistent subjectivism (the transcendental). In this [latter] form it is at the same time objectivism [of a deeper sort], in that it represents the claims of whatever objectivity is to be demonstrated.[27]

Thinking "subjectivism" all the way out rules out appeals to that which is cut off from us in principle, making the reality we experience reality full stop. This reintroduces "subjective" qualities like "beautiful" or "useful" into the world as full-fledged features of reality. Heidegger's later work emphasizes the role language plays in our experience, to the same conclusion as Wittgenstein: "it is language that tells us about the essence of a thing."[28] It isn't that we are presented with a pre-sorted world where categories kneel for us to affix words to them like Adam naming the animals, but that we are always already in a linguistic world. We cannot sift out pristine reality from our reality, making the distinction empty.[29]

Radical immanence acknowledges as real only that which we can encounter, at least in principle. For Heidegger, being means manifesting or appearing in the clearing.[30] We can and often have to interpret appearances, but not in order to throw them over in favor of what cannot appear. Wittgenstein refrains from this kind of definition, preferring to show us when our endeavors are driven by pictures whose application we don't quite grasp and which cannot do what we imagine them to do—similar to what the *Tractatus* called for: "the correct method in philosophy would really be the following: to say nothing except what can be said . . . and then, whenever someone else wanted to say something metaphysical, to demonstrate to him that he had failed to give a meaning to certain signs in his propositions" (T 6.53).

Wittgenstein's later thought can be seen as working out the implications of his request, "let us be human" (CV 30). What happens to our understanding of reality and knowledge once we have divested ourselves of metaphysical preconceptions, of the vestigial pretense to divinity instilled in the discipline from centuries of trying to think from God's point of view? One possible inspiration for this project is Kierkegaard, a philosopher admired by both Wittgenstein and Heidegger.[31] For Kierkegaard, our limitedness presents us with a choice: we can either flee from it to imagine ourselves as pure objective thought surveying the world and history *sub specie aeterni*, or we can concentrate all of our energy and thought on embracing and coming to terms, albeit not to peace, with our situation. The latter means making all of our thinking and acting bear the stamp of our finitude: "every subject is an existing subject, and therefore this must be essentially expressed in all of his knowing."[32] We must keep at this, despite an intrinsic dissatisfaction with our mortal condition: "every human being has a strong natural desire and drive to become something else and more."[33] Kierkegaard's main target is Hegel and then-prominent Danish Hegelians who tried to "contemplate world history—from God's point of view" (1992, 395). Far more important, and more difficult, than becoming God is becoming human, giving up reassuring objective security to live in the "fear and trembling" of decisions made without foundations or guarantees. Like Wittgenstein's image of an ideal thoroughfare we can only look toward enviously from our congested road which is endlessly under repair, Kierkegaard compares Hegel to a man who has built a magnificent palace yet sleeps in a decrepit shack next to it. In a phrase that clearly anticipates Wittgenstein's, Kierkegaard asks one thing of his readers: "let us be human beings."[34]

The essential fact about our existence is that it cannot be rationally accounted for without remainder; our being thrown into existence is *essentially* groundless.[35] We seek God's benediction for and approval of our righteous smiting of the wicked and the irrational; we want our beliefs to mirror the structure of the universe, making our beliefs absolutely right and others' frivolously or maliciously wrong. We want to know that our way of acting and thinking comes from our truest self, from what is highest and most divine in us, so as to make every alternative not just wrong but a form of self-betrayal, a scorning of God or the world or humanity. I see the birth of metaphysics at the moment when Plato watched a jury of his peers condemn the greatest man alive to death—and then go home to enjoy a hot meal, a good night's sleep, and a long, happy self-satisfied life. Plato needed

to know that, even if the jurors and all of their friends felt completely justified, even if they suffered neither punishment nor ignominy nor pangs of
guilt, still, *they were Wrong*. Maybe not by the standards of Athenian culture
or their own consciences, yet it must somehow be objectively true that they
did wrong. *This* Truth must be set into the very fabric of reality, whereas
their merely human verdict was written in sand which, like all that transpires in this half-formed world of decay and ruin, will be washed away in
the currents of time.

Giving up metaphysical solace is difficult. Since all philosophical
accounts of why we do the things we do necessarily bottom out at brute fact,
Wittgenstein stops the project at or very near the start; for many activities
"there is no why. . . . This is how I act."[36] We do not subscribe to our most
basic orienting "beliefs" because we have judged them to be reasonable, but
because nonrational contingent processes like training and socialization
have formed us so. They're not worryingly ungrounded knowledge because
they're not knowledge at all. "You can't in fact call language or grammar
unsupported because there is no question of its being supported."[37] We
cannot get behind our language-games and form of life to ground them in
something stronger, deeper, truer, despite the ancient pull to do so. "It is so
difficult to find the *beginning*. Or, better: it is difficult to begin at the beginning. And not try to go further back."[38] Part of Wittgenstein's therapy is to
cure us of "our disease . . . of wanting to explain" (RFM 333).

Accepting our groundless grounds forms a kind of ethics, as I discussed in chapter 5. It is no accident that Wittgenstein and Heidegger
were profoundly interested in philosophers of nihilism, Schopenhauer
and Nietzsche respectively. Both express a kind of Romantic *Weltschmerz*:
Wittgenstein's foreword to his *Philosophical Remarks* and the epigraph of
*Philosophical Investigations* recoil from the notion of progress, linked in the
former to "the vast stream of European and American civilization" and in
the latter to "the darkness of this time."[39] Much of *Being and Time* is soaked
with an existential despair about a structural lack of integrity and a societal
lack of something like honor or *gravitas*, while Heidegger's later works often
lament the desolation of our time.

They connect these cultural concerns with scientism, the idea that science gives us the one true description of reality. This description, especially
in its classic Cartesian–Newtonian form, is of a cold atomistic universe,
whereas Heidegger and later Wittgenstein emphasize the rich, holistic
world we live in—a world that is far better captured in artworks than in
scientific formulas. "In the age of world impoverishment, a botanist sees
in the blossoming of a flower only a sequence of chemical processes."[40]

Wittgenstein was repulsed by modernity's glorification of scientists rather than composers or writers,[41] while Heidegger repeatedly praises the work of poets (and philosophers) far above that of scientists.[42] Wittgenstein once "summed up my attitude to philosophy when I said: philosophy ought really to be written only as a poetic composition" (CV 24), which comes close to Heidegger's idea that only poets can be as great as thinkers (Badiou makes this comparison, 2011, 178).

Whereas scientific and metaphysical explanations take us away from our experience—think of how different molecular motion is from a languidly hot afternoon, or wavelengths of energy from Matisse's colors[43]—artists remind us of the meaningful world we live in. This harmonizes with Heidegger and Wittgenstein's methods of reminding us of what we already know, returning us to where we already are by calling our attention to inconspicuous aspects of thought and life.[44] According to their Perceptual Model of Thinking, we do not experience meaningless scratches or mere bodily motions or representations; we dwell among meanings, people, and things. The threat of nihilism only appears once philosophers have switched to theoretical contemplation, once they "are, so to speak, fascinated by the radical division between Being and value, and do not notice that they have only theoretically broken the bridges between the two spheres, and now stand helpless on one of the banks."[45]

Heidegger and Wittgenstein's goal is to help us return to where we already are, and truly *be* there for the first time, to echo one of Eliot's famous lines.[46] Compare Wittgenstein's comment on his early metaphor,

if the place I want to get to could only be reached by way of a ladder, I would give up trying to get there. For the place I really have to get to is a place I must already be at now,

with Heidegger's claim that we have

leapt, out of the familiar realm of science and even, as we shall see, out of the realm of philosophy. And where have we leapt? Perhaps into an abyss? No! . . . On that soil upon which we live and die, if we are honest with ourselves. A curious, indeed unearthly thing that we must first leap onto the soil on which we really stand.[47]

Or Wittgenstein saying "where others go on ahead, I stay in one place," while Heidegger insists that "when philosophy attends to its essence it does not make forward strides at all. It remains where it is in order constantly to think the Same."[48] The solution to nihilism is to realize how artificial it is, how pervasively ideas and people and things solicit our actions. We don't need to figure out how to inject values into a gray landscape; our lives are flooded with Technicolor.

Schopenhauer and Nietzsche use voluntarism to overcome nihilism, though their voluntarisms are very different. The *Tractatus* adapts Schopenhauer's peculiar blend of Buddhism and idealism which, finding no value within the world, gives it up as valueless. Meaning transcends the world; it can only be found in the "godhead" of "my independent I" (NB 74) because it is my attitude—either striving to control what will happen or resolved to whatever does happen—that determines whether my world is happily meaningful or sadly absurd. Do we admire existential heroes like Beckett's tramps or Camus's Sisyphus for courageously maintaining their commitment, futile and absurd as it may be (Vladimir: "We have kept our appointment and that's an end to that. We are not saints, but we have kept our appointment" [Beckett 1994, 91]), or do we take pity upon them because their situation, our situation, is such it can never achieve resolution? In other words, does the world determine one's mental, emotional, and moral state, or does one's state determine the status of the world? While Wittgenstein prescribes absolute passivity, this stance paradoxically bestows absolute power: the vicissitudes of the material world can always betray me, foiling my plans no matter what precautions I take, yet I reign omnipotent over my soul. As the Stoics emphasized, *apatheia* toward my worldly fate gives me a strange kind of mastery over that fate: if I fear nothing, no one can force me to do anything; if I want nothing, nothing can make me unhappy. Recall the story of Alexander the Great granting the Cynic Diogenes anything he wishes: Diogenes asks only that the general move out of the way—he was blocking the sunlight. The moral of this story is that the man living in a barrel is more free, even more powerful, than the ruler of the world at the head of his army since the latter's happiness depends on the vagaries of fate. Wittgenstein reaches the same conclusion: "I cannot bend the happenings of the world to my will: *I am completely powerless.* I can only make myself independent of the world—and so *in a certain sense master it*—by renouncing any influence on happenings" (NB 73, my italics). This is what creates Wittgenstein's paradigmatic religious feeling of absolute safety.

Heidegger sees a temporal theme in the background of these ideas. One of the reasons we cling to the traditional conception of being as constant presence is to quell anxiety over the ephemeral, to quiet our horror at the fact that everything we are and achieve and love will decay and be forgotten. We seek refuge not only from this world's injustices and imperfections, but from the flow of time itself by reposing in the eternal. Viewing ourselves and the moments of time we inhabit as present-at-hand protects them—and so protects us—from dissolution and desolation; consider the proofs of immortality based on the simplicity of the substantial "soul." Wittgenstein's early work clearly subscribes to these ideas, though few of these ruminations make it into the *Tractatus*. His *Notebooks* refer to the way in which living exclusively in the present eliminates "fear and hope," which thus secures *apatheia* and ethical happiness (NB 76, 74), escapes death (NB 75, T 6.4311), and solves the problem of life: "but is it possible for one so to live that life stops being problematic? That one is *living* in eternity and not in time?"[49]

Heidegger's temporal holism—that is, the inextricable intertwinings of the tenses—rules out this strategy since the present only has meaning in the context of future-orienting projects. Yet the suspension of the ongoing flow of our lives during anxiety and the anticipation of death gives us the chance to choose ourselves. There is no escape from the world, but certain fundamental, temporal experiences still allow us to temporarily loosen the worldly entanglements that usually absorb us, so that we can lay claim to our self, so that "Dasein can be *authentically itself.*"[50] We are thrown into a certain range of possibilities, but we can actively decide which projects shall define us. We may bristle at the fact that we have undergone our past passively, yet we can—as with Nietzsche's *amor fati*—retroactively choose them, offering an *ersatz* divine self-creation.

This power fantasy has an epistemological side as well: just as the Stoic who wants nothing can never be harmed, so the philosopher who knows the essence of language can never be surprised—not deeply, not logically. Particular sentences can offer unprecedented combinations, of course—my favorite is Stephen Fry's "Hold the newsreader's nose squarely, waiter, or friendly milk will countermand my trousers," but Chomsky's "Colorless green ideas sleep *furiously*" works just as well—but the entirety of legitimate language has been structurally encompassed in advance. The happy man enjoys a form of omnipotence, the knowledgeable logician a form of omniscience, and the Tolstoyan saint living entirely in the present a form of immortality—all the qualities suitable for a godhead. Discerning the exact borders of my kingdom—what I can control and what I can know—allows me to stay within it, where I reign absolutely.

*Being and Time* gives up the dream of capturing reality as it is beyond all possible experience. It presents a human or Dasein world, how it is to us rather than what might be "present-at-hand for an eternal observer exempt from Dasein."[51] Read as a broadly Kantian enterprise (a reading Heidegger recommends),[52] though, it makes Dasein the center of the world, since it is her projects and actions that set up and keep up the world. Entities show up as either ready-to-hand or present-at-hand depending on her stance, just as our transcendental faculties make phenomena causal and substantial for Kant. This is why the study of Dasein forms the foundation for the study of being, that is, fundamental ontology: the various modes of being emerge from our activities the way a rainbow flows from a prism; a complete understanding of the latter secures an understanding of the full array of possible colors. Although Heidegger does not explicitly state that there can be no other modes of being than those he discusses, he does repeatedly insist that he has captured the essential nature of Dasein once and for all,[53] repeating Kant's strategy of securing the complete and final forms of intuition and concepts of understanding, in order to ensure the application of Euclidean geometry and Newtonian science to everything we will ever encounter. In the end, *Being and Time*'s set of existentialia perform a similar function as the *Tractatus*'s general form of the proposition—it allows us to take in being or language in its entirety, to comprehensively encompass all that is comprehensible. Despite his integration of temporality into Dasein, he still wants to capture our nature and reality *sub specie aeterni*, to see us as we *really* are, beneath the dispersion of our daily mass existence.[54]

Heidegger explicitly connects this strategy with metaphysics and science in his later work.

Today a world dominates in which the decisive question runs: How do I have to represent nature in the sequence of its appearances to myself, so that I am in a position to make secure predictions about all and everything? The answer to this question is that it is compulsory to represent nature as a totality of energy particles of existing mass, the reciprocal movements of which are to be mathematically calculable. Descartes already says to the piece of wax that he holds before his eyes: "You are nothing other than an extended, flexible, and mutable thing," and thus I proclaim myself to know everything about you that there is to know of you.[55]

The attempt to achieve exhaustive knowledge by only admitting what fits our categories is like pasting a target to the end of your rifle, ensuring a perfect score in such a way that it compromises the game. (I believe I first found this image in Wittgenstein, but the location eludes me.) Moreover, this world-picture invites the runaway voluntarism of technology by letting us think of the world exclusively in the categories that promise us greater and greater control. For Heidegger, this situation represents the culmination of the entire history of metaphysics since Plato, which intensified considerably in modernity: Descartes focused intensely on the utility of abstract mathematical representations of reality, Kant made the transcendental self the center and unconscious creator of phenomenal reality, Nietzsche transferred this creativity to the conscious will of the strong.[56]

Nietzsche proposes as the solution to nihilism that we use our own values to pump up the deflated world once God, like the center pole of a circus tent, has withdrawn; but Heidegger considers that the ultimate form of nihilism. This move collapses our attempts to live a meaningful life into a tautological circle of wanting to get what we want, an eternal recurrence of our own desires echoed back to us like the reflection between facing mirrors. *"All that is left is the solitary superficies of a 'life' that empowers itself to itself for its own sake.* If metaphysics begins as an explicit interpretation of beingness as *idea*, it achieves its uttermost end in the 'revaluation of all values.'"[57]

Understanding gets assimilated to the project of unbridled technological consumption, as seen most clearly in Descartes's goal of making ourselves "the lords and masters of nature" (Descartes 1985, 142–143) and in Nietzsche's occasional pragmatic identification of truth with what increases power. Thus, metaphysics joins technology in the unbounded demand for explanation.

The unique unleashing of the demand to render reasons threatens everything of humans' being-at-home and robs them of the roots of their subsistence, the roots from out of which every great human age, every world-opening spirit, every molding of the human form has thus far grown. . . . The claim of the mighty Principle [of Reason, that everything has a reason and thus must be rationally judged] of rendering reasons withdraws the subsistence from contemporary humanity. We could also say that the more decisively humans try to harness the "mega-energies" that would, once and for all, satisfy all human energy needs, the more impoverished becomes the human faculty for building and dwelling in the realm of what is essential. There is an enigmatic interconnection between the demand to render reasons and the withdrawal of roots.[58]

Modern autonomy requires that everything answer to us and serve our comprehension and control. But tragically, once everything is maximally accommodating to our projects, none have any weight to them.

Man . . . is continually approaching the brink of the possibility of pursuing and promulgating nothing but what is revealed in ordering, and of deriving all his standards on this basis. Through this the other possibility is blocked—that man might rather be admitted sooner and ever more primally to the essence of what is unconcealed and to its unconcealment, in order that he might experience as his essence the requisite belonging to revealing. . . . Where everything that presences exhibits itself in the light of a cause-effect coherence, even God, for representational thinking, can lose all that is exalted and holy, the mysteriousness of his distance.[59]

Technology creates an "unbearable lightness of Being," cheapening being itself to the point that it can no longer sustain meaningful lives.[60] The best it can do is resemble the *Republic*'s city for pigs, where the only value that qualities like nobility or excellence can have lies in their (supposed) productivity, their exchange-rates for efficiency and convenience; where glens and dales are bulldozed for Starbucks and McDonalds and "nature becomes a gigantic gasoline station, an energy source for modern technology and industry" (DT 50). One need not be a Luddite to acknowledge that something important is being lost.

But this philosophical/technological control fantasy cannot be the final truth about us due to the essential, unavoidable moment of passivity. In keeping with the Perceptual Model of Thinking and the groundlessness of our grounds, all of our thinking is "sent" to us in that we have to rely on how ideas and goals appear to us. Even the quest for autonomy, the attempt to rid ourselves of dependence on anything, depends on seeing this project as sensible and desirable, which turns modern humanism inside out.[61] Poetic quietism helps us escape from metaphysical and nihilistic fantasies, allowing being to send us what it will rather than what we will: "an example of an outstanding non-objectifying thinking and speaking is poetry. . . . Simple willingness that wills nothing, counts on no successful outcome."[62]

Our project, according to Heidegger, must be to return to where we are, to give up metaphysical dreams for human reality. "Rational living beings must first *become* mortals."[63] We must accept that there are fundamental limits to our understanding—not limits that can be definitively surveyed and used to master a limited whole, but brute facts that do not yield to comprehension. The very fact that we are alive, and that we live as humans, "stares [us] in the face with the inexorability of an enigma."[64] For Heidegger, our being open to experiencing anything at all is ultimately contingent and gratuitous, which should fill us with awestruck gratitude. We should celebrate and protect this deepest possible mystery from attempts to ground it which are inevitably futile and which, more importantly, exile us from the space of wonder. Wittgenstein wants to eradicate wonder, it is true, but this is because he believes that it tempts us beyond ourselves, seducing us toward an airless space outside world and time: "all that philosophy can do is to destroy idols. And that means not creating a new one—for instance as in 'absence of an idol'" (PO 171). Ultimately, the later Heidegger and Wittgenstein are alike trying to let us live and think as humans, at last.

# Notes

## Introduction

1. For Heidegger, see Husserl's 1931 letter to Alexander Pfänder: "I placed the greatest hopes in Heidegger . . . presumably my one true student. . . . I was virtually convinced that the future of phenomenological philosophy would be entrusted to him and that he not only would become my heir but also would surpass me. . . . When it came down to choosing my successor, obsessed as I was with the idea of assuring the future of the transcendental phenomenology I had founded, I saw him as the only one who was up to the task, and so I had to decide unconditionally in his favor" (Sheehan and Palmer 1997, 480–481; see also Levine 2008, 10). For Wittgenstein, see Russell's 1912 letters to Ottoline: "I love him and feel he will solve the problems that I am too old to solve" (Monk 1996, 252; see also 259, 264, 272, 274, 279–280). Rorty traces a parallel development between the two branches' "heretical followers" (1979, 167; see also 1991, 32 n.9; 1992, 35; Pinkard 1999, 190–191).

2. Heidegger's close reading of primary texts was innovative and earned him a reputation before he had any significant publications, while Wittgenstein's classes consisted in his extemporaneously thinking through issues. Both emphasized and practiced slow, intense analysis. Heidegger said, "patience is the truly human way of being thoughtful about things. Genuine patience is one of the basic virtues of philosophizing—a virtue which understands that we always have to build up the pile of kindling with properly selected wood so that it may at one point catch fire" (HPS 73). For Wittgenstein, "in philosophy the winner of the race is the one who can run most slowly" (CV 34; see also CV 57, 68, 80, Z §382).

3. Dale Jacquette describes Wittgenstein's legacy well: "the list of those who attended his lectures and whose intellectual and personal lives he touched, even while dissuading many of them from philosophy to more practical pursuits, reads like a who's who of some of the most prominent thinkers of the last half-century" (1998, 8). Richard Wolin wrote a book on four of Heidegger's students, *Heidegger's Children: Hannah Arendt, Karl Löwith, Hans Jonas, and Herbert Marcuse*, a list that doesn't include Hans-Georg Gadamer, arguably his most influential student.

4. I am hardly alone here. In a poll conducted in 1999, *Philosophical Investigations* and *Being and Time* were ranked the first and second most important books in philosophy in the twentieth century respectively, with the *Tractatus* coming in fourth (Lackey 1999, 331; see also "Heidegger and Wittgenstein Break Away from the Pack" (http://schwitzsplinters.blogspot.com/2010/04/heidegger-and-wittgenstein-break-away.html)). I can't think of any other philosophers who have entire books devoted to buildings they were associated with, like Heidegger's Black Forest cabin (Sharr 2006) and the Stonborough house that Wittgenstein designed (Wijdeveld 1993; Leitner 2000; Paden 2007; Last 2008; Oxaal, 2010).

5. There has been some secondary literature on this pairing, though to my mind surprisingly little. Aside from a number of articles, Simon Glendinning (1998) compares their views of Being with others, Stephen Mulhall (1990) connects their treatments of seeing aspects, Anthony Rudd (2003) discusses their views on skepticism, James C. Edwards (1990) analyzes their views on language and nihilism, and George F. Sefler (1974) provides a more general study of the two.

6. Gadamer 1995, xxxvi n.13, see also 557; 1977, 126–127; Hahn 1996, 19, 22; von Wright 1982, 204.

7. In his analysis of the nature of analytic philosophy, Hans-Johann Glock calls the later Wittgenstein a "borderline case" (Glock 2008, 15; see also 162, 226; Gier 1981, 2). Glock wrote an earlier article titled, "Was Wittgenstein an Analytic Philosopher?" (Glock 2004), while Anat Biletzki titled a paper, "Wittgenstein: Analytic Philosopher?" (Biletzki and Matar 1998, 197–208), and Dale Jacquette has "Wittgenstein as Trans-Analytic-Continental Philosopher" (Reynolds et al. 2010; see also Badiou 2011, 70–71). Tom Rockmore (2006, 142) similarly argues that he cannot be classified.

8. Ayer refers to his "oracular sayings" (1985, 28); Russell wrote (with some personal animus): "he, himself, as usual, is oracular and emits his opinion as if it were a Czar's ukase, but humbler folk can hardly content themselves with this procedure" (Russell 1959a, 118; see also Glock 2004, 432; Copi and Beard 1966, 219; Fogelin 1995, xi). When Russell encouraged Wittgenstein to argue for his claims in the *Tractatus* rather than merely state them, Wittgenstein replied that "arguments spoil its beauty, and that he would feel as if he was dirtying a flower with muddy hands" (Monk 1996, 264). The power of Wittgenstein's personality forced this attitude onto some unlikely figures, such as Carnap: "when finally, sometimes after a prolonged arduous effort, his answer came forth, his statement stood before us like a newly created piece of art or a divine revelation. . . . The impression he made on us was as if insight came to him as through a divine inspiration, so that we could not help feeling that any sober rational comment or analysis of it would be a profanation" (Fann 1967, 34–35; see also Bouswma in Fann 1967, 151; Malcolm in Fann 1967, 72; Copi and Beard 1966, 229, 247; Dummett 1996, 173; Glock 2008, 172, 175–176, 194, 218; Staten 1986, 66; Edwards 1990, 142; Yourgrau 2005, 31). Try imagining how analyti-

cally trained philosophers might react to such a statement concerning, say, Derrida or Heidegger, and you start to see the exceptional status Wittgenstein enjoys.

9. Sluga and Stern 1996, 442; see also Stern 2004, 2; Biletzki 2003, 7–8; Hacker 1996, 239; Landini 2007, 1.

10. "The literature on the Tractatus is beginning to resemble the literature on the real meaning of the White Whale" (Thomson in Copi and Beard 1966, 217; see also Ashdown 2001, 318 n.10).

11. To take one prominent example, Saul Kripke's *Wittgenstein on Rules and Private Language: An Elementary Exposition* has become a canonical work even though it consists in "'an elementary exposition' of what I take to be the central thread of Wittgenstein's later work" (1984, vii; see also ix; Kripke also eschews any claim to represent Wittgenstein's own argument [ibid., 5, 6n. 7]). The only other primarily exegetical analytic work that has become important in its own right that I can think of is Strawson's *The Bounds of Sense: An Essay on Kant's Critique of Pure Reason*. Has any other work in the analytic tradition inspired anything like Hacker and Baker's highly regarded four-volume commentary on *Philosophical Investigations*? One is reminded of John Searle's response upon meeting a phenomenologist: "I am an analytic philosopher. I think for myself."

12. In Fann 1967, 34. Wittgenstein himself said that the *Tractatus* "is strictly philosophical and at the same time literary" (McGuinness 2005, 288).

13. See Jacquette 2005, 249–261. Scholars such as Ray Monk, Allan Janik, and Stephen Toulmin have pointed out the importance of figures such as Kraus or Herz, but I am focusing on philosophers here.

14. In 1919, Wittgenstein wrote to Ludwig von Ficker that "the book's point is an ethical one"; the account of language which sets the limits of effability is entirely in the service of that which is not included because ineffable. This attitude comes out clearly in the final sentence of his 1929 "A Lecture on Ethics" which holds that while religious and ethical statements are nonsense, they spring from "a tendency in the human mind which I personally cannot help respecting deeply and I would not for my life ridicule it" (PO 44; see also LO 36).

15. See LWVC 68–69; Murray 1978, 80–81. Ayer (1986, 18, 30–31) and Carnap (Fann 1967, 36) have conceded the point.

16. P. M. S. Hacker, as thorough a commenter on Wittgenstein as one can imagine, wrote that "although the young Wittgenstein was influenced by such diverse figures as Boltzmann, Paul Ernst, Hertz and Schopenhauer, his first masterpiece was inspired by, and written in reaction to, the works of Frege and Russell" (1996, 12; see also Biletzki 2003, 166–167; Lawn 2007, xvii n.2; Janik and Toulmin 1973, 9, 145; Glock 2008, 35, 79–80, 132, 149; Apel 1980, 10, 38 n.7, 38 n.9, 152–153; Taylor 1995, 73).

17. For example: "my views are, on almost every point of mathematical theory, diametrically opposed to those of Kant" (Russell 1996, 456; see also Russell 1959b, 11–12, 38, 54, 74, 172; Hylton 1990, chaps. 3–5; Hanna 2001, 58; Braver 2007, 23–30).

18. Many have noted this. On the first page of his two-volume study of Wittgenstein, David Pears writes that "the simplest general characterization of his philosophy is that it is critical in the Kantian sense" (Pears 1987, 3; see also 90, 147; Goodman 2007, 108; Dilman 2002, 9; see Tang 2011, 598n.1 for a thorough list).

19. His unpublished works contain more extensive references to various authors than do his published works or recorded statements (see Stern 1996, 472 n.14); we know that he spent considerable time on Kant's first *Critique* (see Monk 1990, 158, 322; Drury in Rhees 1984, 158; Jacquette 2005, 250; Stern 1995, 113 n.77).

20. Russell Goodman (2007) has written an entire book on Wittgenstein's relationship to William James.

21. Conv 46, CV 53; Malcolm 2001, 106; Monk 1990, 283, 310, 463; von Wright in Fann 1967, 28; Drury in Rhees 1984, 157–158. He once called Kierkegaard "by far the greatest philosopher of the nineteenth century" (Fann 1967, 70; Rhees 1984, 87–88), a particularly interesting comment in light of the fact that Frege can be classified as a nineteenth-century thinker.

22. See BT 492 n.iv; 494 n.vi; 495 n.xii; 497 n.iii.

23. PI §108, §116; see also §120, §235.

24. Von Wright in Fann 1967, 23; see also Arrington and Glock 1992, 74; Baker and Hacker 1991, 5, 345. Jacquette coins the word—"unpigeonholeable"—to capture the fact that Wittgenstein has "a fundamentally different aim and orientation than can reasonably be attributed to any other thinker in the history of philosophy" (Reynolds et al. 2010, 161, 170).

25. LPP 47; Hacker 1996, 100, 135; Pears 1987, 41; Glock 2004, 440.

26. PO 103, 436, PG 293, PI §402, Z §357, §414; Gier 1981, 66, 127.

27. PI §305, PO 327, 333–334.

28. BT 63/39; see also BT 199/157, 209/165, 211/167. Hacker differentiates analytic philosophy from, among other things, Heidegger's "obscurities" (Hacker 1996, 3), while producing three volumes of exegesis on the *Investigations* due to the fact that it is "so difficult to fathom" (1996, 239).

29. PG 283; see also Z §455, LC 41; Rhees 1984, 208.

30. HCT 222–223; see also HCT 166–167, BT 63/39, 170/132, 250–251/207–208, IM 107, BP 65–66, 69, 124, 157, 167, 175, 255, 297, KPM 165, BW 217–218, 237.

31. Russell 1959a, 63; see also 11–12, 54.

32. David Stern is the best on this point: "philosophers in search of Wittgenstein's theory of language or experience or practice focus on a relatively small number of much-discussed remarks in which he appears to summarize his real reasons for accepting (or rejecting) a specific view, looking for 'evidence' of his 'underlying commitments' without giving sufficient consideration to the context from which those quotations are taken" (Sluga and Stern 1996, 442–443; see also 444–447, 457; Stern 1995, 3–6, 97–98; 2004, 168–170; Pears 1987, 192; Pears 1988, 227–228, but compare Pears 1988, 397).

33. 1929's "Some Remarks on Logical Form" (PO 28).

34. One is reminded of Derrida's famous objection to Heidegger's emphasis on Nietzsche's *Nachlass* (Derrida 1981, 123). Stern briefly mentions this connection, as well as Foucault's challenge to the notions of text and author as self-evident (Stern 1996, 474 n.28, 458). See Stern 1995, 95–96; 1996, 448, 455; Baker and Hacker 1985, 3–4.

35. Stern makes this point as well at 1991, 204; 1995, 5–6; 1996, 445–446, 449; Baker and Hacker 1985, xi.

## 1  What Is Philosophy?

1. See Husserl's 1931 moving letter to Alexander Pfänder: Heidegger

behaved entirely as a student of my work and as a future collaborator, who, as regards all the essentials of method and problematic, would stand on the ground of my constitutive phenomenology. . . . I had been warned often enough: Heidegger's phenomenology is something totally different from mine; rather than furthering the development of my scientific works, his university lectures as well as his book are, on the contrary, open or veiled attacks on my works, directed at discrediting them on the most essential points. When I used to relate such things to Heidegger in a friendly way, he would just laugh and say: Nonsense! . . . I devoted two months to studying *Being and Time*, as well as his more recent writings. I arrived at the distressing conclusion that . . . he may be involved in the formation of a philosophical system of the kind which I have always considered it my life's work to make forever impossible. . . . For almost a decade he was my closest friend; naturally this is all over. . . . This reversal in professional esteem and personal relations was one of the most difficult ordeals of my life. (Sheehan and Palmer 1997, 480–482)

2. Russell's decision to retire his ambitious project and retire is all the more remarkable given that he did not grasp the point of Wittgenstein's criticism: "I couldn't understand his objection—in fact he was very inarticulate—but I feel in my bones that he must be right, and that he has seen something I have missed" (Monk 1996, 197). Of course, once he did appreciate it, it only made matters worse: "his criticism . . . was an event of first-rate importance in my life, and affected everything I have done since. I saw he was right, and I saw that I could not hope ever again to do fundamental work in philosophy. My impulse was shattered, like a wave dashed to pieces against a breakwater. I became filled with utter despair" (Monk 1996, 301–

302; see also 80–81, 272–274, 279–281, 290, 295–302; Monk 1990, 63, 80–83). Russell made a number of bitter remarks later in his career, especially regarding Wittgenstein's later method and the fact that Wittgenstein's reputation had eclipsed his own (Russell 1959a, 214, 216–217).

3. Wittgenstein notes the way his ideas intertwine with each other, complaining about "the crowd of thoughts which cannot come out, because they all want to rush forward and thus get stuck in the exit" (PO 123; see also LC 7; von Wright 1982, 139). Heidegger points to the hermeneutic circle of parts and whole involved in grasping any complex thought, an idea anticipated by Schopenhauer who wielded great influence over the young Wittgenstein (Schopenhauer 1969, xii–xiii).

4. PI x. Biographies attest to his urgent need to confess and correct even the slightest miscommunication. I don't think it a coincidence that he begins the book meant to correct his widely influential but "gravely mistaken" work with *Confessions*. Fania Pascal writes that "to make a confession must have appealed to Wittgenstein as the most radical way of relieving his mind of an oppressive burden of guilt" (Rhees 1984, 36; see also 120).

5. Glock in Glock 2001, 15; see also Fogelin 1995, 108–110; Edwards 1982, 4. Louis A. Sass takes this metaphor literally, comparing Wittgenstein's interlocutors to schizophrenics (1994, 8–9, 13).

6. He clearly assigns it this role in the midst of the richest discussion of philosophy in all of his *oeuvre*, PI §§89–133. Given his rudimentary knowledge of the canon, the *Tractatus* represents one of the few philosophical books Wittgenstein knew in detail.

7. T ix–x. Carnap admits that the Vienna Circle made the same mistake (Fann 1967, 38). Frank Ramsey points out Russell's error in his highly regarded 1923 review.

8. T 5.5563; see also T 5.4733, PI §98.

9. T 3.2, 3.201.

10. T 4.002, 4.112, PO 29, LO 50; von Wright 1973, 50.

11. NB 99. Were one inclined to psychoanalyze philosophers based on their symptomatic views, as Nietzsche occasionally recommends, one might attribute Wittgenstein's demand that propositions be completely candid about their true function to the extraordinary standard of absolute honesty he required in himself and his friends. Fania Pascal writes that she "never met anyone more incapable of telling a lie," describing the way his less than forthcoming description of having struck a girl in the Austrian school he briefly taught became a "crisis . . . burdening his conscience forever" (Rhees 1984, 37–38). Note that it is his "lie," not the blow, that haunts him.

12. Schopenhauer, a thinker the young Wittgenstein greatly admired, foreshadowed and possibly inspired some of these ideas, even the particular metaphor used: "gram-

mar explains only the clothing of the forms of thought . . . ; their function is to express these forms of thought with all their modifications. They are the instrument, the clothing, of the forms of thought, which must be made to fit their structure accurately, so that that structure can be recognized in it. . . . Philosophical grammar has to tell us about the precise mechanism of the expression of the thought-forms, just as logic has to inform us about the operations with the thought-forms themselves" (Schopenhauer 1969, 478–480). I was lead to this passage by Hannan 2009, 100–101.

13. Wittgenstein endorses Russell's theory at T 3.24, immediately prior to the book's second mention of the method of proposition analysis at T 3.25. He later confirms this as the model he had in mind (PG 211) and broaches the topic early in PI (§§39–40; see also McManus 2006, 22). Frege also emphasizes this point: "languages are unreliable on logical questions. It is indeed not the least of the logician's tasks to indicate the pitfalls laid by language in the way of the thinker" (GB 126; see also GB 58; Burge 2005, 219).

14. T p. 3; see also T 3.324.

15. These include conflating different "modes of signification" due to a single symbol standing for multiple meanings (T 3.323, 5.4733; see also GB 171; Fogelin 1995, 63), mixing up propositions and names since their signs look similar (T 3.143), and mistaking the arguments of functions for the "affixes of names" (T 5.02).

16. One of the few philosophical works Wittgenstein knew in detail was the first *Critique*, having studied it at length in an Italian prison camp he occupied for part of the First World War (Monk 1990, 158, 322; Rhees 1984, 157–158; Genova 1995, 8; Stern 1995, 113 n.77; PG 404, NB 15, T 6.6.36111). Like the preface to the *Tractatus*, Kant also brags that "there is not a single metaphysical problem which has not been solved, or for the solution of which the key at least has not been supplied" (C1 A xiii). Russell too has "no doubt that, in so far as philosophical knowledge is possible, it is by such methods that it must be sought; I have also no doubt that, by these methods, many ancient problems are completely soluble" (Russell 1945, 834; see also 831; Russell 1929, 259–260; 1959b, 14–15; in Ayer 1959, 33).

17. T p. 3, 4.003, 6.53, BB 59.

18. See Kenny 1973, 35; O'Hear 2000, 235; Livingston 2008, 50–54.

19. T 6.52; see also T 6.521, NB 74.

20. See T 3.317, 3.33, 6.12, 6.124, 6.126, NB 55; Diamond 1991, 2.

21. T 3.42, 4.023, 6.124.

22. T 6.13, 6.54. There are obvious echoes here of Kant's problem of tracing phenomena back to noumenal sources without using phenomenal categories like substance, existence, or cause, a problem pointed out by among others Schopenhauer

(1969, 435–436). Graham Priest (2002) argues that such self-referential paradoxes (including Russell's paradox and Heidegger's discussions of being) are an inevitable side-effect of any attempt to set limits to thought or language since, as Wittgenstein and Hegel argue, setting a limit requires us to have some sense of the outside, thus transgressing it.

23. T 3.334; see also T 3.326, 3.262, 6.113, 6.122, 6.211, NB 105–109, 115, 121, 127, 130, LO 59. This would also solve Russell's paradox without the *ad hoc* theory of types (NB 108–109; Churchill 1994, 392–393, 406 n.11; Livingston 2008, 54–55; McManus 2006, 25) which Wittgenstein found not just wrong but, I think, offensive, desecrating logic's austere perfection as much as ornamentation would sully the Stonborough House he designed for his sister.

24. T 3.331, 5.132, 5.452, 5.535, NB 91, 104.

25. T 4.115, T 4.1272, T 6.53, T 5.61, NB 45, 108, LWVC 183–184.

26. Briefly, Frege treated propositions as functions which combine an unsaturated or incomplete concept like "is a horse" with a self-sufficient object like "Trigger." Concepts cannot be the subject of a proposition, which means that the rule forbidding such a construction must use the very structure it forbids, indeed *in* its very forbidding of it, as in, "The concept 'is a horse' cannot serve as the subject of a proposition." This problem is reminiscent of the scene in Monty Python's *Life of Brian* where a rabbi reads out the charges against a man about to be stoned for saying the forbidden word, "Jehovah," and promptly gets stoned.

27. "Logical so-called propositions *shew* [the] logical properties of language and therefore of [the] universe, but *say* nothing. This means that by merely looking at them you can *see* these properties; whereas, in a proposition proper, you cannot see what is true by looking at it" (NB 107).

28. T 4.126, 6.122, NB 106, 108, 115, 121.

29. T 5.535, 5.5561, NB 130.

30. T 5.473, 5.53, 5.5303, 5.533, 6.232, NB 19, 130.

31. A mistake made by Frege (GB 170).

32. T 4.411, 4.441.

33. T 4.0312; see also T 4.0621, 4.441, 5.4, 5.44, 5.461, NB 99; Copi and Beard 1966, 244. He also believes that logical operators dissolve into truth-tables that show their significance (T 4.31, NB 19, 101; Fogelin 1995, 42).

34. T 5.473, 5.4733, PO 35; Copi and Beard 1966, 242, 246.

35. In a rather Kantian moment, Wittgenstein says that "logical laws are *forms* of thought and space and time *forms* of intuition" (NB 117).

36. T 6.124; see also LWVC 80, 228, 240; Diamond 1991, 4.

37. T xix. Similarly, Frege's concept writing "has, as a result of genuine thought, been so developed that it does the thinking for us, so to speak" (Frege 1980, IV; see also 103, GB 116; Diamond 1991, 31). Several of these ideas can be found in Descartes as well. He argues that many philosophical confusions and disagreements arise from unclear uses of language (*Rules* XIII, 433), requiring a language built up out of ultimate simples, albeit simple ideas rather than propositions, which would effectively think for us: "if someone were to explain correctly what are the simple ideas in the human imagination out of which all human thoughts are compounded, and if his explanation were generally received, I would dare to hope for a universal language. . . . The greatest advantage of such a language would be the assistance it would give to men's judgement, representing matters so clearly that it would be almost impossible to go wrong" (Letter to Mersenne, 20 December 1629/AT 1–81). Leibniz too dreamt of a notation system to represent all human knowledge and force thought down the right alleys, a kind of colorless Glass Bead Game that would clear up all disputes by translating the issue at hand into symbols which can then be calculated to find the answer. As he wrote in a letter to Galloys (December 1678, quoted in Davis 2000, 16): "this characteristic consists of a certain script or language . . . that perfectly represents the relationships between our thoughts. . . . The characters of this script should serve invention and judgement as in algebra and arithmetic. . . . It will be impossible to write, using these characters, chimerical notions (*chimères*) such as suggest themselves to us." Wittgenstein writes in a similar spirit, "I used to believe that philosophy had to give a definitive dissection of propositions so as to set out clearly all their connections and remove all possibilities of misunderstanding" (PG 211; see also T 5.551, T 6.1262), and compares logical proofs to mechanical processes (T 6.1262; as does Russell [2004, 59]), an analogy he will spend much his career undermining. (The possible connections with Alan Turing, who sat in on some of Wittgenstein's classes, are intriguing.) In words echoing his description of the *Tractatus*, Russell praises Leibniz's "*Characteristica Universalis*, by means of which thinking could be replaced by calculation" (1945, 592). Russell explicitly connects Leibniz's vision with its realization in contemporary logic, and with its concomitant rewards: "two hundred years ago, Leibniz foresaw the science which Peano has perfected. . . . The subject which he desired to create now exists. . . . Over an enormous field of what was formerly controversial, Leibniz's dream has become sober fact. . . . Hence many of the topics which used to be placed among the great mysteries . . . are now no longer in any degree open to doubt or discussion" (Russell 2004, 61; see also 1945, 591, 595; 1996, 5). Apparently, Frege's *Begriffsschrift* was also inspired by Leibniz (see Davis 2000, 52, 57). This may simply be my ignorance, but it seems that the history of early analytic thought emphasizes its empiricist roots to the exclusion of sufficient attention to rationalism.

38. "In order that you should have a language which can express or *say* everything that *can* be said, this language must have certain properties" (NB 107; see also 39, 117, T 4.121, 5.511, 6.1233, 6.13; Glock 2008, 35, 79–80, 97; Jacquette 2005, 254).

39. LWVC 216; see also LWVC 183, 213–214, 229, T pp. 3–4, T 4.114, 4.1273, 4.411, 4.51, 5.473, 5.551, 6, 6.001, 6.125–6.1251, NB 33, 75, 89, 112, 116, 122; Copi and Beard 1966, 140, 364–365; Churchill 1994, 398; McGuinness 2005, 227–228, 311. Frege applies the same strategy to arithmetic: once he has defined zero and one nonmathematically, and determined the method for generating consecutive numbers from these, he has fully circumscribed the concept of number and, in principle, all numbers (Frege 1980, 12, 25, 67, 87–90, 115–116). Russell credits Peano and Frege with discovering this method (2004, 60–61).

40. T 4.5–4.51, bracketing numbers added; see also T 5.21, 5.442, 5.45, 5.46, 5.4711, 5.5, 6.001; O'Hear 2000, 239; Diamond 1991, 7. "We ask: 'What is language?,' 'What is a proposition?' And the answer to these questions is to be given once for all; and independently of any future experience" (PI §92).

41. PG 113; see also AWL 12–13, 138, OC §320; Travis 2006, 5–6, 78. This admission is momentous given his earlier commitment to Frege's requirement that any assertion must be completely determinate in order to have any sense at all (GB 105, 159, 170; NB 61–62, 68, 98, T 3.23, 3.3442, PI §99; Churchill 1994, 391). Also rejected is the idea that 'elementary' has a single, determinate meaning rather than shifting with differing purposes (PI §17, §47, §59, §88). Wittgenstein occasionally deploys a Tractarian metaphor to support this anti-Tractarian point: "we remain unconscious of the prodigious diversity of all the everyday language-games because the clothing of our language makes everything alike" (PI II.xi, p. 191).

42. T 6.45; see also T 4.11.

43. See Malcolm 1994, 38–39; Edwards 1990, 138.

44. Monk 1990, 249–251. Tangentially, the arch-Platonist Kurt Gödel, who had been attending meetings of the Vienna Circle, apparently saw Wittgenstein at this lecture (Yourgrau 2005, 28–29). Unsurprisingly, he thought very little of Wittgenstein's views on mathematics, early or late.

45. Russell 1996, 450–451; GB 1960, 122, 127, 131, 145.

46. RFM 45, 266–270, 279, 284, 407–408, LWVC 201–202, AWL 131–132, PG 480–481, PhR 149, 237, PI §352, §426, §516. Michael Dummett defines realism as the commitment to bivalence concerning the truth or falsity of answers, regardless of our ability to ascertain them (Dummett 1981, 434). Frege uses the same idea (GB 105, 126 n., 159, 162, 166, 170).

47. PG 117, 126, 238, 245, 301, 322, 361, 368, 377, 400, 415, 481, LWVC 36, 110, 129, 132, 146, 175–176, 204, AWL 133–134, 179, RFM 228, 267, 279, 320–321, 420.

48. LWVC 154, LWL 12, 30–31, PG 444.

49. PG 66; see also PG 106, 179, PhR 118, PI §18, §65, §304, PI II.xi p. 171.

50. LWVC 124, 132–133, 202, PhR 321, PG 116. Recall that the term "barbarian" originally indicated those who, lacking a genuine language, could only spout gibberish sounding to the Greeks like "barbarbar."

51. RPPI §920, translation slightly altered.

52. PG 334; see also PG 111, 116, 322, LWVC 124, 132–133, 202, PhR 321, PI §§23–24; Medina 2002, 152; Staten 1986, 21.

53. AWL 138; see also AWL 12–13, PG 211, LWPPI §525, LWPPII 44.

54. BB 59; see also PO 161, PI §52, §340; Stern 1995, 39; 2004, 55, 74; Fogelin 1995, 110, 136.

55. PI §116; see also PI §190, OC §260, §406, Z §448; Stern 2004, 12–13, 70, 92.

56. Austin is quite close to Wittgenstein here: "The wile of the metaphysician consists in asking 'Is it a real table?' (a kind of object which has no obvious way of being phoney) and not specifying or limiting what may be wrong with it, so that I feel at a loss 'how to prove' it *is* a real one" (1979, 87).

57. PI §199; see also PI §150, RFM 210, 283, LFM 61, RPPI §875, RPPII §736, OC §355, Conv 23–25, PG 47; Williams 2002, 58, 171; Williams in Williams 2006, 74, 84; Hacker 1996, 127; Baker and Hacker 1985, 65, 75, 104, 149, 159, 161; Wright in Vesey 1982, 226; Mulhall 1990, 36–37; Glendinning 1998, 156 n.11; Dummett 1996, 133, but compare with 159–160; McGinn, 1987, 30–31; Ryle 1949, 41, 54.

58. "We use language without conscious awareness of its rules" (LWL 50; see also LWL 84, 101, LWVC 153, 248, AWL 3, PG 50, 62–63, 85, 96, BB 25, RPPII §417, §603, OC §46, CV 64). Wittgenstein briefly touches on this point in the *Tractatus* (T 4.002, 5.511), but with the goal of overcoming it in order to consciously examine the rules of logic.

59. AWL 115; see also RFM 337, 350–351, 397, 422, PO 381–383, 395, PI §201, §503–506, CV 31, OC §510, LC 62, PG 47, PI §593.

60. PI §78; see also PI §89, §610; Austin 1979, 84–85.

61. PI §43, AWL 29, 48, 78, 87, BB 69, RFM 89, RPPI §1013, OC §61.

62. PI §360, §421, §569, RPPI §586, LPP 51, OC §351; Hintikka and Hintikka 1989, 217–218; Cooper 2003, 173; Goff 1968.

63. LQT 121 n.11.

64. LWL 53; see also LWL 22, 50, 84, 101, LLVC 77, 153, 248, AWL 3, 43, PO 202, 456, PG 50, 62–63, 80, 85, 96, Z §86, §111, §118, Conv 23–25, RFM 210, LFM 61, 183, PI §150, §199, RPPII §417, §603, §736, OC §46, BB 25, LC 68, CV 64; Wright 1980, 261–262; Medina 2002, 80–81; Genova 1995, 51; Rudd 2003, 76–77; Travis 2006, 16. The importance of this topic is shown by the fact that Wittgenstein opens

the first day of his 1930 lectures with it: "philosophic puzzles are irrelevant to our every-day life. They are puzzles of *language*. Instinctively we use language rightly; but to the intellect this use is a puzzle" (LWL 1). Pierre Bourdieu connects this problem to anthropologists' attempts to capture a culture's tacit understanding in explicit theories and interpretations (Bourdieu 1977, 2, 17–19, 96, 106, 109–110, 117, 120, 156). Psychological experiments done by Timothy Wilson found that students' initial ranking of different jams in a blind taste test closely correlated with the preference reached by trained experts at *Consumer Reports* but, when forced to articulate criteria for their ranking, their ordering diverged radically, choosing the expert's worst jam as their favorite (Lehrer 2009, 143–145; Gladwell 2007, 179–182).

65. Conv 28; Fann 1967, 53, 59, 69, 73, 82; Guignon 1990, 650–651; Janik and Toulmin 1973, 205–206; Rhees 1984, 124. He even considered studying medicine himself (von Wright 1977, 132; Rhees 1984, 76–77, 136). When M. O'C. Drury told him of a philosophy student who abandoned his dissertation after deciding that he had nothing original to say, Wittgenstein replied that he should receive a PhD "for that action alone" (Rhees 1984, 109).

66. PO 179; see also PO 161, 255, 449, RFM 92, PI §129, §415, II.xii. p. 195, p. 48 n., LFM 22, CV 13, 17, 39, 63, PG 256; Stern 1995, 16–17, 29; Stroud 2000, 191; Ashdown 2001, 325; Mays and Brown 1972, 259, 262; de Beistegui 2005, 10, 17.

67. Strictly speaking, Heidegger applies this term to equipment that gets absorbed into the task at hand, but this is very similar to his claims about pre-ontological knowledge in general. He also identifies three slightly different forms of unobtrusiveness (BT 102–104/73–74), but the differences do not matter for my purposes here. Some commentators have noted this similarity between Heidegger and Wittgenstein (Mulhall 1990, 147–151; Glendinning 1998, 51, 88).

68. PO 255, PI §§85–86, §139, §§240–242, §349.

69. BB 19; see also BB 25, 27, PI §68, §84, §99–101, PG 117, 238, 300, CV 82, RPPII §639; Staten 1986, 97.

70. NB 61–62, 68, 98, T 3.23, 3.3442, PI §99.

71. Z §111; see also Z §114, §118, RPPI §78, RPPII §234, PI II.xi, p. 193; Pears 2006, viii; Ryle 1949, 7.

72. IM 16. There are rare exceptions to Wittgenstein's hostility; for example, "don't think I despise metaphysics or ridicule it. On the contrary, I regard the great metaphysical writings of the past as among the noblest productions of the human mind" (Drury in Fann 1967, 68).

73. See BT 35/15, BT 96/67, 119/86, 179/140, 415/364, PIRA 359/3, 361/5, 367/15, 369/18, WT 57, BW 109, BaT 15, 159, Supp 113, PIA 62, ITP 1, FCM 13, 22; Sheehan and Palmer 1997, 476.

74. T 6.5, 6.52–6.521, PI §118, §133.

75. BT 215/171; see also BT 85/59, 88/61, 128–129/95–96, 106/75, 185/145, 246/202, 309/264, 412/361, HCT 91, 106–107, 111, 117, 156, 160, 162–163, 185, 218, PS 94, 117–122, BP 109–110, 118, 123, 275, PIK 18–19, 136, LQT 7, 86, 179, 205, IPR 42, 168, 195, 208, 230; FCM 275; Ryle 1949, 26–27. Cavell compares Heidegger with Wittgenstein on this point (1982, 241).

76. HCT 172, 184, BT 122/89; Guignon 1983, 61; Mensch 1996, 16, 29.

77. BT 101/71, 132/99, 245/201, 268/225, 320/275, 363–364/315–316.

78. Guignon puts it nicely: "in Heidegger's view, many of the intractable puzzles that run through philosophy first arise because we uncritically buy into a particular conception of what things are" (Polt 2005, 75).

79. BT 125/92, 130–131/98, 150/114–115, 132/99, 198/156, IPR 170, 188, 217–219, HCT 172, MFL 32.

80. These include language and statements (BT 57/33, 201/159, 269/226, BW 122, FCM 340–341, 314–315, MFL 216–217, BP 210, PS 125, IPR 14), truth as correspondence (85–86/59, 203/160, 257–258/214–215, 261/218, 267/224–225, MFL 124, 127, 217, BP 206–207, BW 127, KPM 87, PS 350; Wrathall 1999, 70; Carman 2003, 259), and logic (BT 166–167/129, PS 174–175, BP 206–207).

81. BT 36/15, 42/21, 72/46, 150/114–115, 245/201.

82. "We must show *why* the kind of Being with which Dasein knows the world is such that it passes over the phenomenon of worldhood" (BT 94/65–66; see also BT 128/95, HCT 219; Taminiaux, 1991, 91).

83. BT 360/312; see also BT 32/12, 36/15, 59/35, 85/58, 245/201, 359/311, 460/408, HCT 149, 152, 196, BP 165, Zo 36, BW 98, 116, 144.

84. PI §128, §599; Michael Polanyi similarly posits what he calls "tacit knowledge" as the solution to Meno's paradox (1967, 22–23).

85. "When Being-in-the-world is exhibited phenomenologically, disguises and concealments are rejected *because* this phenomenon itself always gets 'seen' in a certain way in every Dasein" (BT 85/58; see also 96/67, 119/86, HCT 162, BCAP 184, 188). In his knowledgeable and sympathetic 1929 review of *Sein und Zeit*, Gilbert Ryle writes that Heidegger "is simply telling us explicitly what we must have known 'in our bones' all the time" (Murray 1978, 61). I discuss Ryle's review in more detail in "Analyzing Heidegger: The Analytic Receptions of Heidegger's Work."

86. PIK 16–17, HCT 143–144, 186–187, KPM 7, 50, 159, ITP 57; Zimmerman 1986, 37. In what is perhaps the single best analysis of Heidegger and Wittgenstein, Charles Guignon writes that, "both suggest that these problems arise from a stance of disengaged, theoretical reflection, and both try to dissolve these problems by pro-

viding descriptions of how things show up for us in the course of our ordinary, pre-reflective lives" (Guignon 1990, 652). Charles Taylor (1995, 75) and Stanley Cavell (1995, 138) also note the similarity.

87. BT 37–38/16, 69/43, 184/144, 187/146, 383/334, 402/351, BP 160, HCT 95, 110, 154–155, 170, PRL 92, 227, 246, MFL 126, Zo 142; Baiasu 2009, 686, 691–2.

88. BT 95/67; see also BT 90/62, 140/106, 177/138, 405/354, 409/358, HCT 30, 162, 168, 182–185, PRL 43–44, BCAP 12, Supp 115; Carman 2003, 19, 56, 66, 207; Tamin-iaux, 1991, 42, 61, 170; Zimmerman 1986, 29. Some have noted the similarity with Wittgenstein (Sefler 1974, 88; Apel 1998, 132; Guignon 1990, 651; Cooper 2003, 150). Rorty compares Heidegger's reformation of Husserlian phenomenology with Wittgenstein's transition to his later work on this point (1991, 32 n.9, 50–51).

89. BT 32/12, 98–99/69, 183/143, 245/200–201, 360/312, BP 276, HCT 144, 162, 299, LQT 121 n.11, 229, 236–237, BaT 177–178; Mulhall 1990, 76; Taylor 1995, 170; Polt 2005, 78; Dreyfus 1992, xi, xxvii, xlii.

90. BT 96/67; see also PIRA 362/7, LQT 121–123, 129, PS 100; Dreyfus and Wrathall 2002, 91; Crowe 2008, 64, 89.

91. "We sometimes use the expression 'understanding something' with the signifi-cation of 'being able to manage something,' 'being a match for it,' 'being competent to do something.' In understanding, as an *existentiale*, that which we have such competence over is not a 'what,' but Being as existing" (BT 183/143).

92. BT 88/61, 118–120/85–87, BP 16, 68, HCT 164, 194–195, BP 275–276; Cooper 2003, 114, 126; Okrent 1988, 28, 280–281; Crowell and Malpas 2007, 10.

93. BT 34/13, 61/37, 244/200, 274/231, 361–362/313–314, 424/372. Avrum Stroll writes that no philosopher before Wittgenstein thought to recall obvious facts of everyday life as a solution to philosophical problems (2002, 104, 122), presumably unaware of Heidegger's use of this technique in 1927's *Being and Time*. P. M. S. Hacker claims that Wittgenstein's "non-cognitive conception of philosophy [is] unprecedented in the history of the subject" (1996, 36; see also 42, 100, 118). Such errors and lost opportunities proliferate in the silence between analytic and conti-nental thinkers. On the other hand, see Mulhall 1990, 15, 120.

94. HCT 185; see also HCT 191, 196, 202, 244, LQT 85–86, 341, TDP 56, 174, BP 159, 163, 171, BT 101/71, 104/74, 152/116, 155/119, 191/150, 368/321, 405/354, 416/364, Ont 72, BCAP 24, MFL 127, PRL 147, 170; van Buren 2002, 164–165.

95. BP 165; see also HCT 152, BT 69/43, PIRA 363/8, BCAP 32, LQT 122–123, PR 5, FCM 177, BaT 79, Zo 29, 74.

96. Dahlstrom 2011, 107n.3; Thomson 2011, 8n.2. In an early lecture, Heidegger tells his students that he is "implanting the *instinct for what is self-evident*" (BCAP 5; see also LQT 18, 167–168, 238–239, EGT 59, WT 42). Compare with Wittgenstein:

"God grant the philosopher insight into what lies in front of everyone's eyes" (CV 63).

97. BT 105/75; see also BT 232/187, 406/355, HCT 188.

98. LQT 132; see also LQT 336, HCT 183, BT 128–129/95–96, 147/112, 190/149, 200–201/158, 412/361, TDP 64, 75, 85, 187; Bourdieu 1977, 156.

99. BT 101/71; see also BT 255/212, 269/227, HCT 218.

100. BT 101/71; see also BT 128–129/95–96, 132/99, 141/106, 190/150, 198/156, 320/275, HCT 207, 213, 231, 254–255, LQT 121, PIA 69.

101. Curiously, Gilbert Ryle, who became one of the main proponents of know-how as a distinct and legitimate form of knowledge, criticized Heidegger in 1929, arguing that his "attempt to derive our knowledge of 'things' from our practical attitude towards tools breaks down; for to use a tool involves knowledge of what it is, what can be done [with] it, and what wants doing" (in Murray 1978, 63).

102. BT 269/227; see also BT 255/212, HCT 197, 202. The thematic statement about a piece of chalk "is possible only on the basis of a *re-concealing* of the chalk as a means whereby we deal with things" (LQT 133). I discuss this in more detail and with references to secondary literature in *A Thing of This World* (Braver 2007, 190–198).

103. "The more narrowly we examine actual language, the sharper becomes the conflict between it and our requirement. (For the crystalline purity of logic was, of course, not a *result of investigation*: it was a requirement)" (PI §107; see also PI §94, §101, §§103–105, §107, §§112–113, §115, §154, §170, §177, §402, §427, §607, PI II. xi p. 167, RFM 86). Compare with BT 200/158.

104. Rendering *sein-bei* as "Being-alongside," as Macquarrie and Robinson do, is widely considered to be a problematic translation. *Sein-bei* means almost the opposite of "alongside" which connotes disengagement and separation, as Heidegger points out on the very next page. See HCT 158 for a helpful discussion.

105. Heidegger later develops this attribution of the beginning of metaphysics to Plato in works like *The Essence of Truth* and "Plato's Doctrine of Truth." See Braver 2007, 291–303, for more.

106. BT 88/61; see also LQT 237, PM 26, PIRA 362/7, 385/41, BCAP 146, Supp 84, 95, 115–116, PS 117–122, HCT 188; Sallis 1993, 9.

107. BT 190/149, all italics in original; see also BT 103/73, 129/96, 147/112, 177/138, 200–201/158, 238/193, 413/361–362, 474–475/422–423, HCT 187, 195–196, 219, BW 101–103, LQT 122–123; Rouse 1987, 60–61, 66; Carman 2003, 56, 66, 207; Richardson 1986, 17, 19; Guignon 1983, 201; Versényi 1965, 27; Pöggeler 1970, 293. Heidegger accuses Husserl of building this mistake into his version of phenomenology with the *epochê* (see, e.g., MF 134; Ihde 2010, 43).

108. PO 310, BB 150, 165, PI §114, OC §601.

109. BB 177; see also BB 150, 165, 174, RFM 64, PI §113.

110. PI §132; see also PO 425, BB 66, 174; Malcolm 1994, 73, 82, 87; McManus 2004, 250; Edwards 1990, 140; Sass 1994, 9, 14, 36. Karsten Harries connects the two on this idea (1968, 283–286).

111. PI §175; see also PI §166, §428, §503, §507, RFM 36–37, 41; McGuinness 1982, 41–42; Baker and Hacker 1985, 74; Stroud 2000, 171; Taylor 1995, 167; McDowell 2009, 94.

112. PI §322, PO 212, 434.

113. AWL 132; see also PI §334, Z §8.

114. BB 40; see also BB 142, PG 273, LC 22, PI §607, §633, §693, PI II.xi p. 185.

115. "You *could* say [a philosopher] knows better what a word means than others do. But in fact philosophers generally know *less*. Because ordinary persons have no temptations to misunderstand language" (PO 367; see also McGuinness 1982, 40).

116. PI §607; see also PI §20, §51, §124, §154, §578, §592, BB 34, 41, 45, 56, 80, 115.

117. PO 179; see also PO 114, 173, 179, 453, LWVC 183, DWL 35, AWL 97, PG 256, PhR 65, 153, LFM 22, 44, PI §89, §93, §109, §§126–128, §140, §§654–655, PI II.xi p. 171; Ryle 1949, 7. Wittgenstein even refers to Plato in this context, an important precedent for Heidegger (LPP 45). McGinn says that Wittgenstein "wishes to give a characterisation of what it is actually like to follow a rule, to remind us of the 'phenomenology' of (e.g.) using a word; and so to get away from certain natural philosophical misconceptions" (1984, 20; see also 29; Stern 1995, 16–17; Stroud 2000, 191; Glendinning 1998, 88, 156 n.11; Polt 2006, 78; Apel 1999, 132, 138; Cavell 1995, 138). Wittgenstein used the term "phenomenology" during his transitional phase, but not in the Husserlian or Heideggerian sense (Stern 1995, 99, 137–140).

118. Fann 1967, 52; H 17.

119. PI §90; see also PI II.xi p. 193–194, PG 47, PO 326–327; Malcolm 1994, 78–79. Augustine "knew the technique, but not how to describe it" (LPP 6). Heidegger spent a good deal of time on Augustine early in his career, bringing his notion of pre-ontological understanding to bear on Augustine's worry about knowing time (Zo 36) and his description of the self (BT 69/43 n.i; see also Kisiel 1993, 24–25).

120. Wittgenstein criticizes Socrates' demand that claimants to knowledge be able to supply and defend a consistent definition (BB 20, 26–27, PG 120–121; Rhees 1984, 115; Stern 2004, 13–14; Pears 2006, viii). See Burger (2008, 47–56) for a helpful comparison of Aristotelian and Socratic approaches.

121. BT 96/68, 132/99, 200/158, 245/201, 320/275, PM 9. See especially HCT 219.

122. BT 191/150, HCT 299–300, LQT 238–239, BCAP 186–187.

123. Thus, while Heidegger also sees the need for an explanation (BT 250/206), he has one handy: "this 'seeing in a certain way and yet for the most part wrongly explaining' is itself based upon nothing else than this very state of Dasein's Being" (BT 85/58).

124. AWL 90, 108, BB 46, PG 47, 193–194, PO 189, 367.

125. LWPPI §41; see also LWPPII 46, 86, BB 9–10, 62, PO 214, 222, 235, RFM 75, RPPI §65, RPPII §235, LFM 18, 21, Z §448; Pears 1988, 426–427; Kenny 1973, 164.

126. CV 11, RFM 137, 272, PG 169, RPPI §65, §378, §380, §417, §751, §1015, §1074, AWL 98; McGuinness 1982, 81.

127. BB 41, RPPI §359, §586, LPP 71, PI §427, OC §146, LC 63, RC III §20, PG 149.

128. PI §194; see also PI §349, PO 51, 199, 435, 453, LWL 35, 60, 108, AWL 61–62, RPPII §417, PI §112, §349, §402; Baker and Hacker 1985, 19–20; Stern 1995, 15, 42; Crary and Read 2000, 46, 51 n.15; McDowell 2009, 94. Cavell notes that "Wittgenstein shows us that we maintain unsatisfiable pictures of how things must happen," and finds a similar view in Heidegger (1995, 152). Note that while Heidegger emphasizes the way these confusions arise from natural events in Dasein's life (equipment breakdowns, anxiety, anticipating death), he also places some of the blame on language, especially the way subject–predicate grammar suggests a substance underlying qualities. One reason Heidegger's writing is so laborious is that he is working against the grain of our language, trying to reveal inconspicuous phenomena for which "often not only the words are lacking but the very grammar as well" (HCT 151; see also HCT 202, 228, 249, BT 55/32, 63/39, 199/157, 211/167–168). His early work limits language's corruptive influence by making it secondary to a prelinguistic understanding of beings.

129. I think Wittgenstein would have liked a story I heard about a child who overheard his parents speaking of the 'white man' who crossed the ocean to treat American Indians badly. The child took the subject's definite description literally, imagining a giant chalk-white man striding across the ocean like a colossus, stomping teepees and swallowing buffalo whole.

130. AWL 13; see also AWL 15; Medina 2002, 2, 137, 187; Griffiths 1991, 213; Goldfarb in Williams 2006, 24. "The passages in question were meant to show that the intuitions that fuel such philosophical theories are only compelling if they are left unexamined" (Stern 1995, 175; see also Stern 1995, 24–25, 86–87).

131. PI §464, §524, PO 119, 165, AWL 90, BB 66, 98–99, 144, 182; Livingston 2008, 47; Diamond 1991, 21, 45. This strategy has proved surprisingly effective. Quine infers the indeterminacy of translation from his refusal to take meaning for granted when he spells out exactly what we would have to do in order to translate a new language: "the shadows have favored wishful thinking" (Quine 1970, 10). Much of

Einstein's work is the result of figuring out exactly how we would measure things like simultaneity or length without taking them for granted (Einstein 2006, 23–25, 37, 89). Wittgenstein compares his own emphasis on verification to Einstein's on measurement (PG 458–459, PhR 200). Mark Twain takes notions of heaven literally in "Captain Stormfield's Visit to Heaven," as does Bernard Williams in "The Makropulos Case: Reflections on the Tedium of Immortality" (T 6.4312 alludes to Williams' subject).

132. LWPPI §148; see also AWL 91, BB 56, LFM 199, PI §90, §191, PI II.xi p. 167, II. xi p. 180, RPPI §354, §950, LPP 47, Z §625. These two sources of confusion—pictures and analogies—are by no means mutually exclusive. Indeed, since "pictures of [e.g.] the working of our mind are embodied in many of the forms of expression of our everyday language" (BB 40), they often overlap and reinforce each other.

133. T 4.002, NB 70.

134. NB 7; see also T 5.4541.

135. LWL 54; see also LWL 26, PG 104, PI §126, PI §435, LWPPI §§971–974.

136. PO 185; see also PO 177, PI §122, §182, RFM 113.

137. Stephen Mulhall compares Heidegger's fore-understandings to Wittgenstein's pictures (2003, 37; 2007, 88), as does Karl-Otto Apel (1980, 18, 42 n.26).

138. LWL 25, my italics; see also LWL 45, AWL 77–78, BB 26, 40–41, PhR 82, 172–173, RFM 115, RPPI §498, §824, PI II.xi p. 167; Wisdom in Fann 1967, 47; Fogelin 1995, 109. Jaynes is good on this subject (2000, 44–46, 53–56).

139. BB 108; see also LPP 43.

140. AWL 114; see also Z §605; Ryle 1949, 35.

141. Zo 192; see also HCT 96–97, MFL 134–135; Carman 2003, 102; Mulhall 1990, 8.

142. PM 26, BT 72/46, 405/354, TDP 64, 83–85, 94.

143. PI §103; see also PI §115, §305, §308, §363, §412, §425, §607, PO 221, 264, LPP 45, Z §20, §446; Stern 1995, 42.

144. RPPII §§642–643; see also Z §554, LWPPI §951, LWPPII 61–63, 68–70; Cook 1965, 290–291. One of their responses to the "problem" of this asymmetry is to simply deny it, as we will see in chapter 4.

145. Both see philosophers getting trapped in an implicit disjunctive syllogism where apparently positive characterizations of the mind actually result from the denial of various mundane qualities. In other words, the mind is not *out* in the world like this hairbrush so it must be *inside*; it's not a *material* object like this hairbrush so it must be *ethereal* (BB 47, 69, HCT 160).

146. "We tend to think of the mind as a sort of receptacle in which things are stored" (AWL 77; see also RPPI §193). "Here the subject is thought of as a sort of box with an interior, with the walls of a box, and with an exterior" (MFL 160; see also Supp 163).

147. BT 87/60–61, translation slightly altered; see also BT 79/54, 130/97, 205/162, 250/206, 363/315–316, TDP 64, HCT 157–161, PIA 122–123; Dreyfus and Wrathall 2002, 16, 222. Hegel makes the same point (1977, 47/§74).

148. "An analytic of Dasein must remain our first requirement in the question of Being. . . . We have no right to resort to dogmatic constructions and to apply just any idea of Being and actuality to this entity, no matter how 'self-evident' that idea may be" (BT 37/16; see also BT 75/49, 125–127/92–94, 373/334, BP 123, HCT 156, IPR 195, LQT 273–274).

149. "The 'inner' is a delusion. That is: the whole complex of ideas alluded to by this word is like a painted curtain drawn in front of the scene of the actual word use" (LWPPII 84; see also Z §446; McManus 1999, 325–326).

150. BT 86/59; see also BT 81/54–55, 93–94/65, 96/68, 166–167/129, 200/158, 351/303, 366–368/318–321, 475/423, TDP 73–74, 94, PM 20, PRL 54, HCT 29, 195–196, 219, PIRA 388/44–45, LQT 242, 261, 278.

151. "Consciousness as the inner was thought to be given absolutely as an absolute starting point, from which all the puzzles of 'inner' and 'outer' then arise" (HCT 216; see also HCT 97, BT 170/132, 249–250/205–206; Thomson 2011, 55).

152. HCT 161–162; see also HCT 216, BT 205/162, 250/206, TDP 77, PIRA 363/9, 392/51, LQT 76–77.

153. "But when closer reflection causes this view to go up in smoke, then what turns out is not that the inner is something outer, but that 'outer' and 'inner' now no longer count as properties of evidence. 'Inner evidence' means nothing, and therefore neither does 'outer evidence'" (LWPPII 62; see also BP 66, 170; Taylor 1995, 12). Bill Blattner compares the two on this point (2007, 108). G. H. von Wright says of Wittgenstein, in words that apply equally to Heidegger, "the problem of the external world, one could say, *is* in fact solved before it *can be* raised" (1982, 172). Compare this with: "if Dasein is understood correctly, it defies such proofs, because, in its Being, it already *is* what subsequent proofs deem necessary to demonstrate for it" (BT 249/205).

154. BB 43; see also BB 130, PI §§112–113, §115, §402.

155. WCT 144; see also WCT 41–43, IM 148, LEL 124, 129.

156. This "resolute" reading is associated with thinkers like Cora Diamond and James Conant (a nice collection is Crary and Read's *The New Wittgenstein*), while David G. Stern represents the skeptical (in the ancient sense, not the Cartesian) read-

ing of the later work (2004, 22–26). David Pears raises a good objection to the resolute reading of the early work, citing statements such as "there are two things"
which are forbidden by the *Tractatus*, but certainly not complete gibberish (Pears
2006, 5 n.2; see also McManus 2006, 59).

157. T p. 4, 4.003, 6.5–6.521, NB 74.

158. One difference is that Heidegger believes that it can be expressed, if only
obliquely, in forms of language different from propositional statements of fact such
as poetry or what he calls thinking. I am grateful to Iain Thomson for pointing this
out to me.

159. Engelmann 1967, 7. In his well-known letter to Ficker, he writes, "the book's
point is an ethical one. . . . Where *many* others today are just *gassing*, I have managed in my book to put everything firmly into place by being silent about it" (Engelmann 1967, 143). Engelmann believes that "we do not understand Wittgenstein
unless we realize that it was philosophy that mattered to him and not logic, which
merely happened to be the only suitable tool for elaborating his world picture"
(1967, 96; see also T 6.4321). One cannot help but think of Kant who "found it necessary to deny *knowledge*, in order to make room for *faith*" (C1 B xxx; see also C1
A395, A745/B773). Kant too worried about "just gassing": he considered his critical
project of finding "the outermost boundary of all moral inquiry" essential so that
reason will not "impotently flap its wings in the space (for it, an empty space) of
transcendent concepts which we call the intelligible world . . . and so losing itself
amid phantoms" (Kant 1995, 80/462).

160. T 5.135, 6.373–6.375, NB 73–74, 77–78.

161. PO 41; see also T 6.43, 6.432, LWVC 68; Rhees 1984, 107. Norman Malcolm
relates the story of Wittgenstein seeing a play in which "one of the characters
expressed the thought that no matter what happened in the world, nothing bad
could happen to *him*—*he* was independent of fate and circumstances. Wittgenstein
was struck by this stoic thought; for the first time he saw the possibility of religion"
(2001, 58). For Schopenhauer, "such a man who, after many bitter struggles with his
own nature, has at last completely conquered, is then left only as pure knowing
being, as the undimmed mirror of the world. Nothing can distress or alarm him any
more; nothing can any longer move him; for he has cut all the thousand threads of
willing which hold us bound to the world" (WWRI 390). Tolstoy's *Twenty-Three
Tales*, which Wittgenstein greatly admired (Janik and Toulmin 1973, 195–196; Rhees
1984, 72, 86), tell of the insatiability of desires and of the peace and joy that result
when one stops seeking personal gain, leading one character to proclaim, "no evil
and no good can befall me from anyone but from God" (Tolstoy 2003, 302).

162. NB 73, 75, 81, CV 53; Rhees 1984, 196; Edwards 1982, 44.

163. HE 64–67, NB 73, 86.

164. T 5.631–5.6331, 5.641, NB 50, 73, 80, 86.

165. For a discussion of Frege's, Russell's, and Moore's rebellion against idealism, see Braver 2007, 23–30.

166. Frege boasts that "the concept has a power of collecting together far superior to the unifying power of synthetic apperception" (1980, 61; see also GB 24, 31, 54–55, 85, 113–114, 122, 127, 131–132, 152–154, 171, 180 n.). Kurt Gödel, a staunch Platonic realist, makes a similar comparison between sets and Kant's synthesizing categories (Benacerraf and Putnam 1964, 272 n.40). This passive stance of the knower was important to Russell too, who compares our knowledge of logical relations to empirical perception (Russell 1945, 834–836; 1929, 62–63; 1996, 33, 450–451; 1959a, 98, 130; 1959b, 132, 186, 213).

167. T 5.542–5.5421. This is the problem that subjective factors such as people's knowledge can affect the transitive sense of propositions: if someone does not know that the evening star is the morning star, she can believe that "the evening star is presently visible" and that "the morning star is not presently visible," even though their referential identity means that the truth of either proposition entails the truth of the other.

168. PO 39–40, NB 74–80, T 5.634, 6.37, 6.4, 6.41, 6.421, T 6.432.

169. NB 84. Ironically, his later work corrects his earlier view of tautologies as completely empty since, in certain circumstances, sentences like "war is war" or "a man's got to do what a man's got to do" can convey something, a fact he already exploits here.

170. T 3.01, 4.11, 4.26. A number of metaphors in the *Tractatus*, such as invisible eyes and the mirror of the world (T 4.121, 5.511, 6.13, NB 10–11, 18, 39–40, 107), can be traced back to Schopenhauer, for whom the genius becomes a *"pure knowing subject*, the clear eye of the world . . . the subject purified of will, the clear mirror of the inner nature of the world" (WWRI 186; see also WWRII 370–371). For more on this connection, see Hannan 2009, 16 n.26, 17, 95–101, 107–108, 133–134, 141; Jacquette 2005, 249–261. Russell also describes logic as a mirror (1959b, 213).

171. "The philosophical I is not the human being, not the human body or the human soul with the psychological properties, but the metaphysical subject, the boundary (not a part) of the world. The human body, however, my body in particular, is a part of the world among others, among animals, plants, stones etc., etc. Whoever realizes this will not want to procure a pre-eminent place for his own body" (NB 82). This quest informed his brave, even reckless military service in World War I (McGuinness 2005, 216, 221, 240 254–255, 315). This is an essential part of Schopenhauer's system which bases compassion on piercing the illusory *principium individuationis* to identify others' needs and suffering with one's own (WWRI 372–373, WWRII 371, 609–610). The last of Tolstoy's *Twenty-Three Tales* ends with a Schopenhauerian sermon which "draw[s] aside the veil of delusion [to] let you see

that by doing evil to others you have done it to yourself also. Life is one in them all. . . . You can only improve life in yourself by destroying the barriers that divide your life from that of others, and by considering others as yourself, and loving them. . . . Life knows neither time nor space" (Tolstoy 2003, 342–343).

172. T 5.541; see also T 5.621, 5.63, NB 73, 77. For Schopenhauer, "we *lose* ourselves entirely in this object . . . ; we forget our individuality, our will, and continue to exist only as pure subject, as clear mirror of the object" (WWRI 178–179; see also 390).

173. T 6.4311, NB 76, 83; Rhees 1984, 118; WWR I 195–196.

174. T 6.44, NB 72, 86.

175. NB 73, 75, T 6.43, CV 27. Schopenhauer connects "quietism, that is, the giving up of all willing, asceticism, that is, intentional mortification of one's own will, and mysticism, that is, consciousness of the identity of one's own inner being with that of all things" (WWRII 613).

176. BP 264. I raise this objection to Hubert Dreyfus's powerful and illuminating reading of Heidegger in "Never Mind: Thinking of Subjectivity in the Dreyfus-McDowell Debate" (in Schear, 2011). A couple of years after *Being and Time*, Heidegger anticipated and rejected interpretations that excessively focus on everyday tool-use in division I: "there I took my departure from what lies to hand in the everyday realm, from those things that we use and pursue. . . . It never occurred to me, however, to try and claim or prove with this interpretation that the essence of man consists in the fact that he knows how to handle knives and forks or use the tram" (FCM 177; see also PM 370 n.59).

177. BT 237/192, PIA 68; Olson 1994, 135.

178. BT 33/13, 68/42–43, 119/86, 220/175–176, 237–238/193, CT 6, 8, 10, Supp 122–123. The terms property, proper, appropriating, and appropriateness also resonate in these terms.

179. BT 164/126; see also BT 154/118, 283/239, BW 104.

180. "Being-in-the-world . . . amounts to a non-thematic circumspective absorption in references or assignments constitutive for the readiness-to-hand of a totality of equipment. . . . In this familiarity Dasein can lose itself" (BT 107/76; see also BT 149/113, 220/175, 443/391, Supp 117, 123; Carman 2003, 21). He calls this tendency "fleeing" (BT 229–230/184–185, 303/259, Ont 26).

181. BT 307/263; see also BT 167/129, 232/187, 308/263, 312/268, 354/307, 369/322, 441–442/390.

182. BT 232/188, 308/263–264, 313/268, 434–435/383–384; Dreyfus and Wrathall 2002, 219; Raffoul and Nelson 2008, 133–136.

183. BT 312/268. In an interesting turn of phrase, he says that we contract an "addiction to becoming 'lived'" rather than living (BT 240/196; see also BT 345/299).

184. "The authentic entity of Dasein, the who, is not a thing and nothing worldly, but is itself only a way to be" (HCT 247; see also BT 292/248, 307/262, 393/343, 434/383, CT 13; Raffoul and Nelson 2008, 140; Olson 1994, 161). He compares this to Aristotle's notion of *arête* as an example of "the peculiar category of the *how*" (BCAP 122).

185. "Here everything seems to turn, so to speak, on *how* one wants" (NB 78).

186. BT 152/116, 155/119, 184/144, 187/146, 368/321, 416/364, BP 159, 171, HCT 202, 244, MFL 127, Ont 72, TDP 56, 174; van Buren 2002, 164–165.

187. Anxiety "induces the slipping away of beings as a whole. . . . Where there is nothing to hold onto, pure Da-sein is all that is still there" (BW 101).

188. BT 36/15, 42/21, 61/36, 85/58, 96/67–68, 155/119, 245/201, 285/241, 359/311, 439/387.

189. BT 168/130, 307/262, 314/269, 317/272, 333/287, 344/298, 346/299, 434/383.

190. HCT 110, MFL 126, 161, Husserl 1997, 138, BT 71/44, 81/54, 237/192, BP 227; Baynes 1987, 482–483, Rorty 1989, 110; Haar 1993, 184.

191. BT 186/145, 188/148, BW 101–102, FCM 82, 103, 117, 121, 143; Fell 1979 39, 50–51.

192. T 5.4541, 5.5563.

193. T 5.63; see also NB 73, 77; Young (2002, 12) compares the two on this idea.

194. Rorty also sees a developmental cross, but for somewhat different reasons (1991, 52).

195. BW 119, 129, 132, 295–296, 302–304; Thomson 2005, 63, 161; Zimmerman 1986, xix, 19, 76–77, 134; Young 2002, 96. Poetry, art and philosophy become the world-disclosing agents of Heidegger's later works, resisting the "idle talk" of the early work, itself a version of Husserl's account of manipulating empty intuitions (best expressed in the late "Origin of Geometry"). This fulfills the claim, included but undeveloped in *Being and Time*, that "the ultimate business of philosophy is to preserve the *force of the most elemental words* in which Dasein expresses itself, and to keep the common understanding from leveling them off to that unintelligibility which functions in turn as a source of pseudo-problems" (BT 262/220; see also WCT 126, EHP 48, 55, BQ 181).

196. Derrida 1983, 70. Think of the Hölderlin line that Heidegger likes to quote: "But where danger is, grows / The saving power also" (BW 333). Cavell connects Heidegger and Wittgenstein for their focus on the ordinary as their subject matter (1995, 138), and then a few pages later (1995, 156) contrasts their attitudes since

Heidegger flees ordinary averageness while Wittgenstein seeks it. This switch is due to Heidegger's ambivalence. Minar attributes this view of philosophy to Wittgenstein (1995, 444).

197. "The demand for an ultimate direct givenness of the phenomena carries no implication of the comfort of an immediate beholding" (HCT 87; see also HCT 29, 35, 136, 300).

198. See Braver 2007, 325–331 for more details.

199. "The human being's being-open to being is so fundamental and decisive in being human that, due to its inconspicuousness and plainness, one can continuously overlook it" (Zo 74–75; see also PM 234–236, BW 238, BQ 159, 170, WCT 98, 110, 152, 201–202, 237–239, WIP 73–75, 91, EGT 121–122; Dahlstrom 2011, 52; Thomson 2005, 56).

200. BW 431; see also PS 53, 310, BQ 147, WIP 51, PM 233, Zo 17, 187, CPC 78–80.

201. WIP 85; see also CP 11/§5, 29/§14, 163/§117, 175/§130, 272/§243, 326/§265, 339/§269, P 150, WIP 97, BW 442, FCM 355, BQ 150–151, BP 69, BT 29/9, PM 53–54, EGT 76, BW 129, 150, 153, 191, 200, STF 29–30, 134, ITP 3, 52, CPC 80; Raffoul and Nelson 2008, 135. "Thoughtful wonder speaks in questioning" (EGT 104).

202. NB 86, T 6.44, PO 41; Meillassoux 2008, 41, 48, 72.

203. At the first meeting of the Circle he attended, Wittgenstein refused to discuss logic, insisting instead on reading aloud Tagore's mystical poetry (Janik and Toulmin 1973, 215, 257). I will return to this preference, which was shared by Heidegger, in my conclusion.

204. IM 44; see also BW 341, CP 242/§222, NII 192, WCT 169, NIV 201, FCM 142, 292.

205. LWPPII 86; see also CV 75. Interestingly, his early "Lecture on Ethics" describes the same phenomenon, but there it is respected as an indication of something profoundly true about language and values: "I at once see clearly, as it were in a flash of light, not only that no description that I can think of would do to describe what I mean by absolute value, but that I would reject every significant description that anybody could possibly suggest, *ab initio*, on the ground of its significance. . . . Their nonsensicality was their very essence. For all I wanted to do with them was just *to go beyond* the world and that is to say beyond significant language" (PO 44; see also LWVC 68–69). In his later work, he hews much more closely to his early dictum that "when the answer cannot be put into words, neither can the question be put into words. The *riddle* does not exist. If a question can be framed at all, it is also *possible* to answer it" (T 6.5).

206. BT 35/15, 96/67, 119/86, 179/139–140, 229–230, 415/364, BW 109–110.

207. PI §194; see also PI §412, AWL 90, PG 103, 169, PR 83, PO 189, 212, 280, 367, BB 46, 107, RPPI §138, §1074, LWPPI §240, §675, OC §347, §406, §622.

208. PI §118, §255, AWL 21, PO 167, LFM 14, CV 61, LWPPII 84, LWPPI §756, OC §33, Z §452, LWL 1, 4, 21–22, 53. Robert Fogelin notes Wittgenstein's crusade against wonder, but claims that "Wittgenstein does not develop this view in detail, and, needless to say, he never defends it. Yet it has persistent influence throughout the text" (1995, 209–210). I am arguing that it fits quite logically into Wittgenstein's overall view of philosophy.

209. PG 169; see also PG 108–109, 121, 154–155, BB 46, 150, RPPI §65, §378, §380, §417, §751, §1000, §1015, §1074, PI §§93–94, §170, §175, §194, §275, §428, §607, PhR 88, LPP 45, 48, 113, Z §273.

210. RPPII §289; see also Z §273, RFM 88, 113.

211. PG 47; see also PI §97, §192, §309, §412, PO 181, 258, 327, Z §690, BB 27, 107, AWL 119, RFM 137, 263, 272, CV 11, Z §660, RPPI §378, §417, §751, §1074, LC 28, LPP 3, 14, 26.

212. BW 179; see also BW 191, 200, BQ 144, CP §5/11, §243/272, §269/339.

213. Even the profound respect he had earlier accorded the mystical (PO 44, 116–117, LO 36) is now part of the problem: "what is typical of the phenomenon I am talking about is that a *mysteriousness* about some mathematical concept is not *straight away* interpreted as an erroneous conception, as a mistake of ideas; but rather as something that is at any rate not to be despised, is perhaps even rather to be respected. All I can do, is to shew an easy escape from this obscurity and this glitter of the concepts" (RFM 274; see also PI §§194–197, PI II.xi p. 171, 183, 187, PO 189, 280).

214. BW 204; see also Rorty 1991, 36.

215. T 6.52–6.521; see also NB 74, PI §133.

216. PI §524, RPPI §621, §996, Z §661, PO 327, AWL 58.

217. PI II.xi p. 173, 183–184, LPP 42. He also mentions associating a composer's musical proclivities with his face or name (PI II.vi p. 156, PI II.xi p. 183, 186, LWPPI §713) and of qualities like fat and lean with days of the week (PI II.xi p. 184).

218. CV 11; see also RFM 137, 272, PG 169, RPPI §65, §378, §380, §417, §751, §1015, §1074, AWL 98; McGuinness 1982, 81.

219. PI §133; see also CV 43, PO 165, 175, 258, LWL 34; Rhees 1984, 110. Stern takes this interpretation very far, reading Wittgenstein as a Pyrrhonian with no views of his own (Stern 1996, 29; Stern 2004, 11; Sluga and Stern 1996, 44), even contrasting Wittgenstein with Heidegger on this point (Stern 2004, 165).

220. "It is true that we can compare a picture that is firmly rooted in us to a super-stition; but it is equally true that we *always* eventually have to reach some firm ground, either a picture or something else, so that a picture which is at the root of all our thinking is to be respected and not treated as a superstition" (CV 83).

221. Z §460; see also Z §456, PI §111; Rhees 1984, 77, 160. Though compare CV 80.

222. "Some philosophers (or whatever you like to call them) suffer from what may be called 'loss of problems.' Then everything seems quite simple to them, no deep problems seem to exist any more, the world becomes broad and flat and loses all depth, and what they write becomes immeasurably shallow and trivial. Russell and H. G. Wells suffer from this" (Z §456). There are also a couple of positive mentions of wonder (CV 5, 57). Some commentators find his later work to be attempting to induce wonder in us (Biletzki and Matar 1998, 218; Malcolm 1994, 73, 82, 87; Fann 1967, 71; Bearn 1997; John 1988; Churchill 1994; Pears 1987, 17–18; Edwards 1990, 232, 239; Cooper 1997, 113).

223. BT 130/97, 245/201, HCT 38, MFL 167, BPP 305, OHF 70.

## 2   What Is a Thing?

1. PI §3, §304, §593, Z §444, RPPI §38, LPP 47, AWL 46–47.

2. RPPI §42; see also RPPI §349, PI §559, LWL 59, PG 54, BB 5.

3. PI ix; see also CV 7.

4. Mathieu Marion writes, "it is no exaggeration to say that the whole of Wittgen-stein's later philosophy of language goes against the *Bedeutungskörper* conception of meaning" (Marion 1998, 178). Meredith Williams: "the appeal to the shadow-object . . . only gives the illusion of making intentionality intelligible. For Wittgenstein, it is a perpetuation of a very simple, but compelling, picture of language, and that is that meaning is the object for which the word stands. This, for Wittgenstein, is the greatest illusion of all" (2002, 48; see also Glendinning 1998, 77, 88; Medina 2002, 59; Moyal-Sharrock 2004, 110; Baker and Hacker 1980, 37, 577; Baker and Hacker 1985, 115, 312, 316, 320; O'Hear 2000, 235 n.10; Pears 1988, 492; Teghrarian, Serafini, and Cook 1990, 55; Harris 1998, 7, 17; Bloor 2002, 3, 136; Stroll 2002, 113; Williams 2006, 63; Malcolm 1995, 186–188; Stroud 2002, 177; Mulhall 1993, 39, 46; Livingston 2008, 23, 46, 59–61, 141–143).

5. BT 320/275. Note that Macquarrie and Robinson occasionally capitalize words, "Objectively" here, to preserve distinctions in the German. I will retain these capi-talizations, though frequently their purpose only becomes clear within *Being and Time*.

6. T 3.201, 3.203, 4.221, NB 111.

7. PG 56; see also NB 100, Z §12.

8. T 3.2, 3.21, 3.323–3.325, 4.002, 4.00311, PI §96.

9. NB 3, 45, 64, 68, PO 29.

10. T 2.0123; see also T 2.012, 2.0141. Compare with Leibniz: "the notion of an individual substance includes once and for all everything that can ever happen to it ... by considering this notion, one can see there everything that can truly be said of it, just as we can see in the nature of a circle all the properties that can be deduced from it" (*Discourse on Metaphysics* §13; Leibniz 1989, 44).

11. T 3.221, 3.26, 3.261, LWVC 250; GB 32, 42–43, 126, 151, 180 n.

12. T 3.262–3.263, T 3.326, 4.124, NB 70, 108, 115, 121, LO 59, Z §138.

13. T 2.022, T 2.0231, 2.0271, 2.023, 3.4–3.42, 6.1233, NB 20–21, 24. As Wittgenstein explains in PI §§39–46 (see also T 4.2211, 6.124), one of the reasons that objects must be eternal is to secure referents for all proper names, as demanded by Frege (GB 58 n., 69–70, 104, 170; Frege 1980, 103; Burge 2005, 132), in order to prevent empty definite descriptions.

14. T 3.22, 3.221, 4.0312, NB 70, RPPI §687, GB 188, 196, 231.

15. See NB 7, Fann 1967, 18. This is a case where the picture and state-of-affairs share the same form: space. Pictures can also have forms with no apparent resemblance, like musical notation corresponding to pitches, note-length, and so on (T 4.011, 4.014, 4.0141). A painting-by-numbers instructs by means of correlating numbers with colors; it would rather defeat the purpose were it to indicate the color that particular parts should be painted by marking them with that color.

16. T 2.013, 2.0131; Pears 2006, 9–11.

17. GB 24, 31, 54–55, 113–114, 127, 131–132, 152–154, 171, 180 n.

18. T 2.03, 4.221; see also T 3.141, 4.0311–4.0312, LO 23; von Wright 1973, 23; Anscombe 1963, 108–109; Sellars 1991, 227–228; Copi and Beard 1966, 336.

19. T 2.013, 2.0131, 2.0251, 3.42.

20. T 2.0121, 2.0123–2.0124.

21. We see here the deep interconnection between the book's logical and mystical elements. The mystical gets defined near the end of the book: "to view the world sub specie aeterni is to view it as a whole—a limited whole. Feeling the world as a limited whole—it is this that is mystical" (T 6.45). The book's very first proposition depicts the world in just this manner, as "*all* that is the case" (T 1, my italics).

22. "A proposition must restrict reality to two alternatives: yes or no" (T 4.023; see also T 3.01, 3.23, 3.25, 3.251, 3.42, 4.1, 4.2, 4.25, 4.26, 4.3, 5.153; Moyal-Sharrock 2004, 127). Michael Dummett defines realism by its commitment to bivalence (Dummett 1978, 155; 1981, 434, 505; 1991, 9).

23. "Without complete and final definitions, we have no firm ground underfoot, we are not sure about the validity of our theorems, and we cannot confidently apply the laws of logic, which certainly presuppose that concepts, and relations too, have sharp boundaries" (GB 166; see also GB 105, 110, 159, 162, 170; Frege 1980, 87, 93). Arch-realist that he is, Frege insists that we discover rather than create these sharply bounded sets (GB 85, 122, 127; Pears 1987, 73 n.40).

24. T 4.51. "We can determine the general term of a series of forms by giving its first term and the general form of the operation that produces the next term out of the proposition that precedes it" (T 4.1273; see also T 4.53, 5.3, 5.501, 6.001, 6.002, 6.01, NB 76, 91, 102).

25. NB 122; see also NB 102, T 5.47. Frege also sought maximal economy in logic and mathematics (GB 130–131, 137, 181).

26. T 5.472; see also T 5.47.

27. T p. 3, 4.114; see also T 5.133, 5.551, 5.61, 6.113, 6.1222, 6.124, LWVC 213–214, NB 105.

28. T 6.13, 6.421.

29. T 6.422, 6.423, 6.521.

30. T 5.43; see also T 6.1, 6.11, 6.124.

31. T 3.124. David Pears discusses this passivity which follows from the *Tractatus*'s realism a number of times (Pears 1987, 9, 88; 1988, 209–210, 487; 2006, 8, 16 n.10, 24).

32. T 3.331, 5.132, 5.451–5.452, 5.535, NB 104.

33. T 3.334; see also T 3.325, 4.1213, 4.126, 5.13, 5.515, 5.53, 5.473, 5.4731, 6.113, T 6.121–6.122, 6.232, NB 2–3. Russell praises Peano (before he knew Frege's work) for having "reduced the greater part of mathematics (and he or his followers will, in time, have reduced the whole) to strict symbolic form, in which there are no words at all. In the ordinary mathematical books, there are no doubt fewer words than most readers would wish. Still, little phrases occur, such as *therefore, let us assume, consider*, or *hence it follows*. All these, however, are a concession, and are swept away by Professor Peano" (Russell 2004, 60). This may help explain Wittgenstein's rage at Moore's suggestion to reformulate his early work to fit the criteria of the dissertation necessary for a B.A. degree ("if I'm not worth your making an exception for me *even in some* STUPID *details* then I may as well go to Hell directly; and if I *am* worth it and you don't do it then—by God—you might go there" [McGuinness 2005, 199–200]). Such a revision would require niceties like prefaces and notes where he would have to stop channeling Pure Logic and speak to the reader in his own voice.

34. NB 89–90; see also T 5.2523.

35. T 5.46; see also T 3.311, 5.442, 6.126, NB 116, LWVC 69; Dummett 1978, 170–171.

36. LWVC 213–214; see also NB 105, T 5.133, 5.551, 6.113, 6.1222, 6.124.

37. T 3.1431; see also T 4.0311–4.0312.

38. Russell 1945, 834; 1929, 62–63; 1945, 836; 1996, 33, 450–451; 1959a, 98, 130; 1959b, 132, 186, 213. Much of my *A Thing of This World* traces the evolution and rejection of this idea, which I call "Passive Knower," through continental thought.

39. This refers to a famous anecdote of Russell asking Wittgenstein, brooding and pacing in his office, whether he was "thinking about logic or your sins," to which Wittgenstein replied "both" and resumed his pacing (Monk 1991, 64). Schopenhauer wrote, "no philosophy can leave undecided the theme of quietism and asceticism, if the question is put to it, since this theme is in substance identical with that of all metaphysics and ethics" (WWRII 615). Wittgenstein introduces logic as the border between them.

40. RPPI §349; see also RPPI §42. Ryle makes the same point (1953, 172). Frege often talks about logical or arithmetical objects (GB 144, 181, 235, 244, LWVC 105, LWVC 150).

41. T 2.023; see also T 2.013, 2.022, 2.026, 2.027.

42. PO 356; see also PO 312–313, LPP 69, 78, LWPPII 43; Wisdom in Fann 1967, 46.

43. PI §112; see also PI §90, §402, §427.

44. BB 1; see also BB 18, 26, AWL 44, PI §24, §92, LPP 46; Malcolm 1994, 42; 1995, 4, 186.

45. RPPI §38; see also Z§444, PI §3, §304, §593, AWL 12–13, 46–47, 88, 107, 110, 115, PO 418.

46. AWL 150–151; see also AWL 44, BB 1, PG 108–109, Conv 19, 23–24, PI §264, PO 327.

47. PI §358; see also Z §449.

48. LFM 145; see also AWL 58, 157, BB 36, LWL 32, PI §194, PI II.vi p. 155, PO 303, PG 281, 466, RFM 86–87, 202, PG 356; Williams 2002, 48, 159; Marion 1998, 180–181; McGinn, 1987, 9; Baker and Hacker 1985, 79, 124; Livingston 2008, 59.

49. BB 47; see also Z §287, AWL 44, PO 327, PG 427.

50. LWPPI §843; see also LWPPI §817, RPPI §94, §256, §870, LPP 81, 113. Frege also uses the metaphor of germs in describing his hope to "develop the whole wealth of objects and functions treated of in mathematics out of the germ of . . . eight functions. . . . Our construction (if you like to call it that) is not unrestricted and arbi-

trary; the mode of performing it, and its legitimacy, are established once for all" (GB 181; see also Frege 1980, 24, 101).

51. RFM 83; see also AWL 83.

52. PI §193; see also PI §197, §334, PO 399, LFM 196–199, RPPI §40; Wright 1980, 18; Pears 2006, 32.

53. PI §194; see also RFM 86, LFM 196.

54. PG 55; see also PG 481, BB 39–40, 73–74, PI p. 124 n., RPPI §139, AWL 83. One reason Wittgenstein criticizes the way Frege and Russell explain rules in multiple contexts is that it suggests that the rules may behave differently in different situations, whereas the notion of meaning demands an absolute uniformity that enables us to know how to use it in any circumstance (T 3.42, 4.51, 5.442, 5.451–5.452, 5.46, 5.551, NB 64, 104). Whether or not he lived up to it, Frege too insisted that "logic must reject all piecemeal definition" (GB 162; see also 137, 170).

55. PG 108; see also Z §153, LC 68, PI §§138–139, §191, §§318–320; Stern 2004, 143.

56. "We are taking 'judgment' to mean, not an act performed by a definite man at a definite time, but something timelessly true, even if its being true is not acknowledged by any human being" (GB 126 n.; see also GB 107, 128, 134, 145, 159, 227, 235–237).

57. BT 297/253; see also BT 185/145, 377/329, 474/422, HCT 317.

58. Paul M. Livingston makes a similar point about "anxiety" over "a death of sense" (2008, 1).

59. PG 356; see also PG 281, 427, RFM 267, AWL 189, PO 310, LFM 144–145; Crary and Read 2000, 43.

60. AWL 164–165; see also RFM 45, 85, PG 281, 355–356.

61. PI §188; see also PI §352, LFM 28, 124; Baker and Hacker 1985, 194; O'Hear 2000, 235. Wittgenstein explicitly applies this diagnosis to the *Tractatus*'s formula for converting atomic propositions into molecular ones (PG 466–467).

62. PI §229. "The lightning-like thought may be connected with the spoken thought as the algebraic formula is with the sequence of numbers which I work out from it" (PI §320).

63. BB 142; see also BB 40, PI §598, PI II.ii p. 150, LC 22. "But didn't I already intend the whole construction of the sentence (for example) at its beginning? So surely it already existed in my mind before I said it out loud! . . . But here we are constructing a misleading picture of 'intending,' that is, of the use of this word" (PI §337). The same thing happens with ambiguous words like 'bank': if a question arises as to which sense I had intended, I retroactively place an explicit mental intention of

either financial or river banks inside my earlier speech (PI §334, PI II.xi pp. 184–186; McGinn 1984, 100).

64. BB 143; see also PO 308, AWL 131. The inconspicuousness of our grammatical competence contributes to this picture (AWL 50–51).

65. BT 36/15, 42/21, 85/58, 335–336/289, 340/294, 381/333, 386/337, 439/387. He often associates this interpretation with falling (BT 229–230/184, 295–296/251–252), but the point is rather muddied by the fact that Dasein actually *is* inextricably tied up with, even partially constituted by equipmental webs. This problem stems from what Dreyfus correctly identifies as the tension between Heidegger's commitment to a Hegelian view of society as enabling intelligibility and a Kierkegaardian analysis of the pressure to conform which prevents authentic choices, especially in division I, chapter IV (Dreyfus 1991, chaps. 8 and 13, and appendix).

66. BT 268/225; see also BT 245/201, 254–255/211, 320/275, HCT 219; Richardson 1986, 51, 76.

67. HCT 162–163; see also HCT 91, 106–107, 111, 117, 156, 160, 185, 218, BT 85/59, 88/61, 128–129/95–96, 106/75, 185/145, 215/171, 246/202, 309/264, 412/361, BP 118, 123, 275, PIK 18–19, 136, LQT 7, 86, 179, 205, IPR 42, 168, 195, 208, 230.

68. BT 45/24, 49/26, 126/93, IPR 83, 233; Thomson 2005, 8, 26.

69. BT 129/96; see also BT 48/26, 125/92, PIK 136, HCT 219. Much of his later writings focus on the historical narrative (PM 235, PR 59, QT 127, 169, WT 51, 97, FS 8–9, 13–14, 37, 72, PLT 170, 181, 224, OBT 69, 77, 82, PR 27, 79, EGT 43, Zo 25, 80, 94, 110, WCT 62, 135, M 75, 155, BW 131, 332, 335, 339, ITP 20; Apel 1999, 142; Mulhall 2003, 37; Mulhall 2007, 88; Mensch 1996, 6, 29).

70. BT 250/206, HCT 160–161. Cavell compares the two on this point (1979, 241). Hegel famously ridicules this position (*Phenomenology of Spirit*, §§73–74), also arguing that it presupposes a particular conception of the subject–object distinction and of knowledge as a medium between the two that can be evaluated as a whole.

71. BT 130/97; see also BT 128–129/95–96.

72. BT 125/92, 128/95, 198/156, HCT 172, 218, MFL 32.

73. TDP 64; see also TDP 176, BT 106/75, 189–191/149–150, 200–201/158, 231/186, 412–415/361–364, HCT 195–196, 219; Carman 2003, 219.

74. TDP 73, 85; see also TDP 187, Supp 84, 95, 116, PS 117–122.

75. BT 200–201/158; see also BT 412/361, BP 162, HCT 183; Edwards 1990, 42.

76. HCT 125, 157, 295, 305, BT 65/40, 78–79/53, 226/181, 238/193–194, 275/232, BP 164.

77. T 2.1511, 2.21, 4.05, 4.2, 4.25, 5.134.

78. Apel 1998, 138–139; see also Guignon 1990, 652, 663; Carman 2003, 65 n.25; Rudd 2003, 116 n.16; Pöggeler 1998, 17.

79. PI §454, RPPI §42; see also PI §432, PG 427, BB 3, 5, Z §238; Stroud 2002, 171; Cavell 1995, 164; Crary and Read 2000, 53–54, 66, 69.

80. T 2.0271; see also 2.012, NB 70.

81. CV 44; see also LC 68, PI §117, §264, §607, PI II.x p. 164, Z §343, OC §§349–350, §393, §423, RPPI §488, BB 9.

82. NB 70; see also NB 61, 64, 68–70, 90, T 3.42, 4.023, 5.46, 5.47, 6.124.

83. PI §99; see also PI §§70–71, §88.

84. Although Wittgenstein makes an important break with his earlier way of thinking in the early 1930s, this is a transitional time and he occasionally falls off the wagon. For instance, at one point he plants his earlier insistence that there be no surprises in logic into the later soil of our tacit grasp of ordinary language. Here, it isn't because reality determines logic once and for all that it can never change; rather it is because we know how to speak that "we make our moves in the realm of the grammar of our ordinary language, and this grammar is already there. Thus we have already got everything and need not wait for the future" (LWVC 183; see also LWVC 216, 248). This hybrid theory uses the later notion of grammar to secure the early commitment to preset meaning.

85. PR 306–307; see also LWVC 34–36, 128–129, 146, 175, 204, AWL 50–51, 83, PG 113, 117, 301, 361, 377, 415, 481, AWL 133–134, 179, RFM 228, 267, 279, 320–321, 420, LPP 69, BB 9; Malcolm 1994, 46–47; Bloor 2002, 3, 10; Travis 2006, 28, 52, 60, 77.

86. PI §20, §§68–71, §80, §84, PG 113, 120, LPP 44, 74.

87. PG 282; see also PG 120–121, RFM 228, 320–322, 325, 327, 343–344, 392, 420, PI §69, §71, §75, §135, §§208–210, §362, AWL 131–132.

88. BT 249/205; see also 84–86/57–59, 93–94/65 223/179, 246/202, LEL 123, LQT 242, 261, 278; Pöggeler 1998, 29.

89. BT 203/160; see also BT 85–86/59, 166–167/129, 267/224–225, BP 206–207, MFL 124, TDP 155, FCM 314–315, 340–341, PS 174–175, WT 103, LQT 7, 132.

90. NB 19, PI §432, §454, RPPI §42, PG 427, BB 3, 5, Z §238.

91. I discuss Heidegger's views as objections to Davidson's analysis of interpretation and conceptual schemes in Braver 2007, 228–253.

92. PI §124, §§128–129, PI p. 48 n., §415, §496, §599, PI II.xii p. 195, BB 18, 125, PO 161, 449, NB 115, LWL 26, 34, PG 66, 88–89, 187, RPPI §22, §§256–257, §432, §508, §873.

93. LQT 167; see also LQT 18, 238–239, BT 35/15, 85/58, 119/86, 415/346.

94. PI §607; see also PI §170, §§195–196, §592, §607, §628, §633, §693, PI II.xi pp. 182–183, PhR 83, BB 34, 41, 43, 80, 164, Z §§236–238.

95. PI §20; see also PI §166, §175, PO 316, 453.

96. Stern 1996, 87; see also McGinn 1987, 20, 120; Sefler 1974, 26; Gier 1981, 32, 104; Guignon 1990, 652; Taylor 1995, 75; Minar 1995, 415.

97. PI §232, §314, §383, §§655–656, PI II.ix p. 161, 174.

98. PG 58, 66, PO 339, PI §316, PI II.vi pp. 155–156, PI II.xi p. 186, LPP 113. Russell Goodman (2007) disputes the accuracy of Wittgenstein's depiction of James, whose *Varieties of Religious Experience* he admired, but this is irrelevant for my purposes. Wittgenstein also criticizes introspection for focusing on experiences taking place while reflecting on speech, rather than examining the use itself.

99. PI §66; see also PI §20, §51, §93, §109, §124, §187, §496, §578, §592, §607, §637, PO 453, RFM 43, 299. One may object to this "argument from phenomenological absence," which we will take up in more detail in chapter 4, that even though we are unaware of such processes, still they are necessary to explain successful communication. Donald Davidson sometimes justifies his radical interpretation this way (for a more detailed discussion of this point with references, see Braver 2007, 228–253, 536 n.62). However, it is hard to see what role that mental representations of which we are unaware could play, or even whether such a notion is coherent (more than anyone, Wittgenstein has taught us to be suspicious of entities which are supposed to represent something solely in virtue of intrinsic features rather than how we use them). And if they do not actually occur in communication, then it becomes unclear how they can be said to explain it. The fact that I *could* use such acts or items in understanding does not show that I must or do use them.

100. BT 25/5, 27–28/8, 36/15, 61/37, 167–168, 189/149, 191–192/150, 194–195/153, 210–214/167–170, 213/169, 239/194, 264–267/222–224, 275/232, 315/270, 371/324, 413–414/362–363, HCT 87, 137, 246, 270, 299–300, PIRA 359/2, LQT 232; Mulhall 2003, 37; Mulhall 2007, 88.

101. BT 81/54–55, 86/59, 93–94/65, 96/68, 166–167/129, 475/423, TDP 73–74, 94, PM 20, HCT 195–196, 219.

102. BT 96/67–68; see also BT 150/114–115, PIRA 370/19, LQT 178, 273–274, 339, 341, Supp 144; Polt 2006, 75.

103. Z §87; see also LWPPI §53, §§118–120, §§124–127, PI §38, §113, §132.

104. PI §103, §115, §305, §308, §363, §412, §425, §607, PO 221, 264, LPP 45, 48, 113.

105. BT 245/201; see also BT 140/106, BP 68, 125, 305, MFL 167, HCT 38.

106. BT 29/9, 25/5; see also HCT 137, SFT 98.

107. BT 33–35/ 13–15, 118/86, 120/87, 161/124, 186–187/146, 194/152, 264/221; Caputo 1987, 66–67, 81.

108. PI §109; see also PI §340.

109. BT 359/311; see also BT 61/36, 96/67, 151/115, 155/119, 167/129, 255/212, 265/222, 285/241, 428/376, 439/387, HCT 29, 87, 128–130, 136.

110. LWVC 238; see also LWVC 216, 229, 247, NB 60, 64, 67, 69–70, 94, 99, T 3.23–3.25, PI §46, §88, §91, §§98–101.

111. T 6.125, 6.1251; see also T 4.411, 4.51, 5.473, 5.551, 6.001, NB 33, 89, 112, 116, 122. Wittgenstein is so certain of this property that he sometimes reverses this line of reasoning, arguing from the impossibility of logical surprises to the existence of the general form of propositions (NB 75, 90, T 4.5).

112. PI §219. David Pears describes this well, calling it Platonism: "the idea is that in all our operations with language we are really running on fixed rails laid down in reality before we even appeared on the scene. Attach a name to an object, and the intrinsic nature of the object will immediately take over complete control and determine the correct use of the name on later occasions. Set up a whole language in this way, and the structure of the fundamental grid will inexorably dictate the general structure of the logical system" (Pears 1987, 10).

113. BB 143; see also AWL 57–58, RFM 328–329, 394. As discussed above, some form of passive knower has been endemic to most philosophy up to Kant, and to much philosophy afterward, especially in analytic thought. Russell, for example, makes knowledge by acquaintance, in which "we are directly aware [of sense-data], without the intermediary of any process of inference or any knowledge of truths," epistemologically foundational because it presents me with "things immediately known to me just as they are" (Russell 1959a, 46–47). Minimizing one's interference in the apprehension of reality so as to render "observations and inferences as impersonal, and as much divested of local and temperamental bias, as is possible for human beings" represents "the chief [merit] of the philosophical school of which I am a member" (1945, 836).

114. Wittgenstein's sister Hermine wrote that "right from earliest childhood he suffered almost pathological distress in any surroundings which were uncongenial to him" (Rhees 1984, 11; see also 18, 54, 59–60; von Wright 1977, 57–58). Think of the way he volunteered for the most dangerous posts in World War I, not just to quell a Spengler-induced anxiety about feminine cowardice, but perhaps also to put himself in a situation where reaction could take the place of rumination. Conversely, one is reminded of Kierkegaard's comment that "a soldier standing alone with a loaded rifle at his post near a powder magazine on a stormy night thinks strange thoughts" (1983, 50).

115. Rhees 1984, 71; see also 119–120.

116. In a 1920 letter, Russell makes the insightful observation that "what [Wittgenstein] likes best in mysticism is its power to make him stop thinking" (von Wright 1977, 82).

117. PG 444; see also LWL 12, 30–31, AWL 90, PI §292.

118. RFM 234, 238–239, PhR 226; Dummett 1978, 170–171, Wright 1980, 128–129; Teghrarian and Serafini 1995, 10; Bloor 2002, 10; Pears 1987, 30; Wright 1980, 20.

119. As Pears puts it, Wittgenstein seeks to "destroy the illusion that there is a way of escaping our alarming responsibility for unformulatable accuracy. We have to accept the human predicament, which does, after all, allow us a certain freedom of choice" (Pears 2006, 64). Pears also warns that "anxiety takes over at this point and we feel that it would be outrageous to turn free will loose in the field of rationality" (2006, 84).

120. BT 186/145, 188/148, 232/187, BW 102; Thomson 2005, 170.

121. BT 307/262, 393/343, 434/383, PIA 80–81.

## 3   The Whole Hurly-Burly of Human Actions

1. T 2.0271, 2.024.

2. BT 125/92; see also BT 128/95, 198/156, 413–414/362.

3. Charles Taylor makes this idea the center of his comparison of the two: "my view is, in short, that the dominant conception of the thinking agent that both Heidegger and Wittgenstein had to overcome was shaped by a kind of ontologizing of rational procedure. . . . The result was a picture of the human thinking agent as disengaged, as occupying a sort of proto-variant of 'the view from nowhere.' . . . Both Heidegger and Wittgenstein had to struggle to recover an understanding of the agent as engaged, as embedded in a culture, a form of life, a 'world' of involvements. . . . The world of the agent is shaped by one's form of life, or history, or bodily existence" (Taylor 1995, 61–62; see also 68, 72–73, 169–170; Guignon 1990, 651; Rorty 1991, 59).

4. Russell 1959a, 63; see also 54–55.

5. T 1.21, 2.061–2.062, 5.135, 6.37.

6. T 4.211, 5.134.

7. Such as space, time, color; see T 2.0131, 2.0251, 6.3751, LWVC 214.

8. T 3.4, 3.42, NB 20–21, 24.

9. T 2.1511, 2.15121.

10. NB 3, 45, 64, LWL 120, PO 29; Janik and Toulmin 1973, 213.

11. T 2.061–2.062, 5.134–5.135, LWL 119.

12. T 6.3751, NB 91.

13. Wittgenstein even chastises himself a bit for not following out the line of reasoning that he had begun: "in my old conception of an elementary proposition there was no determination of the value of a co-ordinate; although my remark that a coloured body is in a colour-space, etc., should have put me straight on to this" (PR 111). Frank Ramsey had caught this problem in his 1923 review of the *Tractatus* (in Copi and Beard 1966, 18). See Allaire 1959 for an early discussion of this problem (my thanks to Jon Cogburn for bringing this essay to my attention). See also Medina 2002, 35, 41–42, 47; Teghrarian and Serafini 1995, 20–23; Stern 1995, 14–15, 99, 120; Pears 1987, 86, 193; Pears 2006, 15, 79; Livingston 2008, 58–59. Frege mentions the mutual exclusivity of numbers and colors (Frege 1980, 61), while Heidegger attributes the insight to Aristotle (BCAP 126).

14. LWVC 63–64; see also LWVC 74, 87–89, 149, 185, PG 210–211, PhR 110, 317, PO 32–33; Kenny 1973, 114.

15. LWL 29; see also LWL 37, LWVC 261, PhR 180, Z §228, LPP 17, LWPPI §294, BB 42, Z §228, OC §410.

16. PG 131; see also BB 5, 42, Conv 24, RFM 344, LFM 137, OC §229.

17. PI §23; see also PI §19, §25, RPPI §§561–563, RPPII §624, PO 123, 235, 260, LC 2, 11, RFM 43, 390, OC §229, §§349–350, §413, §423, §461, §465, §553, §622.

18. Z §567; see also LWPPI §913, LWPPII 30, 41–42, 56, LC 8.

19. Pears 1988, vol. II, 208–209; see also Stroud 2000, 177, 220–221; Apel 1994, 28; Hintikka and Hintikka 1989, 189; McManus 2004, 246; Bloor 2002, 99; Williams 2002, 26, 57, 242; Stern 1995, 120, 122, 188; von Wright 1982, 139; Baker and Hacker 1985, 141, 158; Janik and Toulmin 1973, 225; Edwards 1990, 150–153; Travis 2006, 3, 22, 33, 186.

20. Expressed at T 3.3 and approvingly mentioned at PI §49; see also Pears 1987, 99 n.40; Frege 1980, x, 71, 116. Rorty makes the interesting claim that Frege's context principle represents "the beginning of the end for representationalist philosophy" (Rorty 2007, 144), which for him denotes a great deal of the philosophy of the first half of the twentieth century (see also Gerrard in Sluga and Stern 1996, 175; Livingston 2008, 48). Karl Ameriks attributes this breakthrough to Frege's sworn enemy, Kant, for focusing on judgments as the basic epistemological unit rather than simple ideas or impressions (2000, 58).

21. OC §61, §65; see also LWPPI §340, LWL 28, 61–62, PO 51, 235, RFM 335, PI §21, §49, §563.

22. "The difficulty of my theory of logical portrayal was that of finding a connexion between the signs on paper and a situation outside in the world" (NB 19; see also PI §432, §454, RPPI §42, PG 427, BB 3, 5, Z §238).

23. Conv 41; see also RFM 108, PI §21, §49, §316, §563, RPPI §150, LWPPII 46, LPP 99, LWVC 105, 150; Finkelstein in Crary and Read 2000, 66, 106; Stone in Crary and Read 2000, 106; Harris 1988, 43. A number of commentators have used holism to connect Wittgenstein with various continental figures such as Saussure (Harris 1990, 43; Staten 1986, 79; Garver and Lee 1995, 26, 117), or Derrida (Derrida 1973, xxvi; Garver and Lee 1995, 93–94), or as I am doing here, with Heidegger (Sefler 1974, 94; Gier 1981, 79; Taylor 1995, 72, 75; Guignon 1990, 651; Carman 2003, 224).

24. PI §33; see also PI §155, §199, §205, §250, §337, §581, §638, II.xi p. 185, RPPI §155, PO 235, 240–241, 271, 277, 292, 319, 325, 329, 338, 421, 448, RFM 108, 322–323, Z §133, BB 173.

25. Williams 2002, 55–56; see also 79; Cavell 1995, 164.

26. PO 51; see also AWL 61–62, BB 5, 42, PI §21, §49, RPPI §34, Z §135, §173, LPP 17, 76, LWPPI §50, §294, OC §229, Conv 7, 61; Malcolm 1995, 163, 167.

27. PhR §153; see also OC §61, §§64–65, RPPII §150; Fogelin 1995, 145; Baker and Hacker 1985, 21; Malcolm 1994, 46–47; Diamond 1991, 53, 69–70.

28. "It is, incidentally, very important that by merely looking at the little pieces of wood I cannot see whether they are pawns, bishops, castles, etc. I cannot say, 'This is a pawn and such-and-such rules hold for this piece.' Rather, it is only the rules of the game that define this piece" (LWVC 134; see also Baker and Hacker 1985, 142, 159, 177). I have heard that Wilfrid Sellars referred to the possibility of two rather eccentric and wealthy Texas oil tycoons playing chess on a vast field with a small army of helicopters (Haugeland 2000, 247–248 briefly uses this example).

29. LWPPII 48; see also PhR §213, p. 307, RPPI §549; Ashdown 2001, 322, 325; Crary and Read 2000, 66.

30. RPPI §488; see also PI §47, OC §350, §554.

31. Kierkegaard 1992, 195. Kierkegaard, an author Wittgenstein admired, uses this point to object to Cartesian doubt.

32. OC §467; see also OC §229, §237, §334, §§347–350, §413, §461, §465, §§552–553, §622; McManus 2004, 80; Sass 1994, 8–9, 13.

33. PI §349; see also PI §47, §96, PI II.iv p. 152, LPP 51, Conv 7, 14, Z §§234–235, §238, PhR §213, OC §423, §469, RFM 75, RC I §86, III §168, III §§328–331, RFM 135. Medina writes that Wittgenstein "identified decontextualization as the main source of philosophical confusions and argued that we can only achieve philosophical understanding by situating our ideas or concepts in the contexts in which they

function" (2002, 2; see also 137, 141, 187; Malcolm 1995, 149–150; Kenny 1973, 164).

34. Flew 2008, 21–22. Gadamer makes a similar comment about Davidson: "even the model proposition that Davidson employs—'snow is white'—seems strange to me from this viewpoint. Who uttered this, even if it is true?" (Hahn 1996, 129–130). After years of reading and trying to understand Davidson, I finally found a real-world occurrence of his Tarskian deflationary sentences such as "'Snow is white' means that snow is white." After having children, I'm constantly saying things like, "When I told you to wash the dishes, I meant that you should wash the dishes!"

35. PI §116; see also OC §260, §237, §347, §406, §554, PO 167, 193.

36. LWPPI §41; see also LWPPII 46, 86, BB 9–10, 62, PO 214, 222, 235, RPPI §65, RPPII §235, LFM 18, 21; Pears 1988, 426–427; Kenny 1973, 164.

37. RC I §15, II §45, III §63, OC §65, §87, §256, Z §352.

38. AWL 20–21, 27, PO 275, PI §124.

39. PI §125; see also PI §423, LWPPII 46, 86, CV 75, LPP 21, LFM 170; Stern 1995, 175; Stern 2004, 83, 98; Fogelin 1995, 141; Travis 2006, 6, 52, 152; Minar 1995, 420, 431; Dummett 1996, 446. "I'm not saying anything against that picture. We don't yet know how to apply it" (LFM 145; see also PO 217, 222, PI §278, §295, §305; Williams in Williams 2006, 63).

40. RFM 88, 113, 137, 141, 226, 263, 272, 274, 286, 410. Wittgenstein comments on Hilbert's famous refusal to leave Cantor's paradise of infinities, "I would say, 'I wouldn't dream of trying to drive anyone out of this paradise.' I would try to do something quite different: I would try to show you that it is not a paradise—so that you'll leave of your own accord. I would say, 'You're welcome to this; just look about you'" (LFM 103). Infinity is a prime example of something enticing, redolent of mystery, but which actually represents a humdrum component of certain mathematical operations. I particularly like this exchange: "'I bought something infinite and carried it home.' You might say, 'Good lord! How did you manage to carry it?'—A ruler with an infinite radius of curvature" (LFM 142; see also PR 313, PG 403).

41. OC §622; see also OC §553, §423, §469, §554, PI §97, §100, §§105–107, §120. "When we have difficulty with the grammar of our language we take certain primitive schemas and try to give them wider application than is possible. We might say it is the whole of philosophy to realize that there is no more difficulty about time than there is about this chair" (AWL 119).

42. RPPI §516, §372, RPPII §94, PI §350, §591, OC §349, §393.

43. "To get clear about philosophical problems, it is useful to become conscious of the apparently unimportant details of the particular situation in which we are inclined to make a certain metaphysical assertion" (BB 66; see also BB 98, 144, 182).

44. RPPII §342; see also LWPPI §§830–835, LWPPII 46, OC §6, §§10–12, §17, §54, §89, §117, §§154–155, §247, §260, §349, §352, §372, §393, §413, §423, §§552–554, PI §213, §288, PO 266, LC 68–69, RPPII §§342–345, Z §394, §402, §406, §410, PO 271–272, 286, 325.

45. PO 403; see also PO 204, 214, 222, 267, 275, 292, 295, 362–363; McDowell 2001, 316–317; Hintikka 1989, 251.

46. Like searching our feelings to decide which day of the week is the fattest, or which color a vowel is (RPPI §1037, PI II.xi p. 173, PI II.xi p. 184, PI II.xi p. 186, Z §§183–185, LPP 103), or the way a person's face and name can resonate with features of their personality or work (PI II.vi p. 156, PI II.xi p. 183, RPPII §§245–246).

47. Stern makes this point (1995, 6, 175; 2004, 19–21, 119–120; in Sluga and Stern 1996, 445–446, 457; see also Williams 2002, 16; Genova 1995, xvi; Stroud 2000, 227; Hintikka and Hintikka 1989, x; McGinn 1987, 70). David Pears makes a rather surprising comment on this topic: "it would be simplistic to suppose that it is possible to take a late text of Wittgenstein's, cut along the dotted lines, and find that it falls into neatly separated arguments. The structure of his thought is too holistic for that. However, though this is generally true of his later work, his private language argument is something of an exception. It is brief, looks self-contained, and, after it has been cut out of the text of *Philosophical Investigations*, it proves to be memorable and eminently debatable" (1988, 328). Later, he suggests that we stop calling it an argument since this label "has an extraordinary power to blind us to [Wittgenstein's arguments'] actual structures and interrelations" (Pears 1988, 522 n.54; see also Pears 2006, 63; Monk 2005, 87–88).

48. PO 279–280; see also Hintikka and Hintikka 1989, 251.

49. PI §§263–264; see also RPPI §479; Mulhall 1990, 59.

50. PO 266–267; see also PO 193, 385, BB 170.

51. PO 235; see also Hintikka and Hintikka 1989, 254.

52. PO 236, 252, 275, 291, 342, 353, 450, Z §213, PI §294.

53. PI §261; see also PI §256, PO 253, 338, PhR §68; McDowell 2001, 310; Stern 1995, 145–146.

54. Quine 1969, 19, 27–30; 1970, 8.

55. Much of Derrida's work tries to disillusion philosophy of this illusory sense of absolute self-presence and pellucid meaning within one's mind: "pure auto-affection . . . which does not borrow from outside of itself, in the world or in 'reality,' any accessory signifier, any substance of expression foreign to its own spontaneity. It is the unique experience of the signified producing itself spontaneously, from within the self, and nevertheless, as signified concept, in the element of ideality or universality. The unworldly character of this substance of expression is constitutive of this

ideality. . . . This illusion is the history of truth" (Derrida 1998, 20; see also 98, 138, 153–154, 166, 286, 289; Derrida 1973, 22). His emphasis on writing is meant, among other things, to introduce "foreign" elements into the very essence of meaning.

56. PO 307, PI §§370–373, RC I §72, III §127.

57. PI §257; see also PI §§30–32, PO 240, 447–448, LPP 4, LWPPII 64, RPPII §643; Hacker 1996, 132; Williams 2002, 26; Strawson in Pitcher 1966, 23; Mulhall 1990, 54, 59; Minar 1995, 421.

58. LPP 42; see also LPP 34.

59. Meredith Williams is perhaps the best-known commentator on Wittgenstein's idea that the individual mind depends on the social rather than being a privileged source of meaning or knowledge: "the social dimension is not derivative, hence dependent upon the prior assignment of meaning by the individual mind, but basic" (2002, 51; see also 16, 27; Sluga 1996, 341–342; Mulhall 1990, 69, 127, 155). This has been a common view in continental thought since Hegel, as I discuss throughout Braver 2007, esp. chaps. 6–8.

60. PI §244; see also LPP 34.

61. BB 175; see also T 3.334, 3.34, 3.342.

62. BB 172–173; see also PO 235, 240, 269, 329, 447.

63. PO 329, 235; see also PO 240–241, 269, 271, 277, 292, 319, 325, 329, 338, 421, 447–448, BB 5, 172–173.

64. BB 80; see also BB 2, 69, AWL 12–13, 23, 43, LWL 45, PO 54, 421, PI §26, §28, §§33–35, PI p. 12 n., Z §§11–12, LPP 4, RPPII §296; Williams 2002, 80, 92, 147, 173–176, 217; Stern 2004, 163, 177; Dummett 1996, 44, 163; Taylor 1995, 74–75.

65. LFM 182; see also PI §6, §28.

66. "'But one can surely see the figure as an arrow and as a bird's foot, even when one never tells anyone.' . . . Of course I have here purposely chosen a very rare experience. For because it is not one of the everyday experiences, one looks more sharply at the use of the words" (RPPI §156; see also PI §85, §139, §146, §198, §213, §349, §433, §634).

67. "It isn't a *false* appearance either, but rather one that robs us of our orientation" (Z §259).

68. PI §259, §268, PO 205; Stern 2004, 178–179; Mulhall 1990, 54, 63.

69. PI §259, §265, §267.

70. PI §§270–271, PO 408.

71. PI §293, §296, §298, §304, PI II.xi p. 177, PO 295, 321, 353, BB 159.

72. PO 253, 282, 328, 336–338. I discuss both Hegel's objection and its similarity to Wittgenstein (as well as to arguments made by Nelson Goodman, Richard Rorty, Donald Davidson, John McDowell, and Hilary Putnam) in Braver 2007, esp. 79–93.

73. LWVC 209, PhR §6, PO 56, 131, 312, 336, 339–340, LFM 248, PI §58, RPPI §648, §687, §807, Z §260, LPP 49, Conv 23–25. Compare with Derrida: "from the moment that the sign appears, that is to say from the very beginning, there is no chance of encountering anywhere the purity of 'reality'" because "the signified . . . is *always already in the position of the signifier*" (Derrida 1998, 91, 73; see also Derrida 1983, 328; 1973, 49; 1978, 191).

74. PI §§304–305, PO 327.

75. PO 285; see also PO 267, 295, 317, PI §337, PI II.xi p. 187.

76. PI §142, §345, PI II.xii p. 193, LFM 23, RPPII §145, RFM 200, LWPPI §§252–255, §§260–262, §877, PO 239, 245; Baker and Hacker 1985, 183.

77. PO 265, LWPPII 32, 59, 94.

78. PI §§249–250, Z §571, LPP 99, LWPPI §§859–862, §§946–947, LWPPII 42, PO 254, 267, 306, 349.

79. Z §571; see also PI §284, §580, RFM 351, PO 234, 240, 245, 326.

80. PO 233; see also PO 379, 397.

81. PO 298; see also PO 254–255, 279, 298.

82. PI §284, §§249–250, §281, §283, §360, §650, PI II.i p. 148, II.iv p. 152, LWPPI §358, RPPI §561, §563, §580, LPP 82, Z §531.

83. PI §293; see also PI §304, PI II.ix p. 177, PI II.ix p. 189, PO 282, 409, 450.

84. PI §56, §258, PO 278, 338, 340–344, 451, RPPI §530, LPP 22, 34–35, 88; Williams 2002, 40, 51; Malcolm in Fann 1967, 183–185; Pears 1987, 55; Pears 1988, 361, 386–387, 416–417; Ayer in Steele 2002, 330; McGinn, 1987, 48 n.47.

85. PO 454; see also PO 355, PI §§211–212, §289, §374; Ayer in Morick 1967, 86–87, 89–96; Wright 1980, 28–30, 36–38, 355; Fogelin 1995, 180. Colin McGinn makes this point well: "it is true that Wittgenstein himself sometimes exhibits what can only be described as verificationist tendencies (e.g. in the private language argument) and that he commonly characterises use in terms of the application of words on the basis of criteria (ways of telling); but it is not at all obvious that his capacity view of understanding commits him to a full-scale verificationist account of meaning" (McGinn, 1987, 124).

86. LFM 24, 105, 183, 238, LWVC 154–155, LWL 32, 44, 56, 59, 67, AWL 110, PO 86–87, PI §141.

87. A number of commentators share this reading: Williams 2002, 19–22; Hacker 1996, 132; McDowell 2001, 287; Hintikka 1989, 254–255; Sluga 1996, 341–342; Stern 1995, 181–183.

88. PI §564; see also RFM 108–109; Travis 2006, 33, 68–69. Biletzki (2003, 173) compares Wittgenstein and Heidegger on this point.

89. PI §17, §47, §88, §§562–564, LWPPI §385.

90. PO 214; see also PO 204, 267, 279–280, 403, PI §96, §349, LPP 51, Conv 7, 14–15, Z §238.

91. PO 425; see also PI §38, PI §132, LWVC 48, 65, 139, 160, BB 174, LFM 111.

92. RPPI §65; see also PhR 267, 306–307, LPP 51, LWPPII 86, RFM 86–87.

93. PI §116; see also RFM 137, 286, RPPI §65, PO 167, 193, OC §622.

94. PI II.xi p. 181; see also PI II.xi p. 187, §421, §569, RPPI §1013, PO 332.

95. AWL 90, 108, BB 46, PG 47, PO 367.

96. David G. Stern also makes this point (1995, 41; 2004, xii).

97. This of course requires the kind of indefinite *ceteris-paribus* qualifications that all such discussions do. For example, I can play the game with the intention of losing it, in order to shore up my nine-year-old's confidence or to throw a high-stakes game for great remuneration. Note, however, that even in these cases, (1) I still need to have *some* motivation for the action to make sense—there must be *a* point to these actions even if it diverges from the usual one; and (2) my uncommon actions still presuppose the context of chess play with its goal of winning. In other words, I must know that checkmate is the key to victory in order to *avoid* it.

98. PI §11, §14, §360, LC 1.

99. RPPII §655; see also OC §10, PO 362–363, 391, RFM 89; Williams 2002, 56.

100. OC §347; see also OC §348, §553, §622; Medina 2002, 149.

101. AWL 28; see also AWL 36, RPPI §266, RFM 43, LWPPI §291, OC §61, PO 319.

102. BT 42–44/21–22, 128–129/96, 131/98, 439/387, HCT 300, BCAP 16, 51–52, 74, 102.

103. HCT 91–92, 119–123, 187, MFL 134, BT 85–86/59, 246/202, IPR 40, 60–61; Levine 2008, 40.

104. BT 128–129/95–96; see also BT 48/26, 125/92, 268/225, IPR 168, 230, BCAP 26.

105. BT 31/11; see also PIK 136, BP 22, 125, LQT 258, 322.

106. Sefler compares Heidegger and Wittgenstein on this point (Sefler 1974, 94). Aristotle (or Heraclitus) is perhaps the progenitor of this idea: "the whole must be

prior to the part. Separate hand or foot from the whole body, and they will no longer be a hand or foot" (*Politics* bk. I, chap. 2, 1253a 19–22; see also BCAP 221). Heidegger appears to allude to this passage in his 1949 Bremen lectures: "the part joins, with other parts, into the whole. It takes part in the whole, belongs to it. The piece on the other hand is separate. . . . My hand is not a piece of me. I myself am completely in each respective gesture of the hand" (HR 279). Derrida examines Heidegger's discussions of the hand at length in the context of his treatment of animals.

107. BT 37–38/16; see also BT 140/106, 383/334, 402/351, HCT 95, 155.

108. BT 94/66; see also BT 149/113, LQT 183, 192, 341.

109. FCM 215; see also BT 120–121/87, 160/123, 182/143, 236/192; Rouse 1987, 60, 74, 155; Carman 2003, 48, 217; Ihde 2010, 45; Abbott 2010, 496–497. Jeff Malpas compares Heidegger's public equipmental holism with Wittgenstein's private-language argument (Malpas 2007, 85; see also Carman 2003, 224; Dreyfus 2005, 58–59).

110. BT 97–98/68; see also BT 105/74, 114–118/83–86, 403/352, 432/381, BP 162–164, HCT 186–190, 203, 213, TDP 61, BCAP 41, 206–207, LQT 124–125; Caputo 1987, 70; Dreyfus and Wrathall 2002, 220; Okrent 1988, 42. Our lived space is also organized in terms of practical engagement which means in terms of our projects and goals: the pen is out of reach rather than located at coordinates (x, y) because it is too far to be easily used in order to write down notes. Interestingly, recent discoveries in neuroscience back up this idea, showing that different cells fire in response to what is within our immediate reach as opposed to what lies outside of it (Blakeslee and Blakeslee 2008, 140).

111. Sallis 1993, 27.

112. BT 200–201/158; see also BT 238/193, 474–475/422–423, FCM 300, LQT 329, 331–333, 340, BW 101–103, HCT 195–196, 219; Rouse 1987, 66; Richardson 1986, 17, 19; Versényi 1965, 27; Pöggeler 1970, 293; Carman 2003, 56, 66, 207, 219; Guignon 1983, 201; Guignon 1990, 663.

113. BT 190/149; see also BT 85/59, 88/61, 96/67, 103/73, 129/96, 147/112, 177/138, 215/171, 246/202, 309/264, 412–413/361.

114. BT 101/71, 106/75, 118/85, 128/95, 207/164, 268/225, 405/354, 413/362, TDP 46; Raffoul and Nelson 2008, 58.

115. HCT 183. Equipment's "specific kind of being is encountered in use, and it is characteristic of practical usage that *no scrutinizing objectification occurs.* . . . Dwelling in it, that is, having the tool in use, means precisely not having the reference itself objectively" (HCT 191; see also BT 98/69, 104/74).

116. BT 190/149; see also HCT 187, 195–196, 219.

117. FCM 214, BT 97/68, 404/353, HCT 194.

118. BW 359; see also BT 474/422, 479/426.

119. PI §583; see also PI §35, §525, §584, §638, PI II.i p. 148, II.xi p. 185, LWPPI §406, §§861–862, §§946–947, Z §§532–534, RFM 335, 351–322, PO 306, RPPII §345, LC 54. "I always think of it as like the cinema. . . . The present is the picture which is before the light, but the future is still on this roll to pass, and the past is on that roll. . . . Now imagine that there is only the present. There is no future roll, and no past roll. Now further imagine what language there could be in such a situation. One could just gape. This!" (Conv 13). This refutes his early discussion of timelessness as living in the present (T 6.4311).

120. BT 78/53; see also BT 169/131, 238/193, 275/232, 376/328, 402/351, 410/359, BP 164, HCT 157, 202, 251, 305, Supp 166; Gier 1981, 79.

121. "This unity is not a sum in the sense that it comes after the parts and is only the sum of them. Rather, the unity of this multiplicity is a wholeness that precedes the multiplicity and is its origin and that, as it were, first releases parts from that wholeness" (LQT 190; see also LQT 127, BT 65/40, 226/181, 238/193–194, 350/302, HCT 125, 295).

122. BP 207, 278, 297, BT 156/120, 161–162/123–125, HCT 31, 159, 238, 246, 296–297; Kisiel and Sheehan 2007, 231, 284.

123. TDP 73–74; see also BT 87/60, 130/97, 205/162, 363/315–316, HCT 137, 160–161, 306–307. Incidentally, these discussions of prejudices had a significant impact on his student Gadamer.

124. BT 170/132; see also BT 249/205, CT 7.

125. BT 84/57; see also BT 33/13, 92/64, 118–120/86–87, 152/116, 186/146, 223/179, 232/187, 252/209, 264/221, 368/321, 371/324, PM 121–122, HCT 159, 165, 202, 305, PM 108–109, LQT 79–80, 179, 186, 332, 336; Charles Taylor 1995, 12–13, 172–173; Zimmerman 1986, 26; McManus 1999, 325, 339. See esp. HCT 304.

126. BT 81/54–55, 86/59, 93–94/65, 96/68, 166–167/129, 200/158, 351/303, 366–368/318–321, 475/423, TDP 73–74, 94, PM 20, PRL 54, HCT 195–196, 219, PIRA 388/44–45, LQT 242, 261, 278.

127. In Sheehan and Palmer 1997, 138 (bracketed material in original); see also HCT 246, 270, PM 108.

128. Or at least understands its function, a bit of a sticky wicket in the secondary literature which need not concern us.

129. BP 159; see also BP 171, 297, BT 155/119, 163/126, 283/239, 368/321, 416/364, 465/412, MFL 127, HCT 202, 244, 294; Cooper 2002, 181; Kisiel and Sheehan 2007, 285. Compare T 5.63: "I am my world."

130. My favorite Heideggerian joke was told by Steven Wright. Seeing his Boston Red Sox baseball shirt and cap, a talk show host asked him if he was a fan. Wright

responded that he followed the team zealously, owned paraphernalia, watched all of their games, was happy when they won and upset when they lost—but no, he wasn't a fan. This idea also resonates with Gilbert Ryle's near identification of mind with intelligent behavior and a university as nothing else beyond the buildings, faculty, students, etc. (Ryle 1949, 16; see also Mulhall 1990, 114).

131. BT 305–307/261–262, HCT 317–318.

132. BT 193/151, 237/192, 329/284, 371/324, HCT 168, 185, 294–295, 305, 308, LQT 185.

133. BT 378/329, HCT 308, BCAP 186. Sartre put this nicely in saying that we are what we are not (yet), though I think Heidegger would argue that the other half of this slogan—that we are not (no longer) what we are (have been) does not take history seriously enough, as he discusses in his *Letter on Humanism*.

134. BP 123, HCT 156, 216, IPR 195, BT 72/46, 150/114–115, 152/116.

135. BT 166/128; see also HCT 241, 247.

136. BT 68/41, HCT 152–153.

137. BT 151/116; see also BT 365/317.

138. BT 167/129; see also BT 154/118, 164/126, 312/268, HCT 247.

139. BT 345/299; see also BT 240/196.

140. BT 165/127, 239/194, HCT 244–246.

141. BT 351/303, 367/320, HCT 236, 240, BP 175–176.

142. HCT 243; see also BT 161–163/124–125, 205/162, TDP 77.

143. BT 156/120; see also HCT 238–239, FCM 205, BP 168, 296, LQT 196–197, Zo 162, 183. Charles Taylor compares Heidegger and Wittgenstein on this point (Taylor 1995, 76–77, 168–173).

144. BT 166/128; see also BT 436/384, BP 278, HCT 246, BaT 46, 233, Zo 111, 201.

145. BT 153–154/117–118. Even individually tailored items are tokens of a type, that is, this pair of shoes may have been cobbled just for me, but shoeness certainly wasn't. My very request for an individualized item relies on a universal category. If I wanted someone to make something utterly original and unique, I wouldn't be able to ask for it, like the private-linguist reduced to grunts. Specifying the desired item—say, a piece of art—itself compromises absolute novelty.

146. BT 283/239. Incidentally, this is how I have always understood the much-maligned lyrics of The Beatles' "All You Need Is Love." I take lines like, "There's nothing you can do that can't be done," to mean that hanging your sense of self and worth on worldly accomplishments is futile since whatever you do is just some-

thing that can be done, and hence can be done by others, preventing it from making one's life genuinely one's own. Love, on the other hand, is highly individual and gives a unique shape to great swaths of one's life. In an amorous variation on Heraclitus' river, my wife might have loved another had she not met me, but that would not be the same love, nor would she be the same lover. This could illuminate Heidegger's rather cryptic mention of love as a fundamental mood alongside anxiety and boredom, which get far more discussion (BW 99).

147. BT 161/123–124; see also Guignon 1983, 59–60; Hatab 2000, 69; Charles Taylor 1995, 12–13, 172–173; Okrent 1988, 47–51. "This wholeness as such is what primarily determines the human being's mode of being" (Sheehan and Palmer 1997, 138).

148. BT 441/390; see also BT 369–370/322–323.

149. BT 441/390, 308/263; see also BT 357/310, 369–370/322–323, FCM 82, 103, 117, 121, BW 101.

150. BT 157/121, 160/123, 351/303.

151. BT 152/116; see also BT 89/62, 156/120, 162/125, BP 64, 157, 159, 170, 278, 297, 301, HCT 31, 159, 238, 246, Zo 192.

152. Braver 2007, 276–278. Quentin Meillassoux calls this notion "correlationism" and considers Heidegger and Wittgenstein "emblematic representatives" of it (2008, 41, 48; see also Haar 1993, 72).

153. MHC 40; see also IM 31, 147, 173–174, 219–220, OG 107, ET 52, 75, M 119, M 133, 367, BW 211, 228–229, 248, 329, 412, WCT 106, 121, 241–242, PR 70, 94, PM 283, DT 83–84, CP 177/§133, 179/§135, 201/§164, BQ 179, QT 38–39, 130–131, 145–147, PLT 202, N 3:49, N 4:216, TB 12, 38, Z 176–180, ITP 59.

154. M 118, 281, PM 309, BW 235, ID 31–33, IM 130, WCT 79.

155. One is reminded here of Hegel's examination of phenomenalism, Derrida's deconstruction, and Frege's horse paradox.

156. OBT 57; see also OBT 79, N II:80, N II:131, N IV:7, 100, 205, WT 95–96, BW 330, PR 55, 87, 94, CP 169/§122, ET 150, FS 61, WCT 66; Edwards 1990, 93; Schürmann 1990, 4; Thomson 2005, 55, 147; Thomson 2011, 7; Dahlstrom 2011, 107. Hegel anticipates this idea (Hegel 2002, §3).

157. BW 132, 159–160, 167, 174, 180, 187–188, 224–226, 251, 262, 331, 337, ET 155, CP 98/§72, IM 11, N III:19, HH 84, 103, 123–124; Dreyfus in Guignon 1993, 289–316.

158. OC §102, §§140–144, §225, §248, §274, §312, §410, §594, LC 53, 58.

159. WT 78–79; see also WT 39–40, 50, 65, 90, 129, 135, 52, 121, HH 33–34, IM 56, 110, PT 69, PIK 22, QT 117, 176, BQ 48, AM 67, PR 79, EGT 43.

160. BW 354–356, 360.

161. BW 351; Edwards 1990, 96.

## 4  What Is Called Thinking?

1. Wittgenstein says that the *Theaetetus*, where Plato discusses this definition of knowledge, "is occupied with the same problems that I am writing about" (Rhees 1984, 149). Note that it is the problems that are the same, not their solutions.

2. PO 29, T 4.1121, NB 61, 110, 129; Anscombe 1965, 28.

3. T 3.326–3.327; see also 3.262, 3.328, 5.4733, 6.211, NB 21, 23, 111, LO 59; von Wright 1973, 59; Pears 187, 11, 217; Fogelin 1995, 59.

4. T 4.002, 4.0031, PO 29, 34.

5. GB 45, 115, 54–55, 134, 151.

6. Janik and Toulmin 1973, 222–223.

7. PI §73, PI II.xi p. 185; Wisdom in Fann 1967, 47. Like the confusing double role of games in Wittgenstein's writings as both a metaphor for the practical context of speech and the primary example of family resemblance, pictures also have multiple meanings. On the one hand, Wittgenstein's early work posits a picture theory of meaning according to which a thought or proposition's meaningfulness consists in its being an isomorphic representation of a state-of-affairs. On the other hand, his later view of philosophy is that certain pictures or metaphorical illustrations, once we have strayed beyond the province of normal usage, guide our ideas about various subjects, such as the image of a room organizing our thoughts about mental privacy. This becomes acutely confusing when the picture guiding our thoughts about thinking depicts thinking as the possession of a mental picture. Heidegger makes a similarly disorienting dual use of pictures when he uses a photograph as the example in his objections to the early modern idea (HCT 42, BT 260–261/217–218).

8. PO 59; see also LPP 9, BB 33, PG 90, LWPPI §314, §317, §818, LWPPII 41, 70, Z §§235–236, §239, PhR 65, BB 33, LFM 81, 160, 181, 184–185, 193, PI p. 9, 46 n.2, §§422–425, §§663–664, RPPII §576; Williams 2002, 158, 160.

9. PI §§139–140, §141, §146, §198, §213, §§240–242, §433, LFM 20, 107, 182, RFM 342–343, 414.

10. PI §142, §349, PG 147, RFM 40, 79, 389.

11. NB 21, 23, 27, T 3.327, 4.011, 4.014, 4.0141, BB 53.

12. For some examples, see the figures drawn at RFM 47, 54, LFM 71.

13. T 2.172, 3.332, 4.12.

14. LWL 9, 32, 44, 56, 59, 67, AWL 110, PG 47, 70–71, 89–90, 96, 143, 160, PhR 58, 198, BB 3, 12, 89, RFM 79, LFM 24, 183, 238, PI §86, §141. One solution Wittgenstein entertains in his transitional conversations with Friedrich Waismann is to treat rules like logical form, which must be shown rather than said (T 2.03, 2.172, 3.1432), modifying his "fundamental idea . . . that there can be no representation of the *logic* of facts" (T 4.0312). Instead of an additional entity doing the connecting—like mortar between bricks—a rule simply *is* the way different propositions relate to each other (LWVC 154–157, 207, LO 23).

15. LC 67; see also LWL 61, BB 5, 42, Z §231, Conv 24, PI §140, §426, PI II.vi p. 157, PO 309.

16. BB 4–5; see also BB 39, 42, 47, 53, 69, 113, PI §141, §504, §634. He cites a similar motivation for using primitive, simple language-games like the slab-builders' (BB 17).

17. LWVC 51, LWL 23, BB 2, 172, PI §28, §257, PI p. 12 n., RPPII §296, LPP 4, PO 319, 338, 363, 421.

18. RFM 389; see also RFM 40, 79, 249, 341, 406, PI §§85–86, §146, §198, §433, LFM 23, 180, 225, PG 444, BB 33, RPPII §298, §400.

19. PI §85, §146, §213, §433, LFM 23, 225–226, RFM 36, 40, 79, 389–390, LPP 8.

20. RFM 414; see also RFM 249, 341, LFM 145, 241, PI §198.

21. This idea, captured beautifully by Cavell (1979, 178–179, 358–359), will be the topic of chapter 5.

22. AWL 88–89; see also RPPII §297, PO 310.

23. 2009, 81, 100; see also Minar 1995, 441.

24. PI §§334–335, §§633–637, PI II.xi p. 185, RPPII §34, Z §8; Hanfling in Glock 2001, 142.

25. PI §§437–443, §§602–604; Teghrarian et al. 1995, 84.

26. See Medina 2002, 168–169; Marion 1998, 157; Stern 1995, 178; Pears 1988, 467, 499; Pears 2006, 27–28; Eldridge 1997, 100–101; McDowell 2009, 100; Diamond 1991, 39; Biletzki and Matar 1998, 249. Colin McGinn pays Kripke's work the same backhanded compliment that Nietzsche gave to Descartes's, namely, that its clarity "make[s] it an excellent foil against which to put forward an alternative interpretation" (1987, xii; see also 60, 68). Kripke's reading does have some defenders, such as Priest 2003, 210.

27. PI II.xi p. 182, RPPII §464.

28. WCT 4, DT 44–45, PM 318, compare with PI II.xi p. 181.

29. LFM 23, 81, 159, 193, RFM 50, 236, 342–343, 356, 382, 414, Z §355, LWPPI §304, §932, AWL 187, LPP 37, PI §142, §199, §240, §345, PI II.xi p. 192.

30. PI §201; see also Z §231, §§234–235, RFM 397; Griffiths 1991, 48; Williams in Williams 2006, 64; Pears 1988, 440; McGinn, 1987, 117; Taylor 1995, 170.

31. BB 143; see also Z §140, PI §146.

32. RFM 422; see also RFM 337, 351, 406, PI §206, PG 85, 96; Stern 1995, 125; Mulhall 1990, 40–43; Pears 1988, 518–519; Fogelin 1995, 159; Baker and Hacker 1985, 149; Priest 2003, 211; Kaufman 2002, 360. Colin McGinn writes, "the general picture Wittgenstein is here advocating is a sort of *anti-intellectualism* about the activity of using signs in a rule-governed way: he wishes to emphasise the *habitual* character of rule-following and to discourage an overly rationalistic conception of the nature of this form of behavior" (1987, 24; see also 20, 29, 39, 120).

33. NB 2, 61, 67, 70, PI §80.

34. BB 41; see also BB 65, 78, 137, Z §445, PI §329; Stern 1995, 106.

35. PI §154; see also PI §20, §§34–35, §146, §179, §§506–507, §638, §673, PI II.vi p. 155, PI II.xi p. 184, II.xi p. 187, AWL 52, 78, Z §136, §163, §§445–446, §565, §§605–606, BB 112–113.

36. PI §151; see also PI II.ii p. 150, BB 34, PO 308, 349, PG 85.

37. PI §330, §507; Stroud 2000, 171. This problem bothers his earlier work (NB 19).

38. BB 41; see also BB 43, 80, 164, PI §20, §166, §170, §175, §§195–196, §592, §607, §628, §633, §645, §693, PI II.xi p. 184, PhR 83, PO 316, 453, RFM 43, 299.

39. BB 34; see also BB 156, PI II.ii p. 150, RPPI §232, RPPII §6, Z §100, §136; Williams 2006, 158; Finkelstein in Crary and Read 2000, 65; Malcolm 1995, 4, 15, 188; Malcolm 1994, 108; Edwards 1990, 168; McDowell 2009, 86; but see Wright (Preston 2008, 132).

40. LPP 8; see also LPP 35, 55, 72, PG 182.

41. PG 71, 255, 283–284, PI §90, §370, §587, PI II.xi p. 186, RPPI §472.

42. PG 85, 165–167, 182, BB 165, RPPI §166, §295, PI §106, §442, §596, §§602–603, Z §202, LPP 104.

43. PI §503, LWPPI §120; Malcolm 1995, 71, 86; Williams 2002, 26; Fogelin 1995, 206.

44. Dreyfus 2005, 53, 55. For more on this topic, see my "Never Mind: Thinking of Subjectivity in the Dreyfus-McDowell Debate" in Schear 2011.

45. PG 50; see also PG 47, 71, PO 456, LC 22, AWL 3, 49, 78, LWL 50, 84, 101, RFM 210, 283, LFM 61, PI §150, §199, RPPI §87, §875, RPPII §736, Conv 23–25, BB 25, 41, 43, 65, 80, 143, 156, LWVC 153.

46. Williams 2002, 152; see also Ashdown 2001, 325–326; Mulhall 1990, 36.

47. RFM 397; see also PI §481, §486, LWPPII 46, OC §§510–511; Baker and Hacker 1985, 163; Kenny 1973, 214; von Wright 1982, 172, 177–179; Jaynes 2000, 40–43; Noë 2009, 127–128.

48. PI §505; see also PI §486, PhR 198, AWL 90.

49. Oddly enough in light of his later work, Gilbert Ryle raises this very objection to *Being and Time* (Murray 1978, 59, 63). For more on Ryle's review, see my "Analyzing Heidegger: The Analytic Receptions of Heidegger's Work" (Dahlstrom 2011).

50. BT 85/59, 88/61, 91–92/63, 129/96, 215/171, 246/202, HCT 160–163, 185, MFL 134–135, BCAP 40.

51. Note that Heidegger's later work adds a third "layer" to the ontological difference between beings and their ways of being, what is sometimes called being itself. See Braver 2007, 326–330.

52. BT 62/38; see also PIA 46, HCT 72.

53. BT 90/62; see also BT 246/202, 409/358, HCT 162, BP 157, KPM 165; Dreyfus and Wrathall 2002, 18.

54. BT 246–247/202, 249–250/205–206.

55. HCT 196; see also HCT 30, BT 95/66–67, 101/171, 177/138, 191/150, 405/354, BP 163, 309, LQT 121 n.11, BCAP 12, PIK 15. Anthony Rudd compares Heidegger with Wittgenstein on this point (Rudd 2003, 74, 88).

56. BT 98/69; see also BT 95/67, 177/138, 182–183/143, 191/150, 245/200–201, 405/354, 409–410/358–359, HCT 30, 144, 162, 168, 182–185, 299, PRL 43–44, BCAP 12, BP 276, PIRA 362/7, LQT 121–123, 129, 228, 236–237; Carman 2003, 21; Guignon 1990, 665–666; Jaynes 2000, 34, 47.

57. OC §110; see also OC §148, §196, §204, §232, §395, §431, LWPPII 46; McGinn 1998, 54.

58. BT 185/145. Glendinning notes the philosophers' shared view of understanding as an ability (1998, 159 n.11), as does Mulhall, who compares Wittgenstein's analysis of the immediate grasp of a word's meaning to Heidegger's readiness-to-hand (1990, 36–37, 44–45, 76, 140, 148–149). See also Dreyfus 1990, 184; Polt 2005, 78.

59. This tension is already present in chapter IV of division I, but it comes out in full force in division II.

60. BP 264; see also BCAP 55, 68–69.

61. BB 97; see also PG 287; Stroud 2000, 173.

62. PI §140, §152, PG 140, BB 41, 113.

63. PhR 198; see also AWL 90, PI §486, §505.

64. PG 70–71, 96, PhR 58, RFM 406–407, LFM 24, 105, 183, 238, BB 3, 12, 14–15, 89, 97, LFM 183; Bloor 2002, 46–47.

65. BB 34; see also BB 73, 88, 143, PI §292, PG 160.

66. Caputo calls *Being and Time* "the central document in the development of hermeneutics in this century" (1987, 7).

67. BT 61/37, 96/67, 187/147, 414/362, Supp 74, 160, 175, BaT 195.

68. HCT 87, 300, PM 4, BT 192/150, 213/169–170.

69. BT 189–190/148–149, HCT 57, 63, 78, 157, 206–207, 260–261, 272, PS 99, 126.

70. HCT 91, 111, 117, 187, MFL 134, BT 58–56/59, 246/202, IPR 40, 60–61, 208; Carman 2003, 70–71.

71. HCT 195; see also HCT 163, BT 412–414/361–363; Crowell and Malpas 2007, 11–12. Some have compared Heidegger and Wittgenstein on this topic (Apel 1998, 139; Mulhall 1990).

72. HCT 219, BT 75/49, 85–86/59, 93/65, 96/68, 128–129/96, 150/114–115, 200–201/158, 412/361.

73. BT 101/71, 131–132/98–99, 245/201, 320/275, 363–364/316.

74. BT 201/159, 267/224, BP 206.

75. See Braver 2007, 228–253 for a Heidegger-inspired critique of Davidson. See also Mulhall 1990, 104–122.

76. PI §304, RPPI §824.

77. PI II.xi p. 186; see also Bloor 2002, 19, 46–47.

78. PI §693; see also PI §20, p. 28 n., §80, §154.

79. PG 71; see also PI §148, p. 50 n., §150, PhR 60–61, Z §96.

80. PI §330, Z §§106–107, §139, BB 113, RPPI §488, OC §89; Wright in Williams 2006, 159; Edwards 1990, 195.

81. PI §149; see also PI §141, §165, PI II.vi p. 155, LFM 22, 182, 190, AWL 79, 144, LFM 22–23, 182, 190, PO 306; Malcolm in Fann 1967, 186–187.

82. PI §179; see also PI §152, §157, LFM 24.

83. PI §160, §165, §228, §345,§540, Z §571, PO 218, 232–233, 267, PG 445.

84. PI §294; see also PI §261, §293, §304, §§348–349, Z §213, LC 69–70, BB 65–66.

85. PI §580; see also PI §572, PI II.vi p. 155, PG 445, 469, BB 137, LFM 42, 223, LWPPI §947, §970, PO 233, 240, 298; Williams 2002, 16; Mulhall 1990 61–63.

86. RPPI §215. "I don't know what your thoughts are; why should this interest us more than your digestion?" (LPP 21; see also RPPI §184, §212, §299, §346, §669, §677, §1089, PI §35, §146, §160, §180, §423, §680, PI II.vi p. 155, RPPII §209, §238, §241, §253, §602–603, §643, LWPPI §828, OC §38, §230, §524, Z §88, RFM 325, 395, LWVC 167, BB 65, PG 80, 371–372, PO 204, 217, 235, 349; Malcolm 1994, 62, 71).

87. PI §35, §316, §328, §340, §578, §§581–587, §598, §638, §686, PI II.i p. 148, BB 56, 43, 115, Z §113.

88. PI §155; see also PI §35, §154, §337, §560, §557, PI II.xi p. 187, 191, Conv 61, Z §67, §98, §170, BB 65, 78, 80, LC 62; Lear 1999, 269–270, 290–291.

89. PO 349; see also PI §146, §§151–152, §157, §179, §238, §288, §378, §542.

90. HCT 47. "Our investigation . . . asks about Being itself in so far as Being enters into the intelligibility of Dasein" (BT 193/152; see also BT 292/248).

91. AWL 61; see also RPPI §889, PI §164. Both even describe their target with the metaphor of a symptom of a deeper illness (RPPI §292, BT 52/29, HCT 80), as does Austin (1979, 105).

92. HCT 86; see also HCT 72, 81–85, 112, BT 51–55/28–31, 60/36, IPR 33, 200–202, PIK 68–69, BP 17, 72, MFL 164, 198; Dreyfus and Hall 1992, 96.

93. PI §435; see also PI §92, §126, §559. Baker and Hacker connect this anti-metaphysics with Wittgenstein's methodological commitment to description: "philosophy is purely descriptive. . . . Explanation would be possible only if it made sense to get behind these rules and supply a deeper foundation. . . . But there is no behind. . . . This insight shapes the whole of Wittgenstein's philosophy" (1985, 22).

94. RPPI §509; see also RPPI §256–257, §723, Z §310, §313–315, RFM 254, 333, LPP 90, RPPII §402; Malcolm 1994, 68, 88; Hintikka & Hintikka 1989, 277. Compare with: "the in-being of Dasein is not to be explained but before all else has to be seen as an inherent kind of being and accepted as such" (HCT 165; see also HCT 36, 76, 78, 85, BT 50/28, 58/34, FS 31).

95. BB 143; see also BB 15, 73, 88, AWL 132–133, 179, PG 47, 96, 144, 243, PhR 70, RFM 81, 337, 342, 350–351, 397, 422, LFM 237, PI §217, §377, §481, §506, RPPI §214, Z §136.

96. Z §287; see also Z §135, §139, §173, PI §449, §557, §656, LC 29–30; Baker and Hacker 1985, 144, 180; Mulhall 1990, 40–41, 72, 124; Crary and Read 2000, 65; Travis 2006, 21, 87, 152. I think Wittgenstein would like the story I once heard, about Schumann I believe, who played someone a piano piece and when the listener asked the composer what it meant, he responded, "I'll tell you *exactly* what it meant," and played the piece again (see Rhees 1984, 141; LC 29, CV 58–59, for similar suggestions). Wittgenstein, whose appreciation of music is well known, occasionally compares understanding language to understanding music for, I think, similar reasons (BB 167; Rhees 1984, 160).

97. PI §329; see also PI §445.

98. BT 107/76; see also BT 149/113, 405/354, HCT 185, CT 9; Kisiel and Sheehan 2007, 285.

99. "That in which concern has *fallen* at any given time is not thematically perceived, not thought, not known" (HCT 193; see also HCT 185, 259, 267, BT 107/76, 149/113, 163/125, 220/175, 229/184, 233/189).

100. BT 207/164; see also BT 101/71, PS 288, HCT 35, 39, 60, 68, 210, 266–267, BP 208–209, IPR 6, BW 151–152, 408, EGT 64–66, WCT 129–130, Zo 142; Mulhall 1990, 40–41; Kisiel and Sheehan 2007, 286.

101. TDP 60–61; see also TDP 71, BT 190–191/150, HCT 207, 213, 231, 254, LQT 83, 121, 137, 158, 278.

102. BT 177/138; see also BT 96/67, 98/69, 140–141/160, HCT 70; Dreyfus and Wrathall 2002, 13; Caputo 1987, 62.

103. As Iain Thomson pointed out to me, Heidegger does accept a version of the allegory of the Cave, especially in his discussions of education, but his version diverges from Plato's transcendent metaphysics.

104. RFM 77, 337, LWL 51, PG 47, 96, PhR 70; Rhees 1984, 132; Hacker 1996, 134, 219–220; McGinn, 1987, 16–17; Griffiths 1991, 48.

105. LWPPI §749; see also PI II.xi p. 181; Williams 2002, 158–160; 2007, 64; some commentators have compared the Wittgenstein and Heidegger on this point (Carman 2003, 246; Mulhall 1990, 124, 140; Gier 1981, 109). Russell, like Quine after him, views physical objects as posits or inferences from more immediate sense data (Russell 1959a, 23, 27; Dummett 1996, 80).

106. RPPI §869; see also RPPI §§20–21, §543, RPPII §547, LWPPI §179, §542, §554, §564; McDowell 1998, 276; Genova 1995, 26, 77; in Hiley et al. 1992, 114; in McManus 2004, 102; Mulhall 1990, 16–21, 33–34, 79, 88, 107, 117, 137; Monk 1990, 507–516. A side-effect of the meaning-hungry gaze is that we sometimes see "too much" in arbitrary symbols, the way a composer's name or face takes on the character of his music, or words or vowels accrue physiognomies like fat or lean (RPPI §322, §1064, Z §185, CV 52, PI II.xi p. 173, 186). Heidegger invokes the movement in connection to Husserl at HCT 66.

107. Quoted in Monk 1990, 512.

108. Rhees 1984, 159.

109. PI II xi p. 170; see also PI II xi pp. 165, 168–169, 173, 180, RPPII §378, §390, §462, LWPPI §179, §542, §554, §595, §732, §757.

110. LWPPI 169, 438.

111. "We can also *see* the illustration now as one thing now as another.—So we interpret it, and *see* it as we *interpret* it" (PI II.xi p. 165; see also PI II.xi pp. 179, 181, LFM 159, RPPII §360, §§512–514, §544, LPP 102, LWPPI §179, §555, LWPPII 15; Mulhall 1990, 79). Stephen Mulhall argues that the aspect-blind person is locked into this interpreting mode which the rest of us only resort to under specific circumstances, rather like Dreyfus' analysis of AI (1990, 32, 86, 146).

112. PI II.xi p. 174; see also LPP 103–104; Austin 1979, 110 n.

113. PI II. xi pp. 166, 175, RPPII §305, §359, §436, §511, §§515–517, LPP 106, 108, 111, LWPPI §§52–53, §518, §521, §§533–536, 564, LWPPII 12, 52; Mulhall 1990, 11, 18–21, 23, 42, 88, 121, 135.

114. RPPI §415; see also RPPI §§27–30, §208, §§411–414, §416, §§523–524, §§860–861, §1021–1022, §1028, §1034, RPPII §§304–305, §356, §§358–360, §436, §§510–511, §§515–517, §615, PI §634, PI II.xi p. 166, 175, 179, LPP 104, 106, 108, 111, LWPPI §169, §438, §521, §§533–536, §555, LWPPII 12, Z §208.

115. LWPPI §120; see also Z §130, PI §607.

116. Malcolm 1995, 81; see also 75; Dreyfus 1992, xxviii.

117. PI §289; see also PI §485.

118. BT 200/157; Okrent 1988, 73.

119. BT 190–191/150, HCT 54, 56–58, 63, 70, 84, OTB 78; Schürmann 1990, 67–68; Levine 2008, 18.

120. LQT 123; see also 129, 236–239, HCT 67; Mulhall 1990, 132; Okrent 1988, 76.

121. LWVC 87; see also 65, 146.

122. BB 15; see also 34, 73, 88, 143, 166. Merleau-Ponty makes the same point (1964, 15).

123. Mulhall notes this similarity at Dreyfus and Wrathall 2002, 52.

124. PI §219; see also §201, §506; Edwards 1990, 127, 180, 211.

125. Braver 2007, 312–325; 2009, 60–70; Braver 2011; see also Caputo 1993, 86, 118, 143, 179; Haar 1993, 15, 60, 112, 122–123; Noë 2004, 186, 199, 204; Carman 2010, 141.

126. He claims to have superseded the entire passive–active duality (DT 61, BQ 151, BW 217) by showing their traditional understandings to be incoherent, and I think he is right—perfect activity makes no sense. Our coming to terms with this facts is another form of original finitude. There is no question, though, that what the later work prioritizes is much closer to passivity than activity, although it encompasses elements of both. Heidegger occasionally admits that his early work can be read voluntaristically (FS 40–41, 47, BW 259, P 103, M 257–258, M 287).

127. PO 100–101, all bracketed comments in original. Russell Goodman convincingly shows how Wittgenstein's account of action without explicit thought or decision resembles James' (Goodman 2002, 79–85, 122; see also Stern 1995, 80; Kripke 1982 postscript, esp. 123 n.7; Sass 1994, 69). Gadamer uses the metaphor of games, which he recognizes in Wittgenstein's thought, to move away from transcendental idealism's focus on the subject (Hahn 1996, 27).

128. TDP 56; see also TDP 174, BT 72/46, 366/318, 405/354, WCT 172. Sartre captures this brilliantly in *The Transcendence of the Ego*. Nietzsche says the same thing: "a thought comes when 'it' wishes, and not when 'I' wish, so that it is a falsification of the facts of the case to say that the subject 'I' is the condition of the predicate 'think.' It thinks" (1966, §17; see also 1966, §192; 1968, §477, §484, §487, §531, §547). He also uses the metaphor of lightning where we cannot separate a flashing entity from the flash. Other fellow travelers include Ryle, who claims that grammar misleads us to hypostatize the mind as a separate entity, and Russell, who argues that "the subject-predicate logic" of our language leads to a "substance-attribute metaphysic," even though it is merely an accidental feature of our syntax (Ayer 1959, 38; see also Jaynes 2000, 376).

129. BT 171/133; see also BT 182/143, 214/170, 263/220, 355/307, 401/350.

130. PI II.xi p. 186; see also PI §335, RPPI §73, LWPPI §828, BB 41, LWVC 166.

131. BW 410–411; see also BW 200, 220, 418, 423, PR 47, 96, N III:187, III:214, IV:200, PT 25, PLT 181, 209, PM 236, CP 325/§265, P 49, OWL 76, CPC 47; Edwards 1990, 126–127.

132. PR 24, N:IV 7, N:IV 181, QT 54, WCT 46, 65, 164.

133. BB 155; see also BB 4–5, 34, Z §44, §136, PI §334.

134. N IV:93; see also N III:240, N IV:89, N IV:108, N IV:139, PLT 111, 127, PR 80, WT 97, ID 34, BW 136, 332, EHP 224, Z 266, FS 56, WCT 115, 126, 142, OWL 76, CP 167/§120; Schürmann 1990, 74, 138, 157.

135. PR 24, 87, N III:5, IV:7, IV:180, QT 54, WCT 46, 65, 164, EGT 19, 55, BW 323, CPC 57; Fynsk 1993, 94.

136. Z 217; see also BW 330, 360–361; Schürmann 1990, 61, 73.

137. OWL 76. "To think 'Being' means: to respond to the appeal of its presencing. . . . The responding is a giving way before the appeal and in this way an entering into its speech" (PLT 183–184; see also PLT 6, 209, PM 236, 279, DT 71, 74, PR 23–24, 47, 50, 53, 67, 87–88, 92, 96, P 49, N III:187, N III:214, N IV:200, PT 25, 27, 53, WIP 75–79, PM 279, EGT 19, 55, BW 104–105, 220, 328, 330, 361, 372, 409–411, 418, 423, CP 325/§265, WCT 6, 46, Zo 217, N III:5, III:188, IV:181, QT 54, HR 330, CPC 62). Note that, strictly speaking, Heidegger rejects the distinction between acting and thinking (BW 217–218, 262, QT 40).

138. N IV:214; see also PR 55, 94, BW 217, 384, WCT 115, 126, 132, 151, 232.

139. WCT 233; see also Zo 5, 62, 69, 71. For negations, see BW 104–105, 260, ID 26–27, 39.

140. PR 3; see also PM 293, ID 35, PLT 112, CP 88/§61, 92/§67.

141. For more on this topic, see my "Never Mind: Thinking of Subjectivity in the Dreyfus-McDowell Debate" in Schear 2011. Alva Noë briefly mentions a similar idea (2004, 204).

142. BP 275; see also BT 185/145.

143. HCT 215–216. See BT 88/61, 96/67, 98/69 for tools, and BT 246/202, 249/206, TDP 77–79 for "belief" in the external world; see also Williams 2002, 73; in McManus 2004, 42; Carman 2003, 161.

144. OC §559; see also PI II.xi p. 171, PI II.xi p. 192; Overgaard 2006, 55, 64.

145. BT 249–250/206; see also BT 246/202, Harman 2007, 35, 61, 70; Rouse 1987, 160. "Dasein . . . is in a particular but primarily non-cognitive and not merely cognitive mode of being. . . . Knowing understood as apprehending has sense only on the basis of an already-being-involved-with. This already-being-involved-with, in which knowing as such can first 'live,' is not first 'produced' directly by a cognitive performance" (HCT 162; see also HCT 299).

146. Von Wright 1982, 172.

147. See esp. Dreyfus and Dreyfus 1986, Dreyfus 1996a,b.

148. RPPI §829; see also OC §540, PI §647, LWPII §537.

149. LFM 23; see also LPP 45, 55.

150. Kripke 1982, 22, my italics.

151. Glendinning comments on this feature (1998, 71); see also Garver in Sluga and Stern 1996, 156; Pears 1988, 358; McGinn 1987, 84; Baker and Hacker 1985, 237 n.4; Kaufman 2002, 337; O'Neill 2001, 21; Edwards 1990, 232.

152. RFM 92; see also RFM 43, 61, 253–254, 387, 390, PI §25, p. 48 n., LFM 291.

153. OC §475; see also OC §287, §359, Z §391, §541, §545, RPPII §689; Bloor 2002, 19; Kenny 1973, 176; Baker and Hacker 1985, 237 n.4; Ashdown 2001, 319 n.11; de Lara 2003, 122–123.

154. The *locus classicus* occurs in FCM, which states that "the animal is separated from man by an abyss" (FCM 264; see also FCM 282, BCAP 14–15, 37, 40, 42, 68, 94, 220, Supp 163; Caputo 1993, 126; Haar 1993, 85; Dreyfus 2005, 47, 57, 61, 64 n.39, 65 n.54).

155. BT 125/92, 128/95–96, 190/149, 412/361, 474/422. Nietzsche writes, "a 'scientific' interpretation of the world, as you understand it, might therefore still be one of the *most stupid* of all possible interpretations of the world, meaning that it would be one of the poorest in meaning" (1974, §373). In general, Nietzsche praises the strength to deal with nuances and contradictions rather than the need for the thin gruel of clear, literal meaning.

156. BT 99/69, 173/134, 238/193, 395–396/345, 408–409/357–358.

157. Z §412; see also LC 1, RFM 392–393, RC III §61, III §110, PI II.xi p. 177; Williams 2002, 50, 236.

158. LPP 25, PI §71, §§209–210, §§362–363, PG 118; see also Frege 1980, VIII.

159. Z §304. This conception of teaching often rests upon a naïve faith in ostensive definitions' powers (RPPII §296, PI §28, PI p. 12 n., PO 421).

160. RFM 405; see also RFM 50, 60–62, 79, 321–322, 392–393, LFM 58, 108, 183, 203, BB 89–90, 93, 97, 141, Z §186, §302, §305, §308, §318, §419, §§540–542, §545, PI §§30–31, §143, §185, §231, §338, §597, PI II.xi p. 193, PG 94, PO 352, LPP 25, 37; Williams 2002, 177, 206–207, 218, 233; Priest 2003, 212. Karl-Otto Apel notes this agreement between Heidegger and Wittgenstein (1994, 35).

161. BB 77; see also LPP 52, AWL 102, LFM 107, RFM 117; Moyal-Sharrock 2004, 47, 51; Bloor 2002, 14; Wright in Williams 2006, 168; Hintikka and Hintikka 1989, 199; Sellars 1991, 327; McGinn, 1987, 39, 85; Baker and Hacker 1985, 170; McGuinness 1982, 58; Churchill 1994, 400; Eldridge 1997, 16; Edwards 1990, 158, 165, 170, 183–184.

162. LFM 20; see also LFM 58, 107, 183, 223; Williams in Williams 2006, 71, 81; Pears 1988, 437.

163. LWVC 124, OC §95, §103, §279, §538. See also Bourdieu: "the habitus is precisely this immanent law, *lex insita*, laid down in each agent by his earliest upbringing, which is the precondition not only for the co-ordination of practices but also for practices of co-ordination, since the corrections and adjustments the agents themselves consciously carry out presuppose their mastery of a common code" (1977, 81; see also 85).

164. PI §5; see also AWL 102.

165. "Doubtless the ostensive teaching helped to bring this about; but only together with a particular training" (PI §6; see also PI §9, §§27–32, §§33–34, RFM 41, LWL 48; Bourdieu 1977, 83).

166. Having raised children myself, I am tempted to think that Wittgenstein's frustrating experience as a rural schoolteacher might have shown him that the ability to grasp even simple ideas is an achievement.

167. LFM 60–61. Compare: "I have been trained to react to this sign in a particular way, and now I do so react to it. . . . To understand a language means to be master of a technique" (PI §§198–199).

168. LWL 89, PG 273, 422, Z §295, CV 82; Baker and Hacker 1985, 193.

169. PI §208; see also PI §69, §71, §135, §209, RFM 228, 320–322, 343–344, 420, Z §300, §304, §308, AWL 67, RPPII §298, §§400–401, OC §139; Stern 2004, 13–14; Diamond 1991, 66. Wittgenstein also argues that this is how we do in fact teach (PG 299–300), which serves as another argument in favor of the explanatory sufficiency of examples, if a somewhat circular one: it teaches us that teaching occurs through examples by citing examples of teaching-by-example.

170. Rhees 1984, 115; see also BB 20, 26–27, PG 120–121.

171. OWL 71; see also BW 121–122, 167–169; Baiasu 2009, 687; Zimmerman 1986, 1; Young 2002, 7.

172. BB 89–90; see also LPP 37, AWL 102, Z §187, LWL 48; Polanyi 1967, 5–6; Baker and Hacker 1985, 6; Churchill 1994, 408; Bloor 2002, 14, 46–47; Williams 2002, 50, 177–178, 202, 206, 222, 233; Williams 2006, 71, 81, 168; Griffiths 1991, 54, 212; Edwards 1990, 165, 183–184.

173. Hintikka and Hintikka 1989, 21; see also PI §§240–242, §654–656, PI II.xi p. 171, II.xi p. 192; Stroud 2000, 16; Garver in Sluga and Stern 1996, 164; Stern 1995, 192; Mulhall 1990, 65; Baker and Hacker 1985, 171–172, 179–180, 209, 234; Gier 1981, 31; Wright in Preston 2008, 128–129, 138–140; Churchill 1994, 401; Pears 2006, 19, 28; Travis 2006, 50, 82, 118.

174. BB 141, RFM 50, 196, LFM 21–22, 108, 203, PI §143, §185, §231, Z §302, PO 352, RPPII §397.

175. LPP 37; see also PI §142, PO 397; Hacker 1996, 190; Griffiths 1991, 212–213, 232; Bloor 1983, 2; Dreyfus and Wrathall 2002, 225; Edwards 1990, 199.

176. BB 93, RFM 60, 62, 79, 94, LFM 58, LPP 11, 86.

177. Haugeland 1997, 88; see also 108.

178. Dreyfus 1992, 40–44; 2005, 48–49.

179. PI §§241–242; Griffiths 1991, 54, 212. Scholars working at the intersection of cognitive science and phenomenology often reject the conception of thought as primarily inferential (Noë 2004, 20; Ramachandran and Blakeslee 1998, 132).

180. Some genres such as jokes are actually about what is left out, like a jug's emptiness; the same goes for certain types of fiction, such as Hemingway or Carver's short stories.

181. McGinn 1984, 138; see also Williams 2002, 26; Lear 1999, 249, 290; Hacker 1996, 80.

182. Sluga in Sluga and Stern 1996, 321; see also 341; Stern 1995, 15, 42; Eldridge 1997, 16–17, Apel 1994, 35.

183. BT 161–162/124; see also BT 152/116–117, HCT 243; Raffoul and Nelson 2008, 141; Cook 1965, 290–291.

184. BP 278; see also BT 72/46, BT 150/114, 250/206, 446/394, HCT 246, LEL 36–37, 119, 130.

185. HCT 296–297, BT 152/116, 156–157/119–121, 161–162/123–125, BP 296–297, LQT 196–197, BCAP 45; Sallis 1993, 26; Dreyfus and Wrathall 2002, 223; Austin 1979, 115. This primitive sociality becomes even more important in Heidegger's later work, when he turns to specific epochs and communities.

186. See BCAP 228; Glendinning 1998, 143; Hatab 2000, 148–150. Merleau-Ponty makes the same point (Baldwin 2004, 54–55).

187. BT 192–193/151, 203–204/161, 370–371/324.

188. HCT 162, 168, BT 99/69, 173/134, 176/137, 188–190/148–149, 238/193, 263/220, 382–383/334, 401–402/350, 409/358, BP 164, CT 7, 9, LQT 124; Sallis 1993, 14.

189. N I:51; see also WIP 91, FCM 67–68, 89, 283, LEL 107–108, 112, 125. Kierkegaard agrees: "with respect to existence, thinking is not at all superior to imagination and feeling but is coordinate" (1992, 346–347).

190. BW 100; see also BT 105/75, 173–177/134–138, 232/187, HCT 254–256, 291, N I:99, OTB 199.

191. BT 173/134; see also BT 105/75, 175/136, 177/138, 232/187, 321/276, BW 101, 105, 108, 151, OTB 199, HCT 254–255, 291; Dreyfus and Wrathall 2002, 36, 198. As Hacker writes of Wittgenstein, "thought is essentially bound up with the sentient, affective and conative functions of a being that has a good (welfare and ill fare), is capable of desiring and suffering, can set itself goals and pursue them, and hope to succeed or fear to fail in the pursuit of its purposes" (1996, 134).

192. HCT 239; see also BT 206/163, BCAP 220; Mulhall 1990, 65.

193. BT 154/118, 163–164/126, 168/130, 213/169–170, HCT 246, 270; Guignon 1990, 655–656.

194. BT 151/116, 154–155/118–119, 163–164/126, 167/129, 365/317, HCT 244–245, BCAP 45, 102, CT 8, 17. Recent discoveries in neuroscience dispute the notion that, in Heidegger's words, "the bounds of the human being run along the surface of his skin" (LEL 124). The picture now emerging is one of a flexible identity, where mirror neurons connect us with others at the preconscious level and body maps quite literally incorporate tools and the space of activity surrounding us into our body sense. Neuroscientist Marco Iacoboni argues that mirror neurons show a "*primary* intersub-

jectivity" as opposed to the "individualistic, solipsistic framework that has taken for granted the assumption of a complete separation between self and other" (Iacoboni 2008, 155; see also 203, 267; Blakeslee and Blakeslee 2008, 3, 110, 133, 140; Noë 2009, 67–95; Clark 2004, 26–28). Austin makes the same point (1979, 103, 109, 115).

195. HCT 245; see also BT 167/129, Supp 164.

196. BT 163–164/126, HCT 244–245. I saw a fascinating documentary on animal intelligence where scientists separately showed an ape and a child how to work a mechanism to get a piece of candy, but the scientists included a step that patently played no role. The ape skipped that step while the child imitated the scientist exactly. Here, the ape is behaving more intelligently—grasping how the procedure works well enough to eliminate unnecessary motions—but the human reaps benefits in the long run from the less intelligent, "monkey see, monkey do" imitation.

197. HCT 244, BP 159, 301, BT 155/119, BCAP 186, CT 9; Sallis 1993, 25; Dreyfus and Wrathall 2002, 223–224.

198. BT 161/123–124; see also BT 154/118. Heidegger often argues that our primary relations with others occurs through conversation (BT 206/163, BCAP 33, 43, 76, CT 8), rejecting the two-step theory of perception applied to words as well as things (HCT 210, 266–267, LQT 197, BP 207; Mulhall 1990, 104, 124).

199. RPPII §170; see also RPPII §219, §385, §550, §§558–560, §566, §570, RPPI §§137–139, §247, §267, §878, §919, §§961–962, §1017, §§1066–1069, PG 176, PI II.v p. 153, Z §225, LWPPI §320, §325, §767, §769, RC I.63–64, II.270–271, LWPPII 32–33, 67, 92, 94, NB 84; Glendinning 1998, 147; Malcolm 1995, 67; McDowell 2001, 384, 387, 392–393; Mulhall 1990, 72–73, 88, 116; Rudd 2003, 6, 101, 114–115; Pears 1988, 400; Polanyi 1967, 30–31; Apel 1980, 32–33; McManus 2004, 283, 289; Stroll 2007, 137–138; Hacker 1996, 134, 218–221; Cavell 1979, 368–370; Overgaard 2006, 65.

200. PI §303, §420, PI II.xi p. 190, LWPPII 59.

201. PI II.iv p. 152; see also PI II.v p. 153, PI II.xi pp. 190–191, RPPI §268, RPPII §386, §602, §642, Z §537, §575, LWPPI §321, §324, LWPPII 84, 92; Lurie in Biletzki and Matar 1998, 213; in McManus 2004, 31, 289; McGinn 1998, 53.

202. As Wittgenstein's account accurately reflects our experience, it is not surprising that other phenomenologists make similar analyses. For example, Merleau-Ponty:

My interlocutor gets angry and I notice that he is expressing his anger by speaking aggressively, by gesticulating and shouting. But where is this anger? People will say that it is in the mind of my interlocutor. What this means is not entirely clear. For I could not imagine the malice and cruelty which I discern in my opponent's looks separated from his gestures, speech and body. None of this takes place in some otherworldly realm, in some shrine located beyond the body of the angry man. It really is here. . . . Anger inhabits him. . . . It is only afterwards [i.e.: RRR], when I reflect on what anger is and remark that it involves a certain (negative) evaluation of another person, that I come to the following conclusion. Anger is, after all, a thought . . . and this thought, like all others, cannot—as Descartes has shown—reside in any piece of matter and therefore must belong to the mind. (2004, 63–64; see also 1962, 66–67, 214–215, 356; Bourdieu 1977, 80)

Compare this with Wittgenstein's famous saying, "the human body is the best picture of the human soul" (PI II.iv p. 152; see also PI §281). Others have noted this similarity (see Hammond, Howarth, and Keat 1991, 207–208; Overgaard 2006, 63).

203. Cavell 1979, 45. Wittgenstein also argues that the grammar of these terms undermines the idea of first- and third-person asymmetry which awards me absolute and immediate access to my own "inner" thoughts or emotions but only indirect access to others, forcing me to infer others' mental states (PI II.xi pp. 189–190, LWPPII 40, RPPI §§137–139, LWPPI §831–834, LWPPII 84, OC §243; see also Austin 1979, 97).

204. Z §545; see also PO 381, 395.

205. Z §541; see also CV 31, RPPI §151, RPPII §689, LWPPI §325, §769; Malcolm 1994, 64, 91; Malcolm 1995, 67, 79, 82; in McManus 2004, 283.

206. LWPPII 55, OC §34, §160, §263, §283, §310, §329, §344, §374, §450, §472; Polanyi 1967, 60–62.

207. OC §392; see also RPPII §§588–591, PG 147, LFM 81, PI §85, §87, §213, §349, RFM 249, 341, 414, LFM 241; Griffiths 1991, 228.

208. Recent neurological discoveries about "mirror neurons" back up Wittgenstein's and Heidegger's views on this point by providing "an unreflective, automatic simulation . . . of the facial expressions of other people, and this process of simulation does not require explicit, deliberate recognition of the expression" (Iacoboni 2008, 111–112). Rather, "it is an *effortless*, automatic, unconscious inner mirroring" (Iacoboni 2008, 120). And, specifically on the privacy of pain: "although we commonly think of pain as a fundamentally private experience, our brain actually treats it as an experience shared with others" (Iacoboni 2008, 124; see also 265; Varela 1999, 23; Blakeslee and Blakeslee 2008, 166–167, 177–179). Iacoboni concludes that "mirror neurons seem to explain why and how Wittgenstein and the existential phenomenologists were correct all along" (2008, 262; see also 16–18, 55–56). Shaun Gallagher, in his discussions of how cognitive science and phenomenology can "mutually enlighten" each other, reviews recent discoveries about the many ways in which we are neurologically hard-wired for sociality (Gallagher 2004; see also Gallagher and Varela 2003; Gallagher and Meltzoff 1996; Hatab 2000, 69–70, 145–148; Meltzoff and Moore in Bermúdez, Marcel, and Eilan 1995, 53–55). Meltzoff and Moore also argue that infants' perception is teleologically organized (Bermúdez, Marcel, and Eilan 1995, 54, 61–63).

209. RFM 341–342, italics in original, bracketed comments added; see also RFM 350–351, 430, PG 47, 147.

210. Gadamer 2001, 51; Gadamer 1995, 368, 385; Gadamer 1977, 57. I discuss these two conceptions of reading in "Davidson's Reading of Gadamer: Triangulation, Conversation, and the Analytic-Continental Divide" (in Malpas 2011).

211. PIRA 377/29, 381/35, PS 112. For discussions of Heidegger's appropriation of Aristotle, see Kisiel and van Buren 1994, 195–227; Volpi in Macann 1995, 27–66; Gadamer 1994, 31–33, 140–141; 1977, 201–202; Caputo 1993, 64; Caputo 1987, 89, 109–110; Dreyfus 2005, 56.

212. PS 45–46, 77–78, 104, TB 78–79, HR 299–300; Gadamer 2001, 105–106. Gadamer reports that he "was even able to persuade Husserl that Aristotle had been a founder of phenomenology" (Hahn 1996, 23; see also 308).

213. *Topics* chap. 14, 105b25–30; NE 1103b26–30, 1105b13–18, 1112a3–4, 1116b4–7, 1139a36–39, 1144b18–32, 1179b2–19. See Burger (2008, 47–56) for a helpful contrast between Aristotle and Socrates.

214. PI II.xi p. 193; see also RPPII §29, §§401–402, §607, §630, RFM 321, LC 6–7. This is one of the reasons Wittgenstein liked the elder Zosima from *The Brothers Karamazov*, whose speeches he knew by heart (Monk 1990, 136). Dostoevsky's first description of the character says that his many years of experience gave him "such fine discernment that he could tell, from the first glance at a visiting stranger's face, what was in his mind, what he needed, and even what kind of suffering tormented his conscience" (Dostoevsky 1990, 29). Wittgenstein told a friend, "you know there really have been people like the Elder Zosima who could see into people's hearts and direct them" (Rhees 1984, 86).

215. NE 1094b13–14; see also NE 1098a27–35, 1104a1–11, 1143b11–14. "The standard applied to what is indefinite is itself indefinite" (NE 1137b29–30). One of the ways to define the right kind of action is by reference to the actions done by the right kind of person (1105b7–9, 1113a30–34, 1140a25). Since this model is circularly defined as the person who does the right kind of thing in the right way, there is no way to bootstrap up to an understanding starting from nothing.

216. NE 1109b21–24; see also NE 1103a5–9, 1104a5–9, 1106a30–1106b7, 1110b5–9, 1126b3–10, 1137b7–32, 1141b9–24, 1142a27–28, 1143a8–10, 1143a32–35, 1180b7–12, PS 34, 93–94, 96, 100–101, 110, 112; PG 62, RPPII §607, PI II p. 193, LWPPI §§925–927; Dreyfus 2005, 51.

217. Heidegger quotes *Metaphysics* bk. IV, 1006a ff. at BW 449, PR 13. See also NE 1098b1–4, 1143b11–14.

218. NE 1139b28–32; *Posterior Analytics* bk. I, chap. 2, 71b20–24; bk. I, chap. 3, 72b19–24.

219. The passage from which I derived "the Primacy of the Whole" argues that "the state is both natural and prior to the individual" (*Politics* I.2, 25–26; see also NE 1097b8–14, 1142a9–10, 1169b13–23).

220. NE 1179b24–32; see also NE 1095b4–10, 1103b20–26, 1104b11–13, 1137a5–9, 1179b33–1180a18.

221. NE 1103a24–26, cf. Moyal-Sharrock 2004, 82; Stern 1995, 192.

222. NE 1111b1–3, 1144a32–36.

223. NE 1112a3–4, 1114a4–7, 1114b22–24, 1119b9–11.

224. "We ought not to follow the proverb-writers, and 'think human, since you are human,' or 'think mortal, since you are mortal.' Rather, as far as we can, we ought to be pro-immortal, and go to all lengths to live a life that expresses our supreme element. . . . Each person seems to be his understanding, if he is his controlling and better element" (NE 1177b34–1178a2; see also NE 1166a23–24, 1177a7–22, 1178b22–24). You can't get much farther from original finitude than that.

225. NE 1179a19–23, brackets in original; see also NE 1096b30–36, 1098a26–35, 1104a1–9, 1112b8–10, 1137b14–17, 1180b11–13. Jacques Taminuaux points out that what I call the "*pharmakon* logic" of Dasein's relations with others can be seen as an internal tension between Aristotelian and Platonic proclivities (1991, 130–132, 141–142, 162). Gadamer discusses *phronêsis* in terms of what I am calling "original finitude": "the Socratic legacy of a 'human wisdom,' had to be taken up again in my own hermeneutical theory-formulation, a legacy which, when measured against the godlike infallibility of science, is, in the sense of *sophia*, a consciousness of not knowing. What Aristotle developed as 'practical philosophy' can serve as a model for this fallible and merely human wisdom . . . articulated in a reflection that neither starts at a zero point nor ends in infinity" (Hahn 1996, 31).

## 5   The Essence of Ground

1. LO 24; Travis 2006, 201.

2. PO 73, 408; Rosen 1999, 17–22; Minar 1991, 209.

3. T 6.1251; see also T4.5, 5.451, 5.47, 5.4711, NB 75, 89–90, 116. I trace the development of this idea, which I call Realism of the Subject, from Kant to Derrida in Braver 2007.

4. T 6.1233; see also T 5.473, NB 2, 11; O'Neill 2001, 4.

5. PG 481; see also LFM 103, 131–132, 170–171, PR 237, PI §352, §426, RFM 45, 64, 249, 268, 408; Wright 1980, 18–20; Marion 1998, 181–183. Kant makes the same argument in the cosmological antinomy (C1 A522–523/B550–551).

6. PI §107, PO 391, OC §47, §260, §572, PG 187.

7. RFM 267; see also RFM 115, 269.

8. PI §352; see also PI §§422–425, §663, PI II.vii p. 157; Minar 1995, 419, 430.

9. PI §211; see also PI §377.

10. PI §485; see also PI §289, AWL 5, OC §358.

11. PI §219; see also PI §228, §292, §323, PO 381, 395, PG 47, RFM 326, 330, 337, 350–351, LFM 199, 234, 289.

12. PI §228; see also RFM 46.

13. Z §358. See Forster 2004 for an informative discussion.

14. PG 246; see also AWL 4, 65, LWL 44, 104, RFM 96, 131, RC I §§72–74, III §127, LPP 49–50; Sellars 1991, 356; Stern 2004, 116; Baker and Hacker 1985, 22, 37, 40, 63, 164, 166, 330; Kenny 1973, 176; Baker and Hacker 1985, 330–331; O'Neill 2001, 6; Rosen 1999, 19; Malcolm in Vesey 1982, 259; Pears 2006, 66; Travis 2006, 170. Note that upon his return to philosophy in the late 1920s, Wittgenstein initially distinguished between systems that do answer to reality (such as physics or war-making) and those that do not, labeling only the latter arbitrary (LWVC 62, 103–105, 126, 162–163, 170, 240, AWL 4, 83–84, 139, LWL 49).

15. AWL 139; see also RFM 99, LFM 14, 22, 82, 139, 190, LPP 5, 38, 43, RC III 293, PI §17.

16. LWL 44, LFM 135; see also LWL 41, 85.

17. PI §§47–48, §59, LFM 154.

18. PhR 54–55; see also PG 255, 283–284, OC §145, §130, Z §333, RPPI §644, OC §§196–198, §292, PG 224–227, 443, AWL 28, 98 n.; Pears 1988, 462; Guignon 1990, 665–668; McManus 2004, 34; Diamond 1991, 56, 68–69. See esp. LPP 49–50.

19. PI §257; see also RFM 381.

20. PG 415; see also LFM 39, 56, WT 90, PIK 22; Kober in Sluga and Stern 1996, 429.

21. Graham Priest (2003) examines this paradox in Russell, the *Tractatus*, and Heidegger, among others.

22. LWL 47, 79, 86, 95, PO 70–71, RC III 86, PG 186, 255, LFM 248, PR 55, RFM 162, 381; Travis 2006, 160.

23. PG 97; see also PG 215, 313–314, 324, OC §191, LWVC 186, 226, PO 56, 312, AWL 106–107, LFM 248. "Like everything metaphysical the harmony between thought and reality is to be found in the grammar of the language" (PG 162). See also Medina 2002, 48, 78; Hacker 1996, 80, 119; Malcolm in Vesey 1982, 259; Hintikka and Hintikka 1989, 277; Garver in Sluga and Stern 1996, 148; Bloor 2002, 22, 30, 34–35; Williams 2002, 27, 51; Mulhall 1990, 127; Rudd 2003, 153; Arrington and Glock 1992, 70, 81; Pears 1987, 30, 189–190; McGinn 1987, 88.

24. PI §374; see also PI §84, PG 245, Z §§440–441, BB 19, 25, 27.

25. PI §371, §373; see also PO 307, RFM 65, 75–76, PG 314; BB 57, 70, 109, PI §303; Garver in Sluga and Stern 1996, 143.

26. RPPI §§548–550, Z §458, §461.

27. PG 184; see also PO 83, 312, RFM 131, PI §58, §251, §370, §§383–384, §§401–402, PI II.xi p. 174, LPP 92.

28. LWVC 226; see also OC §199; Pears 1987, 189–190.

29. BT 51–55/28–31, 60/35, 62/38, BP 17, HCT 72, 81–85, IPR 33, 200–202, PIK 68–69, MFL 164, 198; Apel 1994, 35, 49 n.95, 83–84. This becomes more complicated in his later work, where being itself is never exhausted by any particular epoch's understanding of being, though neither is being something beyond and independent of them (Thomson 2005, 27d–8, 117). See below.

30. AWL 70; see also AWL 129, 162, 178, LFM 138–139, PI §242, RFM 38, 96, 200, PG 111, 184–185, 322, 334, 352, 401, LC 59, LWVC 103–105, 126, LWL 104–105; Wright 1980, 61, 69; Hacker 1996, 121; Baker and Hacker 1985, 54, 105, 163; Arrington and Glock 1992, 77, 81; Pears 1988, 437, 446; Rouse 1987, 62, 124, 160, 210; O'Neill 2001, 3, 7; Gier 1981, 42; Stern 1995, 49; Griffiths 1991, 215; Minar 1995, 439; Minar 1998, 330. Echoing a point made in the *Tractatus* (T 6.341–6.342), he does occasionally say that the ease or difficulty encountered in applying different forms of measurement can suggest very general facts about nature (PO 449, Z §364) as well as, presumably, human nature.

31. RFM 234; see also RFM 238–239, PhR 226; Dummett 1978, 170–171; Wright 1980, 128–129; Teghrarian and Serafini 1995, 10; Bloor 2002, 10; Pears 1987, 30, Wright 1980, 20; Travis 2006, 187.

32. Of course, which circumstances count as normal can only be decided circularly as those which provoke little hesitation or disagreement.

33. PI §§68–71, §80, §142, LPP 44, 74, PG 112–113, 117, 125, 236, 300, LFM 263, LWVC 36, 110, 129, 132; Staten 1986, 97; Crary and Read 2000, 65; Diamond 1991, 69.

34. AWL 179; see also LFM 223, RFM 274, LWVC 134; Wright 1980, 60–63; Hintikka and Hintikka 1989, 234; Gerrard in Sluga and Stern 1996, 172; Travis 2006, 28, 32, 52, 60, 77.

35. "Frege somewhere says that the straight line which connects any two points is really already there before we draw it; and it is the same when we say that the transitions, say in the series +2, have really already been made before we make them orally or in writing—as it were tracing them" (RFM 45; see also RFM 361, GB 58, 122, 127, 145).

36. Von Wright 1982, 114, 125, 132; Glock 2001, 16. One of the inspirations for his return to philosophy was attending a lecture on mathematics by Brouwer, the main

figure of mathematical intuitionism which overlaps with some of Wittgenstein's ideas, especially concerning the role of mathematical proofs (Fann 1967, 22).

37. LFM 104; see also LFM 255, 271, PI §208, LPP 69, PG 321, 480, AWL 192, LWL 89–90, PR 149, 212, RFM 408; Marion 1998, 181–192.

38. LWVC 34–35, 63, RFM 50, 99, 111, 136, 267, 270, 362, LFM 22, 39, 82–83, 138–139; Wright 1980, 240–241; Baker and Hacker 1985, 10; Dummett 1996b, 446, 451. Compare with Russell: "all knowledge must be recognition, on pain of being mere delusion; Arithmetic must be discovered in just the same sense in which Columbus discovered the West Indies, and we no more create numbers than he created the Indians" (Russell 1996, 450–451; see also GB 1960 122, 127, 131, 145).

39. Glendinning 1998, 102; see also Griffiths 1991, 215; Priest 2003, 213; Sluga and Stern 1996, 386; Stern 1995, 115; Pears 2006, 66–67, 80.

40. LFM 183; see also LFM 97, 101, 236–237, 275, 290–291, PO 352, 395, PI §145, p. 124 n., OC §304, §§496–497, §637, §651, RFM 90, 199.

41. PI §186, BB 142, RFM 79, PG 184, 303, RPPII §§398–402.

42. RFM 205; see also RFM 159, LFM 180; Wright 1980, 99–103.

43. PG 184–186; see also PG 124, 303, 322, 378, OC §497, §510, PO 52, 266, 383, PhR 178–180, 328, Z §320, §331, LWL 19, 57, 90, 92–93, BB 27–28, 69–70, 73–74, RFM 37, 94, 236–237, 274, 366, RPPI §488, RC I §6, I §14, II §10, III §42, III §§86–88, III §123, III §§127–128, III §293, III §296, LWVC 36, 119, 129, 132, 175, LFM 82, 184, 191–192, 194, 203, 214, 218–219, 237, 249–250, PI §194, AWL 65, LWPPI §42, LWPPII 44, 51, PI II.xi p. 192, Z §340, CV 64; Diamond 1991, 30–31.

44. PG 301; see also PG 113, 117, 321, 377, RPPI §547, OC §362, RFM 163, PI §186, LWVC 146, 204.

45. BB 143; see also BB 15, 34, 73, 166, PO 354, RFM 199, 326, 394, LFM 31, PI §141, §190; Williams 2002, 230; Stroud 2000, 13, 16; Marion 1998, 225; Stern 1995, 114; Baker and Hacker 1985, 188; Gier 1981, 102; Crary and Read 2000, 44: Dummett 1996b, 448. Guignon compares the two on this point (Guignon 1990, 669–671).

46. RFM 395; see also RFM 80, 395, PG 109, 126, PO 254, AWL 187, RPPI §896, LWPPI §42, LFM 20, 58, 66, 75, 107, 139, 235, 249, LWL 8, 48, OC §344, §358.

47. RFM 355; see also RFM 200, 228, 253, 342–344, 352–353, 365, 379, 382, 389–390, 406, PI §224, §§240–242, PI II.xi p. 192–193, Z §319, §430, LFM 29, 107; Dummett 1978, 179–180, Medina 2002, 155; Williams in Williams 2006, 79–80; Williams 2002, 51; Malcolm 1995, 157; Stroud 2000, 85; Fogelin 1995, 163; Baker and Hacker 1985, 247.

48. OC §512; see also OC §5, §§80–83, §88, §§95–96, §167, §196, §§210–211, §245, §308, §368, §378, §404, §628, §641, §655, §657, AWL 16, 86, 160, 174, PG 224, 320,

415, LFM 39, 41, 47, 56, 83, 98–99, 104–107, 124, 129, 290–291, RFM 50, 78, 82, 98–99, 160–161, 165–166, 170, 199–201, 224–226, 238, 251, 309, 324–325, 350, 392, 430, 437, PI §50, §79, RC I 32, III 19, III 348, PO 375, LWVC 62, 194, 198–199; Dummett 1978, 170–171; Gerrard in Sluga and Stern 1996, 179; Wright 1980, 318–341.

49. See LFM 232, RFM 245, 338 PG 404.

50. LWL 88; see also LWL 104–105, AWL 4–5, PG 97, 110–111, 184–185, 303–304, 322, 334, LFM 95, 107, RFM 44, 381, 397, 401, LWVC 124, 133, PO 352, 418, OC §§81–83, §105, §108, §110, §§150–151, §167, §603, BB 89; Baker and Hacker 1985, 180; Genova 1995, 44; Stroud 2000, 93; Medina 2002, 152; Malcolm in Vesey 1982, 254, 259, 262.

51. LFM 190; see also LFM 278.

52. Descartes 1985, 114.

53. RPPI §643; see also PI II.xii p. 195, Z §351, RFM 236, RC II 10, III 121–124; Malcolm in Vesey 1982, 254, 257, 261–262.

54. LWPPI §200, §259, LFM 291.

55. RPPI §47, LPP 4.

56. CV 37; see also CV 74.

57. RFM 255; see also LWPPI §525, OC §670.

58. LWVC 119–120, 125, 194, LFM 176, 179, 206–207, 213, RFM 254–255, Z §685, §687.

59. LWVC 194, 201, LPP 116, LFM 207–209, Z §688, PG 303.

60. Russell 1959a, 76. Frege warns his readers of the dangers of undiscovered contradictions (Frege 1980, 87, 105–106, 108, 112, 119), foreshadowing just the kind of disaster that befell him: the failure to find a contradiction among one's definitions, he writes, "shall, at bottom, never have achieved more than an empirical certainty, and we must really face the possibility that we may still in the end encounter a contradiction which brings the whole edifice down in ruins" (1980, ix, compare with GB 234). If logic could accommodate tragedy, this is surely what it would look like.

61. RFM 120; see also RFM 213, 370, LFM 206–207, RPPI §1132.

62. PG 303, LFM 28, 124, RFM 215, PhR 319, 338.

63. LFM 103–104, 107, 131–132, 138–139, 171, 209–211, RFM 408, PI §352, LWVC 120, 174, 199–200, PG 303.

64. LFM 209; see also LFM 201, 220.

65. LFM 138–139; see also LFM 47, 66, 83, 95, 107, 126, 132, 179, 202, 235, 258, AWL 67, 84, PG 304, RFM 99, 267, 270. "Only within a mathematical structure

which has yet to be erected does the question allow of a *mathematical* decision" (RFM 279). Karsten Harries compares this idea in Wittgenstein to Heidegger's understanding of poetry (1968, 288–289). Iain Thomson made the interesting suggestion that there could be something like an improvisatory game that could reclaim "Calvinball" as playable, if unorthodox. I am turning to just such considerations in my next book.

66. AWL 71; see also LWL 19; Dummett 1978, 168, 178.

67. LFM 189; see also LFM 237, RFM 122, 211, 254–256, 369–370, PG 303, OC §375, RPPII §290, AWL 71–72; Monk 1990, 545. This is why I disagree with Hacker's assertion that for Wittgenstein, "fundamental propositions of logic, such as the law of non-contradiction . . . are renounceable only at the cost of renouncing all thought and reasoning" (1996, 217). Wittgenstein also argues that contradictions are just as good as tautologies for laying out the structure of logic (T 4.461, 6.12, 6.1202), meaning that, for example, Russell's logic could consist entirely of contradictions rather than tautologies and still be exactly as effective (LWVC 131, Z §689, LFM 214). So why the fuss about one and this complaisance with the other?

68. LFM 271; see also LFM 227–230, 260, RFM 378, 400; Diamond 1991, 8.

69. RFM 401; see also RFM 371, 374, 378, LWVC 129, 139, 149, 195.

70. LWVC 125; see also LWVC 120, RFM 119, 159, 204–205, 375, 378, 400, LFM 210, 217, PO 437.

71. BT 270/227; see also BW 123–124.

72. PIA 123; see also PIA 83–84, OC §163; Levine 2008, 42.

73. BT 213/169–170; see also BT 32/12, 61/37, 72/46, 150/114, 167–168/129–130, 189/149, 191–192/150, 211/168, 239/194, 245/201, 250/206, 315/270–271, 345/299, 360/312, 414/362, 460/408, HCT 246, 299–300, H 17, IM 124, BP 10, 60, 72, 278, BCAP 196, PM 104–105, PIK 158, LQT 228, 234, 280.

74. BP 22; see also BP 117, LQT 232, Supp 74, 160, 174–175, BT 192/150, 250/206, HCT 128–130.

75. BT 195/153; see also BT 27/7, 195/153, 285/241, 362–363/314–315, KPM 15, 160–161, BW 144, ITP 56–57; Zimmerman 1986, 29.

76. Guignon 1983, 40; Hatab 2000, 2.

77. OC §110; see also OC §148, §196, §204, §232, §344, §431, Z §277, §416, RPPI §151, LWPPII 21.

78. HCT 162; see also HCT 168–169, 185, 187, 191, 299, BP 165, 275, 309, BT 95/67, 98/69, 104/74, 122/88, 156/120, 185/145, 405/354, PIK 16; Dreyfus 1991 51, 93.

79. HCT 144, 164, 194–195, 210–211. Compare OC §138, §143, §152, §§160–162, §167.

80. TDP 78–79; see also BT 170/132, 250/206.

81. OC §337; see also §355, §375, §392.

82. Descartes compares his unfortunate state of having uncritically accepted many beliefs with the possibility of having "had the full use of our reason from the moment of our birth, and if we had always been guided by it alone" (Descartes 1985, 117). Whereas this is a contingent matter for Descartes, and an actuality for Augustine, Wittgenstein argues that it is conceptually impossible.

83. BT 38/17, 171/133, 224/180, 237/192, 274–276/231–233, 279/236, 293/249, 309/264, 343/297, 351–352/304, 370/323, 384/335, HCT 152, BP 59, 227, 308, PM 110; Guignon 1983, 61–63.

84. BT 264/221, 233/189, 308/263, 320/275, 317/273, 357/310, 364/316, 443/391, KPM 163, HCT 277, 282, 291–293, 313, 316, BW 103, 109.

85. BT 232/188, 307/262–263, 311–313/267–268, 333/287, 370/323, FCM 143, 314/269, 317/272, 321–322/277, 369–370/322–323, BW 101–102, HCT 318, FCM 143, 165, 171.

86. BT 329–330/284, PIK 158; Bourdieu 1977, 216 n.24.

87. BT 312–313/268; see also BT 164/126, 240/196, 345/299, 354/307, 435–437/383–386, 441–442/390, 448/396, HCT 313, 318–319; Rorty 1991, 61. For more on this, see Braver 2007, 211–221.

88. IM 219–220, ID 31–32, BW 100, 228–229, DT 84, PR 68, 70, 86, 93, WCT 124, 132–133, 142, 149, STF 98, QT 42, BaT 104, 106, 137, 157.

89. CP 168/§120; see also CP 227/§202, WT 67, 90, PIK 22, BQ 80, 181, FS 8, P 7, BW 238, PR 41; Young 2002, 9 n.4, 31; Thomson 2005, 9, 54, 114 n.76. For more on this, see Braver 2007, 261–273.

90. TB 9, 28–29. CP 34/§19, 53/§34, 208/§172, 212/§176, FS 78.

91. BW 239; see also EHP 57, QT 153, IM 149, DT 77–78, PM 334 (in Sallis 1970, 26), HH 124; Thomson 2011, 197.

92. TB 32; see also FS 13, 70, CP 320–321/§264.

93. WT 39–40, IM 56, EP 14–15, M 91, ET 104, BW 186, PR 29, 62, 79, 91, 94, EGT 43, QT 168, 176, STF 31–32, 58, 167, ITP 1–2.

94. STF 30, 54, WT 74–75, OBT 59–60.

95. BW 65–66, 168, 354, N III:56, M 199, PM 321, WCT 66, Zo 6, 187; Ihde 2010, 42.

96. PM 279; see also BW 217, 234, 240–241, 256, 260, 384, 416, HH 91, CP 169/§122, IM 166–167, WCT 126, 151, P 76–77, N III:68, N IV:152, N IV:218, BQ 147, DT 46,

64, 74, PM 135, M 276; Young 2002, 23, 83; Zimmerman 1986, 113, 146; Pinkard 1999, 208.

97. WCT 22, 136, 176, BCA 6, BW 234, 246, 263.

98. BQ 139; see also TB 35, 45, FS 47, Z 207, QT 128, 151, 153, DT 77–78, PM 285, 334, P 138, N III:221.

99. BW 226, 232–233, 254, 314, WCT 161, M 19, 37, 268–269, 333, STF 171, 187, PM 279, CP 120/§85, WT 78–79; Schürmann 1990, 11, 25, 74.

100. M 300, 322–323, 375, TB 37, ITP 5, 15, 58.

101. EGT 60, 99, 122, QT 115, PM 232, 287, N IV:7, OBT 57, EP 90, BW 247, N IV:211–212, PM 278, 288, AM 8, 102, ITP 16; Young 2002, 23–29; Zimmerman 1986, 23.

102. ET 6; see also EP 14–15, M 91, PR 89, 105; Schürmann 1990, 50; Young 2002, 86; Thomson 2005, 8, 23, 39, 41, 142; Ihde 2010, 31. Gadamer will make this notion axiomatic for his hermeneutics. Interestingly, Kant makes a similar argument (Kant 2000, 19–20/20:216, 275/5:405, 311/5:445).

103. PT 69; see also Zo 286, QT 37, 176, PR 100–101, HR 257, 306; Rorty 1991, 16, 40; Schürmann 1990, 7. Although there is much to admire in Graham Priest's *Beyond the Limits of Thought*, he gets Heidegger wrong on this point: "Heidegger simply identifies Logic with the received logical theory of his day, forgetting that it, too, is a product of a fallible history. It is an irony that a thinker of the acuity of Heidegger, who was so critical of his historical heritage, should have been blind to the possibility that people had got Logic wrong" (Priest 2003, 248). In fact, Heidegger restricts logic to particular epochs and argues that it is valid only for presence-at-hand. Karsten Harries compares him with Wittgenstein on this point (1968, 282–283).

104. PR 79, 87, 105, EGT 43, PT 57, CP 120/§84, OBT 58; Malpas 2006, 289.

105. LEL 74; see also LEL 68. Karl-Otto Apel compares the two on this idea (Apel 1998, 140).

106. PO 408; see also PO 73.

107. I find Heidegger conflicted on this idea. He does offer narratives of the increasing forgetfulness of being across history, while also opposing the use of transhistorical criteria to compare epochs' understandings of being (TB 52, BW 433, IM 30, 110, FS 9, CP 171/§125, M 17, 206, PR 79, 91, 108, WIP 63, QT 39, 117, OBT 58, BQ 48, AM 67). Caputo (1993) gives an illuminating account of this tension.

108. PR 49; see also PR 108, 110, 113, 125, STF 170, PM 132, 278 n.b, BW 432, ID 32, 57–60; Thomson 2005, 117.

109. N IV:193; see also N III:90, PR 68, 94, BQ 53, PM 232, BaT 204, CP 265/§242, P 150; Schürmann 1990, 19–20, 34; Olson 1994, 129.

110. LWL 104; see also PO 406, PI §374; Minar 1995, 439; McGinn 1998, 48; Cavell 1979, 45.

111. PR 51; see also PR 37, 59, 111, 125, M 240/§74, PM 104na, P 150; Raffoul and Nelson 2008, 61; Dahlstrom 2011, 54, 58, 136n4.

112. STF 170–171; see also PLT 180, BW 412; Young makes roughly this comparison (2002, 8), as does Harries (1968).

113. BQ 147; see also HH 90, Z 266; Malpas 2007, 194, 222; Rorty 1991, 15; Schürmann 1990, 41.

114. TB 6, 33, 52; Thomson likens them on this point (2005, 146).

115. WCT 153. He even calls "tautological thinking . . . the primordial sense of phenomenology" (FS 80; see also WCT 172, 233, PR 43, TB 42, BW 415, PLT 179–80, CPC 60–61, 90–91, BaT 71, OWL 106, Zo 35, 85, 186; Malpas 2006, 194, 222; Levine 2008, 37; Ihde 2010, 55). For more on this, see Braver 2009, 106–115.

116. BW 415; see also DT 67.

117. T p. 3, 4.114, 4.463, 4.466, 5.143.

118. RFM 199; see also RFM 102–103, 205, 323, OC §212.

119. KPM 202; see also KPM 15, 151–152, 160–162, 166, 207, STF 41, LQT 224, 243, BT 271/228, 330/284, N III:119, PR 65, FS 18, HPS 105, AM 27; PFM 65, §36, C1 B145–146; Dreyfus and Hall 1992, 96; Schürmann 1990, 118, 130. Gier compares Wittgenstein's forms of life and Heidegger's thrown categories to Kant (1981, 32, 44).

120. *Prolegomena* 65, 99; C1 B145–146, B421–422; Kant 1995, 77/459.

121. HR 328, BP 23, PM 31, HCT 6–7, WIP 67–71, QT 157–158, 181, IM 132–133, CP 168/§120, EP 14–15, M 91, N II:186, ID 41, 43–45, 47–48, WT 42–43.

122. BP 23, PM 31, HCT 6–7, WIP 67–71, QT 157–158, 181, IM 132–133, CP 168/§120, EP 14–15, M 91, N II:186, ID 41.

123. PR 105, OBT 131–132, 157, 179, QT 172–173, M 47, N III:164, N III:187, N IV:221, WCT 121, CP 123/§87,168/§120, 318/§262, 348/§273, ID 66–67, BW 186, 238, 436, EGT 27, ET 150, 228, BQ 35, 38, IM 26, 45, 62, 96–97, BT 192/150, PR 45.

124. Drury in Rhees 1984, 158; see also Fann 1967, 54, 58, 60–61, 84.

125. OC §65, §87, §§96–99, §256, §336, Z §352, §438, PI §18.

126. PI §115, PO 183–187, 199, CV 15.

127. AWL 98, CV 79, LPP 47.

128. Glock 2008, 97, 100; Williams in Vesey 1982, 87; Malcolm in Vesey 1982, 254, 257, 261–262; Baker and Hacker 1985, 240, 243, 328, 335; Apel 1998, 129, 143; Apel 1980, 22; Janik and Toulmin 1996, 245.

129. See Malcolm on Wittgenstein:

what was gained by the invention of the fictitious tribe was the realization that there could be a concept of pain that deviated from ours. This helps to free us from the assumption that our concept is "absolutely the correct one"; but also it helps us to understand our own concept better; for we are now able to perceive how it is rooted in our own form of life—that is, in our instinctive, unlearned, reaction. . . . In describing forms of life, world-pictures, language-games, real or imaginary, that differ from our own . . . we distance ourselves from our concepts and view them from the outside. (In Vesey 1982, 261–262; see also 254, 257; Young 2002, 43)

130. Some commentators argue that Wittgenstein uses these thought experiments as a *reductio* of the idea of incommensurable ways of thinking (Medina 2002, 146–147; Wright 1980, 304–305; Williams 2002, 236–237). Others, like Jonathan Lear, give a Kantian interpretation according to which we cannot give any content to the idea of "other-mindedness," since the only kind of reasonability we can talk about is our own, even though we can acknowledge that the way our form of life grounds our mindedness is ultimately contingent. Other tribes then would not present real possibilities so much as heuristic devices to illuminate our own mindedness (1998, 250, 258, 277, 298; Vesey 1976, 84–85, 91–92; Griffiths 1991, 53; Stroud 2000, 10–14; Stern 2004, 34 n.7, 161).

131. Vesey 1976, 87, though qualified at 91; see also LC 55, 58, 63, LPP 24, OC §§80–81, §154, RFM 37, 80–81, 89, LFM 231, RPPII §398; Wright 1980, 66–67; Moyal-Sharrock 2004, 74; Travis 2006, 172.

132. RC II §42, III §63, III §127, III §296, LC 58, RFM 348. At one point, he argues that the loose family resemblance of our concepts allows significant leeway in the identification of concepts in different language-games (RFM 39), which shows that Baker and Hacker's interpretation of constitutive internal relations between concepts or rules and specific ways to follow them is still too close to the meaning-object view (Baker and Hacker 1985, 313, 317–318, 322, 327, 333, somewhat qualified at 323).

133. OC §336, RPPI §366, LWL 104.

134. PI §142, LFM 283, 291.

135. Z §§378–381, LWPPII 43–44, LPP 52; Mulhall 2007, 89; Baker and Hacker 1985, 229.

136. RPPI §643, PI II.xii p. 195, Z §350, LWPPI §209, §212, OC §63, §617, RFM 82.

137. Z §352, §§387–388, LWPPI §205, §221, §727, LWPPII 46, RC III 130; Williams in Vesey 1976, 86–87; Baker and Hacker 1985, 21, 320; O'Neill 2001, 10.

138. PO 389; see also LC 64, OC §498, §609, §611, §667, RPPI §587, §622.

139. PO 106, 119, 141, LC 58–59; Drury in Rhees 1984, 93, 119. Drury tried to read *The Golden Bough* with Wittgenstein, but Wittgenstein's repeated outraged outbursts made it impossible (Monk 1990, 310–311).

140. PO 121, 123, 125, 129, 137, 153, 395–397, LC 57–58, OC §110, §148, §196, §204, §232, §395, §402, §477, PI §477, PI II.v pp. 153–154, PG 106, 110, LFM 183–184, 291–292, Z §310, §391, §416, §§540–541, §345, LWPPI §§353–355; Malcolm 1994, 90; Williams 1996, 30–21; Cavell 1982, 45–46.

141. LFM 110, OC §§6–7, §107, §229, §239, §292, §336, §344, §395, §431, LC 53–54, 55, 58, 62–63, 70, AWL 129, PO 123, RPPI §366, Conv 57, LWPPII 59, RFM 43, 253, LWVC 117–118, CV 85; Malcolm in Vesey 1982, 255–256; Preston 2008, 74–76; Medina 2002, 152; Griffiths 1991, 215; Crary and Read 2000, 302.

142. CV 64. Kierkegaard anticipates Wittgenstein here: "truth in the sense in which Christ is the truth is not a sum of statements, not a definition etc., but a life" (1991, 205). One of Heidegger's best discussions of this topic is his description of the Greek temple (BW 167–169). For more on this, see Braver 2009, 39–57.

143. See Rouse 1987, 60–61, 66, 211, 234; Rouse in Dreyfus and Wrathall 2005, 174–176.

144. OC §83, §§102–103, §§140–144, §225, §274, §449, §558.

145. OC §§355–356, §358; see also OC §2, §32, §87, §159, §206, §232, §370, §411, §414, §419, §446, §§481–482, §498, §514, §521, §554, §§613–614, RC III, 348, PO 60, Z §393, LWPPII 46, 86, PI §481, §486; McDowell in Crary and Read 2000, 46, 51 n.15; Malcolm 1995, 78–79; Pinkard 1999, 204–205, 208.

146. OC §141; see also OC §94, §§159–162, §279, LWVC 105, 114; Genova 1995, 51.

147. OC §§94–95, §103, §143, §152, §298.

148. OC §72, §136, §151; Edwards 1990, 58.

149. OC §205; see also OC §82, §94, §§130–131, §§140–142, §144, §162, §248, §253, §307, §§358–359, §514.

150. OC §150, §235, §358, §375, §392, §446, §509.

151. OC §§96–99, §163, §341, §509, §655, RFM 199.

152. OC §559; see also PI II.xi p. 192, LC 58, Conv 4–5, 37; Rouse 1987, 160.

153. BW 97; see also BT 166–167/129, 203/160, 209/165.

154. BW 449, PT 25–26, from *Metaphysics* 1006ff.

155. IM 127; see also PM 235, Zo 217, PIA 123–124. Compare with Wittgenstein: "Aristotelian logic brands a contradiction as a non-sentence, which is to be excluded

from language. But this logic only deals with a very small part of the logic of our language" (LWPPI §525; see also LWPPII 44).

156. Heidegger believes that the Principle of Non-Contradiction is based on the Principle of Reason (PR 30, 123; Sallis 1995, 100; Meillassoux 2008, 71).

157. M 237/§74; see also MFL 214–215, IM 5, BCA 39, 178, KPM 199.

158. ITP 48; cf. Hahn 1996, 43.

159. OC §105; see also OC §146, §167, §292, §337, §603, PO 437; Malcolm in Vesey 1982, 254–255, 259; Malcolm 1994, 76–78; Hintikka and Hintikka 1989, 237 n.5; Wright 1980, 373–376; Williams 1996, 4; Priest 2003, 210–212; Rouse 1987, 62, 124, 160, 210.

160. PR 30; see also PR 3, 20, 22, 33, 37, 123, FS 67, STF 98. Gadamer uses the same metaphor to compare his work to Wittgenstein (Hahn 1996, 22).

161. PR 24, 33, BCA 179–180.

162. PR 6, 11, KPM 199, IM 5–6.

163. PT 47; see also WCT 65, BW 324, FS 67, M 133, 350, MFL 104.

164. DT 82–83; see also DT 65, PR 62, 75, 84.

165. WCT 151, P 147, FS 73, PM 279, 294, DT 64, PR 69, 75, CP 167/§120; Thomson 2005, 72.

166. Zo 217; see also BW 330, 361, KPM 165, STF 148–149, 154–155; Edwards 1990, 129.

167. PM 234; see also M 240–241.

168. Compare: "there is *one* thing of which one can say neither that it is one metre long, nor that it is not one metre long, and that is the standard metre in Paris" (PI §50).

169. PR 111; see also P 150, M 43, 240, PM 279, 294, PLT 180.

170. OC §271; see also OC §317.

171. DT 50; see also BT 29–31/9–10, WT 65–111. Kuhn's (in)famous phrase reads, "the proponents of competing paradigms practice their trades in different worlds" (Kuhn 1996, 150). Heidegger even uses Kuhn's key term "paradigm" in a discussion of science (ET 46). I discuss this similarity in Braver 2009, 70–81.

172. OC §92, §107, §233, §262, §§609–612, LC 27–28; see also Rhess 1984, 206.

173. DT 68; see also DR 62–63, ID 41. Wittgenstein says something similar: "in every serious philosophical question uncertainty extends to the very roots of the

problem. We must always be prepared to learn something totally new" (RC I §15; see also RC III §45, III §63).

174. PT 52–53; see also WCT 46, 65, 135–136, 151, 154, 234–235, DT 58–59, IM 123–124, ID 35, FS 56, 62–63, 74–75, QT 37, 128, 151, 168–169, OTB 188, BW 320, 323–326, EP 100–101, P 103, HR 272, 278, PM 235, 293, 300, N IV:22, N IV:28, N IV:86, N IV:103, WT 97, 100, 106, CP 119–120/§82, 179/§134, 221/§193, 325/§265, HH 90, PR 76–77, BW 332; Polanyi 1967, xi, 60–62, 80, 91; Edwards 1990, 178–181, 188. For more on this, see Braver 2007, 303–325; Braver 2009, 70–97.

175. DT 50; see also DT 55, QT 42–43, N III:181.

176. BW 333; see also ID 36–37, 40; BW 315.

177. PI §108; see also OC §108, LC 64, PO 73, 408. See Michael Dummett: "if Wittgenstein were right, it appears to me that communication would be in constant danger of simply breaking down" (1978, 176–177).

178. OC §253; see also PG 110.

179. OC §108; see also OC §458, §560, RFM 118, PO 66; Sluga and Stern 1996, 424–425, 428–429; Stroud 2000, 93.

180. Lear 1998, chaps. 11–12; Vesey 1976, 76–95; Sluga and Stern 1996, 375, 429.

181. RFM 80; see also RFM 196, 348, LFM 110, OC §92, §162, §217, §233, §262, §609, §612, LC 58, LWL 104.

182. LFM 243; see also LFM 261, PI p. 46 n., PI §141.

183. OC §§609–612; see also OC §92, §138, §233, §262, §292, §495, §498, Conv 4–5, 37, 57, Z §318, §352, LFM 58, 236, Z §461, PI §144, LC 64, LWPPII 53; Rhees 1984, 201.

184. LWL 60, PI §88, §§562–564, LFM 205, 235, PG 184–185; Kober in Sluga and Stern 1996, 432–433.

185. STF 138; see also QT 117, IM 110, BQ 48, AM 67, WT 90, PIK 22.

186. LFM 203–204; see also LFM 207, Z §320, §322, OC §131, §287, §359, §474, RC 58–59, CV 64; Bouveresse in Preston 2008, 5; Pinkard 1999, 206, 217 n.33. "Is there only one way of correlating them? If there are more, which is the logical way?—You can do any damn thing you please" (LFM 159).

187. PO 123; see also PO 139, PI §467, PI II.ix p. 161, PI II.xi p. 193, RFM 37–38, 95, 379, Z §322, §700, PG 109, LWPPII 46; Malcolm 1994, 60; Fogelin 1995, 175–176; Kenny 1973, 176–177; de Lara 2003, 113, 116–117; O'Neill 2001, 9.

188. PO 129; see also PO 106, RFM 95, CV 64, PI §§496–497. This view sets Wittgenstein apart from Carnap's idea that "external" questions about which linguistic framework to use are based on purely practical considerations (Rorty 1992, 73–74,

79, 83; Stroud 1984, 188–190; Williams 1996, 30–31); as well as Quine's evaluation of conceptual schemes (Quine 1980, 44–45, 79; Stroud 1984, 214, 219–220). Goodman makes a similar distinction between Wittgenstein and William James: "whereas James holds that our most basic beliefs are ultimately grounded in scientific inquiry, Wittgenstein finds that our 'way of acting' is 'ungrounded'" (2002, 31).

189. See Lyotard 1988, xiii, 55, 130.

190. Z §309; see also PI §71, §483, OC §28, §39, §§128–129, §148, §254, §294, §551. As Robert Fogelin puts it, "the italicized demonstrative is the *leitmotiv* of Wittgenstein's later philosophy" (Fogelin 1995, 206).

191. LC 25; see also RPPI §49, Z §700, LWPPI §878.

192. RFM 333; see also RFM 323, Z §314, RPPII §314, §402, §453.

193. Moore had already used it (Hacker 1996, 122, 303 n.29; Monk 1991, 451).

194. Z §315; see also PO 86, 217.

195. NB 72; see also T 6.371–6.372, LO 35, LWVC 115, OC §95; Malcolm 1994, 84–85.

196. PG 110–111; see also PG 94, 184–185, 322, 334, 401, PI §§654–656, PI II.xi p. 171, PI II.xi p. 192, RPPII §453, LWL 104–105.

197. BQ 7; see also OWL 12.

198. OC §471; see also RFM 102–103, 199, 323, RPPI §257, §509, §723.

199. PT 55–56; see also BW 204, CP 171/§125, M 17, 206, WIP 63, QT 39, TB 52, BW 433, IM 30, DT 55, STF 138; Ferry and Renault 1990, 140–141; Edwards 1990, 106, 109; Young 2002, 59–60.

200. BT 443/391; see also BT 320/275; cf. Kant 1995, 48, Ak. 431; 75, Ak. 457; 79, Ak. 461; Dahlstrom 2011, 28; Young 2002, 92; Zimmerman 1986, xxv, 116–118; .

201. PLT 170–171, FS 8, 37, BW 129, 153, PM 235, WCT 142.

202. BQ 159–160; see also BW 131–132, 172, 228–229, 332, DT 50, 56, PR 80, M 137, P 75, 137, 156, N III:178, N:III 190–191, N IV:241, QT 79–80, 84, 100, PLT 111.

203. OTB 77, ID 72; see also OTB 193–194, PR 30–31, BW 251, 262, FS 56, 77, IM 167, QT 102–103, 111, 134, N IV:203.

204. PR 51, 111, PM 134, 232, DT 83, N III:90, N III:119, NIV:155, N IV:193, M 73/§19, HCT 291, ID 68; Ferry and Renault 1990, 142.

205. N III:188, DT 82, QT 115, PM 130, 232; McGuinness 1982, 59; Schürmann 1990, 29, 35; Thomson 2005, 19, 59, 146.

206. Wittgenstein told a friend that "he could not sit down and read Hume—he knew far too much about the subject of Hume's writings to find this anything but a

torture" (Fann 1967, 61). I'm not sure how to read this—that Wittgenstein was in great agreement with Hume and so found his works gratingly redundant, or that Hume appeared terribly naïve compared with our more advanced knowledge of psychology or linguistics or Wittgenstein's own ruminations. Given the widespread and often very direct similarity between them, I incline toward the former reading. In any case, my claims here do not rest on or imply direct influence or knowledge.

207. Compare Hume: "take any action allow'd to be vicious: Wilful murder, for instance. Examine it in all lights, and see if you can find that matter of fact, or real existence, which you call *vice*. In which-ever way you take it, you find only certain passions, motives, volitions and thoughts. There is no other matter of fact in the case" (HT 468; see also HT 618, HE 165, 287–290), with Wittgenstein's linguistic version: "if for instance in our world-book [i.e., the collected descriptions of all facts] we read the description of a murder with all its details physical and psychological, the mere description of these facts will contain nothing which we could call an *ethical* proposition" (PO 39–40; see also T 6.41, 6.421).

208. Compare Hume's well-known conclusion with Wittgenstein's: "there is no possible way of making an inference from the existence of one situation to the existence of another, entirely different situation. There is no causal nexus to justify such an inference" (T 5.135–5.136). Wittgenstein even borrows Hume's example of the sun rising tomorrow as a surprisingly contingent fact (T 6.36311).

209. T 5.1362, 6.373–6.374; HE 64–69.

210. "We cannot infer the events of the future from those of the present" (T 5.1361; see also T 1.21, 5.135, 5.136, 5.1361, 5.634, 6.3631, 6.36311; HE 29–30, 63, 74, HT 94). Both single out the incompatibility of different colored dots occupying the same space for discussion (HT 41; NB 91, T 6.3751). See also Pears 1991, 27.

211. T 5.5421, 5.631–5.633; HT 207, 252–253, 634–635, 657; Kripke 1982, 122–123; Jacquette 2005, 258. Since Hume establishes this point on the proto-phenomenological grounds of introspection, it is hardly surprising that Heidegger notes the same absence: "what is decisive is that simple inspection does not discover anything like an 'I.' What I see is just that 'it lives'" (TDP 56; see also TDP 57, 174).

212. T 4.461, 4.462, 6.1, 6.11, 6.362, 6.37, 6.375; HE 25–26, 163.

213. T pp. 3–4, T 7; HE 165.

214. HE 156; see also HE 157, HT 214; Williams 1996, 8, 12, 26–27.

215. HE 41, 47, 158–159, HT 218, 268–269.

216. HE 271, 234 n.; see also HT 619.

217. HE 251; see also HE 220; HT 579, 588–589, 592, 605, 619; though see HT 576. We see again the fulfillment in recent neuroscientific discoveries: "'vicarious' is not a strong enough word to describe the effect of these mirror neurons. When we see

someone else suffering or in pain, mirror neurons help us to read her or his facial expression and actually make us feel the suffering or the pain of the other person. These moments, I will argue, are the foundation of empathy and possibly of morality, a morality that is deeply rooted in our biology" (Iacoboni 2008, 4–5; see also Blakeslee and Blakeslee 2008, 166–167, 177–179).

218. PI §420; see also PI §303, PI II.iv p. 152, II.xi p. 190.

219. HT 457; see also HT 547, 579, 620, HE 214, 281, 301.

220. HT 104; see also HT 97 n.

221. Pears 1988, 508–509, 514–517; Pears 1991, vii, 14, 25, 98; Kripke 1982, 62–69, 107–109; McGinn, 1987, 40, 87.

222. HE 33, 63–64, 74; HT 111, 139, 168, 400, 468–471.

223. HE 27, 42; HT 265, 650–651.

224. HT 170; see also Kaufman 2002, 336–337, 355–356.

225. HT 134, 183; see also HT 92, 149, 225, 652, 679, HE 32, 43, 151.

226. HT 179; see also HE 41–42, 46–47, 55, 108, 159.

227. HT 103; see also HT 92, 149, 178–179, 183–184, 205–206, 225, 265, 627.

228. OC §287; see also OC §359, §475, §499.

229. HE 108; see also HE 39, 106–107, 151, HT 176, 397.

230. PI §472, §477; see also PI §481.

231. HE 35–36. Heidegger makes this point (PT 47, WCT 65, BW 324).

232. HE 219–220 n.; see also HE 43, 293, HT 13, 590.

233. HT xviii; see also HT 646; compare with Locke's account of empiricist humility (Locke 1996, 5).

234. HT 13; see also HT 64, 159, 169.

235. PR 30–31, DT 48–49, OWL 13, N III:181, M 211, 308.

236. HT 267; see also HT 184.

237. HT 186; see also HT 222–225, HE 162.

238. RFM 350–351; see also RFM 337, 341, 414, 430.

239. HT 269; see also HT 187, 216–218, HE 158–160.

240. HE 151; see also HT 84.

241. HT 183; see also HT 116, 657, HE 41–42, 47, 155 n., 158–160.

242. HT 67, 212, 634; HE 152–153.

243. PI §106; see also PI §116, §235.

244. BT 94/66; see also BT 37–38/16, 69/43.

245. HE 72; see also HE 81, 146, 162.

246. HE 160; Williams 1996, 4; Pears 1991, 97–98.

### Conclusion: Original Finitude

1. PI §89; see also RFM 40, LFM 271, Z §452.

2. PI §52; see also PI §107, §340.

3. PI §§105–106; see also PI §§435–436.

4. PI §426; see also T 3.031, 5.123, PhR 149, 212, 237, PO 94, LC 71; Baker and Hacker 1985, 212; Staten 1986, 14, 151; Rorty 1991, 53; Dummett 1996, 450–451. Russell explicitly articulates this aspiration: "I think we can, however imperfectly, mirror the world, like Leibniz's monads; and I think it is the duty of the philosopher to make himself as undistorting a mirror as he can. . . . To achieve such impartiality [as a god might have] is impossible for us, but we can travel a certain distance towards it. To show the road to this end is the supreme duty of the philosopher" (Russell 1959b, 213).

5. Edwards 1990, 191; see also 139, 200; Diamond 1991, 68–69.

6. PI §352; see also PI §222, RFM 45–46, 64, 266–269, PO 94, 435, PG 481, LFM 131–132; Wright 1980, 220, 275–276, 312, 372; Baker and Hacker 1985, 236; Dummett 1978, 185.

7. PI §128. This is where Cora Diamond seems to "chicken out" from the extreme version of her interpretation, correctly in my view: "leaving everything as it is is consistent with showing that the interest of a game rests on mythology or fantasy or a failure of understanding of what it is for our own real needs to be met" (1991, 22). This kind of correction can require considerable argumentation before one can see the error of their ways, opening the way for Wittgenstein to make arguments and claims.

8. RFM 408; see also OC §436, LFM 103–104, 170–171, RPPI §139, PI II.xi p. 185, PI II.xi p. 192; Edwards 1990, 139; Wright 1980, 187–189.

9. BT 255–256/212, 269–270/227.

10. LFM 95, 107, 137–139, RFM 50, 267, 270, 279.

11. Except when grammatically ruled out.

12. OC §554; see also OC §349, §393, §406, §423. Austin calls this idea "the original sin . . . by which the philosopher casts himself out from the garden of the world we live in" (1979, 90).

13. OC §260, §482; see also OC §§347–350; Williams 1996, 8, 12, 26–27, 47; Rudd 2003, 89, 153; Staten 1986, 67.

14. OC §191; see also OC §215, PO 208–209; Wright 1980, 220.

15. "We are asking ourselves: what do we do with a statement 'I *know* . . .'? For it is not a question of mental processes or mental states. And *that* is how one must decide whether something is knowledge or not" (OC §230; see also OC §10, §38, §243, §245, §601).

16. Crary and Read 2000, 46. Cavell centers his analysis on the point that "in Wittgenstein's work, as in skepticism, the human disappointment with human knowledge seems to take over the whole subject" even as it assures us "that nothing at all is wrong with the human capacity for knowledge . . . that our lives, and the everyday assertions sketched by them, are in order as they are" (Cavell 1982, 44; see also Cavell 1990, 92; Sluga and Stern 1996, 385; Bloor 2002, 20; Williams in Vesey 1976, 79; Dummett in Clark and Hale 1994, 55–57; Guignon 1990, 651, 660–661).

17. OC §595; see also PhR 61. Compare with Nietzsche: "the 'in-itself' is even an absurd conception; a 'constitution-in-itself' is nonsense; we possess the concept 'being,' 'thing,' only as a relational concept. . . . We possess no categories by which we can distinguish a true from an apparent world. (There might only be an apparent world, but not *our* apparent world)" (Nietzsche 1968, §583A). I discuss this in Braver 2007, 151–159.

18. OC §347, §423, §469, §553, §622.

19. FCM 6; see also FCM 143, 165, 171–172, BT 186/145, 188/148, EHF 163, BW 101–102, KPM 18, 151–154, PIA 80–81, PM 116, STF 38; Sheehan 2010, 188; Fell 1979, 39, 50–51.

20. BT 193/152; see also BT 51–55/28–31, 141/106, 177/138, HCT 85–86; Haar 1993, 43.

21. Heidegger says of "mere appearance" that "probably no word has caused as much havoc and confusion in philosophy" (HCT 81).

22. BP 17, 72, BT 60/36, EHF 161, 168, M 348–349/§123, IPR 200–202.

23. HCT 72, 81, 85–86, 112, BT 51–55/28–31, 62/38, BP 72; Schatzki in Dreyfus and Hall 1992, 96; Versényi 1965, 46; Carman 2003, 32–33, 171; Braver 2007, 181–198. Another inexplicable statement made by a Wittgenstein scholar about Heidegger is Newton Garver's comment that Heidegger agrees with Plato, against Wittgenstein, that metaphysics explains "the difference between appearance and reality" (Garver

in Sluga and Stern 1996, 159). A great deal of Heidegger's thought, throughout his career, aims at undermining this very distinction.

24. PIK 68–69; see also MFL 164, 198.

25. LEL 68; see also LEL 74, PLT 181, 200, Zo 184, M 73, 348–349.

26. Putnam 1990, 25; see also Putnam 1995, 39; Gier 1981, 13, 39, 88; Apel 1998, 128. It has been suggested that Wittgenstein invented Putnam's internal realism (McManus 2004, 45).

27. Welton 1999, 334, all bracketed comments in original; see also HCT 207, 213, 231, 254–255, TDP 41, BP 66, 69, 124, 157, 167, 175, 255, 297, BT 170/132, KPM 165, HCT 166–167, 222–223.

28. BW 348; see also BW 167–168, 354, IM 15, 57, 86, 167, 183, 198, BaT 46, 84, EHP 59–60, WCT 120, 123, 202, OWL 64–66, 73, 155, Zo 16, 64, 140, 185, 200; Apel 1994, 49 n.95, 83–84; Mulhall 1990, 69, 127; Mulhall 2007, 93; Sefler 1974, 188; Gier 1981, 35; Dahlstrom 2011, 221, 226; Young 2001, 34–36. Cf. "*essence* is expressed in grammar" (PI §371; see also PI §§373–374, RFM 50, PO 307, LFM 145).

29. McManus 2004, 169, 176; Sluga and Stern 1996, 358; Pears 1987, 189–190; Mulhall 1990, 124, 155. David E. Cooper compares the two on this point (1997, 115; see also Baiasu 2009, 691).

30. N III:49, TB 38, QT 130–131, M 178, EGT 96, ID 31–32, BW 228–229, 235, DT 84, Zo 176–180, CP 169/§123; Zimmerman 1986, 107.

31. Wittgenstein admired Kierkegaard so much that he learned some Danish in order to read him in the original (Lee 1979; Rhees 1984, 88; my thanks to Jonathan Beale for this reference). Large parts of *Being and Time* practically plagiarize Kierkegaard, especially *Concluding Unscientific Postscript*.

32. Kierkegaard 1992, 81; see also 86, 120, 351, 356; Taylor 1995, 61–62, 68, 169–170; Guignon 1990, 653–654. Kierkegaard also subscribes to the distinction between abstract thinking which is improper to our way of existing and engaged concrete existence (Kierkegaard 1992, 301).

33. 1992, 130; see also 35 n., 44, 86, 279; Mulhall 1990, 89. This idea that we have a constitutional yearning for what we cannot achieve obviously has Kantian roots. Cavell has been the interpreter who most emphasizes this aspect of *Philosophical Investigations*.

34. 1992, 114; see also 51, 159, 163, 346, 523.

35. 1992, 15, 52, 109, 120, 306, 316, 330, 571.

36. OC §148; see also LWL 87, LWPPII 40; McDowell in Crary and Read 2000, 43; Malcolm 1994, 68, 88; Travis 2006, 104; Dummett 1996, 448.

37. LWL 104; see also OC §342, §477, PO 352, 406, PhR 310; Stroud 2000, 16.

38. OC §471; see also RFM 102–103, 199, 323.

39. PhR 7, PI x; see also CV 6–7, 56, compare with CPC 136.

40. FS 9; see also FS 37, 72, 74, DT 50, WCT 42, Z §438; Cooper 1997, 118–121.

41. PI p. x, CV 36, Conv 39; Fann 1967, 13, 35, 73–74; Rhees 1984, 112.

42. "The great poets Dante, Shakespeare, Goethe, Homer have achieved far more than any scientist" (BaT 128).

43. BW 172, BaT 120–123, LC 17 n.3, 24, 27.

44. On this topic, see Thomson 2011, 76. Wittgenstein occasionally compares his work to the way instruction in art appreciation highlights unnoticed details (PO 106, LC 20, 27).

45. TDP 46; see also BT 87/60, 161–162/124, 170/132, 200–201/158, 250/206, 412/361, PR 80, HCT 201–202, 219; Guignon 1983, 61.

46. "We shall not cease from exploration / And the end of all our exploring / Will be to arrive where we started / And know the place for the first time" (T. S. Eliot, "Little Gidding," ll. 241–244).

47. CV 7, WCT 41; see also WCT 174, 228, PM 319, 257, BW 241, PM 319, OWL 85, 93, PLT 190, HCT 186–187, CPC 78–80, 111, 115, ITP 3, 52, Zo 17, 109, 187, P 150.

48. CV 66, BW 238; see also PhR 7, WT 73–74, 242, BQ 146, QT 180.

49. NB 74. This idea is also found in the twelve basic tenets of Tolstoy's *The Gospels in Brief*, a book Wittgenstein constantly carried with him during the First World War: "8. THE TRUE LIFE IS OUTSIDE OF TIME,—IT IS ONLY IN THE PRESENT. . . . 10. MAN MUST STRIVE TO DESTROY THE DECEPTION OF THE TEMPORAL LIFE OF THE PAST AND OF THE FUTURE" (Tolstoy 2004, xvi–xvii).

50. BT 308/263; see also BT 317/272, 333/287, 357/310, 370/323, FCM 82, 103, 117, 121, 143, BW 101–102; Fell 1979 39, 50–51; Caputo 1993, 79–80, 172; Haar 1993, 13, 15, 35, 44; Schürmann 1990, 70, 73; Fynsk 1993, 28–30, 37–38. There are occasional hints of a more open approach in the early work, for example, BCAP 205–206, BT 49/26, 488/437. Compare this with early Wittgenstein: "only death gave life its meaning" (McGuinness 2005, 240).

51. BT 140–141/160; see also BT 38–39/17, 193/152, HCT 218, BP 228, 274, 280, PS 439–440; Krell 1986, 32–33, 56.

52. PIK 48, 252, 289, KPM 141–142, BP 73, 155; Husserl 1997, 138; Versényi 1965, 23; Caputo 1987, 98; Macomber 1967, 29; Rorty 1989, 109–110; Richardson 1986, 12–13; Guignon 1993, 6; Blattner 1999, 261; Weatherston 2002, 25; Sherover 1971; Carman 2003, 11–13, 155; Lafont 2000, xiii, 154; Wolin 1990, 70; Glazebrook 2000,

39, 42; Wrathall and Malpas 2000, 44; Carr 1999, 130; Okrent 1988, 28, 271; Schürmann 1987, 143; Rudd 2003, 69; Zimmerman 1986, 35, 107. See also Braver 2007, chapter 5.

53. BT 38/17, 171/133, 224/180, 237/192, 274–276/231–233, 279/236, 293/249, 309/264, 351/304, 370/323, HCT 152, BP 59, 227.

54. BT 422/371, 441/389–390. Recall Heidegger's criticism of idle talk and Wittgenstein's claim that the central achievement of his early work is that it remains silent about the essential topics that others are gassing about.

55. FS 8; see also FS 37, 72, 75, BW 129, 153, PM 307, N III:89, BaT 126, 166, Zo 19, 25, 80; Schürmann 1990, 116–118, 143–144.

56. See Braver 2007, 291–306 for a more detailed discussion of this lineage; see also Fynsk 1993, 74–75.

57. N III:176; see also N III:179–180, IV:44, IV:102, CP 348–349/§274, QT 67, 95, 104, CPC 5, 122, 138, ITP 8, 20, 34, 62–64, PLT 91–92; Krell 1986, 106; Fynsk 1993, 87.

58. PR 30–31; see also DT 48–49, OWL 13, HH 167, HR 325, 330, ITP 24.

59. BW 331; see also BW 262, BaT 47. Interestingly, Wittgenstein expressed an intense dislike of Esperanto (Conv 47; see also CP 54/§36) and made a similar point about the limits of our technological control (CV 42).

60. Edwards makes this point, though he (1990, 225–226) and Rorty (1991, 51, 70, 75) see Heidegger's later focus on Being or language as falling back into the trap of metaphysics which is eluded by Wittgenstein's later work, whereas I believe that a full appreciation of the ontological difference absolves Heidegger of the charge. Cooper defends Heidegger well on this point (1997, 122–123).

61. BW 235, 251, FS 47, PM 361, CP 123/§88, 169/§122, 315/§262, 317/§262, Zo 194; Haar 1993, 99; Krell 1986, 7, 60; Fynsk 1993, 72, 78–79.

62. PT 30; see also DT 62, 68, ITP 15.

63. PLT 179; see also CPC 144; Schürmann 1990, 55–56, 60, 79, 89.

64. BT 175/136; see also BT 271/228, 321/276, PIK 59.

# References

## Martin Heidegger

Heidegger, Martin. 1956. *What Is Philosophy?* Trans. Jean T. Wilde and William Kluback. New Haven, Conn.: New College and University Press.

Heidegger, Martin. 1959. *An Introduction to Metaphysics.* Trans. Ralph Manheim. New Haven: Yale University Press.

Heidegger, Martin. 1962. *Being and Time.* Trans. John Macquarrie and Edward Robinson. San Francisco: HarperSanFrancisco.

Heidegger, Martin. 1966. *Discourse on Thinking.* Trans. John M. Anderson and E. Hans Freund. San Francisco: Harper Torchbooks.

Heidegger, Martin. 1967. *What Is a Thing?* Trans. W. B. Barton, Jr. and Vera Deutsch. Chicago: Henry Regnery.

Heidegger, Martin. 1968. *What Is Called Thinking?* Trans. J. Glenn Gray. New York: Harper & Row.

Heidegger, Martin. 1969. *Identity and Difference.* Trans. Joan Stambaugh. New York: Harper Torchbooks.

Heidegger, Martin. 1970. *Hegel's Concept of Experience.* New York: Harper & Row.

Heidegger, Martin. 1971. *On the Way to Language.* Trans. Peter D. Hertz. San Francisco: HarperSanFrancisco.

Heidegger, Martin. 1971. *Poetry, Language, Thought.* Trans. Albert Hofstadter. New York: Harper & Row.

Heidegger, Martin. 1972. *On Time and Being.* Trans. Joan Stambaugh. New York: Harper Torchbooks.

Heidegger, Martin. 1973. *The End of Philosophy.* Trans. Joan Stambaugh. New York: Harper & Row.

Heidegger, Martin. 1975. *Early Greek Thinking: The Dawn of Western Philosophy.* Trans. David Farrell Krell and Frank A. Capuzzi. San Francisco: HarperSanFrancisco.

Heidegger, Martin. 1976. *The Piety of Thinking.* Trans. James G. Hart and John C. Maraldo. Bloomington: Indiana University Press.

Heidegger, Martin. 1977. *Martin Heidegger in Conversation.* Ed. Richard Wisser. Trans. B. Srinivasa Murthy. New Delhi: Arnold-Heinemann.

Heidegger, Martin. 1977. *The Question Concerning Technology and Other Essays.* Trans. William Lovitt. New York: Harper Torchbooks.

Heidegger, Martin. 1979, 1982, 1984, 1987. *Nietzsche.* 4 vols. Ed. David Farrell Krell. San Francisco: HarperSanFrancisco.

Heidegger, Martin. 1982. *The Basic Problems of Phenomenology.* Trans. Albert Hofstadter. Bloomington: Indiana University Press.

Heidegger, Martin. 1985a. *History of the Concept of Time.* Trans. Theodore Kisiel. Bloomington: Indiana University Press.

Heidegger, Martin. 1985b. *Schelling's Treatise on the Essence of Human Freedom.* Trans. Joan Stambaugh. Athens, OH: Ohio University Press.

Heidegger, Martin. 1990. *Kant and the Problem of Metaphysics*, 5th enlarged ed. Trans. Richard Taft. Bloomington: Indiana University Press.

Heidegger, Martin. 1991. *The Principle of Reason.* Trans. Reginald Lilly. Bloomington: Indiana University Press.

Heidegger, Martin. 1992a. *Parmenides.* Trans. Richard Rojcewicz and André Schuwer. Bloomington: Indiana University Press.

Heidegger, Martin. 1992b. *The Concept of Time.* Trans. William McNeill. Malden, Mass.: Blackwell.

Heidegger, Martin. 1992c. *The Metaphysical Foundations of Logic.* Trans. Michael Heim. Bloomington: Indiana University Press.

Heidegger, Martin. 1993. *Basic Concepts.* Trans. Gary E. Aylesworth. Bloomington: Indiana University Press.

Heidegger, Martin. 1993. *Basic Writings*, rev. ed. Ed. David Farrell Krell. San Francisco: HarperSanFrancisco.

Heidegger, Martin. 1993. *Heraclitus Seminar.* Coauthored with Eugene Fink. Trans. Charles H. Siebert. Evanston: Northwestern University Press.

Heidegger, Martin. 1994. *Basic Questions of Philosophy: Selected "Problems" of "Logic."* Trans. Richard Rojcewicz and André Schuwer. Bloomington: Indiana University Press.

Heidegger, Martin. 1994. *Hegel's* Phenomenology of Spirit. Trans. Parvis Emad and Kenneth Maly. Bloomington: Indiana University Press.

Heidegger, Martin. 1995. *Aristotle's* Metaphysics Θ *1–3: On the Essence and Actuality of Force.* Trans. Walter Brogan and Peter Warnek. Bloomington: Indiana University Press.

Heidegger, Martin. 1995. *The Fundamental Concepts of Metaphysics: World, Finitude, Solitude.* Trans. William McNeill and Nicholas Walker. Bloomington: Indiana University Press.

Heidegger, Martin. 1996. *Hölderlin's Hymn "The Ister."* Trans. William McNeill and Julia Davis. Bloomington: Indiana University Press.

Heidegger, Martin. 1997. *Phenomenological Interpretation of Kant's* Critique of Pure Reason. Trans. Parvis Emad and Thomas Kalary. Bloomington: Indiana University Press.

Heidegger, Martin. 1997. *Plato's Sophist.* Trans. Richard Rojcewicz and André Schuwer. Bloomington: Indiana University Press.

Heidegger, Martin. 1998. *Pathmarks.* Ed. William McNeill. New York: Cambridge University Press.

Heidegger, Martin. 1999. *Contributions to Philosophy (From Enowning).* Trans. Parvis Emad and Kenneth Maly. Bloomington: Indiana University Press.

Heidegger, Martin. 1999. *Ontology: The Hermeneutics of Facticity.* Trans. John van Buren. Bloomington: Indiana University Press.

Heidegger, Martin. 2000. *Elucidations of Hölderlin's Poetry.* Trans. Keith Hoeller. Amherst, NY: Humanity.

Heidegger, Martin. 2000. *Towards the Definition of Philosophy.* Trans. Ted Sandler. New York: Athlone.

Heidegger, Martin. 2001a. *Phenomenological Interpretations of Aristotle: Initiation into Phenomenological Research.* Trans. Richard Rojcewicz. Bloomington: Indiana University Press.

Heidegger, Martin. 2001b. *Zollikon Seminars: Protocols—Conversations—Letters.* Trans. Franz Mayr and Richard Askay. Evanston: Northwestern University Press.

Heidegger, Martin. 2002a. *Mindfulness.* Trans. Parvis Emad and Thomas Kalary. New York: Continuum.

Heidegger, Martin. 2002b. *Off the Beaten Track.* Trans. and ed. Julian Young and Kenneth Haynes. New York: Cambridge University Press.

Heidegger, Martin. 2002c. *Supplements: From the Earliest Essays to "Being and Time" and Beyond.* Ed. John van Buren. Albany: SUNY Press.

Heidegger, Martin. 2002d. *The Essence of Human Freedom: An Introduction to Philosophy*. Trans. Ted Sadler. New York: Continuum.

Heidegger, Martin. 2002e. *The Essence of Truth: On Plato's Cave Allegory and "Theaetetus."* Trans. Ted Sadler. New York: Continuum.

Heidegger, Martin. 2003. *Four Seminars*. Trans. Andrew Mitchell and François Raffoul. Bloomington: Indiana University Press.

Heidegger, Martin. 2005. *Introduction to Phenomenological Research*. Trans. Daniel O. Dahlstrom. Bloomington: Indiana University Press.

Heidegger, Martin. 2009a. *Basic Concepts of Aristotelian Philosophy*. Trans. Robert D. Metcalf and Mark B. Tanzer. Bloomington: Indiana University Press.

Heidegger, Martin. 2009b. *Logic as the Question Concerning the Essence of Language*. Albany: SUNY Press.

Heidegger, Martin. 2009c. *The Heidegger Reader*. Ed. Günter Figal. Trans. Jerome Veith. Bloomington: Indiana University Press.

Heidegger, Martin. 2010. *The Phenomenology of Religious Life*. Trans. Matthias Fritsch and Jennifer Anna Gosetti-Ferencei. Bloomington: Indiana University Press.

Heidegger, Martin. 2010. *Being and Truth*. Trans. Gregory Fried and Richard Polt. Bloomington: Indiana University Press.

Heidegger, Martin. 2010. *Country Path Conversations*. Trans Bret W. Davis. Bloomington: Indiana University Press.

Heidegger, Martin. 2010. *Logic: The Question of Truth*. Trans. Thomas Sheehan. Bloomington: Indiana University Press.

Heidegger, Martin. 2011. *Introduction to Philosophy—Thinking and Poetizing*. Trans. Phillip Jacques Braunstein. Bloomington: Indiana University Press.

## Ludwig Wittgenstein

Wittgenstein, Ludwig. 1961. *Notebooks, 1914–1916*. Trans. G. E. M. Anscombe. Oxford: Blackwell.

Wittgenstein, Ludwig. 1967. *Lectures and Conversations on Aesthetics, Psychology, and Religious Belief*. Ed. Cyril Barrett. Berkeley: University of California Press.

Wittgenstein, Ludwig. 1969. *On Certainty*. Ed. G. E. M. Anscombe and G. H. von Wright. Trans. Denis Paul and G. E. M. Anscombe. New York: Harper Torchbooks.

Wittgenstein, Ludwig. 1969. *The Blue and Brown Books: Preliminary Studies for the "Philosophical Investigations."* Malden, Mass.: Blackwell.

Wittgenstein, Ludwig. 1970. *Zettel*. Ed. G. E. M. Anscombe and G. H. von Wright. Trans. G. E. M. Anscombe. Berkeley: University of California Press.

Wittgenstein, Ludwig. 1973. *Letters to C. K. Ogden with Comments on the English Translation of the* Tractatus Logico-Philosophicus. Oxford: Blackwell.

Wittgenstein, Ludwig. 1975. *Philosophical Remarks*. Ed. Rush Rhees. Chicago: University of Chicago Press.

Wittgenstein, Ludwig. 1976. *Wittgenstein's Lectures on the Foundations of Mathematics: Cambridge 1939*. Ed. Cora Diamond. Chicago: University of Chicago Press.

Wittgenstein, Ludwig. 1977. *Remarks on Color*. Ed. G. E. M. Anscombe. Berkeley: University of California Press.

Wittgenstein, Ludwig. 1979. *Ludwig Wittgenstein and the Vienna Circle: Conversations recorded by Friedrich Waismann*. Oxford: Blackwell.

Wittgenstein, Ludwig. 1980. *Wittgenstein's Lectures: Cambridge, 1930–1932*. Ed. Desmond Lee. Chicago: University of Chicago Press.

Wittgenstein, Ludwig. 1980. *Culture and Value*. Trans. Peter Winch. Chicago: University of Chicago Press.

Wittgenstein, Ludwig. 1980. *Remarks on the Philosophy of Psychology*, vol. I. Ed. G. E. M. Anscombe and G. H. von Wright. Trans. G. E. M. Anscombe. Chicago: University of Chicago Press.

Wittgenstein, Ludwig. 1980. *Remarks on the Philosophy of Psychology*, vol. II. Ed. G. H. von Wright and Heikki Nyman. Trans. C. G. Luckhardt and Maximilian A. E. Aue. Chicago: University of Chicago Press.

Wittgenstein, Ludwig. 1982. *Last Writings on the Philosophy of Psychology*, vol. 1: *Preliminary Studies for Part 2 of "Philosophical Investigations."* Ed. G. H. von Wright and Heikki Nyman. Trans. C. G. Luckhardt and Maximilian A. E. Aue. Chicago: University of Chicago Press.

Wittgenstein, Ludwig. 1983. *Remarks on the Foundations of Mathematics*, rev. ed. Ed. G. H. von Wright, R. Rhees, and G. E. M. Anscombe. Cambridge, Mass.: MIT Press.

Wittgenstein, Ludwig. 1986. *Wittgenstein Conversations 1949–1951*. O. K. Bouwsma. Indianapolis: Hackett.

Wittgenstein, Ludwig. 1989. *Wittgenstein's Lectures on Philosophical Psychology, 1946–47*. Ed. P. T. Geach. Chicago: University of Chicago Press.

Wittgenstein, Ludwig. 1992. *Last Writings on the Philosophy of Psychology*, vol. 2: *The Inner and the Outer*. Ed. G. H. von Wright and Heikki Nyman. Trans. C. G. Luckhardt and Maximilian A. E. Aue. Cambridge, Mass.: Blackwell.

Wittgenstein, Ludwig. 1993. *Philosophical Occasions, 1912–1951*. Ed. James Klagge and Alfred Nordmann. Indianapolis: Hackett.

Wittgenstein, Ludwig. 2001. *Wittgenstein's Lectures: Cambridge, 1932–1935*. Ed. Alice Ambrose. Amherst, N.Y.: Prometheus Books.

Wittgenstein, Ludwig. 2001. *Philosophical Investigations*, 3rd rev. ed. Trans. G. E. M. Anscombe. Malden, Mass.: Blackwell.

Wittgenstein, Ludwig. 2001. *Tractatus Logico-Philosophicus*. Trans. D. F. Pears and B. F. McGuinness. New York: Routledge.

Wittgenstein, Ludwig. 2005. *Philosophical Grammar*. Ed. Rush Rhees. Berkeley: University of California Press.

## Other Authors

Abbott, Matthew. 2010. The poetic experience of the world. *International Journal of Philosophical Studies* 18 (4): 493–516.

Allaire, Edwin B. 1959. *Tractatus* 6.3751. *Analysis* 19 (5):100–105.

Ameriks, Karl. 2000. *Kant and the Fate of Autonomy: Problems in the Appropriation of the Critical Philosophy*. New York: Cambridge University Press.

Anscombe, G. E. M. 1963. *An Introduction to Wittgenstein's* Tractatus, 2nd ed. New York: Harper & Row.

Apel, Karl-Otto. 1980. *Towards a Transformation of Philosophy*. Trans. Glyn Adey and David Frisby. London: Routledge & Kegan Paul.

Apel, Karl-Otto. 1994. *Selected Essays*, vol. 1: *Towards a Transcendental Semiotics*. Atlantic Highlands, N.J.: Humanities Press.

Apel, Karl-Otto. 1998. *From a Transcendental-Semiotic Point of View*. New York: Manchester University Press.

Aristotle. 1985. *Nicomachean Ethics*. Trans. Terence Irwin. Indianapolis: Hackett.

Aristotle. 1987. *A New Aristotle Reader*. Ed. J. L. Ackrill. Princeton: Princeton University Press.

Arrington, Robert L., and Hans-Johann Glock. 1992. *Wittgenstein's* Philosophical Investigations: *Text and Context*. New York: Routledge.

Ashdown, Lance. 2001. Reading *On Certainty*. *Philosophical Investigations* 24 (4):314–329.

Austin, J. L. 1979. *Philosophical Papers*, 3rd ed. New York: Oxford University Press.

Ayer, A. J. 1959. *Logical Positivism*. New York: Free Press.

Ayer, A. J. 1985. *Wittgenstein*. New York: Random House.

Badiou, Alain. 2011. *Wittgenstein's Antiphilosophy*. New York: Verso.

Baiasu, Roxana. 2009. Puzzles of discourse in *Being and Time*: Minding gaps in understanding. *International Journal of Philosophical Studies* 17 (5):681–706.

Baker, G. P. 1991. *Meaning and Understanding: Wittgenstein's Philosophical Invention (Essays on the* Philosophical Investigations *vol. 1)*. Oxford: Wiley-Blackwell.

Baker, Gordon P., and P. M. S. Hacker. 1980. *Wittgenstein, Understanding and Meaning: Volume 1 of an Analytical Commentary on the* Philosophical Investigations. Chicago: University of Chicago Press.

Baker, Gordon P., and P. M. S. Hacker. 1985. *Wittgenstein: Rules, Grammar, and Necessity*. Oxford: Blackwell.

Baldwin, Thomas, ed. 2003. *Maurice Merleau-Ponty: Basic Writings*. New York: Routledge.

Baynes, Kenneth, James Bohman, and Thomas A. McCarthy, eds. 1987. *After Philosophy: End or Transformation?* Cambridge, Mass.: MIT Press.

Bearn, Gordon C. F. 1997. *Waking to Wonder: Wittgenstein's Existential Investigations*. Albany: SUNY Press.

Beckett, Samuel. 1994. *Waiting for Godot: A Tragicomedy in Two Acts*. New York: Grove Press.

Benacerraf, Paul, and Hilary Putnam. 1964. *Philosophy of Mathematics: Selected Readings*. New York: Cambridge University Press.

Bermúdez, José Luis, Anthony Marcel, and Naomi Eilan, eds. 1995. *The Body and the Self*. Cambridge, Mass.: MIT Press.

Biletzki, A. 2003. *(Over)Interpreting Wittgenstein*. Leiden: Kluwer.

Biletzki, Anat, and Anat Matar, eds. 1998. *The Story of Analytic Philosophy: Plot and Heroes*. New York: Routledge.

Blakeslee, Sandra, and Matthew Blakeslee. 2008. *The Body Has a Mind of Its Own: How Body Maps in Your Brain Help You Do (Almost) Everything Better*. New York: Random House.

Blattner, William. 2007. *Heidegger's* Being and Time: *A Reader's Guide*. New York: Continuum.

Bloor, D. 1983. *Wittgenstein: A Social Theory of Knowledge*. New York: Columbia University Press.

Bloor, D. 2002. *Wittgenstein, Rules & Institutions*. New York: Routledge.

Bourdieu, Pierre. 1977. *Outline of a Theory of Practice*. New York: Cambridge University Press.

Braver, Lee. 2007. *A Thing of This World: A History of Continental Anti-Realism*. Evanston: Northwestern University Press.

Braver, Lee. 2009. *Heidegger's Later Writings: A Reader's Guide*. New York: Continuum.

Braver, Lee. 2011a. Never mind: Thinking of subjectivity in the Dreyfus–McDowell debate. In *Is the Mental a Myth?* Ed. Julian Schear. New York: Routledge.

Braver, Lee. 2011b. Analyzing Heidegger: The analytic receptions of Heidegger's work. In *Interpreting Heidegger*, ed. Daniel Dahlstrom. New York: Cambridge University Press.

Brill, Susan B. 1994. *Wittgenstein & Critical Theory: Beyond Postmodern Criticism and Toward Descriptive Investigations*. Athens: Ohio University Press.

Burge, Tyler. 2005. *Truth, Thought, Reason: Essays on Frege*. New York: Oxford University Press.

Burger, Donna. 2008. *Aristotle's Dialogue with Socrates: On the* Nicomachean Ethics. Chicago: University of Chicago Press.

Caputo, John D. 1983. The thought of being and the conversation of mankind: The case of Heidegger and Rorty. *Review of Metaphysics* 36:661–687.

Caputo, John D. 1987. *Radical Hermeneutics: Repetition, Deconstruction, and the Hermeneutic Project*. Bloomington: Indiana University Press.

Caputo, John D. 1993. *Demythologizing Heidegger*. Bloomington: Indiana University Press.

Carman, Taylor. 2003. *Heidegger's Analytic: Interpretation, Discourse, and Authenticity in Being and Time*. New York: Cambridge University Press.

Carman, Taylor. 2010. Heidegger's anti-Neo-Kantianism. *Philosophical Forum* 41:131–142.

Cavell, Stanley. 1979. *The Claim of Reason: Wittgenstein, Skepticism, Morality, and Tragedy*. New York: Oxford University Press.

Cavell, Stanley. 1990. *Conditions Handsome and Unhandsome: The Constitution of Emersonian Perfectionism*. Chicago: University of Chicago Press.

Cavell, Stanley. 1995. *Philosophical Passages: Wittgenstein, Emerson, Austin, Derrida*. Oxford: Wiley-Blackwell.

Churchill, John. 1994. Wonder and the end of explanation: Wittgenstein and religious sensibility. *Philosophical Investigations* 17 (2):388–416.

Clark, Andy. 2004. *Natural-Born Cyborgs: Minds, Technologies, and the Future of Human Intelligence*. New York: Oxford University Press.

Clark, Peter, and Bob Hale, eds. 1994. *Reading Putnam*. New York: Blackwell.

Cook, John W. 1965. Wittgenstein on privacy. *Philosophical Review* 74 (3):281–314.

Cooper, David E. 1997. Wittgenstein, Heidegger, and humility. *Philosophy* 72 (279):105–123.

Cooper, David E. 2002. *The Measure of Things: Humanism, Humility, and Mystery*. New York: Oxford University Press.

Copi, Irving M., and Robert W. Beard, eds. 1966. *Essays on Wittgenstein's Tractatus*. London: Routledge & Kegan Paul.

Crary, Alice, and Rupert Read, eds. 2000. *The New Wittgenstein*. New York: Routledge.

Creegan, Charles L. 1989. *Wittgenstein and Kierkegaard: Religion, Individuality, and Philosophical Method*. New York: Routledge.

Crowe, Benjamin D. 2008. *Heidegger's Phenomenology of Religion: Realism and Cultural Criticism*. Bloomington: Indiana University Press.

Crowell, Steven, and Jeff Malpas. 2007. *Transcendental Heidegger*. Stanford, Calif.: Stanford University Press.

Dahlstrom, Daniel, ed. 2011. *Interpreting Heidegger*. New York: Cambridge University Press.

Davis, Martin. 2000. *The Universal Computer: The Road from Leibniz to Turing*. New York: W. W. Norton.

de Beistegui, Miguel. 2005. *The New Heidegger*. New York: Continuum.

de Lara, Philippe. 2003. Wittgenstein as anthropologist: The concept of ritual instinct. *Philosophical Investigations* 26 (2):109–124.

Derrida, Jacques. 1973. *Speech and Phenomena: And Other Essays on Husserl's Theory of Signs*. Trans. David B. Allison. Evanston: Northwestern University Press.

Derrida, Jacques. 1981. *Spurs: Nietzsche's Styles / Eperons: Les Styles de Nietzsche*. Trans. Barbara Harlow. Chicago: University of Chicago Press.

Derrida, Jacques. 1983. *Dissemination*. Trans. Barbara Johnson. Chicago: University of Chicago Press.

Derrida, Jacques. 1987. *The Post Card: From Socrates to Freud and Beyond*. Trans. Alan Bass. Chicago: University of Chicago Press.

Derrida, Jacques. 1998. *Of Grammatology*. Trans. Gayatri Chakravorty Spivak. Baltimore: The Johns Hopkins University Press.

Descartes, René. 1985. *The Philosophical Writings of Descartes*, vol. I. Trans. John Cottingham, Robert Stoothoff, and Dugald Murdoch. New York: Cambridge University Press.

Diamond, Cora. 1991. *The Realistic Spirit: Wittgenstein, Philosophy, and the Mind.* Cambridge, Mass.: MIT Press.

Dilman, Ilham. 2002. *Wittgenstein's Copernican Revolution: The Question of Linguistic Idealism.* Basingstroke: Palgrave.

Donagan, Alan, Anthony N. Petrovich, and Michael Wedin, eds. 1986. *Human Nature and Natural Knowledge: Essays Presented to Marjorie Grene on the Occasion of her Seventy-Fifth Birthday.* Dordrecht: D. Reidel.

Dostoevsky, Fyodor. 1990. *The Brothers Karamazov*. Trans. Richard Pevear and Larissa Volokhonsky. New York: Farrar, Straus & Giroux.

Dreyfus, Hubert L. 1991. *Being-in-the-World: A Commentary on Heidegger's "Being and Time," Division I*. Cambridge, Mass.: MIT Press.

Dreyfus, Hubert L. 1992. *What Computers Still Can't Do: A Critique of Artificial Reason.* Cambridge, Mass.: MIT Press.

Dreyfus, Hubert L. 1996a. The current relevance of Merleau-Ponty's phenomenology of embodiment. *Electronic Journal of Analytic Philosophy* 4:1–16.

Dreyfus, Hubert L. 1996b. A phenomenology of skill acquisition as the basis for a Merleau-Pontyian non-representationalist cognitive science. http://socrates.berkeley.edu/~hdreyfus/pdf/MerleauPontySkillCogSci.pdf.

Dreyfus, Hubert L. 1999. The primacy of phenomenology over logical analysis. *Philosophical Topics* 27 (2): 3–24.

Dreyfus, Hubert L. 2000. Merleau-Ponty's critique of Husserl's (and Searle's) concept of intentionality. In *Rereading Merleau-Ponty: Essays Beyond the Continental-Analytic Divide*, ed. Lawrence Haas and Dorothea Olkowski, 33–52. Amherst, N.Y.: Humanity.

Dreyfus, Hubert L. 2005. Overcoming the myth of the mental: How philosophers can profit from the phenomenology of everyday expertise. *Proceedings and Addresses of the American Philosophical Association* 79 (2):47–65.

Dreyfus, Hubert L., and Stuart E. Dreyfus. 1986. *Mind Over Machine: The Power of Human Intuition and Expertise in the Era of the Computer.* New York: The Free Press.

Dreyfus, Hubert L., and Harrison Hall, eds. 1992. *Heidegger: A Critical Reader.* New York: Blackwell.

Dreyfus, Hubert L., and Mark Wrathall, eds. 2002. *Heidegger Reexamined*, vol. 4: *Language and the Critique of Subjectivity*. New York: Routledge.

Dummett, Michael. 1978. *Truth and Other Enigmas*. Cambridge, Mass.: Harvard University Press.

Dummett, Michael. 1981. *Frege: Philosophy of Language*. Cambridge, Mass.: Harvard University Press.

Dummett, Michael. 1991. *The Logical Basis of Metaphysics*. Cambridge, Mass.: Harvard University Press.

Dummett, Michael. 1996a. *Origins of Analytical Philosophy*. Cambridge, Mass.: Harvard University Press.

Dummett, Michael. 1996b. *The Seas of Language*. New York: Oxford University Press.

Dwyer, Philip. 1997. *Sense and Subjectivity: A Study of Wittgenstein and Merleau-Ponty*. Leiden: E. J. Brill.

Edwards, James C. 1982. *Ethics without Philosophy: Wittgenstein and the Moral Life*. Tampa: University of Southern Florida Press.

Edwards, James C. 1990. *The Authority of Language: Heidegger, Wittgenstein, and the Threat of Philosophical Nihilism*. Tampa: University of Southern Florida Press.

Einstein, Albert. 2006. *Relativity: The Special and the General Theory*. Trans. Robert W. Lawson. New York: Penguin.

Eldridge, Richard. 1997. *Leading a Human Life: Wittgenstein, Intentionality, and Romanticism*. Chicago: University of Chicago Press.

Engelmann, Paul. 1967. *Letters from Ludwig Wittgenstein with a Memoir*. Oxford: Blackwell.

Fann, K. T. 1967. *Ludwig Wittgenstein: The Man and His Philosophy*. Atlantic Highlands, N.J.: Humanities Press.

Fell, Joseph P. 1979. *Heidegger and Sartre: An Essay on Being and Place*. New York: Columbia University Press.

Ferry, Luc, and Alain Renaut. 1990. *French Philosophy of the Sixties: An Essay on Antihumanism*. Amherst: University of Massachusetts Press.

Figal, Günter, and Jerome Veith. 2009. *The Heidegger Reader*. Bloomington: Indiana University Press.

Flew, Antony. 2008. *There Is a God: How the World's Most Notorious Atheist Changed His Mind*. New York: HarperOne.

Fogelin, Robert. 1995. *Wittgenstein*, 2nd ed. New York: Routledge.

Frege, Gottlob. 1960. *Translations from the Philosophical Writings of Gottlob Frege*. Ed. Peter Geach and Max Black. Oxford: Blackwell.

Frege, Gottlob. 1980. *The Foundations of Arithmetic*, 2nd rev. ed. Trans. J. L. Austin. Evanston: Northwestern University Press.

Foucault, Michel. 1996. *Foucault Live: Collected Interviews, 1961–1984*. Ed. Sylvère Lotringer. Trans. Lysa Hochroth and John Johnston. New York: Semiotext(e).

Fynsk, Christopher. 1993. *Heidegger: Thought and Historicity*, exp. ed. Ithaca: Cornell University Press.

Gadamer, Hans-Georg. 1977. *Philosophical Hermeneutics*. Ed. and trans. David E. Linge. Berkeley: University of California Press.

Gadamer, Hans-Georg. 1994. *Heidegger's Ways*. Albany: SUNY Press.

Gadamer, Hans-Georg. 1995. *Truth and Method*, 2nd rev. ed. Trans. J. Weinsheimer and D. G. Marshall. New York: Crossroad.

Gadamer, Hans-Georg. 2001. Gadamer. In *Conversation: Reflections and Commentary*, ed. and trans. Richard E. Palmer. New Haven: Yale University Press.

Gallagher, S., and A. N. Meltzoff. 1996. The earliest sense of self and others: Merleau-Ponty and recent developmental studies. *Philosophical Psychology* 9:211–233.

Gallagher, S., and F. Varela. 2003. Redrawing the map and resetting the time: Phenomenology and the cognitive sciences. *Canadian Journal of Philosophy, Supplementary* 29: 93–132. (Published online in *The Reach of Reflection: The Future of Phenomenology*, ed. Steven Crowell, Lester Embree, and Samuel J. Julian. Electronpress.)

Garver, Newton, and Seung-Chong Lee. 1995. *Derrida and Wittgenstein*. Philadelphia: Temple University Press.

Genova, Judith. 1995. *Wittgenstein: A Way of Seeing*. New York: Routledge.

Gier, Nicholas F. 1981. *Wittgenstein and Phenomenology*. Albany: SUNY Press.

Gladwell, Malcolm. 2007. *Blink: The Power of Thinking without Thinking*. Boston: Back Bay Books.

Glazebrook, Trish. 2000. *Heidegger's Philosophy of Science*. New York: Fordham University Press.

Glendinning, Simon. 1998. *On Being with Others: Heidegger—Derrida—Wittgenstein*. New York: Routledge.

Glendinning, Simon. 2001. *Arguing with Derrida*. New York: Blackwell.

Glendinning, Simon. 2007. *The Idea of Continental Philosophy*. Edinburgh: Edinburgh University Press.

Glock, Hans-Johann, ed. 2001. *Wittgenstein: A Critical Reader.* New York: Blackwell.

Glock, Hans-Johann, ed. 2004. Was Wittgenstein an analytic philosopher? *Metaphilosophy* 35 (4):419–444.

Glock, Hans-Johann, ed. 2008. *What Is Analytic Philosophy?* New York: Cambridge University Press.

Goff, Robert Allen. 1968. Wittgenstein's tools and Heidegger's implements. *Man and World* 1 (3):447–462.

Goodman, Russell B. 2007. *Wittgenstein and William James.* New York: Cambridge University Press.

Griffiths, A. Phillips, ed. 1991. *Wittgenstein: Centenary Essays.* New York: Cambridge University Press.

Guignon, Charles. 1983. *Heidegger and the Problem of Knowledge.* Indianapolis: Hackett.

Guignon, Charles. 1990. Philosophy after Wittgenstein and Heidegger. *Philosophy and Phenomenological Research* 50 (4):649–672.

Guignon, Charles. 1993. *The Cambridge Companion to Heidegger.* New York: Cambridge University Press.

Haar, Michel. 1993. *Heidegger and the Essence of Man.* Trans. William McNeill. Albany: SUNY Press.

Hacker, P. M. S. 1996. *Wittgenstein's Place in Twentieth-Century Analytic Philosophy.* Oxford: Wiley-Blackwell.

Hahn, Lewis Edwin, ed. 1996. *The Philosophy of Hans-Georg Gadamer.* Library of Living Philosophers, vol. 24. Chicago: Open Court.

Hammond, Michael, Jane Howarth, and Russell Keat. 1991. *Understanding Phenomenology.* Oxford: Blackwell.

Hanna, Robert. 2001. *Kant and the Foundations of Analytic Philosophy.* Oxford: Clarendon.

Hannan, Barbara. 2009. *The Riddle of the World: A Reconsideration of Schopenhauer's Philosophy.* New York: Oxford University Press.

Harries, Karsten. 1968. Wittgenstein and Heidegger: The relationship of the philosopher to language. *Journal of Value Inquiry* 2 (4):281–291.

Harris, Roy. 1988. *Language, Saussure and Wittgenstein: How to Play Games with Words.* London: Routledge & Kegan Paul.

Hatab, Lawrence. 2000. *Ethics and Finitude.* New York: Rowman & Littlefield.

Haugeland, John, ed. 1997. *Mind Design II: Philosophy, Psychology, and Artificial Intelligence*. Cambridge, Mass.: MIT Press.

Haugeland, John. 2000. *Having Thought: Essays in the Metaphysics of Mind*. Cambridge, Mass.: Harvard University Press.

Hegel, G. W. F. 1969. *Hegel's Science of Logic*. Trans. A. V. Miller. London: G. Allen & Unwin.

Hegel, G. W. F. 1977. *Hegel's Phenomenology of Spirit*. Trans. A. V. Miller. New York: Oxford University Press.

Hegel, G. W. F. 2002. *Hegel's The Philosophy of Right*. Trans. Alan White. Newburyport, Mass.: Focus Philosophical Library.

Hiley, David R., James F. Bohman, and Richard Shusterman, eds. 1992. *The Interpretive Turn: Philosophy, Science, Culture*. Ithaca: Cornell University Press.

Hintikka, Merrill B., and Jaakko Hintikka. 1989. *Investigating Wittgenstein*. New York: Blackwell.

Horn, Patrick Rogers. 2005. *Gadamer and Wittgenstein on the Unity of Language: Reality and Discourse Without Metaphysics*. Burlington, Vt.: Ashgate.

Hume, David. 1975. *Enquiries Concerning Human Understanding and Concerning the Principles of Morals*, 3rd ed. Ed. P. H. Nidditch. New York: Oxford University Press.

Hume, David. 1978. *A Treatise of Human Nature*, 2nd ed. Ed. P. H. Nidditch. New York: Oxford University Press.

Hume, David. 1998. *Dialogues Concerning Natural Religion: The Posthumous Essays of the Immortality of the Soul and of Suicide*, 2nd ed. Ed. Richard Popkin. Indianapolis: Hackett.

Husserl, Edmund. *Ideas Pertaining to a Pure Phenomenology and to a Phenomenological Philosophy: First Book*. Trans. F. Kersten. Boston: Kluwer Academic.

Husserl, Edmund. 1997. *Psychological and Transcendental Phenomenology and the Confrontation with Heidegger (1927–1931)*. Ed. and trans. Thomas Sheehan and Richard E. Palmer. Boston: Kluwer Academic.

Hylton, Peter. 1990. *Russell, Idealism, and the Emergence of Analytic Philosophy*. New York: Clarendon.

Iacoboni, Marco. 2008. *Mirroring People: The New Science of How We Connect with Others*. New York: Farrar, Straus & Giroux.

Ihde, Don. 2010. *Heidegger's Technologies: Postphenomenological Perspectives*. New York: Fordham University Press.

Jacquette, Dale. 1998. *Wittgenstein's Thought in Transition*. West Lafayette, Ind.: Purdue University Press.

Jacquette, Dale. 2005. *Philosophy of Schopenhauer*. Montreal: McGill-Queen's University Press.

Janik, Allan, and Stephen Toulmin. 1973. *Wittgenstein's Vienna*. New York: Simon & Schuster.

Jaynes, Julian. 2000. *The Origin of Consciousness in the Breakdown of the Bicameral Mind*. Boston: Houghton Mifflin.

John, Peter C. 1988. Wittgenstein's "wonderful life." *Journal of the History of Ideas* 49 (3):495–510.

Kant, Immanuel. 1929. *Critique of Pure Reason*. New York: St. Martin's Press.

Kant, Immanuel. 1950. *Prolegomena to Any Future Metaphysics*. Ed. Lewis White Beck. Upper Sadle River, N.J.: Prentice Hall.

Kant, Immanuel. 1995. *Foundations of the Metaphysics of Morals*, 2nd Ed. Trans. Lewis White Beck. Upper Sadle River, N.J.: Prentice Hall.

Kant, Immanuel. 2000. *Critique of the Power of Judgment*. New York: Cambridge University Press.

Kaufman, Daniel A. 2002. Reality in common sense: Reflections on realism and anti-realism from a "common sense naturalist" perspective. *Philosophical Investigations* 25 (4):331–361.

Kenny, Anthony. 1973. *Wittgenstein*. Cambridge, Mass.: Harvard University Press.

Kenny, Anthony. 1986. *The Legacy of Wittgenstein*, new ed. Oxford: Wiley Blackwell.

Kierkegaard, Søren. 1983. *Fear and Trembling / Repetition*. Ed. and trans. Howard V. Hong and Edna H. Hong. Princeton: Princeton University Press.

Kierkegaard, Søren. 1991. *Practice in Christianity*. Ed. and trans. Howard V. Hong and Edna H. Hong. Princeton: Princeton University Press.

Kierkegaard, Søren. 1992. *Concluding Unscientific Postscript 1*. Ed. and trans. Howard V. Hong and Edna H. Hong. Princeton: Princeton University Press.

Kisiel, Theodore J. 1993. *The Genesis of Heidegger's* Being and Time. Berkeley: University of California Press.

Kisiel, Theodore J., and John van Buren, eds. 1994. *Reading Heidegger from the Start: Essays in His Early Thought*. Albany: SUNY Press.

Kisiel, Theodore J., and Thomas Sheehan, eds. 2007. *Becoming Heidegger: On the Trail of His Early Occasional Writings, 1910–1927*. Evanston, Ill.: Northwestern University Press.

Kolb, David. 1986. *The Critique of Pure Modernity: Hegel, Heidegger, and After*. Chicago: University of Chicago Press.

Korsgaard, Christine M. 1996. *Sources of Normativity*. New York: Cambridge University Press.

Krell, David Farrell. 1986. *Intimations of Mortality: Time, Truth, and Finitude in Heidegger's Thinking of Being*. University Park: Pennsylvania State University Press.

Kripke, Saul A. 1984. *Wittgenstein on Rules and Private Language: An Elementary Exposition*. Cambridge, Mass.: Harvard University Press.

Kuhn, Thomas. 1996. *The Structure of Scientific Revolutions*, 3rd ed. Chicago: University of Chicago Press.

Lackey, Douglas P. 1999. What are the modern classics? The Baruch poll of great philosophy in the twentieth century. *Philosophical Forum* 30 (4):329–346.

Lafont, Cristina. 2000. *Heidegger, Language, and World-Disclosure*. New York: Cambridge University Press.

Lamb, David. 1980. *Language and Perception in Hegel and Wittgenstein*. New York: St. Martin's Press.

Landini, Gregory. 2007. *Wittgenstein's Apprenticeship with Russell*. New York: Cambridge University Press.

Last, Nana. 2008. *Wittgenstein's House: Language, Space, and Architecture*. New York: Fordham University Press.

Lawn, Chris. 2007. *Wittgenstein and Gadamer: Towards a Post-Analytic Philosophy of Language*. New York: Continuum.

Lear, Jonathan. 1998. *Open Minded: Working out the Logic of the Soul*. Cambridge, Mass.: Harvard University Press.

Lee, H. D. P. 1979. Wittgenstein 1929–1931. *Philosophy* 54 (208):211–220.

Lehrer, Jonah. 2009. *How We Decide*. Boston: Houghton Mifflin Harcourt.

Leibniz, G. W. 1989. *Philosophical Essays*. Indianapolis: Hackett.

Leitner, Bernhard. 2000. *The Wittgenstein House*. New York: Princeton Architectural Press.

Levine, Steven, ed. 2008. *On Heidegger's* Being and Time. New York: Routledge.

Livingston, Paul M. 2008. *Philosophy and the Vision of Language*. New York: Routledge.

Locke, John. 1996. *An Essay Concerning Human Understanding. Abridged*. Indianapolis: Hackett.

Lyotard, Jean-François. 1988. *The Differend: Phrases in Dispute*. Minneapolis: University Of Minnesota Press.

Macann, C. 1995. *Critical Heidegger*. New York: Routledge.

Macomber, W. B. 1967. *The Anatomy of Disillusion: Martin Heidegger's Notion of Truth*. Evanston, Ill.: Northwestern University Press.

Malcolm, Norman. 1994. *Wittgenstein: A Religious Point of View?* Ithaca: Cornell University Press.

Malcolm, Norman. 1995. *Wittgensteinian Themes: Essays 1978–89*. Ithaca: Cornell University Press.

Malcolm, Norman. 2001. *Ludwig Wittgenstein: A Memoir*, 2nd ed. New York: Oxford University Press.

Malpas, Jeff. 2007. *Heidegger's Topology: Being, Place, World*. Cambridge, Mass.: MIT Press.

Malpas, Jeff, ed. 2011. *Dialogues with Davidson*. Cambridge, Mass.: MIT Press.

Malpas, Jeff, Ulrich Arnswald, and Jens Kertscher, eds. 2002. *Gadamer's Century: Essays in Honor of Hans-Georg Gadamer*. Cambridge, Mass.: MIT Press.

Marion, Mathieu. 1998. *Wittgenstein, Finitism, and the Foundations of Mathematics*. New York: Oxford University Press.

Mays, Wolfe, and S. C. Brown, eds. 1972. *Linguistic Analysis and Phenomenology*. Lewisburg: Bucknell University Press.

McDowell, John. 2001. *Mind, Value, and Reality*. Cambridge, Mass.: Harvard University Press.

McDowell, John. 2009. *The Engaged Intellect: Philosophical Essays*. Cambridge, Mass.: Harvard University Press.

McGinn, Colin. 1984. *Wittgenstein on Meaning: An Interpretation and Evaluation*. New York: Blackwell.

McGinn, Colin. 1987. *Wittgenstein on Meaning: An Interpretation and Evaluation*. New York: Blackwell.

McGuinness, Brian. 1982. *Wittgenstein and His Times*. Chicago: University of Chicago Press.

McGuinness, Brian. 2005. *Young Ludwig: Wittgenstein's Life 1889–1921*. New York: Oxford University Press.

McManus, Denis. 1999. The rediscovery of Heidegger's worldly subject by analytic philosophy of science. *Monist* 82 (2):324–346.

McManus, Denis. 2004. *Wittgenstein and Scepticism*. New York: Routledge.

McManus, Denis. 2006. *The Enchantment of Words: Wittgenstein's* Tractatus Logico-Philosophicus. New York: Oxford University Press.

Medina, José. 2002. *The Unity of Wittgenstein's Philosophy: Necessity, Intelligibility, and Normativity*. Albany: SUNY Press.

Meillassoux, Quentin. 2008. *After Finitude: An Essay on the Necessity of Contingency*. New York: Continuum.

Mensch, James Richard. 1996. *Knowing and Being: A Postmodern Reversal*. University Park: Pennsylvania State University Press.

Merleau-Ponty, Maurice. 1962. *Phenomenology of Perception*. Trans. Colin Smith. London: Routledge & Kegan Paul.

Merleau-Ponty, Maurice. 1964. *The Primacy of Perception*. Evanston, Ill.: Northwestern University Press.

Merleau-Ponty, Maurice. 2004. *The World of Perception*. Trans. Oliver Davis. New York: Routledge.

Minar, Edward H. 1991. Wittgenstein and the "contingency" of community. *Pacific Philosophical Quarterly* 72 (3):203–234.

Minar, Edward H. 1995. Feeling at home in language. *Synthese* 102 (3):413–452.

Minar, Edward H. 1998. Wittgenstein on the metaphysics of the self. *Pacific Philosophical Quarterly* 79 (4):329–354.

Monk, Ray. 1990. *Ludwig Wittgenstein: The Duty of Genius*. New York: Penguin.

Monk, Ray. 1996. *Bertrand Russell: The Spirit of Solitude 1872–1921*. New York: Free Press.

Monk, Ray. 2005. *How to Read Wittgenstein*. New York: Norton.

Moran, Dermot, and Tim Mooney, eds. 2002. *The Phenomenology Reader*. New York: Routledge.

Morick, Harold, ed. 1967. *Wittgenstein and the Problem of Other Minds*. Atlantic Highlands, N.J.: Humanities Press.

Moyal-Sharrock, Danièle, ed. 2004. *The Third Wittgenstein: The Post-Investigations Works*. Burlington, Vt.: Ashgate.

Mulhall, Stephen. 1990. *On Being in the World: Wittgenstein and Heidegger on Seeing Aspects*. New York: Routledge.

Mulhall, Stephen. 2003. *Inheritance and Originality: Wittgenstein, Heidegger, Kierkegaard*. New York: Oxford University Press.

Mulhall, Stephen. 2007. *Philosophical Myths of the Fall*. Princeton: Princeton University Press.

Murray, Michael. 1978. *Heidegger and Modern Philosophy: Critical Essays*. New Haven: Yale University Press.

Nietzsche, Friedrich. 1966. *Beyond Good and Evil*. Trans. Walter Kaufmann. New York: Vintage Books.

Nietzsche, Friedrich. 1968. *The Will to Power*. Trans. Walter Kaufmann. New York: Vintage Books.

Nietzsche, Friedrich. 1974. *The Gay Science*. Trans. Walter Kaufmann. New York: Vintage Books.

Noë, Alva. 2004. *Action in Perception*. Cambridge, Mass.: MIT Press.

Noë, Alva. 2009. *Out of Our Heads: Why You Are Not Your Brain, and Other Lessons from the Biology of Consciousness*. New York: Hill & Wang.

O'Hear, Anthony. 2000. *German Philosophy since Kant*. New York: Cambridge University Press.

Okrent, Mark. 1988. *Heidegger's Pragmatism: Understanding, Being, and the Critique of Metaphysics*. Ithaca: Cornell University Press.

Olson, Alan M., ed. 1994. *Heidegger and Jaspers*. Philadelphia: Temple University Press.

O'Neill, Martin. 2001. Explaining "the hardness of the logical must": Wittgenstein on grammar, arbitrariness, and logical necessity. *Philosophical Investigations* 24 (1):1–29.

Overgaard, Soren. 2006. The problem of other minds: Wittgenstein's phenomenological perspective. *Phenomenology and the Cognitive Sciences* 5:53–73.

Oxaal, Ivar. 2010. *On the Trail to Wittgenstein's Hut: The Historical Background of the Tractatus Logico-Philosphicus*. Piscataway, N.J.: Transaction Publishers.

Paden, Roger. 2007. *Mysticism and Architecture: Wittgenstein and the Meanings of the Palais Stonborough*. Lanham, Md.: Lexington Books.

Pears, David. 1987. *The False Prison: A Study of the Development of Wittgenstein's Philosophy*, vol. 1. New York: Oxford University Press.

Pears, David. 1988. *The False Prison: A Study of the Development of Wittgenstein's Philosophy*, vol. 2. New York: Oxford University Press.

Pears, David. 2006. *Paradox and Platitude in Wittgenstein's Philosophy*. Oxford: Oxford University Press.

Pinkard, Terry. 1999. Analytics, continentals, and modern skepticism. *Monist* 82 (2):189–217.

Pitcher, George, ed. 1966. *The Philosophical Investigations. A Collection of Critical Essays*. Garden City, N.Y.: Anchor Books.

Pöggeler, Otto. 1970. Heidegger today. *Southern Journal of Philosophy* 8 (4):273–306.

Pöggeler, Otto. 1998. *The Paths of Heidegger's Life and Thought*. Trans. John Bailiff. Amherst, N.Y.: Humanity Books.

Polanyi, Michael. 1967. *The Tacit Dimension*. Garden City, N.Y.: Doubleday.

Polt, Richard, ed. 2005. *Heidegger's* Being and Time: *Critical Essays*. New York: Rowman & Littlefield.

Polt, Gregory, and Richard F. H. Fried. 2001. *A Companion to Heidegger's* Introduction to Metaphysics. New Haven: Yale University Press.

Prauss, Gerold. 1999. *Knowing and Doing in Heidegger's "Being and Time."* Trans. Gary Steiner and Jeffrey S. Turner. Amherst, N.Y.: Humanity Books.

Preston, John, ed. 2008. *Wittgenstein and Reason*. Malden, Mass.: Blackwell.

Priest, Graham. 2002. *Beyond the Limits of Thought*, 2nd ed. New York: Oxford University Press.

Putnam, Hilary. 1990. *Realism with a Human Face*. Ed. James Conant. Cambridge, Mass.: Harvard University Press.

Putnam, Hilary. 1995. *Pragmatism: An Open Question*. Cambridge, Mass.: Blackwell.

Quine, W. V. 1966. *The Ways of Paradox and Other Essays*. New York: Random House.

Quine, W. V. 1969. *Ontological Relativity and Other Essays*. New York: Columbia University Press.

Quine, W. V. 1970. *Philosophy of Logic*. Englewood Cliffs, N.J.: Prentice-Hall.

Quine, W. V. 1977. *Ontological Relativity*. New York: Columbia University Press.

Quine, W. V. 1980. *From a Logical Point of View: Nine Logico-Philosophical Essays*, 2nd rev. ed. Cambridge, Mass.: Harvard University Press.

Raffoul, François, and Eric Sean Nelson, eds. 2008. *Rethinking Facticity*. Albany: SUNY Press.

Ramachandran, V. S., and Sandra Blakeslee. 1998. *Phantoms in the Brain: Probing the Mysteries of the Human Mind*. New York: Harper Perennial.

Reynolds, Jack, James Chase, James Williams, and Edwin Mares, eds. 2010. *Postanalytic and Metacontinental: Crossing Philosophical Divides*. New York: Continuum.

Rhees, Rush. 1984. *Recollections of Wittgenstein*. New York: Oxford University Press.

Richardson, John. 1986. *Existential Epistemology: A Heideggerian Critique of the Cartesian Project*. Oxford: Clarendon.

Rockmore, Tom. 2006. *In Kant's Wake: Philosophy in the Twentieth Century*. Cambridge, Mass.: Blackwell.

Rorty, Richard. 1979. *Philosophy and the Mirror of Nature*. Princeton: Princeton University Press.

Rorty, Richard. 1989. *Contingency, Irony, and Solidarity*. New York: Cambridge University Press.

Rorty, Richard. 1991. *Essays on Heidegger and Others: Philosophical Papers*, vol. 2. New York: Cambridge University Press.

Rorty, Richard. 1992. *The Linguistic Turn: Essays in Philosophical Method*. Chicago: University Of Chicago Press.

Rorty, Richard. 2007. *Philosophy as Cultural Politics: Philosophical Papers*, vol. 4. New York: Cambridge University Press.

Rosen, Stanley. 1999. *Nihilism*, 2nd ed. South Bend, Ind.: St. Augustine's Press.

Rouse, Joseph. 1987. *Knowledge and Power: Toward a Political Philosophy of Science*. Ithaca: Cornell University Press.

Rudd, Anthony. 2003. *Expressing the World: Skepticism, Wittgenstein, and Heidegger*. Chicago: Open Court.

Russell, Bertrand. 1929. *Our Knowledge of the External World*. New York: W. W. Norton.

Russell, Bertrand. 1945. *A History of Western Philosophy*. New York: Simon & Schuster.

Russell, Bertrand. 1959a. *My Philosophical Development*. New York: Simon & Schuster.

Russell, Bertrand. 1959b. *The Problems of Philosophy*. New York: Oxford University Press.

Russell, Bertrand. 1996. *The Principles of Mathematics*. W. W. Norton.

Russell, Bertrand. 2004. *Mysticism and Logic*. Mineola, N.Y.: Dover.

Ryle, Gilbert. 1949. *The Concept of Mind*. New York: Barnes & Noble.

Ryle, Gilbert. 1953. Ordinary language. *Philosophical Review* 62 (2):167–186.

Sallis, John. 1995. *Double Truth*. Albany: SUNY Press.

Sallis, John, ed. 1993. *Reading Heidegger: Commemorations*. Bloomington: Indiana University Press.

Sartre, Jean-Paul. 1966. *Being and Nothingness: A Phenomenological Essay on Ontology*, 11th ed. New York: Washington Square Press.

Sass, Louis A. 1994. *The Paradoxes of Delusion: Wittgenstein, Schreber, and the Schizophrenic Mind*. Ithaca: Cornell University Press.

Schear, Julian, ed. 2011. *Is the Mental a Myth?* New York: Routledge.

Schönbaumsfeld, Genia. 2007. *A Confusion of the Spheres: Kierkegaard and Wittgenstein on Philosophy and Religion*. New York: Oxford University Press.

Schopenhauer, Arthur. 1966. *The World as Will and Representation, In Two Volumes*, vol. II. New York: Dover.

Schopenhauer, Arthur. 1969. *The World as Will and Representation, In Two Volumes*, vol. I. New York: Dover.

Schürmann, Reiner. 1987. *Heidegger on Being and Acting: From Principles to Anarchy*. Bloomington: Indiana University Press.

Schürmann, Reiner. 1990. *Heidegger on Being and Acting: From Principles to Anarchy*. Bloomington: Indiana University Press.

Sefler, George F. 1974. *Language and the World: A Methodological Synthesis within the Writings of Martin Heidegger and Ludwig Wittgenstein*. Atlantic Highlands, N.J.: Humanities Press.

Sellars, Wilfrid. 1991. *Science, Perception, and Reality*. Atascadero, Calif.: Ridgeview.

Sharr, Adam. 2006. *Heidegger's Hut*. Cambridge, Mass.: MIT Press.

Sheehan, Thomas, ed. 2010. *Heidegger: The Man and the Thinker*. Piscataway, N.J.: Transaction Publishers.

Sheehan, Thomas, and R. E. Palmer. 1997. *Edmund Husserl: Psychological and Transcendental Phenomenology, and the Confrontation with Heidegger (1927–1931)*. Boston: Kluwer Academic.

Sherover, Charles M. 1971. *Heidegger, Kant, and Time*. Bloomington: Indiana University Press.

Sluga, Hans. 1998. What has history to do with me? Wittgenstein and analytic philosophy. *Inquiry* 41 (1):99–121.

Sluga, Hans D., and David G. Stern. 1996. *The Cambridge Companion to Wittgenstein*. New York: Cambridge University Press.

Soames, Scott. 2005. *Philosophical Analysis in the Twentieth Century*, vol. 2: *The Age of Meaning*. Princeton: Princeton University Press.

Staten, Henry. 1986. *Wittgenstein and Derrida*. Lincoln: University of Nebraska Press.

Steele, David Ramsay. 2002. *Genius in Their Own Words: The Intellectual Journeys of Seven Great 20th-Century Thinkers*. Chicago: Open Court.

Stern, David G. 1991. The "Middle Wittgenstein": From logical atomism to practical holism. *Synthese* 87 (2):203–226.

Stern, David G. 1995. *Wittgenstein on Mind and Language*. New York: Oxford University Press.

Stern, David G. 1996. The availability of Wittgenstein's philosophy. In *The Cambridge Companion to Wittgenstein*, ed. Hans D. Sluga and David G. Stern, 442–476. New York: Cambridge University Press.

Stern, David G. 2004. *Wittgenstein's Philosophical Investigations: An Introduction*. New York: Cambridge University Press.

Stroll, Avrum. 2007. *Wittgenstein*, new ed. Oxford: OneworldPublications.

Stroud, Barry. 1984. *The Significance of Philosophical Scepticism*. New York: Oxford University Press.

Stroud, Barry. 2000. *Meaning, Understanding, and Practice*. New York: Oxford University Press.

Taminiaux, Jacques. 1991. *Heidegger and the Project of Fundamental Ontology*. Albany: SUNY Press.

Tang, Hao. Transcendental idealism in Wittgenstein's *Tractatus*. *Philosophical Quarterly* 61 (244): 598–607.

Taylor, Charles. 1995. *Philosophical Arguments*. Cambridge, Mass.: Harvard University Press.

Teghrarian, Souren, Anthony Serafini, and Edward M. Cook, eds. 1990. *Ludwig Wittgenstein: A Symposium on the Centennial of His Birth*. Wakefield, N.H.: Longwood Academic.

Thomson, Iain. 2001. Heidegger on ontological education, or: How we become what we are. *Inquiry* 44 (3):243–268.

Thomson, Iain. 2005. *Heidegger on Ontotheology: Technology and the Politics of Education*. New York: Cambridge University Press.

Thomson, Iain. 2011. *Heidegger, Art, and Postmodernity*. New York: Cambridge University Press.

Tolstoy, Leo. 2003. *Walk in the Light and Twenty-Three Tales*. Maryknoll, N.Y.: Orbis Books.

Tolstoy, Leo. 2004. *The Gospels in Brief*. Trans. Leo Wiener. New York: Barnes & Noble Books.

Travis, Charles. 2006. *Thought's Footing: A Theme in Wittgenstein's* Philosophical Investigations. Oxford: Clarendon Press.

van Buren, John, ed. 2002. *Supplements: From the Earliest Essays to Being and Time and Beyond*. Albany: SUNY Press.

Varela, Francisco. 1999. *Ethical Know-How: Action, Wisdom, and Cognition*. Stanford, Calif.: Stanford University Press.

Versényi, Laszlo. 1965. *Heidegger, Being, and Truth*. New Haven: Yale University Press.

Vesey, Godfrey, ed. 1974. *Understanding Wittgenstein*. Ithaca: Cornell University Press.

Vesey, Godfrey, ed. 1982. *Idealism Past and Present*. New York: Cambridge University Press.

von Wright, G. H., ed. 1973. *Letters to C. K. Ogden with Comments on the English Translation of the* Tractatus Logico-Philosophicus. Oxford: Blackwell.

von Wright, G. H., ed. 1977. *Letters to Russell Keynes and Moore*. Oxford: Blackwell.

von Wright, G. H. 1982. *Wittgenstein*. Minneapolis: University of Minnesota Press.

Weatherston, Martin. 2002. *Heidegger's Interpretation of Kant: Categories, Imagination, and Temporality*. New York: Palgrave Macmillan.

Welton, Donn, ed. 1999. *The Essential Husserl: Basic Writings in Transcendental Phenomenology*. Bloomington: Indiana University Press.

Wijdeveld, Paul. 1993. *Ludwig Wittgenstein: Architect*. Amsterdam: Pepin Press.

Williams, Meredith. 2002. *Wittgenstein, Mind, and Meaning: Towards a Social Conception of Mind*. New York: Routledge.

Williams, Meredith, ed. 2006. *Wittgenstein's* Philosophical Investigations: *Critical Essays*. New York: Rowman & Littlefield.

Williams, Michael. 1996. *Unnatural Doubts: Epistemological Realism and the Basis of Scepticism*. Princeton: Princeton University Press.

Winograd, Terry, and Fernando Flores. 1986. *Understanding Computers and Cognition: A New Foundation for Design*. Norwood, N.J.: Addison-Wesley.

Wolin, Richard. 1990. *The Politics of Being: The Political Thought of Martin Heidegger*. New York: Columbia University Press.

Wrathall, Mark A. 1999. Heidegger and truth as correspondence. *International Journal of Philosophical Studies* 7 (1):69–88.

Wrathall, Mark A., and Jeff Malpas, eds. 2000. *Heidegger, Coping, and Cognitive Science: Essays in Honor of Hubert L. Dreyfus*, vol. 2. Cambridge, Mass.: MIT Press.

Wright, Crispin. 1980. *Wittgenstein on the Foundations of Mathematics*. Cambridge, Mass.: Harvard University Press.

Young, Julian. 2002. *Heidegger's Later Philosophy*. New York: Cambridge University Press.

Young, Julian. 2001. *Heidegger's Philosophy of Art*. New York: Cambridge University Press.

Yourgrau, Palle. 2005. *A World without Time: The Forgotten Legacy of Gödel and Einstein*. New York: Basic Books.

Zabala, Santiago. 2008. *The Hermeneutic Nature of Analytic Philosophy: A Study of Ernst Tugendhat*. New York: Columbia University Press.

Zimmerman, Michael E. 1986. *Eclipse of the Self*. Athens, Ohio: Ohio University Press.

# Index

Aristotle, 34, 46, 77, 106–107, 116,
145, 168–170, 196, 204, 276n13,
282–283n106, 302n215, 302n219,
303n225, 313–314n155
Atomism, 7, 81–82, 85, 105, 174
Augustine, 33–34, 44, 54–55, 60, 62–63,
67, 100, 105, 156, 158, 256n119,
309n82
Austin, J. L., 61, 99, 251n56, 320n12
Authenticity, 27, 44–47, 115, 190–191,
230, 236, 262n178, 263n184
Autonomy, 146–150, 210, 237–239
Average everydayness, 28, 46, 106, 139–
140, 224–228, 254n93

Blattner, William, 259n153
Braver, Lee, 2, 255n102, 255n105,
261n165, 264n198, 269n38, 272n91,
273n99, 281n72, 289n44, 290n49,
290n51, 291n75, 296n141, 302n210,
311n115

Cavell, Stanley, 3, 179, 196, 257n128,
263n196, 271n70, 288n21, 320n16,
321n33
Contradictions, 185–187, 200, 308n67,
313–314n155–156
Cooper, David E., 91, 321n29, 323n60

Davidson, Donald, 71, 134, 164, 197,
272n91, 273n99, 278n34, 281n72,
291n75, 302n210

Derrida, Jacques, 46, 85, 111, 158,
203, 243n8, 245n34, 279–280n55,
286n155
Descartes, René, 2, 27, 34, 38, 66, 87–
88, 91, 95, 114, 162, 173, 184, 188,
200, 220, 237–238, 249n37, 281n73,
288n26, 309n82
Description versus explanation, 47,
71–75, 130, 139–140
Diamond, Cora, 259n156, 319n7
Dreyfus, Hubert, 128, 152, 160–161,
262n176, 271n65, 289n44, 294n111,
296n141
Dummett, Michael, 7, 250n46, 267n22,
315n177

Edwards, James C., 242n5, 323n60
Explanation. *See* Description versus
explanation

Fogelin, Robert, 265n208, 316n190
Form of life, 46, 84, 159–162, 233
Framework Argument, 180, 194–196,
199–200, 202, 205
Frege, Gottlob, 4, 6, 20, 25, 42, 55–57,
63–64, 69, 84–85, 120, 160, 185, 197,
243n16, 247n13, 248n26, 249n37,
250n39, 250n41, 250n46, 261n165,
267n13, 268n23, 268n33, 269n40,
270n54, 270n56, 276n13, 276n20,
286n155, 305n35, 307n60

Gadamer, Hans-Georg, 3, 133, 168,
    241n3, 278n34, 284n123, 295n127,
    302n210, 302n312, 303n225,
    310n102, 314n160·
Glendinning, Simon, 181, 242n5,
    290n58, 296n151
Goodman, Russell, 244n20, 273n98,
    295n127, 316n188
Groundless grounds, 11, 194–211, 215–
    221, 233
Guignon, Charles, 253n78, 253n86,
    306n45

Hegel, Georg Wilhelm Friedrich, 98,
    165, 196, 205, 232, 271n65, 271n70,
    281n72, 286n155
Heidegger, Martin
  being-with (see Social self)
  breakdowns, 32–33, 45–46, 48, 66, 73,
    97, 104, 134, 257n128
  circumspection, 28, 108–9, 131–134,
    145–146, 150–155, 168
  das Man, 114–117, 164, 215
  Destruktion, 14, 40, 74, 78, 105
  falling, 43–46, 114–115, 141, 271n65
  history of being, 117–118, 191–200,
    310n107
  tools, 23, 29–31, 103–104, 106–110,
    112, 131, 144, 283n115, 285n145
Hermeneutics, 8, 47, 73–74, 110, 133,
    145, 187–188, 246n3, 291n66,
    303n225, 310n102
Hume, David, 11, 42, 161, 168, 211–
    221, 316–317n206–211
Humpty-Dumpty Thesis, 110–112,
    115
Husserl, Edmund, 6, 13, 42, 45, 59,
    95, 104, 106, 111, 134, 143, 145,
    150–151, 188, 231, 241n1, 245n1,
    255n107, 263n195, 293n106

Inconspicuous, 24, 28–30, 39, 45, 47,
    52, 71, 75, 85, 95–97, 104–107,

    125, 131–139, 164, 192, 197, 234,
    257n128, 264n199, 271n64
Inescapable Ambiguity. See Thesis of In-
    escapable Ambiguity
Interpretation Aporia, 122–125, 134,
    140–143, 153, 156–157, 161, 167

Jacquette, Dale, 241n3, 242n7, 244n24

Kant, Immanuel, 4–6, 15, 18, 42, 48,
    76, 87, 98, 138, 174, 178, 189, 191,
    192, 196, 210, 229–230, 236–237,
    244n17–19, 247n16, 247n22,
    248n35, 260n159, 276n20, 311n119,
    321n33
Kehre or turning, 1, 9, 47, 191
Kierkegaard, Søren, 6, 42, 44, 104, 106,
    114, 116, 149, 165, 188, 230, 232,
    244n21, 271n65, 274n114, 299n189,
    313n142, 321n31–32
Know-how, 22–29, 43, 72, 108–9, 128,
    131, 146, 156, 161, 168
Kripke, Saul, 122, 124, 153, 243n11,
    288n26

Language-game, 83–85, 102–103,
    128, 185, 196–211, 312n129–130,
    312n132
Leibniz, Gottfried, 55–56, 63, 156, 201,
    249n37, 267n10, 319n4
Logical Stoicism, 57, 63, 75–76,
    120–121, 140, 174, 178, 180, 182,
    235–236

Malcolm, Norman, 260n161, 312n129
Malpas, Jeff, 283n109
McDowell, John, 123, 228, 262n176,
    281n72, 289n44, 296n141
McGinn, Colin, 161, 256n117, 281n85,
    288n26, 289n32
Meaning-object, 35, 53–65, 68–70, 84,
    105, 123, 153, 156, 174, 180, 213,
    228, 266n4

Merleau-Ponty, Maurice, 294n122,
    299n186, 300n202
Moore, G. E., 7, 82, 88, 103, 198–199,
    204, 261n165
Mulhall, Stephen, 242n5, 254n93,
    258n137, 290n58, 294n111,
    294n123

Names, 13, 31, 54–56, 60, 62, 66–67, 85,
    93–96, 100, 231
Nietzsche, Friedrich, 6, 46, 78, 104,
    114, 116, 142, 149, 154, 165, 190,
    230, 232, 236–238, 245n34, 246n11,
    288n26, 297n155, 320n16
Nihilism, 63, 65, 76, 123–124, 128,
    153–154, 167, 174, 205, 210, 215,
    233–235, 238–239
Non-self-reference paradox, 353

Original finitude, 9, 66, 116, 153, 179,
    196, 223–239

Pears, David, 84, 244n18, 260n156,
    268n31, 274n112, 275n119,
    279n47
Perceptual Model of Thought, 139–146,
    150, 163–164, 169, 188, 200, 213,
    215, 234, 239, 248, 300–301n202–
    203, 301n208
*Pharmakon*, 46–47, 132, 165, 303n225
Phenomenological ontology, 37, 138–
    139, 179, 187–188, 229–231,
    320n21
*Phronêsis*, 11, 34, 77, 141, 168–170, 180,
    211, 303n225
Plato, 26, 28, 34, 46, 59, 61, 63–66,
    77, 86, 119–120, 142, 154, 158,
    168, 170, 229, 232, 237, 255n105,
    256n117, 287n1, 293n103, 303n225,
    320n23
Poets, 46, 48, 148, 234, 239, 263n195,
    322n42
Pragmatism, 102–104, 198, 206–209

Presence-at-hand, 27, 30–35, 47, 52, 54,
    65–66, 73, 81, 104–105, 108, 112,
    117, 212, 310n103
Primacy of the Whole, 106, 110, 115–
    117, 162, 302n219
Putnam, Hilary, 66, 138, 281n72,
    321n26

Quine, W. V. O., 94, 134, 153, 178, 197,
    257n131, 293n105, 316n188

Readiness-to-hand, 10, 29–31, 106–7
Reminders, 10, 28, 33–40, 46, 71–73,
    101–102, 105, 127, 130, 209, 219,
    227, 234, 256n117
Retrospective Rational Reconstruction,
    30–34, 73–74, 79, 123, 127, 139,
    144, 166, 224
Rorty, Richard, 228, 241n1, 254n88,
    263n194, 276n20, 281n72, 323n60
Rouse, Joseph, 198
Rules-Exception Ratio Law, 98–99, 136,
    160
Russell, Bertrand, 7, 13–15, 17, 20, 42,
    57, 59–60, 82, 88, 90, 158, 160, 185–
    186, 241n1, 242n8, 243n16, 245n2,
    246n2, 246n7, 247n13, 248n22,
    250n39, 261n165, 266n222, 268n33,
    269n39, 293n105, 295n128, 306n38,
    308n67, 319n4
Ryle, Gilbert, 140, 255n101, 269n40,
    270n54, 275n116, 285n130, 290n49,
    295n128

Sartre, Jean-Paul, 45, 285n133, 295n128
Schopenhauer, Arthur, 4, 41–45, 56–57,
    59, 77, 108, 233, 235, 246n3, 246–
    247n12, 247n22, 260n161, 261–
    262n170–172, 262n175
Skepticism, 38–40, 51, 70–71, 111–112,
    265n219
Social self, 114–117, 162–167, 169–170,
    214–220, 299n185, 299–300n194,